Free Speech in the American Workplace

Free Speech in the American Workplace

From the Dawn of Workers' Rights to the Age of Social Media

Randy Bobbitt

BLOOMSBURY ACADEMIC
NEW YORK • LONDON • OXFORD • NEW DELHI • SYDNEY

BLOOMSBURY ACADEMIC
Bloomsbury Publishing Inc, 1359 Broadway, 12th Floor, New York, NY 10018, USA
Bloomsbury Publishing Plc, 50 Bedford Square, London, WC1B 3DP, UK
Bloomsbury Publishing Ireland, 29 Earlsfort Terrace, Dublin 2, D02 AY28, Ireland

BLOOMSBURY, BLOOMSBURY ACADEMIC and the Diana logo are trademarks of Bloomsbury Publishing Plc

First published in the United States of America 2025

Library of Congress Cataloging-in-Publication Data

Names: Bobbitt, Randy, 1955- author
Title: Free speech in the American workplace : from the dawn of workers' rights to the rise of social media / by Randy Bobbitt.
Description: New York, NY : Bloomsbury Academic, 2025. | Includes bibliographical references and index. | Summary: "This book examines both the legal and ethical issues that can arise when employees express opinions that conflict with those of their employer through analysis of cases across seven different sectors of employment"—Provided by publisher.
Identifiers: LCCN 2025010667 (print) | LCCN 2025010668 (ebook) | ISBN 9781666951080 cloth | ISBN 9781666951103 paperback | ISBN 9781666951097 ebook | ISBN 9798765152157 pdf
Subjects: LCSH: Freedom of speech—United States | United States. Constitution. 1st Amendment | Civil rights—United States | Employee rights—United States | Industrial relations | Social media—Law and legislation—United States | Educational law and legislation—United States
Classification: LCC KF4772 .B63 2025 (print) | LCC KF4772 (ebook) | DDC 342.7308/53—dc23/eng/20250424
LC record available at https://lccn.loc.gov/2025010667
LC ebook record available at https://lccn.loc.gov/2025010668

ISBN: HB: 978-1-6669-5108-0
ePDF: 979-8-7651-5215-7
eBook: 978-1-6669-5109-7

Typeset by Deanta Global Publishing Services, Chennai, India

For product safety related questions contact productsafety@bloomsbury.com.

Contents

Preface

More than thirty years ago, a man who was brutally beaten by Los Angeles police watched as the streets of the city erupted in violence after the officers accused of the crime were acquitted. When the turmoil spread to other cities and debates over racial justice filled newspaper opinion pages and television and radio airwaves, Rodney King, the victim of the police violence, expressed a sentiment that is applicable when following the case studies presented here: *Can't we all just get along?*

As a career-long researcher in the field of workplace communication and observer of communication in my own workplaces, I've concluded that "getting along" is something at which we don't try very hard. Sometimes, we don't try at all.

Like most of my books, the idea for this one was prompted by my work on a previous project. For fifteen months in 2019 and 2020, I researched a book that told the story of three university professors in New Hampshire who were caught up in a free-speech conflict (discussed in more detail in Chapter 8). Like many of the other individuals whose stories are chronicled in this book, their troubles began when they simply chose to do the right thing, both legally and ethically. After they wrote letters and testified in court in a highly publicized criminal case involving a friend and professional colleague—not defending what she had done, but rather to shed additional light on her circumstances—the professors found their careers and even their lives threatened.

I had researched and taught the issue of free speech in the workplace for years, but the New Hampshire case prompted me to begin researching another book on workplace speech in a variety of fields. I was surprised to learn that few books had been written on the subject, and even fewer were recent enough to include content on the role played by social media. The result is the chapters that follow.

The bulk of the research for this book was conducted in the library at the University of West Florida. As with my previous books, I am grateful for the assistance of research librarians Britt McGowan, Kellie Sparks, and Shari Johnson for their help in tracking down some of the most obscure journal articles ever requested. I also thank the staff of the Escambia County (Florida)

Law Library for allowing me access to parts of the collection usually available only to working attorneys.

Other helpful colleagues at UWF included former chairs Bruce Swain and Kurt Wise from the Department of Communication, where I once taught. I was also fortunate to locate three primary sources who were helpful in providing meaningful quotes as well as assistance with fact-checking. Although it wasn't planned this way, they approached the task from three different professional perspectives: employment attorney Mark F. Kluger, management professor Bruce Barry, and author and social media expert Samuel Greengard. I also thank the acquisition editors at Bloomsbury Publishing (formerly Rowman and Littlefield), Nicolette Amstutz and Jessie Tepper.

Introduction

Odd Couple

At first glance, Trevor Keezor and Lawrence Summers would appear to have little in common. In 2009, Keezor was a twenty-year-old employee of Home Depot in Okeechobee, Florida, making less than $30,000 a year and living a lower-middle-class existence. Four years earlier, Summers, a former Secretary of the Treasury under President Bill Clinton, was president of Harvard University and a frequent guest on television news-interview programs.

What the two now have in common is notoriety and being the subject of news stories that, in hindsight, they would have preferred to stay out of. Keezor was fired from his job for refusing to remove a button stating "One Nation Under God" from his company-issued apron. Keezor insisted that he was merely expressing his love for the country and showing support for a family member serving in the military. But the company claimed that despite his intent, the button violated the company's policy about wearing any items on their aprons or personal clothing that advocated a political or religious viewpoint. Because Home Depot is a private employer and not a government agency, the employee had no claim that his First Amendment rights were violated.[1]

Summers was an invited speaker at a January 2005 conference on women and minorities in the sciences and opined that women were underrepresented in the field because of "innate differences in scientific and mathematical aptitude," analogizing the disparity to the scarcity of Catholics in banking, white men in professional basketball, and Jews in agriculture.[2] The focus of the conference was on systemic discrimination in the field, and Summers's comments rankled not only conference attendees but also the Harvard Board of Trustees. Summers kept his job, but resigned the following year after a "no-confidence" vote of the Harvard faculty.[3]

"His remarks would have been protected from reprisal under academic freedom had they been made by a regular professor, but being a university president involves additional responsibilities," wrote civil rights advocate

Suzanne Nossel in a 2020 book, *Dare to Speak: Defending Free Speech for All*. "Having made the comments in an official capacity, Summers could not argue that they did not reflect on his leadership at Harvard."[4]

Dividing Line Blurred

For more than a century, court rulings have drawn a dividing line between public and private employers. Public employers, such as federal, state, and local governments, as well as regulatory agencies, public universities, and school boards, cannot (or are not supposed to) limit the speech rights of their employees or punish them after the fact for alleged harmful speech. In contrast, private employers can and do limit the speech of their employees and provide appropriate punishment for resulting harm.

At least that's the theory. In reality, the dividing line is not as sharp as it might appear. Some government agencies, while constitutionally prohibited from encroaching on the speech rights of their employees, do so anyway, using a variety of justifications. Examples include branches of the military that limit the speech of their members in the interest of "maintaining order and discipline," law-enforcement agencies that limit the speech of their employees in order to "maintain the trust of the public," and public universities that attempt to limit the controversial speech of faculty members in order to protect the reputation of the institution, provide a "comfortable learning environment" for students, and adhere to the letter and spirit of Title IX, a 1972 law dealing with sex discrimination in higher education.

In contrast, some private employers, while not obligated to do so, encourage free speech and debate among their workers in the interest of promoting healthy debate in the meeting rooms and around the water cooler.

This book will examine both paradigms and will cover seven areas of employment: corporations, government (local, state, and federal), the military, law enforcement, K–12 education, college professors and administrators, and sports. In addition, it will deal with how technology has affected this area of the law. While free speech in the workplace has always been controversial, the phenomenon of social media has caused the number of cases to explode in the last decade, as disgruntled employees take to Facebook, Instagram, Twitter, TikTok, and their own personal blogs to criticize their employers, sometimes behind a veil of anonymity and sometimes not.

There are three issues that come up in multiple chapters. The first is political involvement, as it would be difficult to produce a complete book on the topic of workplace expression without spending many pages discussing that hornets' nest. Here, politics is found in four of the nine chapters.

In Chapter 3, which deals with corporations, the focus is on whether private employers can regulate the political activity or speech of their employees in the form of campaign buttons on clothing, display of campaign materials on vehicles or in offices or cubicles, or conversations in the break room or around the water cooler.

In Chapter 4, which deals with government employees, the focus is on how government employers deal with the same issues, as well as the age-old issue of patronage—the hiring or firing of employees based on their membership in political parties. In Chapters 7 and 8, which deal with education, the focus is on how employees, from kindergarten teachers up to graduate school professors, are maligned for using social media platforms to express opinions on a variety of political issues, some related to their areas of expertise and some not.

The second aspect of workplace expression that comes up in multiple chapters is employees' use of social media to opine about a variety of topics—again, sometimes related to their jobs or areas of expertise and sometimes not. In addition to that dichotomy, one critical detail involved in all of these cases is where, when, and how the expression took place: in the workplace or outside, on company time or the employee's personal time, and using company equipment or their own personal devices. The centuries-old rule advice that you should "think before you speak" applies today in the form of "think before you email," "think before you text," and "think before you post on social media." Many years ago, one of my favorite graduate school professors explained that the most valuable function in any electronic mail application is "save as draft" and the most dangerous is "reply all."

The third concept that appears in multiple chapters is whistleblowing, as it occurs in nearly every type of workplace.

There are a few issues this book does not cover. As mentioned at the opening of Chapter 8, it does not deal with opinions that are part of classroom teaching or academic research. There is a brief mention of these ideas in that chapter, but only to contrast them with other issues that are covered.

It also does not deal with offensive comments made off the top of one's head, such as those made by a politician during a heated exchange at a news conference or campaign rally, or by an athlete during the heat of competition. An example of the latter is a homophobic slur made by a professional golfer after missing a short putt (this case is mentioned briefly in Chapter 9, but only to contrast it with other more serious cases). Instead, these chapters will deal with "premeditated" comments or opinions that a person stands behind and does not apologize for.

Bristle While You Work

Depending on which survey you believe, American adults spend somewhere between one-third and one-half of their waking hours at work. According to Cynthia Estlund, author of a 1995 article in *Indiana Law Journal*, that means free-speech rights in the workplace "enhance human development and well-being no less than freedom of expression in our civic life."[5]

As far back as 1960, workplace sociologist Howard K. Vollmer noted this trend as a result of research he conducted throughout the American workplace in the late 1950s. "Employees tend to have more at stake in the employment relationship in terms of career orientation within a professional or semi-professional occupation; at the same time, they have less at stake in terms of deep personal commitments," he wrote in his book, *Employee Rights and the Employment Relationship*.[6]

Another factor is that for the last half-century, Americans have become hypersensitive to other people's speech—even if it is legal and ethical—simply because it upsets their own sense of right and wrong, especially when it comes to delicate topics such as politics, race, and sex.

One of the first academic journals to address the issue of workplace speech was *Harvard Business Review*. Its 1975 article identified the late 1960s and early 1970s as marking a turning point for employee rights. "Once, differences of opinion between an employee and his or her employer concerning policies and practices were resolved within the organization," the article stated. "It was the manager's place to arbitrate and the employee's place to accept the manager's decision. The only proper course of action for an employee who could not abide by the decision was to resign." Now, the article added, employees have substantially more rights, but often need help from their unions or personal attorneys to assert them.[7] What the article could not have possibly anticipated is how the issue has exploded in the age of social media.

In his 2007 book, *Speechless: The Erosion of Free Speech in the American Workplace*, Bruce Barry identified six trends contributing to the increase in litigation regarding workplace expression since the turn of the new millennium: (1) employment being less stable and more transitional, (2) a decline in unionization, meaning fewer advocates for employee rights, (3) an increase in political participation of corporations, which may not like employees taking opposing positions, (4) a desire by companies for their employees to show more loyalty, (5) the availability of more workplace technology, and (6) the trend of people spending more time at work and less at home.[8]

Free-speech protection covers good-faith whistleblowing (also protected by other federal laws), criticism of employer policy that may not involve public safety but matters of public concern, and comments unrelated to the company's industry. It does not protect defamation, harassment, release of information that includes confidential business information, or comments related to personal grievances.

Sometimes even public comments that are legal and made with the best of intentions backfire on the speakers and subject them to disciplinary action from their employers as well as threats and harassment from strangers on social media. One such case occurred in New Hampshire in 2018, when three college professors and four public-school employees spoke in support of a high school guidance counselor accused of sexually assaulting a student. They clarified that their comments were not meant to excuse her behavior—to which she had already pleaded guilty—but rather to provide the court with information that would be helpful in her sentencing. That didn't sit well with the statewide media and advocacy groups for women and children, who accused her of "protecting a predator," and bloggers and trolls added their own vitriol. (This case is discussed in more detail in Chapter 8).

A similar case occurred in 2023, when an executive with U.S. Figure Skating was demoted in her job based on four years of Facebook comments—most of them posted before she was hired—in which she supported a friend, skater John Coughlin, who had been accused of sexually assaulting at least four female skaters prior to his death by suicide in 2019. Like in the New Hampshire case, Kelsey Parker Gislason claimed her posts, which carried hashtags such as #Justiceforjohncoughlin and #TheJohnIKnew, were not intended to argue for his innocence, but rather to provide critics with "another side of the story." That explanation, along with a public apology, wasn't good enough for USFS officials, who allowed Parker Gislason to keep her job but relegated her to a less prestigious position in which she would not have direct contact with athletes.[9]

Parker Gislason's critics included Senator Richard Blumenthal of Connecticut, a leading advocate for sexual assault survivors, and Olympic skater Ashley

Wagner, one of his accusers. "This individual (Parker Gislason) was extremely vocal against the truth of our experiences," Wagner posted on Instagram. "As soon as you put that out on social media, you should become unhireable for certain positions."[10]

Defining Our Terms

Two related legal terms are critical here: "employment at will" and "state action."

At-will employment, which is largely a function of state law, refers to a class of employees who are working without the benefit of any contract or promise of ongoing employment. A popular expression is that they "may be dismissed for any reason, or no reason at all," but the second half of that phrase is a misnomer. While in most states employers don't have to give a specific reason for terminating an at-will employee, the most defensible cases are related to an employee's competence or attitude, workplace chemistry, or the employer's financial status. Recent cases, discussed in this chapter as well as Chapters 3 and 4, involve support for political and social causes (as demonstrated by buttons on clothing or bumper stickers on vehicles parked on employer property) that the employer finds objectionable. Business journalist Kelley Holland contends these at-will cases are the most troubling, considering the value that society and the courts place on political expression. "Most employees in the private sector have little or no legal protection against discrimination based on political activity or even political speech," she wrote in a 2006 article in *The New York Times*. "They can even be fired or turned down for a job for their political beliefs."[11]

An at-will termination can even be for something as trivial as support for a specific sports team; talking about your love of the Boston Red Sox could get you fired if your boss is a fan of the New York Yankees.

Impermissible reasons for termination not allowed under the at-will concept include:

- *Federally protected classes such as age, race, sex, sexual orientation, religion, nationality, marital status, veteran status, disability, or pregnancy.*
- *Political beliefs.* Employers may prohibit display of political messages on clothing in workspaces, but political leanings and party affiliations are generally protected.
- *Good-faith whistleblowing* (discussed in Chapters 1, 5, and 7).

- *Union activity* (sometimes referred to as "concerted activity"). Employers cannot discipline or fire employees for criticizing their working conditions, such as pay, scheduling, safety, or other workplace conditions; or comments related to advocacy of or opposition to a union. Those comments are protected the same whether they take place on social media, in-person in a break room, or off-property.
- *Lifestyle discrimination*. This is a relatively new term and varies by state; some examples are provided in Chapter 1.

Here's the catch: there are nearly invisible dividing lines between some of the permissible and impermissible justifications. An employee can be terminated for speaking ad nauseum about support for gay rights, for example, but not for being gay. He or she can be fired for over-sharing religious beliefs about abortion, but not for being an evangelical Christian. In all such cases, courts require plaintiffs (employees) to prove their termination was based on illegal motivations; the defendants (employers) don't have to prove their motivations were justifiable—although their attorneys will make sure before their first court appearance that motivations are defensible if questioned. The chapters that follow provide numerous examples of that murkiness.

There are other nuances in the law. One is the exception that requires private employers to honor the constitutional rights of their employees in cases in which they enjoy government contracts. The most common examples are defense contractors that provide products and services to the military. Those situations are often decided on a case-by-case basis, with examples discussed in Chapter 4.

"Because the at-will employment doctrine gives employers the power to discharge employees at any time for any reason, including speech disliked by the employer, employers have tremendous power over employees who often silence themselves fearing termination if they do not," wrote Lawrence Soley, a professor of communication law at Marquette University, in a 2002 book. "Under the at-will employment doctrine, this threat is ubiquitous."[12]

There are two other exceptions that seldom apply but are worth mentioning. One involves cases in which there is an "implied contract" that arises when employers make promises about job security in employment handbooks or other written statements. The final exception involves the dismissal of a long-term employee that "violates the implied covenant of good faith and fair dealing."[13] The latter is so vague that it is difficult to enforce.

"This same doctrine (at-will) does allow private-sector employers to terminate employees if they don't like their political or social views," says Mark F. Kluger, author of a number of articles in professional newsletters and a partner in the firm of Kluger Healey, LLC in Montclair, New Jersey. "In an at-will environment, if an employee espouses views on social media on politics or social issues, with which their employer disagrees or feels may harm the employer's reputation, there is little if anything an employee can do if they are terminated based on their posts."[14] Kluger uses the recent examples of employees attending the 2017 Charlottesville "Unite the Right" rally as well as public protests in support of Black Lives Matter and against the 2020 killing of George Floyd.

State action refers to cases in which a federal, state, or local government entity is the party attempting to prohibit or punish speech. When the government entity takes such action overtly, it is easy to label it as "state action," but cases become murky when the action is taken by a private employer performing a government function, such as when a state "privatizes" functions such as charter schools, prisons, or lotteries; or when the U.S. Department of Defense grants contracts to companies to manufacture weapons or other specialized technology (Chapter 4 deals with this issue in more detail). The concept of state action became part of employment law through a series of cases in the late 1800s in which the Supreme Court drew a dividing line between public and private employers, determining that public employers had to respect the constitutional rights of their employees, while private employers did not.[15]

One example of a "concerted activity" is found in the 1962 Supreme Court case of *NLRB v. Washington Aluminum*, in which employees were engaged in "concerted activity" when they walked out due to cold conditions on the manufacturing floor. Although the case involved a refusal to work rather than workplace speech, the case is still cited in speech cases because of the "concerted activity" principle; the conduct in question was directly related to working conditions.[16]

The concept of "concerted activity" includes an "exception to the exception" provision: a seldom-used rule regarding "unnecessary disloyalty to an employer."[17] At first glance, that might sound like a catch-all claim that employers could use to oppose just about any speech they didn't like, but in a 1953 case, *NLRB v. Local Union No. 1229*, the Supreme Court provided clarity. In that case, electricians at a Charlotte, North Carolina television station were involved in contract negotiations with management. They did not go on strike but instead peacefully picketed outside the station, at first protesting the station's refusal to negotiate in good faith but later shifting to criticisms of the station's programming. The management claimed that the new focus of the protest showed disloyalty to the station and terminated the employees, prompting them to sue in federal district court. When the case reached the Supreme Court, the justices ruled in favor of station management, determining that criticizing programming decisions was unrelated to the original labor dispute.[18]

One of the most bizarre applications of at-will employment rules applied to free-speech issues did not involve an employee who was denied the right to speak, but instead one who refused to speak. In the 1950s, Peter Petermann was employed by the Teamsters Union of California as a business agent. When he was called to testify to a state legislative committee, union leaders provided him with a list of anticipated questions and recommended answers—many of them falsehoods. When he refused to answer questions from the prepared list and instead spoke truthfully, he was fired. He sued the union, losing in district court but winning at the appeals level.[19]

Two cases involving nurses that illustrate the concept of state action (or the lack of it) are discussed in Chapter 3, but here are brief summaries. The 1973 case of *Rafferty v. Philadelphia Psychiatric Center* began when a nurse at a state-run psychiatric hospital was fired after being quoted in a local newspaper about staff conduct and the quality of patient care at a state-run psychiatric hospital. The article quoting Linda Rafferty led to animosity among her superiors and coworkers and met the definition of "workplace disruption" that in other cases would have justified her firing. But in this case, the court overlooked the workplace disruption angle and ruled in her favor, determining first that the hospital received public funding, which qualified Rafferty's comments for First Amendment protection, and second, she was "engaging in precisely the sort of free and vigorous expression that the First Amendment was designed to protect."[20]

Fifteen years later in Arizona, a court made a different ruling in *Jones v. Memorial Hospital.* The nurse at the center of the case was unsuccessful in her claim that the hospital violated her First Amendment rights when it fired her after a local newspaper published her letter to the editor that was critical of hospital policy. The plaintiff's attorneys claimed the hospital held a number of government contracts and that qualified it as a public employer under the concept of "state action," but the court did not equate that relationship as the same as that between a private contractor that held contracts with branches of the military.[21]

Master and Servant

While most public-sector employees enjoy some First Amendment protections for their controversial expressions, their counterparts in the private sector do not, as the doctrine of "at-will" employment means they serve at the pleasure of their employers.

English labor attorney Lucy Vickers analogizes the unbalanced relationship to that of master and servant in her 2002 book, *Freedom of Speech in Employment*. Her examples are mostly from the English legal system, but similar examples are found in the United States. "The employer controls the activities of the employee during the period during which the employee is contracted to work, and sometimes beyond," Vickers wrote. "The control exerted by the employer over the employee can, for the most part, be viewed as a fair exchange for the wages received by the employee. In effect, the employee forfeits personal autonomy in return for financial security."[22]

Many legal scholars agree. "U.S. society is a paradox," wrote civil liberties attorney David W. Ewing in his book, *Freedom Inside the Organization*, published nearly a half-century ago.

> The Constitution and the Bill of Rights light up the sky over political campaigners, legislators, civic leaders, families, church people, and artists. But not so over employees. The employee sector of our civil liberties universe is much like a black hole, with rights so compacted, so imploded by the gravitational forces of legal tradition, that, like the giant black stars in the physical universe, light can scarcely escape.[23]

Labor attorneys claim that the situation has greatly improved since the 1960s. Thomas Emerson, professor emeritus at Princeton University, wrote in the 1970s that "A system of freedom of expression that allowed private bureaucracies to throttle all internal discussion of their affairs would be seriously deficient. There seems to be general agreement that at some points the government must step in. In any event, the law is moving steadily in that direction."[24]

In *Speechless*, Barry described the at-will concept as "an employer's leeway to hire and fire without dwelling over niceties such as due process and other constitutional rights."[25] Earlier in the same book, Barry wrote that "a toxic combination of law, conventional economic wisdom, and accepted managerial practice has created an American workplace where freedom of speech—that most crucial of civil liberties in a healthy democracy—is something you do after work, on your own time, and even then (for many) only if your employer approves."[26]

In Lewis Maltby's book on the same topic, Barry adds that "Your boss can fire you for your politics, the books you read, or even the baseball team you root for, and there's usually nothing you can do about it."[27]

"Every industrial organization is at one time or another faced by the problems of a few, or perhaps more than a few, troublesome employees who refuse to cooperate in a way satisfactory to management," wrote Vollmer in his 1960 book.[28]

In discussing the phenomenon of employers punishing employees for behavioral issues that occur off-hours and off-property, Vollmer used the hypothetical example of an employee who was arrested following a bar fight and was terminated when his supervisor heard about it. The author interviewed a number of workers who identified as peers of the terminated employee as well as those in supervisory roles or human resources management. The former group all sided with the terminated employee, pointing out that the man's behavior did not affect his work (assuming he was out of jail in time to clock in the next day) and did not affect the reputation of the company. Conversely, the latter group sided with the supervisor, claiming that even off-hours and off-property behavior was related to an employee's judgment and character.[29]

Fast-forward six decades and one could see the lines have blurred between on-hours and off-hours behavior, especially when it comes to political involvement and social media activity.

"Employment contracts are not always ideally voluntary agreements, since realities of the employment market often place significantly more power in the hands of the employer than in the hands of the individual prospective employee," wrote philosophy professors Joseph R. Des Jardins and John T. McCall in a 1985 article in the *Journal of Business Ethics*. When an employer says "accept my offer," they added, the employee often reacts as though an armed robber has said "your money or your life."[30]

The Sword of Damocles and the Chilling Effect

A book titled *Tusculan Disputations*, authored by the Roman philosopher Cicero in 45 BC, includes a parable about a man who must work with a razor-sharp sword over his head that is dangling by a single strand of horsehair. One wrong move, the man knows, will result in the sword falling on his head and ending his life. The parable, titled "The Sword of Damocles," describes how many employees feel about the threat that awaits them when they express their free-speech rights. Modern-day labor law experts use the term "chilling effect" to describe the reluctance of employees to speak out for fear of losing their jobs. To use another metaphor, they know the deck is stacked against them, meaning they must weigh the benefits of expressing themselves against the risk of losing their jobs.[31]

One reason behind the reluctance of employees to challenge workplace rules regarding their free-speech rights is the inconsistency in results for those who have done so previously. With outcomes so uncertain, employees must weigh the benefit of speaking out against the risks involved, and in many cases, the "chilling effect" works to suppress their speech. Added to that is the employers' use of free-speech sanctions as an excuse to discharge employees for being the wrong race, gender, religion, or sexual orientation. Terminated employees can sue for discrimination under appropriate state or federal laws, but once in court the burden of proof is on them to establish the real reason behind the dismissal.[32] "The chilling effect is very real," said Annalee Newitz, a policy analyst for the Electronic Frontier Foundation, in a 2005 article in *USA Today*. "We don't want people to feel like they can't express their feelings."[33]

A 2023 study by LeanIn.org, a nonprofit organization co-founded by Facebook CEO Sheryl Sandberg, found that workplace speech issues are especially problematic for women, making them less likely to speak up in male-dominated workplaces. "Women self-shield or self-monitor, meaning they change the way they act or look, tone down what they say, or hide aspects of their identity to protect themselves from mistreatment," stated the report, titled *Women in the Workplace*.[34]

The study also found that nearly half of LGBTQ women admitted they toned down what they say to avoid being "unlikeable" and nearly half of women with disabilities didn't speak up or share opinions so they would not be labeled by supervisors or coworkers as "difficult." The report concluded that such tendencies not only result in less workplace satisfaction for women but also contribute to health problems such as stress and high blood pressure.[35]

In cases discussed in Chapter 6, police officers cited the "chilling effect" to describe their reluctance to speak out after seeing what happened to coworkers who challenged their working conditions.

Not a Hill to Die On

Nossel says that the chilling effect is not necessarily a bad thing. "We owe it to one another to be mindful of what we say, in light of who may hear it," she wrote in *Dare to Speak*. "If we willfully dodge that duty—firing off a drunken tweet, failing to reread a mass email before hitting 'send,' or wading into a public debate on a subject we know little about—we may pay a price."[36]

Plymouth State University Professor Gary Goodnough made a similar decision heavily influenced by the chilling effect during a 2018 conflict with the university's administration. While two colleagues continued to press their free speech cases against the university, Goodnough chose a less confrontational approach. "While there was some temptation to fight it, I decided that my overarching objective was to get on with my career," Goodnough said. "As I said to many people, it was not a fight that I was willing to give up my career for."[37]

Notes

1 "Home Depot Employee Claims He Was Fired Over 'One Nation Under God' Pin," *New York Daily News,* October 28, 2009.

2 Suzanne Nossel, *Dare to Speak: Defending Free Speech for All* (New York: Dey Street Publishing, 2020), p. 30.

3 Ibid.

4 Ibid., p. 40.

5 Cynthia L. Estlund, "Free Speech and Due Process in the Workplace," *Indiana Law Journal* 71, no. 1 (Winter 1995): pp. 101–51. See also: Rudy Nydegger, *Clocking In: The Psychology of Work* (Santa Barbara, CA: Greenwood Publishing, 2018), p. 54.

6 Howard M. Vollmer, *Employee Rights and the Employment Relationship* (Berkeley, CA: University of California Press, 1960), p. 86.

7 Kenneth Walters, "Your Employees' Right to Blow the Whistle," *Harvard Business Review,* July–August 1975, pp. 26–34 and 161–3.

8 Bruce Barry, *Speechless: The Erosion of Free Speech in the American Workplace* (San Francisco: Berrett-Koehler Publishers, 2007), pp. 22–3.

9 Christine Brennan, "USFS Employee Apologies for Skater Support," *USA Today,* June 29, 2023, p. 4-C.

10 Ibid.

11 Kelley Holland, "How Office Politics and Real Politics Can Mix," *The New York Times,* October 8, 2006.
12 Lawrence Soley, *Censorship, Inc.: The Corporate Threat to Free Speech in the United States (*New York: Monthly Review Press, 2002), pp. 55–6.
13 Bruce Barry, "The Cringing and the Craven: Freedom of Expression in, Around, and Beyond the Workplace," *Business Ethics Quarterly* 17, no. 2 (2007): pp. 263–96. See also: Clyde W. Summers, "Employment at Will in the United States: The Divine Right of Employers," *University of Pennsylvania Journal of Business Law* 3 (2000): pp. 65–86.
14 Mark F. Kluger, interview with the author, January 2, 2024.
15 Barry, "The Cringing and the Craven."
16 *NLRB v. Washington Aluminum*, 370 U.S. 9 (1962).
17 *NLRB v. Local Union No. 1229,* 346 U.S. 464 (1953).
18 *NLRB v. Local Union No. 1229.* See also: Barry, *Speechless*, pp. 51–2.
19 *Petermann v. International Brotherhood of Teamsters*, 344 P. 2d 25 (1959).
20 *Rafferty v. Philadelphia Psychiatric Center*, 356 F. Supp. 500 (1973).
21 *Jones v. Memorial Hospital* (746 S.W. 2d 891 (1988)).
22 Lucy Vickers, *Freedom of Speech and Employment* (New York: Oxford University Press, 2002), p. 2.
23 David W. Ewing, *Freedom Inside the Organization: Bringing Civil Liberties to the Workplace* (New York: E.P. Dutton, 1977), p. 5.
24 Robert Ellis Smith, *Workrights* (New York: E.P. Dutton, Inc., 1983), p. 82. See also: Thomas I. Emerson, *The System of Freedom of Expression* (New York: Random House, 1970), p. 677.
25 Barry, *Speechless*, p. 97.
26 Ibid., p. 5.
27 Lewis Maltby, *Can They Do That? Retaking Our Fundamental Rights in the Workplace* (New York: Penguin Group, 2009), p. 5.
28 Vollmer, *Employee Rights and the Employment Relationship*, pp. 118–21.
29 Ibid.
30 Joseph R. Des Jardins and John T. McCall, "A Defense of Employee Rights," *Journal of Business Ethics* 4, no. 5 (1985): pp. 367–76.
31 Estlund, "Free Speech and Due Process in the Workplace."
32 Ibid.
33 Stephanie Armour, "Warning: Your Clever Little Blog Could Get You Fired," *USA Today*, June 14, 2005.
34 Jessica Guynn, "Microaggressions Take a Major Toll," *USA Today*, October 12, 2023, p. 1-B.

35 Ibid.

36 Nossel, *Dare to Speak*, p. 28.

37 Randy Bobbitt, *The View From Under the Bus: A Case Study in Media Influence, Public Opinion, and Moral Outrage* (Pensacola, FL: Windchase Bay Publishing, 2020), p. 52.

1

Legal Framework

The First Amendment, Whistleblowing, and Unionization

The First Amendment to the U.S. Constitution provides that "Congress shall make no law respecting an establishment of religion, or prohibiting the free exercise thereof; or abridging the freedom of speech, or of the press, or the right of the people peaceably to assemble, or to petition the government for a redress of grievances." Now more than 230 years old, the amendment may be the most controversial fifty-four words ever composed.

Many First Amendment scholars contend that the speech clause is at the heart of what James Madison had in mind when he penned the amendment in 1791. He was most concerned with the rights of individuals to criticize the government in essays or oratory. But when employees in the private sector try to use the First Amendment as a defense, different rules apply.

"Our system of constitutional law generally fails to protect civil liberties, including free speech, from actions that threaten or infringe among them when those actions are committed by private parties," Bruce Barry wrote in his 2007 book, *Speechless: The Erosion of Free Expression in the American Workplace.* "Employers in the private sector have no obligation to respect the expressive rights or impulses of those who work for them. Even in public-sector jobs, where government is the employer, the reach of the First Amendment is quite limited."[1]

In cases in which private industry employees challenge their companies or bosses on issues related to free speech, they find that one of the general rules that apply in other free-speech cases does not help them. Under the concept of "strict scrutiny," a local, state, or government entity wishing to enforce a law that restricts someone's speech bears the burden to prove why such a law is necessary. A simple hypothetical: A city council passes an ordinance limiting to four the number of political yard signs allowed on one property owner's lawn.

If a property owner wanted to display more than four and chose to challenge the law, the city council—not the property owner—would have to explain to the court's satisfaction why the ordinance was necessary and how it arrived at the limitation of four.

That burden of proof applies in nearly every other application of First Amendment law— except when it comes to the speech of employees who work in the private sector, especially in states where the "at-will" concept is written into state law. If an employer wanted to enact a company-wide rule prohibiting employees from giving newspaper interviews without their supervisors' permission, for example, the employees challenging the rule would have to demonstrate to the court why the rule was unfair. Unless it was discriminatory, such as in cases in which female employees had to have permission but male employees did not, it is unlikely the employees would prevail.

Within the English legal system in the early 1700s, judge and legal scholar William Blackstone advocated a philosophy allowing for near-absolute freedom of speech, but it came with a caveat: while citizens should feel free to say anything they wanted to, they must still be held accountable after the fact for any harm that resulted from their speech.[2] Three hundred years later, business and technology writer Samuel Greengard suggested that philosophy should be the general rule applied to employees who chose to discuss workplace issues on their personal blogs. "Firms could give employees the freedom to post what they want, but hold them accountable for it," Greengard wrote in a 2005 article in *Workplace Management.* "If they post something that does damage to the company or its causes, there will be consequences. That could include a reprimand, disciplinary action or, in a worst-case scenario, termination."[3]

Bill Lueders, editor of *The Progressive*, adds that "reasonable people may disagree about what the First Amendment requires or protects, but two things are true: the government is not supposed to infringe on free speech, and no one is ever free of consequences for what they say and do."[4]

Courts are careful to draw the line between "speech" and "conduct"—regulating the former is more difficult than regulating the latter. One example of "conduct" is what labor lawyers call "lifestyle discrimination," referring to an employer who determines a person's ability to do the job is affected by smoking, obesity, or other health risks; or one who makes value judgments about an unmarried couple's decision to live together; or one who makes judgments about an unmarried woman who becomes pregnant. Financial guru Dave Ramsey, for example, has terminated employees, including on-air personalities on his radio program, for having extramarital affairs or becoming pregnant without being married. Several states have enacted laws prohibiting lifestyle discrimination, but Ramsey's home state of Tennessee is not among them. When employees who are terminated for violating his rules or leave the company for other reasons, he doubles down and enforces non-disparagement rules—signed at the time of hiring—that prohibit former employees from publicly criticizing him, his family, his company, or its sponsors. Those agreements do not bar those individuals from seeking legal remedies. According to media accounts, between 2015 and 2022, Ramsey settled at least a dozen wrongful termination suits (based on alleged lifestyle discrimination) without going to court.[5]

There are two types of employment agreements that arise in some free-speech cases.

A non-disclosure agreement, sometimes referred to as a confidentiality agreement or proprietary information agreement, is a document signed by a new employee when the employment relationship begins.

Non-disparagement agreements, which apply mainly to employees who resign from a company or are involuntarily terminated, prohibit those individuals from publicly criticizing the employer. Such documents are more difficult to enforce than non-disclosure agreements. In many cases, courts find disparagement agreements vague and overbroad; instead of allowing employers to enforce them, they require employers to pursue cases using state laws dealing with libel and slander. The courts' tendency to side with employees is based on the idea that free-speech rights are so fundamental to individual liberty that employees can't sign them away, even if they wanted to.

There are two sticking points that arise in cases where employees challenge the validity of agreements they signed. The first is to what degree the agreement is enforceable, and for what period of time, after the employment relationship is terminated. Court rulings are mostly consistent, determining that NDAs are enforceable in perpetuity, regardless of the conditions under which the relationship ended. The second issue involves whistleblower protection, and in those cases the courts provide limited protection for the employee; once a court or regulatory agency determines that the whistleblower is making a good-faith claim, the employer cannot counter that claim by attempting to enforce the non-disclosure or non-disparagement agreement. In December 2022, President Joe Biden signed into law the Speak Out Act, which prevents the enforcement of non-disclosure agreements in cases related to claims of sexual assault or sexual harassment.[6]

Non-disclosure and non-disparagement agreements do beg the question: If you run your business honestly and ethically and treat employees well, why do you need to swear them to silence?

The Devil in the Details

Even within organizations that claim to encourage employee expression, there are five general exceptions that employers can use to either shut down speech before it does harm and/or use to defend themselves against lawsuits when terminating the offending employees. Those exceptions involve communication that (1) disrupts the climate or operation of the workplace, (2) exposes the employer to charges of discrimination or harassment, (3) is defamatory, (4) is based on personal grievances rather than matters of public concern (whistleblowing), or (5) constitutes threats to managers, coworkers, or customers.[7]

Some literature in the fields of workplace law or human resources management list another exception—communication that compromises intellectual property, trade secrets, or other confidential information—but there is little case law to illustrate it. These guidelines provide some degree of predictability regarding the outcome of court cases.

Just because cases involving intellectual property and trade secrets are hard to find doesn't mean they have never happened. Barry says the difficulty in finding cases might be a result of the reluctance of companies to publicize cases so as to not draw more attention to them[8] and Kluger adds, "If an employee is going to reveal intellectual property or trade secrets, they are far more likely to do so in a non-public communication and one that will be for their potential personal gain not for revenge. Remarkably, it is not uncommon for those kinds of breaches to occur using the employee's company email account through the employer's server."[9]

Courts generally not only allow employers to limit speech in cases that fall within those five guidelines but also look to see if the rules apply equally to all employees. "If speech devolves into harassment or discrimination, that's typically a violation of company policy and the employee can be subject to discipline or firing," said labor attorney Kelly Dobbs Bunting in a 2023 interview with *SHRM News*. "But those policies have to be applied evenly to all workers. Otherwise, you could face discrimination or retaliation allegations."[10]

Chapters 3 through 9 include discussions of how those general legal guidelines apply to specific fields, along with guidelines that belong specifically to cases in that chapter. There are exceptions for each principle, however, and those, too, are included. Some are the result of hair-splitting exercises on the part of the courts, while others are simply outliers that lead to head-scratching for any readers not familiar with the nuances of the law.

Workplace Disruption. As a general matter, the courts have ruled that the potential for "employee disharmony" or "workplace disruption" is often overstated and results from "oversensitivity to criticism" or "bureaucratic paranoia," although this applies mostly to government agencies, schools, and first responders rather than private employers.[11]

A 1995 article in *Indiana Law Journal* points out that employers must recognize the dividing line between constructive commentary and harmful expressions such as "personal insults, divisive gossip, racial slurs, sexual taunts, propositions, innuendo, and the like" that may harm coworkers and affect morale and productivity.[12]

Discrimination and Harassment. One common rationale for employers monitoring their employees' computer usage is the issue of online hate and harassment. A 2023 study by the Anti-Defamation League found that the number of Americans reporting being harassed online increased from 40 percent in 2022 to more than 50 percent the following year, and that more than half of the vitriol took place on Facebook. ADL warns employers that if prosecutors can "connect the dots" and trace the conduct back to employer-owned computers, those employers can be liable as well.[13]

"I do think some guardrails around free speech are necessary," adds Greengard. "In my opinion, hate speech and threats should NOT be protected free speech. Yet anything involving reasonable political discourse should be permitted. It's the price we pay to live in a free society."[14]

Just as a supervisor's off-the-cuff comments can be subject to defamation suits, they might also be used in cases involving discrimination or harassment. In the 1994 case of *Cooley v. Carmike Cinemas*, for example, an older employee claiming he was terminated as part of a company's efforts to "purge older employees" used a supervisor's comments to make his case. Michael Patrick, president of a national chain of movie theatres, was already known for his dislike of older employees, making public comments such as "I don't like being around old people" and "everybody over thirty years old needs to be put in a pen or confined to a concentration camp."[15] Employee Aaron Cooley had worked at the company for more than forty years. Upon his termination, he sued the company for age discrimination and won a $516,000 judgment.[16]

"Racist speech in the workplace, in both the public and private sectors, may be subject to penalties because it is intertwined with discriminatory conduct," wrote civil libertarian Rodney A. Smolla in his 1992 book on free speech. "Society is entitled to enact legislation for the purpose of encouraging 'racism-free' and 'sexism-free' workplaces."[17]

In 1995, a federal court ruled that a company was guilty of harassment by failing to prevent a supervisor from pushing his religious views on a subordinate. Shirley Peck sued Sony Pictures Corporation after she was terminated for allegedly complaining about her supervisor, James Nevius, telling her she was a "sinner who needed to repent." Peck also complained about an employee engaging in unwelcome religious discussions on company timethe employee told others they were "sinners and had to repent." Peck also complained that Nevius sang religious songs in her presence and prayed over her desk. The court ruled in Peck's favor, and Nevius was terminated.[18]

In a 2004 case, an employee of Hewlett-Packard sued the company after he was terminated for complaining that HP's diversity initiatives, which included support for gay and lesbian employees, violated his religious beliefs. Richard Peterson had worked in the Boise, Idaho, offices of HP for more than two decades when it began decorating walls with posters celebrating the diversity of its employees in terms of age, race, nationality, and sexual orientation. Peterson objected the most to the latter and responded by decorating his own work cubicle, in clear view of coworkers, with Bible verses denouncing homosexuality. Peterson's supervisor told him the verses violated the company's anti-discrimination policy that prohibited communication "related to a person's race, gender, religion, disability, age, sexual orientation, or ethnic background that fail to respect the dignity and feelings of individuals."[19] When he refused to remove the offending materials, he was fired.

Peterson sued the company in federal district court, claiming it did not accommodate his religious views. The court found in favor of the company, determining that his termination was due to insubordination and that HP's policy on workplace discrimination was applied in a reasonable manner, as it offered him the opportunity to remove the offending material. The court also found that the company's need to maintain office civility outweighed Peterson's right to speak about his religious views.[20]

Anti-discrimination laws also prohibit employers from establishing an "official language" or disciplining employees for speaking in their native languages in break rooms, common areas, or other non-work-related situations.[21]

Defamation. The concepts of "libel" and "defamation" are more often associated with the fields of journalism and broadcasting, but decades of case law have determined they can also be used by employees to sue their employers: libel in cases of official company publications and defamation in cases involving email and face-to-face speech. For the last two decades, court rulings have consistently ruled that defamation that takes place on social media, whether individuals do so at work or on their own time, is treated the same way as in cases a century ago. As U.S. Justice Department official Andrew Oosterbaan said in a 2004 media interview, "The Internet has changed the way the law is broken, but it has not changed the law."[22]

Even before the advent of the Internet and social media, the courts made fairly consistent rulings about defamation in non-journalistic venues, such as in business correspondence. In the 1974 case of *Arnett v. Kennedy*, for example, the Supreme Court ruled that federal employees were not protected by the First Amendment when they made allegedly defamatory remarks. The case involved Wayne Kennedy, a Chicago field representative for the federal government's Office of Economic Opportunity. He accused Regional Director Alvin J. Arnett and other officials of conflicts of interest, taking bribes, and violating treaties between the federal government and Native American tribes in the Midwest. He was fired and filed a lawsuit against Arnett. Lower courts sided with Kennedy, but the Supreme Court overturned those rulings and determined that Kennedy's comments were potentially libelous and did not have to be proven so in a defamation case to be classified as unprotected. Arnett claimed Kennedy's termination was allowed under the Lloyd-LaFollette Act, a 1912 law that allowed for federal employees to be dismissed in the interest of "promoting the efficiency of service." Kennedy argued that the law was unconstitutionally vague and overbroad, but the Court disagreed.[23]

In the 2001 case of *Meloff v. The New York Life Insurance Company*, a federal court determined that the rule about defamatory comments not being protected as free speech applied to the employer as well as the employee.[24] The plaintiff was Phyllis Meloff, a service consultant for New York Life, who was fired for using a company-issued credit card to pay personal expenses for which she did not reimburse her employer. The evidence against her was indisputable, but abuse of the policy was unethical, not illegal. That would have been the end of the case if not for an internal email message that was originally sent to only seven people but was later forwarded to others. The message carried the one-word subject line "FRAUD," and that term was repeated in the message itself. Because "fraud" is a legal term and not an ethical one, she was able to win a $1.25 million libel judgment against the company.[25]

While false accusations of a crime are a common complaint in libel cases, plaintiffs have a more difficult case in claims involving less serious accusations. In the 1998 case of *Lian v. Sedgewick James of New York, Inc.*, for example, a terminated employee was allowed to continue to use his office and computer while seeking a new job. When his supervisor sent a company-wide email that misstated the conditions of his termination and why he was allowed to maintain the office, Philip Lian disputed the language in the email and claimed it made it appear as though he acted unethically while servicing clients. When the "he said/he said" case went to federal district court, it was determined that while the supervisor's explanation included factual errors, it didn't rise to the level of defamation.[26]

The issue of defamation has become a larger problem in the era of social media. When employees use company computers to post defamatory information on the Internet, the company may not be directly liable for the damages but may still find itself in legal hot water. In 2006, for example, an employee of a Miami-based stock brokerage firm used a company laptop to alter the Wikipedia biography of professional golfer Fuzzy Zoeller, posting that he had abused drugs as well as his wife and children. Federal law prevented Zoeller from suing Wikipedia for the false information, but his lawyers were able to force the company to trace the source of the posts, which led to the stock brokerage firm. Unable to trace the posts to a specific person, however, Zoeller eventually dropped the case.[27] In another Florida case, a company executive didn't like what one specific employee said about him in a chat room, so he sued the Internet service provider involved and forced it to reveal the employee's identity.[28]

Charges of defamation often surface in cases involving union activity, but court rulings are typically in favor of employers, determining that union officials can safely criticize employers for their policies and practices but cannot make comments that are defamatory (based on state laws).[29]

Personal Grievances. Many cases of workplace speech leading to an employee's termination begin when an individual claims to be whistleblowing (defined later in this chapter), but upon further scrutiny, turn out to be based not on matters of public concern but rather an employee's personal grievance(s). A school teacher pointing out problems with the school system's financial planning is speaking about a matter of public concern, for example, whereas the same teacher would be treated differently when complaining about not getting a pay increase.

In 1926, a garage mechanic in Kentucky found that the principle of free speech didn't protect him from being sued when he posted signs in his window claiming a local veterinarian owed him money and wouldn't pay. The court ruled against him, determining that his speech was related to a private matter rather than a public concern, and the result was a violation of the veterinarian's privacy.[30]

In the 1970 case of *Kelly v. Florida Judicial Qualifications Commission*, the Florida Supreme Court ruled that a state district court judge could be disciplined for his criticisms of other judges because his comments were not motivated by concern for the public interest or judicial efficiency, but rather his own political ambitions. The court also dismissed the judge's claim that he was a whistleblower because his claims lacked "the whistleblower ethic—a desire to improve the performance and quality of public service." The case was decided by a narrow 4-3 vote, with the dissenting justices disagreeing with the majority's finding that the case was about the plaintiff's self-interest. Both sides, however, acknowledged that determining an individual's motive was "a difficult but critical task, since it differentiates the true whistleblower from the employee whose real object is harassment or blackmail."[31]

The landmark case in this area of the law began in Louisiana in 1980 and resulted in a 1983 Supreme Court case. The case involved Sheila Myers, an assistant district attorney, who circulated a questionnaire asking for employees of the office to comment on employee morale. After she was fired by District Attorney Harry Connick Sr., she sued, claiming the termination violated her First Amendment rights. A lower court ruled in Myers's favor and ordered her reinstated, but the Supreme Court reversed, determining that the questionnaire was motivated by her being transferred to another office against her wishes, and was therefore of personal, and not public, concern[32] (the case is discussed in more detail in Chapter 4).

That same year, a federal district court in Kansas made a similar ruling in *Mahaffey v. Kansas Board of Regents*. Ben Mahaffey had been an agricultural sciences professor at Kansas State University for more than a decade, and while popular among his students, he was disliked by his colleagues and administrators, who labeled him as a "chronic complainer." Unhappy with his salary and teaching assignments, he repeatedly availed himself of the university's grievance procedure.

Administrators allegedly retaliated against him by assigning him to teach lower-level classes, moving him to a smaller office, and restricting his access to university resources. When he filed suit, a federal district court ruled that his complaints were all based on personal gripes rather than matters of public concern.

A more recent case took place in Mississippi in 2012, when the court ruled against a police officer who criticized budgetary decisions made by her supervisor, determining that her comments were a "personal rant" rather than constructive comments on public policy (this case is discussed in more detail in Chapter 6).

Threats. Although the case law in this area is rather thin compared to the other exceptions, the courts take the matter just as seriously. In the 1996 case of *Smyth v. The Pillsbury Company,* for example, a federal district court ruled that overt threats were not protected by the First Amendment or an employer's promise of confidentiality in internal communications. Michael A. Smyth, an at-will employee of the Pillsbury Company, was at home and "off the clock" when he exchanged a series of emails with his supervisor. The supervisor described the emails as "inappropriate and unprofessional," but a closer reading revealed Smyth was threatening to kill his coworkers. When Smyth sued for wrongful termination, his claim was not that he didn't make the threats or that his comments were protected by the First Amendment, but rather that the company violated its own policies that promised that email communication was "confidential and privileged." The court ruled that the company's promise was not legally binding and that employees had no expectation of privacy, even though the confidentiality promise was part of the company's written policies. In addition, the threatening nature of the communication outweighed his claims of privacy and free speech.

Chapter 3 describes five cases—three involving nurses and two involving emergency medical technicians—whose comments, made as a result of frustrations with their working conditions, resulted in their termination. However, when they attempted to use the "workplace frustration" defense in court, they lost. The courts found their comments, even though they were made "in the heat of the moment," constituted legitimate threats to patient safety.

A Word to the Wiseguy: Squeaky Wheels Don't Always Get the Grease

One often unspoken rule about whistleblowing is that it must be done in good faith and not related to personal grievances. When done in good faith, whistleblowers perform a vital service in alerting the public, through either reports to regulatory authorities or disclosures to the media, of problems that may cost lives, or in the case of government agencies, taxpayer money.[33]

In a 1999 publication, the National Employee Rights Institute clarifies that, in order to be protected by law, whistleblowing "needs to be a violation of law, rule, or regulation, gross mismanagement, a gross waste of funds, an abuse of authority, or a substantial and specific danger to public health or safety."[34] Thomas Hanna, an attorney and author of a 2007 book that advises employers on labor law, wrote that "when an employee action purports to be in protest of something the company has allegedly done or failed to do, that is your signal to seek legal advice to determine if there is any likelihood of legally protected activity on the part of the employee."[35]

As in all areas of the law, there are many gray areas. Hanna cites the example of a work stoppage in order to protest unsafe working conditions as something that "may or may not be protected."[36]

Barry adds that whistleblowing must be "reporting on illegal, unethical, dangerous, or otherwise inappropriate behavior" and can be related to "a violation of the law, a regulatory infraction, a danger to public health or safety, an abuse of authority, financial malfeasance, a violation of corporate policy, or gross mismanagement."[37] The first two examples on Barry's list are related to illegal acts, whereas the other five are more nebulous. Whether a company's actions at the heart of the claim are illegal or simply unethical is significant, as some state laws deal with both while others deal only with the illegal.

Kenneth D. Walters, an attorney and professor of business at the University of Washington, explored the issue of whistleblowing in a 1975 article in *Harvard Business Review*.[38] Although the origin of the term is unclear, Walters gave credit for its creation to two books published three years earlier and bearing similar titles: *Whistle-Blowing* by Ralph Nader, Peter J. Petkas, and Kate Blackwell[39] and *Blowing the Whistle* by Charles Peters and Taylor Branch.[40] Peters and Branch described a whistleblower as "a muckraker from within, who exposes what he considers the unconscionable practice of his own organization."[41]

Even though private industry employees do not enjoy the same free-speech protections as their public-sector counterparts, they are protected when acting in good faith to warn their supervisors, the media, or regulatory agencies about workplace situations involving discrimination, defective products, or employee safety. Employees lose that protection when they cross the line into disruptive conduct or comments that are defamatory or threatening.

One of the first Americans to make the whistleblower concept famous was A. Ernest Fitzgerald, a civilian employee at the Pentagon, who testified in Congress about waste and fraud, caused mainly by a lack of oversight of the work of defense contractors. He lost his job and successfully sued to get it back.

For more than three decades, Fitzgerald was America's best-known whistleblower (his case is discussed in more detail in Chapter 5). In 2000, due to a major motion picture and the star power of Julia Roberts, he lost that distinction to a young paralegal named Erin Brockovich.

Brockovich exposed the problem of groundwater contamination caused by a public utility, and in both the film and the true story on which it was based, Brockovich did exactly what she was supposed to do: following the chain of command by first bringing the matter to the attention of company managers, then their superiors, and finally government regulators and the media.

While the Fitzgerald case was based in the military, the first whistleblowing case involving a private employer began in 1971 when a commercial bus driver in California became so frustrated with the mechanical condition of the company's vehicles that he took his concerns to a local television station. He claimed to have first told his superiors about the problems but got no response. After the segment aired, the driver was fired based on the company's "loyalty rule," which prohibited employees from using "words or acts of hostility to the company, its officers, agents, or employees, its services, equipment or its condition, or criticisms of the company to others than superior officers."[42]

While state officials sympathized with his plight, none was in a position to help. The office of the California attorney general said the loyalty rule was unfair but it was unable to overturn the decision. The state's Public Utility Commission said it was concerned about the public safety issue involved, but it also lacked the authority to help the terminated employee. Only pressure from the drivers' union and the television station that aired the original story resulted in the driver being reinstated.[43]

The following year, a pilot for Eastern Airlines also traveled a long and difficult path to reinstatement. The pilot, whose name was never released, complained to company management about the automatic pilot system in the Lockheed 1011 aircraft. Not happy with the response from his immediate supervisors, he kept taking his concerns further and further up the organizational chart until he reached the airline president. After being rebuked at every level, he took the issue to the National Transportation Safety Board. After being demoted to co-pilot for no reason other than his reputation as a "squeaky wheel," he sued the airline, which caused him to be grounded. He could not be fired because of the clout of the airline pilots' union. He told the court that he acted in good faith to follow the chain of command and keep his concerns within the company and went public only out of concern for public safety. He was not, as the airline claimed, making defamatory comments about Eastern or Lockheed. After years of litigation, he won his lawsuit and remained with Eastern throughout the rest of his career. The aircraft problems were corrected after other pilots reported similar issues.[44]

The 1974 case of *Geary v. U.S. Steel* began when George Geary, who had been selling the company's products for fourteen years, went to his superiors with his concerns that some of the company's products had not been adequately tested and posed a safety risk to customers. His concerns were ignored, and he was labeled a "boat-rocker."[45] He eventually took his concerns higher up the organizational chart to a vice president, where he was certain he would find a sympathetic ear. He did—somewhat. The company eventually fixed the problem, likely saving lives and millions of dollars for his employer, but instead of receiving praise from management, Geary received a termination notice.

Geary took his case to state court, and he eventually found himself before the Supreme Court of Pennsylvania. There he found three sympathetic ears, but that wasn't enough. The court ruled 4-3 in favor of the company, determining that the "at-will" nature of his employment was the primary factor in its decision and that it was not the role of the court to judge the merits of his concerns.[46]

The court system recognizes the importance of whistleblowers in both public and private workplaces. In a 1994 case that involved a nurse who reported problems with patient care at a public hospital, Supreme Court justice Sandra Day O'Connor wrote that "government employees are often in the best position to know what ails the agencies for which they work; public debate may gain much from their informed opinions."[47]

In a 1990 book on business ethics, Richard T. DeGeorge included an entire chapter on whistleblowing, and within that chapter addressed the once-prevailing view that whistleblowing, no matter how well-intentioned, was an act of disloyalty. "To be disloyal to one's employer is to bite the hand that feeds one—hardly an admirable or praise-worthy action," he wrote. "The flaw in that argument of those who claim that whistleblowing is always immoral is that they make loyalty to a firm the worker's highest obligation and consider it to be always overriding."[48] DeGeorge, a professor of philosophy and co-director of the International Center for Ethics in Business at the University of Kansas, added that whistleblowing was an act of loyalty because the employee doing so was helping to improve the company or government agency (whether his or her actions were welcome or not) and that blowing the whistle was not only a right but a moral imperative.[49]

Civil rights attorney and New York University Law School Professor David A. J. Richards equates whistleblowing with the rights of free speech and frames it as "the inalienable right of conscience."[50] Many professional organizations, especially those in the field of business communications, echo this sentiment. The Public Relations Society of America, for example, states in its code of ethics that "a professional communicator's obligation to the law and public interest always takes priority of his or her duty to a client or employer."[51]

Cases of whistleblowing in government and the military are discussed in those respective chapters because the culture of those fields dictates that employees know they are less likely to be successful in whistleblowing cases and are therefore less likely to be whistleblowers.

The National Employee Rights Institute's 1999 publication, *The Federal Employees Survival Guide*, suggests a three-step process to pursue whistleblowing within a federal government agency: (1) report the issue to a supervisor, (2) contact the inspector general within the department, and (3) contact the Office of the Special Counsel.[52] The OSC is an independent agency that reviews cases and offers a whistleblower hotline. At lower levels, there is no provision for confidentiality, but confidentiality does apply once the case gets to the OSC. Although not mentioned in the NERI publication, other sources suggest government whistleblowers try to resolve issues internally before going to outside regulatory agencies or the media. That same rule applies to whistleblowing in private companies or nonprofit organizations.

At the state level, many whistleblowing laws encourage but do not require employees to try to resolve issues internally before taking them to government regulators or the media. The courts apply that standard inconsistently. In some cases, lower-level state and federal courts question why that wasn't the employees' first step, while in others, they see that the employees followed an established procedure but were ignored. That was the case when Fitzgerald resorted to taking his concerns to the media after being rebuffed by his superiors.

In other cases, courts appear to see little value in internal procedures. In 1968, for example, the Supreme Court did not agree with the school board's requirement that employees first attempt to resolve issues within its established grievance procedure, calling that requirement too "narrowly drawn" to be helpful.[53]

Labor attorneys point out the dichotomy that exists between making constructive, money-saving suggestions and those who point out problems, even when those concerns are related to public safety and calling attention to them may save lives. "Employees who make cost-cutting suggestions are rewarded, but employees who focus attention on corporate problems that turn into disasters later are generally vilified," wrote attorney Robert Ellis Smith in his 1983 book, *Workrights*. His examples include employees fired for informing their bosses about environmental violations or other issues related to employee or public safety, even if they follow the correct internal procedures.[54]

In 1978, Congress passed the Civil Service Reform Act, which provided federal protection for whistleblowers. In subsequent decades, many state legislatures passed laws that mirrored or reinforced that protection.[55] In 1989, Congress amended the CSRA to include anti-retaliation provisions that prohibit employers from punishing employees for speaking out. Examples of retaliation include demotion or cut in pay, transfer to less glamorous positions or work shifts, or verbal harassment. Employers also may not "gaslight" employees into thinking they caused or contributed to the problem they are reporting.[56]

Protections for public-sector whistleblowers go back to the nineteenth century, but for those in the private sector, protections have been in place only for a few decades. Prior to that, employees of private companies had to follow a safe and narrow path: bring the issue to the attention of management, and if that didn't work, keep their mouths shut and go back to work, or in serious cases, resign. Bringing the issue to the attention of government regulators or the media was often a job-ending (or sometimes career-ending) decision.[57]

Most anti-retaliation provisions in state law are similar to those attached to laws that protect complainants in sexual harassment cases. A legitimate whistleblowing claim and its anti-retaliation corollary are exceptions to the employment-at-will concept.[58]

The 1999 case of *Liberatore v. Melville Corporation* began when a pharmacist in the District of Columbia complained to his supervisor that drugs were being improperly stored in a part of the store where variations in temperature may have damaged their effectiveness. When the supervisor failed to act, James Liberatore went further up the chain of command, but after his concerns were ignored at every level, he threatened to report the situation to the Food and Drug Administration.

Before Liberatore could do that, the pharmacy's parent company sent workers into the pharmacy after hours to remove about $250,000 worth of drugs and hide them off-property. No records were kept of the removal, and instead, the company reported they had been stolen, contacted the local police, and identified Liberatore as a suspect. His attorney claimed the company's actions were like the "firing of a warning shot" in hopes Liberatore would back down from his claims.[59]

When that didn't work, the company discharged Liberatore. Unable to prove the claim of theft, they instead listed the cause for termination as the lapse of his pharmaceutical license. When he sued the company for wrongful termination, his attorney claimed the license issue was a pretext, as several of Liberatore's coworkers had allowed their licenses to expire but were still permitted to work.

The trial court in the District of Columbia ruled in favor of the company, based largely on the "employment at will" principle, but the U.S. Court of Appeals overturned that decision, determining that Liberatore acted in good faith to act on a matter of public safety, and those interests outweighed the "at-will" provision.[60]

When employees or former employees are successful in their lawsuits, it is often because the courts determine that the public interest in knowing about a company or government agency's misdeeds outweighs the employers' claims of workplace disruption.[61]

In the cases of *Rafferty v. Philadelphia Psychiatric Center* (mentioned in the Introduction and discussed in more detail in Chapter 3) and *Downs v. Conway School District* (discussed in more detail in Chapter 7), courts ruled the workplace disruption was minimal, overstated by the defendant, or non-existent.[62]

"Whistleblower protections as a matter of law have spread from rare to everywhere, but availing oneself of those protections remains legally challenging, financially costly, and markedly hazardous to one's career health," Barry wrote in *Speechless*.[63]

There are some narrowly drawn exceptions to whistleblower protection. A private or public employer may discipline or dismiss a whistleblower—even one who believes he or she is acting in good faith—if the speech crosses the line into conduct and the employer can demonstrate to the court that the conduct interfered with the orderly functions of that company or government agency.[64]

In order to qualify as good-faith whistleblowing, the information disclosed about workplace conditions must be related to a genuine concern over employee safety, not just conditions an employee finds unpleasant. Employees concerned that equipment not kept in working order presents a physical danger to themselves or others would easily meet that test, but employees complaining about having to work overtime would not.[65]

Although there are different rules and procedures for public and private entities, the definition and principles of whistleblowing apply to corporations, nonprofit organizations, and government agencies at all levels. Although not specifically mentioned in the law, the agencies that deal with whistleblower cases, as well as the courts, do not pursue cases that appear to be based on personal grievances rather than larger, more serious issues.[66]

Much like the broader issue of workplace speech, whistleblowing is subject to exceptions, albeit not as many. In a 1992 journal article on whistleblowing, James Madison University Professor Richard Lippke pointed out that federal law and legal precedents have established specific conditions on whistleblowing: it must not defame the organization, violate the privacy of any of its employees, disclose trade secrets, or be based on personal grievances.[67]

Two federal laws protect whistleblowers. The Sarbanes-Oxley Act of 2002 protects employees in publicly traded corporations who report their employers for possible insider trading violations or other financial issues, while the Occupational Safety and Health Act of 1970 protects employees against retaliation after they report safety issues to federal regulators.

State of the Unions

The National Labor Relations Act, also known as the Wagner Act, is a 1935 federal law that created the National Labor Relations Board and prohibits workplace discrimination and interference with union activities. In addition, many states have laws prohibiting employers from punishing employees for joining a union or recruiting new members.

As a general rule, the NLRB and the courts have sided with unions and employees seeking to form unions, ruling that those activities are protected under two clauses of the First Amendment: the assembly clause (because forming unions became protected as the courts expanded the concept of "right to assemble" to also mean "right to associate") and the speech clause, as they determine that walking a picket line is speech, not conduct.[68]

In addition, the Supreme Court ruled in a 1988 case that union members could legally distribute handbills (in this case, discouraging shoppers from patronizing a shopping mall) as long as they did not coerce individuals walking by nor block them from entering a place of business.[69] Courts have ruled, however, that the First Amendment rights of unions and their members do not protect them from being sued for defamation when they disseminate falsehoods orally while on the picket line, in printed materials, or in media interviews.[70]

Although unions had long respected the privacy rights of individuals running the companies against which they were striking, the concept didn't find its way into case law until 1987. In *French v. Amalgamated Local Union 376*, a federal court ruled that while a union had the right to set up picket lines, it did not have the right to do so outside the home of an executive whose company was the target of the strike. Connecticut law had a statute prohibiting such activity, but the union did so nonetheless, claiming the law violated its First Amendment rights. When Gary French, the president of a company that manufactured firearms, asked the court to enjoin the picketers from staging their protest on the public street in front of his home in Vernon, the case set up a debate between the rights of picketers to express their views and the rights of the president to his privacy. The court agreed, requiring the picketers to limit their protest to company property, because of not only the protest's effect on French and his family but also the rights of his neighbors to enjoy the peace of their residential neighborhood.[71]

In the early 1990s, Fieldcrest Cannon, a North Carolina-based towel manufacturer, was able to prevent its employees from unionizing but was annoyed when employees continued to sing union songs on the production floor. They threatened to suspend the participating employees, despite the fact that the noisy machinery prevented the singing from being heard by anyone more than a few feet away.[72]

At the Frontier Hotel and Casino in Las Vegas in 1997, employees were told not to bring "union shit" into the workplace and that security personnel would be watching and videotaping them if they distributed union materials in the parking lot.[73] In 1999, United Parcel Service disciplined employees for distributing union materials in lounges and meeting rooms, while other employees were allowed to distribute materials on fishing contests, football pools, and golf tournaments.[74]

The NLRA does not apply to government employees, including those who work at state universities. It does, however, apply to those at private universities.[75] Faculty at public universities are governed by state labor laws. In many states, public employees are allowed to unionize but not allowed to strike.[76]

One unusual provision of the NLRA is that plaintiffs who believe an employer violated the law by prohibiting union activity or punishing them for it cannot pursue cases on their own—they concede that authority to the NLRB.[77]

All Politics Is Vocal

Because of the amount of time individuals spend at their jobs, it is inevitable that workplace conversations will eventually include political beliefs. In many cases, those discussions may lead to discrimination, ridicule, and harassment. When individuals from diverse backgrounds come together in the workplace, it's only natural that they talk about current issues and events. And conversations often go beyond preferences for political candidates and into social issues related to race, religion, education, and science.

"As we all know, the lines between our work lives and personal lives are increasingly blurred," wrote Johnny C. Taylor, a human resources expert and columnist for *USA Today*. "And when you add camera phones and social media to the mix, the things we do on our non-work time—such as attending a rally or sharing a few choice words with an elected official at a city council meeting—are no longer exclusively private activities."[78] To avoid potential problems, many employers prohibit their employees from wearing campaign buttons on their clothing or displaying campaign posters, literature, and other religious or political materials in their workspaces.

A CareerBuilder poll taken just prior to the 2014 mid-term elections found that 42 percent of respondents said they avoided talking about politics at work, and 44 percent said they talked about it but then backed away if it got heated. Only 14 percent said they engaged in "lively political debates" at work.[79]

Even before the advent of social media, employees engaging in water-cooler conversations about political issues or other possible hot-button topics presented a lose-lose dilemma for employers. If they allow such discussions to get heated, they invite problems with employee morale, productivity, and turnover and, in extreme cases, charges of sexual or religious harassment. But if they try to eliminate discussions around the water cooler and other places, they get accused of stifling free speech. Today, with employees eager to share opinions on their social media pages, the dangers are even greater, with the newer hot-button issues being related to faith, abortion, gay and transgender rights, immigration, and the presidential elections of 2020 and 2024.

The list of sensitive topics has been getting longer in the last decade, according to the Society for Human Resources Management (SHRM), and it's not just because of presidential politics. Comments about police violence against African Americans might lead to an argument between Black Lives Matter supporters and critics. An employee showing off an outfit she bought for her child's same-sex wedding might provoke a coworker's objection to gay marriage or even the accusation that the subject offended another employee's religious beliefs. Labor lawyer Tom Fredrickson told SHRM News that "a political discussion can quickly morph into something that is actually harassment of someone who's a member of a protected legal class."[80]

The phenomenon of employers attempting to influence the voting choices of their employees dates back to the 1860s, when southern voters in post-Civil War elections were told by their employers to vote for candidates who opposed rights for newly freed slaves.[81]

During the 2004 presidential election campaign, Lynne Gobbell of Moulton, Alabama, was fired by the insulation company Enviromate for refusing to remove a Kerry-Edwards bumper sticker from her car. The termination decision was made by the owner of the company, Phil Geddes, a supporter of incumbent George W. Bush, who also distributed campaign literature explaining why employees should vote for Bush. Conversely, Gobbell did not discuss politics with her coworkers; her only advocacy was the bumper sticker. In media interviews, Gobbell quoted Geddes as telling her, "You can either work for me or work for Kerry," which turned out to be prophetic. When news of her firing became a nationwide story, she was hired by the Kerry-Edwards campaign.[82]

During the 2012 election cycle, Republican presidential candidate Mitt Romney faced no consequences for telling small-business owners they should "make it clear to employees what you believe is in the best interest of your enterprise and therefore their job and their future in upcoming elections." Romney's comments struck a bipartisan tone when he added, "Whether you agree with me or you agree with President Obama, or whatever your political view, I hope you pass those along to your employees. Nothing illegal about you talking to your employees about what you believe is best for your business."[83]

Romney's comments caught the attention of political commentators and columnists, who, despite the bipartisan phrasing, believed it was legal but unethical. "There's a fine line between an employer telling an employee, 'Vote Romney!' and a boss telling a subordinate 'Vote Romney, or else!'" wrote Adam Clark Estes in *The Atlantic*.[84] Paul Secunda, associate professor at Marquette University Law School, added that "subjecting employees to political information is legal, but making explicit or implicit threats against employees who vote for the 'wrong' candidate is not."[85]

An article in the *GlobalPost*, a liberal online news source, expanded on the Romney comments with anecdotes about employers who warned employees that if "unfavorable" candidates (i.e., Democrats) were elected, the result would be higher gasoline prices, runaway inflation, and job layoffs. According to the article, the CEO of Westgate Resorts warned employees that the company would not be responsible for the company downsizing that would be likely if Barack Obama was re-elected.[86]

In the lead-up to the 2016 election, an article in an SHRM publication posed the question: Should employers and HR managers keep political talk out of the workplace? The answer was no—for two reasons. From a legal perspective, any effort to limit workplace discussion would likely violate National Labor Relations Board rules. From a practical perspective, it simply wouldn't work. "But employers still have a responsibility to make sure workers feel comfortable at work," the article stated. "And it's a delicate balance, employment lawyers say, because one person's free speech is another person's loud-mouthed bullying."[87]

In 2020, two social issues came to the forefront and served to produce workplace discussion and discord. The first was the Memorial Day murder of George Floyd, an unarmed Black man, at the hands of a Minneapolis police officer. The tragedy became a new issue for Black Lives Matter, a social movement demanding justice for African Americans who died at the hands of police officers. The second issue was the coronavirus pandemic, which set off workplace debates and litigation based on mandatory vaccines and mask usage, and in some cases, business closures and employee layoffs.

Labor attorney Kelly Dobbs Bunting points out that a rule against employee involvement in political campaigns and causes is more important for those in upper management than those on the lower levels of the organizational chart, as outsiders assume that managers are more likely to be speaking for the company. "Even though you might think that's not a political matter, other employees will," said labor attorney Kelly Dobbs Bunting in a 2023 article in SHRM News. "Think about what the impact your decision is going to be on your workforce."[88]

Notes

1 Bruce Barry, *Speechless: The Erosion of Free Expression in the American Workplace* (San Francisco: Berrett-Koehler Publishers, 2007), p. 3.
2 Randy Bobbitt, *Exploring Communication Law*, 2nd ed. (New York: Taylor & Francis, 2018), p. 73.
3 Samuel Greengard, "The Virtual Pen is Not Mightier Than the Ax," *Workplace Management*, March 1, 2005, pp. 74–6.
4 Bill Lueders, "Speech and Consequences," *The Progressive,* October/November 2022, pp. 20–1.
5 Brinley Hineman, "Can Employers Police Their Workers' Personal Lives?" *USA Today,* April 16, 2021, p. 2-B. See also: Hineman, "Can You Be Fired Over Your Sex Life? Dave Ramsey Thinks So," *The Nashville Tennessean*, March 28, 2021.
6 "Speak Out Act Targets Wall Street's Silencing of Sexual Harassment," *The Seattle Times*, November 16, 2002.
7 Thomas M. Hanna, *The Employer's Legal Advisor* (New York: American Management Association, 2007), p. 133. See also: Patricia Graves, "Ask an Expert: Online Behavior," *SHRM News,* May 27, 2021. Terry Collins, "TikTok Got Me Fired: The Pitfalls of Talking Work on Social Media," *USA Today,* July 19, 2022, p. 4-B.
8 Barry, interview with the author, January 3, 2024.
9 Mark F. Kluger, interview with the author, January 2, 2024.
10 Leah Shepherd, "How to Handle Political Speech in the Workplace," *SHRM News,* June 12, 2023.
11 *Dendor v. Board of Fire and Police Commissioners*, 197 N.E. 2d 316 (1973), *Roberts v. Lake Central School Corporation*, 317 F. Supp 63 (1970), and *Murray v. Vaughn*, 300 F. Supp 688 (1973). See also: Kenneth D. Walters, "Your Employees' Right to Blow the Whistle," *Harvard Business Review*, July–August 1975, pp. 26–34 and 161–2.
12 Cynthia L. Estlund, "Free Speech and Due Process in the Workplace," *Indiana Law Journal* 71, no. 1 (Winter 1995): pp. 101–51.
13 Itzel Luna, "Survey: Hate, Harassment Surges," *USA Today*, June 30, 2023, p. 6-A.
14 Samuel Greengard, interview with the author, January 4, 2024.
15 *Cooley v. Carmike Cinemas*, 25 F. 3d 1325 (1994). See also: Marisa Anne Pagnattaro, "What Do You Do When You Are Not at Work? Limiting the Use of Off-Duty

Conduct as the Basis for Adverse Employment Actions," *University of Pennsylvania of Labor and Employment Law* 6, no. 3 (2004): pp. 625–84.

16 *Cooley v. Carmike Cinemas*, See also: Pagnattaro, "What Do You Do When You Are Not at Work?"

17 Rodney Smolla, *Free Speech in an Open Society* (New York: Alfred A. Knopf, 1992), p. 163.

18 *Peck v. Sony Music Corporation*, 68 Fair Employment Practice Cases 1025 (1995).

19 *Peterson v. Hewlett-Packard*, 358 F. 3d 599 (2004).

20 *Peterson v. Hewlett-Packard.*

21 Shari Lau, "Shari's Solutions: Can We Prohibit Political Discussions at Work in This Heated Election Season?" *SHRM News*, June 1, 2016.

22 "Feds Cracking Down on Pornography." Knight-Ridder report, April 5, 2004.

23 *Arnett v. Kennedy*, 416 U.S. 134 (1974). See also: Lawrence Rosenthal, "Permissible Content Discrimination Under the First Amendment: The Strange Case of the Public Employee." *Hastings Constitutional Law Quarterly*, Vol. 25, Issue 4 (Summer 1998), pp. 528-84.

24 *Meloff v. The New York Life Insurance Company*, 240 F. 3d 138 (2001). See also: Charles J. Muhl, "Workplace E-Mail and Internet Use: Employees and Employers Beware." *Monthly Labor Review*, February 2003, pp. 36-45.

25 *Meloff v. The New York Life Insurance Company, 240 F. 3d 138 (2001). See also: Charles J. Muhl, "Workplace E-Mail and Internet Use: Employees and Employers Beware." Monthly Labor Review, February 2003, pp. 36-45.*

26 *Lian v. Sedgewick James of New York, Inc.*, 992 F. Supp. 644 (1998). See also: Muhl.

27 Ryan Herrington, "Not Fit For Print." *Golf World*, February 2007, p. 17.

28 Ryan Herrington, "Not Fit For Print." *Golf World*, February 2007, p. 17.

29 *Lewis Maltby, Can They Do That? Retaking Our Fundamental Rights in the Workplace.* New York: Penguin Group (2009), p. 11.

30 *Brent v. Morgan*, 299 S.W. 967 (1927). See also: Lori Andrews, *I Know Who You Are and I Saw What You Did: Social Networks and the Death of Privacy.* New York: Free Press (2011), p. 84.

31 Kelly v. *Florida Judicial Qualifications Commission, 238 So. 2d 565 (1970). Connick v Meyers*, 461 US 138 (1983). See also: Henry Cohen, *Freedom of Speech and Press: Exceptions to the First Amendment.* New York: Nova Science Publishers, Inc. (2008), pp. 50-51.

32 *Connick v Meyers*, 461 US 138 (1983). See also: Henry Cohen, *Freedom of Speech and Press: Exceptions to the First Amendment.* New York: Nova Science Publishers, Inc. (2008), pp. 50-51.

33 *Smyth v. The Pillsbury Company*, 914 F. Supp. 97 (1996). See also: Charles J. Muhl, "Workplace E-Mail and Internet Use: Employees and Employers Beware," *Monthly Labor Review*, February 2003, pp. 36–45.

34 Estlund, "Free Speech and Due Process in the Workplace."
35 Joseph V. Kaplan, *Federal Employees Legal Survival Guide* (Cincinnati, OH: National Employee Rights Institute, 1999), p. 131.
36 Hanna, *The Employer's Legal Advisor*, p. 133.
37 Ibid.
38 Barry, *Speechless*, p. 85.
39 Kenneth D. Walters, "Your Employees' Right to Blow the Whistle." *Harvard Business Review*, July-August 1975, pp. 26-34 and pp. 161-62.
40 Charles Peters and Taylor Branch, *Blowing the Whistle* (Westport, CT: Praeger Publishing, 1972).
41 Ibid., p. 4.
42 David W. Ewing, *Freedom Inside the Organization: Bringing Civil Liberties to the Workplace* (New York: E.P. Dutton, 1977), p. 7. See also: Ewing, "Employee Rights: Taking the Gag Off," *Civil Liberties Review*, Fall 1974, p. 56.
43 Ewing, *Freedom Inside the Organization*, p. 7. See also: Ewing, "Employee Rights: Taking the Gag Off."
44 Patricia H. Wehane, *Persons, Rights, and Corporations* (Englewood Cliffs, NJ: Prentice-Hall, 1985), pp. 113–14.
45 *Geary v. U.S. Steel*, 319 A2d 174. See also: Ewing, *Freedom Inside the Organization*, pp. 219–20; Lewis Maltby, *Can They Do That? Retaking Our Fundamental Rights in the Workplace* (New York: Penguin Group, 2009), pp. 7–8.
46 *Geary v. U.S. Steel*, 319 A2d 174.
47 *Waters v. Churchill*, 511 U.S. 661 (1994).
48 Richard T. DeGeorge, *Business Ethics* (New York: MacMillan, 1990), p. 206.
49 Ibid.
50 David A. J. Richards, *Toleration and the Constitution* (New York: Oxford University Press, 1986), p. 169. See also: Richard Lippke, "Speech, Conscience, and Work," *Social Theory and Practice* 18, no. 3 (Fall 1992): pp. 237–58.
51 Public Relations Society of America Code of Ethics (www.prsa.org/ethics).
52 Kaplan, *Federal Employees Legal Survival Guide*, p. 132.
53 *Pickering v. Board of Education*, 391 U.S. 563 (1968). See also: Randy J. Kozel, "Reconceptualizing Public Employee Speech," *Northwestern University Law Review* 99, no. 3 (Spring 2005): pp. 1007–51.
54 Robert Ellis Smith, *Workrights* (New York: E.P. Dutton, Inc., 1983), p. 79.
55 McWhirter, *Your Rights at Work*, p. 129.
56 Kaplan, *Federal Employees Legal Survival Guide*, p. 132.
57 Barry, *Speechless*, p. 107.
58 Ibid., pp. 85–6.
59 *Liberatore v. Melville Corporation*, 168 F.3d 1326 (1999).

60 Ibid.
61 Walters, "Your Employees' Right to Blow the Whistle."
62 *Rafferty v. Philadelphia Psychiatric Center* 356 F. Supp. 500 (1973), and *Downs v. Conway School District*, 329 F. Supp. 338 (1971). See also: Walters, "Your Employees' Right to Blow the Whistle."
63 Barry, *Speechless*, p. 210.
64 *American Bar Association Guide to Workplace Law* (New York: Random House, 1977), pp. 131–3.
65 Estlund, "Free Speech and Due Process in the Workplace."
66 Kaplan, *Federal Employees Legal Survival Guide*, p. 364.
67 Lippke, "Speech, Conscience, and Work," pp. 237–58.
68 *Senn v. Tile Layers Protective Union*, 301 U.S. 468 (1937) and *Thornhill v. Alabama*, 310 U.S. 88 (1940). See also: Ken I. Kersch, "How Conduct Became Speech Became Conduct: A Political Development Case Study in Labor Law and Freedom of Speech," *Journal of Constitutional Law* 8, no. 2 (2006): pp. 1–44.
69 *DeBartolo Corporation v. Florida Gulf Coast Trades Council*, 485 U.S. 568 (1988).
70 *Salzhandler v. Caputo*, 316 F. 2d 445 (1963).
71 *French v. Amalgamated Local Union 376*, 203 Conn. 624 (1987).
72 Lawrence Soley, *Censorship, Inc.: The Corporate Threat to Free Speech in the United States* (New York: Monthly Review Press, 2002), p. 62.
73 Ibid., p. 63.
74 Ibid., p. 62.
75 *NLRB v. Yeshiva University*, 444 U.S. 672 (1980).
76 Ibid.
77 Estlund, "Free Speech and Due Process in the Workplace."
78 Johnny C. Taylor, "Off-Work Politics May Hurt Your Job," *USA Today*, July 10, 2018, p. 5-B.
79 Susan Milligan, "Political Debates in the Workplace: Where to Draw the Line," *SHRM News*, May 12, 2015.
80 Ibid.
81 Eugene Volokh, "Private Employers' Speech and Political Activity: Statutory Protection Against Employee Retaliation," *Texas Review of Law & Politics* 16, no. 2 (2011): pp. 296–336.
82 Adrienne Fox, "Politics in the Office," *SHRM News*, October 1, 2008. See also: Timothy Noah, "A Kerry Fan Gets Fired, Then Hired, for Her Politics," *Slate.com*, September 14, 2004.
83 Jessica Phelan, "Mitt Romney Tells Employers to 'Make it Very Clear' to Employees How to Vote," *GlobalPost*, October 18, 2012.

84 Adam Clark Estes, "Romney Told Bosses to Tell Their Employees How to Vote," *The Atlantic*, October 17, 2012.

85 Phelan, "Mitt Romney Tells Employers to 'Make it Very Clear' to Employees How to Vote."

86 Ibid.

87 Milligan, "Political Debates in the Workplace."

88 Shepherd, "How to Handle Political Speech in the Workplace."

2

Social Media as the Twenty-First-Century Water Cooler

Career Crash

Just as Trevor Keezor and Larry Summers had little in common in the vignette at the beginning of the Introduction, the same could be said about the grouping of nonprofit executive Lindsey Stone, public relations manager Justine Sacco, and golf administrator Ted Bishop. What they now have in common is public vitriol caused by their career-altering social media gaffes.

In 2012, thirty-year-old Stone was visiting Arlington National Cemetery when she asked a coworker to take a photo of her pretending to scream while displaying her middle finger next to a sign asking visitors to show "silence and respect." A pro-military group found the photo online and within hours created its own Facebook page titled "Fire Lindsey Stone." Within days, the site had more than 19,000 "likes." Across other social media platforms, calls to "fire Lindsey Stone" morphed into comments such as "set fire to Lindsey Stone," "cut out her uterus," "rape her," and "she should rot in hell."[1]

Her employer, a Massachusetts nonprofit organization that serves individuals with disabilities, eventually fired both Stone and the woman who took the picture. Stone said that in the aftermath of the shaming, she didn't leave her house for almost a year, was unable to date, and was reluctant to go on job interviews because her past would likely be known to prospective employers. One journalist noted that "five seconds of her life became her entire Internet presence."[2]

Two years later, Sacco lost her job over a few careless thoughts posted on Twitter while on her way to visit her family in South Africa. She began a series of tweets describing her experiences in airports as well as during the transatlantic crossing. Prior to the last leg of her flight, from London to Cape Town, she tweeted, "Going to Africa. Hope I don't get AIDS. Just kidding, I'm white!"[3]

Sacco recalls turning her phone off and sleeping for most of the flight. When she awoke and got off the plane, she found her tweet had created an international social media controversy. A Twitter hashtag emerged with the title #HasJustineLandedYet.

Strangers from around the world posted critical and threatening responses, and even friends and coworkers piled on. The toughest response came from her employer, the parent company of a number of online news and social media services. She was fired before returning to the United States. The tweet followed her for years, making it difficult for her to find subsequent employment.[4]

Much like Stone and Sacco, Bishop saw a solid career spoiled by careless social media comments that took him only a few minutes to compose in October 2014. Bishop was serving as president of the Professional Golfers Association of America[5] when he read a blog comment by English golfer Ian Poulter that disparaged fellow Englishman Nick Faldo and American golfer Tom Watson. Bishop reacted quickly, pointing out the difference in careers—Faldo had forty-three worldwide wins compared to Poulter's seventeen—and calling Poulter a "Lil Girl." Restricted by Twitter's character limit, Bishop then doubled down and expanded his criticism on Facebook, this time also defending Watson, his close friend. "He (Poulter) sounds like a little girl squealing during recess," Bishop wrote.[6]

The next morning, Bishop was reprimanded in a conference call with the group's leadership. That afternoon, he was asked to resign but refused. Even though he apologized profusely and had only one month remaining in his two-year term, the PGA Board of Directors removed him from office by a vote of 18-0 with one abstention. The only reason he was given was the inconsistency between his comments—labeled sexist and derogatory—and the PGA's public commitment to diversity and inclusion. The irony was that many of the organization's diversity and inclusion programs had been developed by Bishop. In addition, throughout his forty-year career in golf, Bishop had initiated programs to introduce golf to women and minorities at various clubs where he was employed.[7]

Because the controversy took place during professional golf's off-season, golf journalists focused more attention on it than they might have if it had happened during a busier time. Golf writers—many of them familiar with Bishop's career and character—questioned not only what he said but also why he felt it necessary to say anything at all. In addition to losing his leadership position in the PGA, Bishop saw a major manufacturer of golf equipment cancel contracts with his golf course in Indiana. Fellow professionals and other leaders in the golf industry who once quickly returned his phone calls no longer did so. "I was embarrassed," Bishop wrote in his 2016 autobiography. "I was humiliated. I was enraged at times. I felt betrayed. I felt like a victim. I felt lonely. I felt like a complete fool for letting my emotions drive my irresponsible use of social media. My life changed in the wink of an eye."[8]

Much of the "Internet problem" involves not what employees say to outsiders, but what they say to each other. Professor and author Christine Porath, in a 2016 book on workplace civility, cites academic studies indicating that more than 70 percent of workers believe the Internet is to blame for the increase in negative workplace behavior.[9]

"We must realize we can work more effectively if we practice e-civility," Porath wrote. "Be more thoughtful about your electronic communications. As with behavior generally, small steps can make a big difference. Practice civility with every email, and you'll gradually make your virtual workplace every bit as pleasurable and affirming as your physical one."[10]

For most employers, the use of social media by their employees is a double-edged sword. When employees engage in social media usage on company time, there is a verifiable loss of productivity. But many employers are willing to overlook that issue in hopes that using social media in moderation allows employees brief periods of escape. In addition, employers don't want to be seen as the "big brother" that monitors and scrutinizes how employees spend their working hours; if they are meeting deadlines and accomplishing priority tasks, employers are willing to accept the downside.[11]

The popularity of social media may not have affected employer-employee relations as much as we think, as employees will always want to criticize their employers, and those employers will always want to stop it. "While the media will change, I don't anticipate that human nature will," says employment attorney Mark Kluger. "Employers will never be tolerant of employees bashing them in any forum although they have already become more accustomed to it. From a legal perspective, the topics on which employer bashing must be tolerated will evolve."[12]

Kluger also points out that the NLRB is a politically influenced agency and its decisions on labor law topics often shift back and forth depending on which political party controls the White House. "Ultimately, the courts will provide sufficient clarity, at least for a period of time, so that we employment lawyers will be able to safely advise employers regarding what they must tolerate and when they can terminate employees for their social media posts," Kluger says.[13]

Employees in all fields are finding that the metaphor of the double-edged sword applies to them as well. On the positive side, platforms such as Facebook, Twitter, and Instagram allow them to connect with like-minded coworkers who need to vent and, in some cases, find opportunities to move on to better jobs elsewhere. But the venting, even when done anonymously, can sometimes have consequences in the form of reprimand, demotion, or termination.

- Corporate workers complain about their bosses, coworkers, customers, job duties, working hours, and, in some cases, problems with their unions or lack of the opportunity to unionize.
- Doctors and nurses use social media to complain about hospital management and issues in the insurance industry. During the Covid-19 pandemic in 2020–1, health-care workers were found on both sides of the debates over masking and vaccine mandates, complaining that their employers were either not doing enough to keep them safe or doing too much—requiring steps that they believed were unnecessary and interfered with patient care.
- Workers in the restaurant industry complain about working hours, low pay, company-mandated uniforms, and customers who under-tip or leave no tip at all.
- K–12 teachers vent about their students, their teaching schedules, the lack of support from administration, and interference from "helicopter parents."
- University professors use social media to complain about students who come to their institutions unprepared because of failing high schools. Other easy targets are their schools' budgeting priorities and problems with the tenure system—comments that ironically contribute to the denial of tenure.
- Even lawyers, who should theoretically "know better" when it comes to issues involving free speech, are not immune from employer sanctions when they complain about their clients, judges, prosecutors, or fellow attorneys in their jurisdiction.

"Most employees have a false understanding of free speech associated with social media and may feel a sense of freedom or protection in posting controversial statements on online platforms," wrote Patricia Graves, a human resources consultant and contributor to SHRM's online newsletter. "Discriminatory, false, or disparaging statements posted on personal social media pages aren't beyond an employer's reach. Violating a company's policy or code of conduct will generally support an employer's request to have a post removed."[14]

In 2022, Mary Gundel was a store manager at a Dollar General in Tampa, Florida, where she was lauded by the company management for guiding the store through a two-year stretch of employee turnover and supply chain problems associated with the Covid-19 pandemic. She even earned compliments for her series of TikTok videos in which she chronicled how she balanced her work and family life, and along the way praised the company for its support. But all of that goodwill gradually disappeared when her video diary morphed into a series of rants about the stresses of the job, undependable subordinates, and difficult customers. The company fired her, stating publicly that it provides "many avenues" for employees to complain and make suggestions to improve store operations and that Gundel did not attempt to use those channels first. After she was let go, dozens of Dollar General store managers across the country took up her cause and posted their own work diaries on TikTok—but did so anonymously.[15]

"When you post on social media, you may feel like you're just venting or sending a message to a bunch of your friends or family," wrote attorney Lewis Massey in his firm's online newsletter in 2016. "However, it's important to remember that there is nothing private about your posts—even if you've activated the highest privacy settings. Any one of your 'friends' could forward your post to someone, and even a time-limited post (like a Snapchat) could be saved and transmitted by a third party."[16]

Author Samuel Greengard adds,

> There's no question that many critics, complainers and trolls hide behind the anonymity of the Internet. Anonymity cuts both ways: positive and negative. It gives employees a chance to express (often legitimate) complaints without the fear of being reprimanded or fired. However, it also allows disgruntled employees to trash employers. I'm not sure how to fix any of this. It's similar to online reviews for restaurants, hotels, etc. Most are at least somewhat valid, though it's clear that some people have a chip on their shoulder and are looking to destroy the reputation of a business. Sometimes these are other restaurants or businesses that somehow think they gain by dragging others down.[17]

Employees should not automatically assume their social media comments are protected, as the NLRB and courts often split hairs when determining what is fair commentary about workplace conditions and what is just misplaced angst. In cases discussed in the Chapter 3 section concerning restaurant workers, for example, the courts found that servers complaining about pay, working hours, and even the manager's sloppy handling of tax paperwork were protected, but servers complaining about customers who were bad tippers could be legally fired. Other punishable acts include those that are defamatory or represent verifiable workplace disruption. Another pair of examples: An employee who opines to coworkers that the company "doesn't treat employees fairly" or "doesn't help me advance in my career" is on safe ground, but one who falsely accuses a manager of sexual misconduct or insurance fraud is not. Also unprotected are comments that violate company policies on sexual, racial, or religious harassment, defame competitors, or disclose confidential company information or trade secrets.

Birth of a Catchphrase

The phenomenon of employees being fired for their online postings is so common that it's generated its own jargon term: *doocing.* The term is based on the title of a blog established by Heather Armstrong, a so-called "mommy blogger" who established her platform in 2001 to share thoughts about her working conditions and her life as a divorced working mother. One post in Dooce described "one of the 10 vice-presidents in this 30-employee company wasn't born with an 'indoor voice' but rather a shrill, monotone, speaking-over-a-passing-F16 outdoor voice . . . and he loves to hear himself speak, even if just to himself."[18]

After her coworkers at the technology startup complained about being ridiculed on her blog, she lost her job as a webpage designer and graphic artist. She replaced the lost income by selling advertisements on Dooce, which eventually attracted 8.5 million followers.[19] After operating the blog for more than two decades, during which she expanded her content to include her struggles with alcohol addiction and depression, she committed suicide in 2023.[20]

Other examples of online gaffes include a social worker fired in 2012 for venting on her Facebook account about the frustrations of her job.[21] The woman's comments did not receive First Amendment protection because they were not made as a private citizen but rather as a government employee, and her employers were concerned that her public comments might affect her credibility as a witness in criminal trials (this case is discussed in more detail in Chapter 6).

Comments posted on social media need not fall into one of the five "exception categories" (listed in Chapter 1) in order to be problematic. In 2022, for example, a Colorado woman was fired from her job within her first month after posting TikTok videos in which she bragged about her new salary. Even though the National Labor Relations Act specifies that an employee discussing his or her salary is considered protected speech, Lexi Larson decided to move on with her career rather than fighting for her job. The National Labor Relations Board clarifies that while discussing salaries or other workplace conditions is protected, employers can still prohibit employees from doing so on company time and using company-owned computers.[22]

"It's important to separate yourself from your employer," stated a 2011 article in the online edition of *Forbes*. "Acting on their behalf on social media can lead to serious consequences." Adds Jenna Wells, a San Francisco-based human resources professional: "You should really not be presenting your own opinions or beliefs in a way that can be construed to represent those of the company."[23]

To Blog or Not to Blog

In 2003, Ellen Simonetti was a flight attendant for Delta Airlines when she began a blog titled "Queen of the Sky" that documented her work and activities during her non-working hours. Posted without the company's permission, the blog included provocative photographs of her in uniform along with lengthy posts about the positives and negatives of her job. The latter was free speech, the airline acknowledged, but the photographs of her on board the plane, interacting with passengers and coworkers, were grounds for her dismissal[24] (this case is discussed in more detail in Chapter 3).

The treatment of Simonetti might have been the most well-publicized case of an employee being fired for blogging, but it was not the first. The previous year, Michael Hanscom was a low-level contract worker for Microsoft, where his job entailed working mostly in the copy shop. He frequently passed by the loading dock, and one day took a photograph of Apple computers being off-loaded and posted it on his personal blog, along with the caption, "Even Microsoft Wants G5s." He was careful to crop the photograph to remove any clues as to where it was taken, but that wasn't enough to prevent his termination—nor was his apology and offer to remove the photograph. Washington has employment laws more favorable to the employee than those in Georgia (that helped decide the Simonetti case), but in the end the state's at-will provision prevailed.[25]

In 2004, a newcomer to Washington, D.C., took the workplace blog a step further. Jessica Cutler was a twenty-five-year-old intern working in the office of Ohio senator Mike DeWine when she started a blog titled "Washingtonienne," allegedly on government time and using a government computer. On the blog, she published stories of her social life, including her sexual encounters with powerful men—some named and some not. The blog quickly attracted the attention of the national media, with the *Philadelphia News* labeling her as "the D.C. slut" and others using harsher terms. "I'm sure I am not the only one who makes money on the side this way," she told *The Washington Post*. "How can anybody live on $25K/year??"[26] Before a formal ethics investigation could take place, DeWine fired her for inappropriate use of a government computer.

As they apply to the workplace, there are two types of blogs. The first is one that is sponsored by the company, hosted on the company's website, written on company time and using company equipment, and related to the industry in which the company competes. The second is produced on the employee's own time and includes content related to both work and personal issues.

The distinction is critical: the former will most likely include only content that has been approved by management, and in some cases legal counsel, and serves to promote the company's products and services or address political or regulatory issues important to that company. Those blogs seldom cause problems. The latter is fraught with dangers, as the content is not approved and may expose the company to liability if it results in accusations of defamation and harassment. If the employee's personal blog uses the company logo or other identifiable information, readers may be unable to differentiate between a company-sponsored blog and an employee's personal one.[27]

"Companies must understand that blogging isn't just a random hobby that a few people are engaging in," wrote business and technology journalist Samuel Greengard in 2005. "It's becoming a mainstream and widespread form of communication. Employers must recognize that unless they accommodate blogging, they risk losing good people."[28]

A 2006 article by Reuters News Service quoted a Microsoft executive as saying that "blogging is a natural extension of what is in our corporate DNA"[29] and claimed there were more than a thousand employees who had blogs that were either personal, workplace-related, or a combination thereof. Had the company learned a lesson from the Hanscom case, which did not result in a lawsuit but did generate negative publicity? Perhaps so. Another Microsoft employee, Michael Scoble, had been writing his blog, titled "Eclecticism," for more than two years, beginning shortly after Hanscom had been shown the door. Scoble's blog became well known within the industry and had the blessing of management, even though it wasn't all positive. He praised some company products and services, criticized others, and even wrote positive content about Microsoft competitors. That amount of leeway was in contrast with the draconian treatment of Hanscom, and pleasantly surprised even Scoble. "It seems like the harsher I got, the more support I got from management," he wrote in a new iteration of his blog, titled "Scobleizer," after leaving Microsoft in 2006 to join a startup technology firm.[30]

Many companies require employees to obtain permission to link their blogs to the company's website, but with the dividing line between a personal blog and what is a company blog so tenuous, enforcing such a policy is difficult. What is easier to enforce is a common rule requiring common sense: employee blogs should not use photographs taken on company property or photographs that show other employees and should not use the company logo without permission. It is also common for employers to prohibit the release of information regarding products still in development that may tip off competitors or affect stock prices. And the biggest common-sense request: don't post any information that shows the company in a bad light.

A study titled "Pew Internet and American Life Project" found that about 37 percent of bloggers base their content on their "life and experiences," and within that the content is evenly split between family topics and work topics (it is the latter that gets bloggers in trouble with their employers). In both cases, many bloggers see themselves as leaders of online support groups for individuals navigating similar challenges.[31]

The study also found that the blogging population is mostly young, evenly split between men and women, and racially diverse. While some bloggers are able to make money off their work, for most it is a hobby rather than something that consumes their lives. Slightly less than half post content under their real names; the majority use pseudonyms to protect their personal safety and to safeguard against employer retaliation.[32]

And speaking of the workplace, only 7 percent of bloggers admit to blogging while at work, but that applies to blogs that are personal in nature and does not include blogs that are employer-authorized and are based on what is happening in the company or industry. In those cases, blogging is done in the office, uses company equipment, and may take up the majority of the employees' workday. For personal bloggers, it is mostly a nights-and-weekends activity.

About half of personal bloggers believe their audience is mostly people they know, meaning that because of the unreliability of privacy settings, they might be unaware of their reach—another factor that might cause problems with employers.[33]

Academic researchers are somewhat divided on what the expansion of blogging means for the culture. "Some suggest that blogging is nothing more than the next step in a burgeoning culture of narcissism and exhibitionism spurred by reality TV and other elements of the modern media environment," the study reported. "But others contend that blogging promises a democratization of voices that can now bypass the institutional gatekeepers of mainstream media."[34]

"When an employee posts something offensive, HR professionals are often on the front line of protecting the employer's brand," wrote human resources professional June D. Bell in a 2018 article in a professional newsletter. She added that the role includes scrutinizing potential employees in the HR pipeline. "Hiring managers also may be expected to act as defenders of the company if a candidate's online posts have the potential to reflect poorly on the organization's image," she wrote.[35]

While technology companies are aware of blogging and generally supportive of their employees who do it, they have little patience for workers who include details of the company's inner workings, whether confidential or not.

Two years after the Hanscom case at Microsoft, Mark Jen had been working at Google for just ten days when he was fired for posting information about yet-to-be-released products, as well as salary and benefit packages offered to employees.[36]

"There is some hesitation about employee blogs because an employee may disclose confidential business information, talk negatively of other employees or of the company, or display an interest that is in conflict with your business policies," wrote technology journalist Tiffany Black in a 2020 column in *Inc.* "There is a thin line between the company's best interests and violation of your employees' First-Amendment right to free speech."[37]

To Screen or Not to Screen

The rule about "being careful what you post" applies not only to current employees but also to future ones. Ever since the dawn of social media just after the beginning of the new century, employers have been using search engines like Google and Yahoo to conduct background checks on prospective employees. Numerous surveys have indicated that a majority of employers include a search of a candidate's social media history in their hiring decisions. Red flags include photographs of individuals in provocative dress, drinking in excess, or engaging in reckless behavior. As a result, career counselors at colleges and universities are warning students about to enter the job market to clean up their social media profiles, including Facebook, Instagram, and TikTok. The discovery of embarrassing or poorly thought-out social media posts could limit a graduate's interview opportunities—even if those posts are several years old.[38]

"One of the things people don't realize is that social media is the place where a lot of employers go first to find out about people," said Candace Moody, vice president of communications for WorkSource in Jacksonville, Florida, in a 2011 article by Gannett News Service. "If you've got party photos, if you've got embarrassing posts, if you've got posts that are talking trash about previous employers, you're in bad shape."[39] The author of the GNS article added that "no matter how much you think you've nailed the interview, your social media websites will nail you if you've been bad online."[40]

Some students scoff at the suggestion, citing privacy settings, but anecdotal evidence supports the belief that privacy settings are not infallible. "College students often post risqué or teasing photographs and provocative comments about drinking, recreational drug use, and sexual exploits in what some mistakenly believe is relative privacy," wrote Alan Finder in a 2006 article in *The New York Times*. "When viewed by corporate recruiters or admissions officials at graduate and professional schools, such pages can make students look immature and unprofessional, at best."[41]

Quoted in the same *New York Times* article is Trudy Steinfeld, director of the Center for Career Development at New York University, who added that many employers she's spoken with use the term "red flags" and ask, "Is there something about their lifestyle that we might find objectionable or that we might find goes against the core values of our corporation?" As one example, the article cited the case of an international student who was puzzled by the lack of employer interest in him, despite his graduating near the top of his class in engineering. At first, he thought he was being discriminated against because of his Asian heritage, but at the suggestion of a counselor, he looked at his social media postings going back several years. One item he found was an essay titled "Lying Your Way to the Top," and shortly after he deleted it, invitations for job interviews started coming his way.[42]

The Finder article pointed out that that scenario is common, as employers seldom tell an applicant why he or she was rejected, and most will not connect the dots for years—or maybe never. Employers do tell college career centers about the "red flags" they see, but only in general terms without mentioning specific cases.[43]

Human resources professionals claim the idea is not to disqualify candidates based on their social media activity, but simply to get a more complete picture of the person they might be hiring—a perspective that is unlikely to be apparent in reference letters or face-to-face interviews.

The Society for Human Resources Management, the largest professional association in the field, frequently publishes research on how prospective employees are evaluated. The processes of criminal background checks and drug screening are now augmented by perusing a candidate's social media activity. With the number of social media platforms constantly expanding, some human resources departments are hiring outside consultants to do the dirty work for them. And some of it is quite dirty: younger candidates coming straight from their senior years in college are advised to remove photos taken at fraternity or sorority parties or during spring break trips. Photographs showing students in partial (or full) stages of undress are frowned upon, as are photographs indicating excessive alcohol consumption. The more traditional and conservative the employer, the less likely they are to be tolerant of such behavior. SHRM reports and legal publications are full of cases in which employees fired for offensive social media content offer a standard excuse: "I was using privacy settings so only my family and friends would see it." The same precautionary advice should be heeded by those seeking jobs: privacy settings don't always work.[44]

In addition to Facebook, Instagram, Twitter, and TikTok, employers look at candidates' personal blogs, which may tell them more than references and interview performances. "Chances are that a candidate's blog will be far more telling than any reference you'll receive from past employers," stated a 2005 article in *Virginia Legal News*. "Neutral job references are the norm, and your shining star may reveal much more on his or her blog than in an interview."[45]

A 2018 study by Careerbuilder.com produced some interesting statistics about employers' use of social media to evaluate potential employees and keep tabs on what current ones are up to. More than 70 percent indicated they check candidates' social media profiles to get another perspective; sometimes before the initial interview but more likely after the interview and before an offer is made. Finding nothing is not necessarily a good thing: in cases in which social media searches are conducted before an interview, more than half of employers said they were less likely to interview candidates who were invisible online.[46]

Embarrassing or offensive social media content is not necessarily a deal-breaker: another study conducted by SHRM found the majority of employers would give candidates the opportunity to explain information of concern before making final hiring decisions. The CareerBuilder study also found that about half of employers indicated they monitor social media sites of current employees and, if necessary, bring negative information or images to the attention of supervisors.[47]

"Do past tweets represent the person who are today? Most would say no," wrote attorney John D. Winer in a 2018 article in *Legal News*. "But whatever you post online will stay online forever, and anything you might have said when you were young or because you were tweeting without using logic can and will come back to haunt you."[48]

Some employers are so concerned about the social media habits of the job candidates that they attempt to circumvent privacy settings by asking—in some cases demanding—that job candidates surrender their social media passwords. They claim their objective is to evaluate what candidates have said about past employers, or in one case involving a man applying for a job as a corrections officer, to see if he had gang affiliations in his past.[49] Privacy experts, however, worry that their intent might be more voyeuristic. Viewing this as a privacy violation, many state legislatures, at the urging of the American Civil Liberties Union, are passing laws prohibiting the gathering of such information.[50]

"I liken this to them saying they want to look at your love letters and your family photos," said Amy Canada, a spokesperson for the Montana chapter of the ACLU, in a 2009 interview with Associated Press.[51]

Federal law requires that employers who decline to hire an otherwise qualified job applicant based on negative financial information from credit-reporting agencies that turns up in a background check must explain their reasons to the applicant and give him or her the opportunity to explain or correct erroneous information. Chris Hoofnagle, a researcher at Berkeley Law School, suggests the law should be expanded to cover a job applicant's old blog posts or other social media activity, but he and other civil libertarians admit such a law would be difficult to enforce.[52]

To Monitor or Not to Monitor

Just because an applicant makes it through a background check that includes an evaluation of social media activity doesn't mean they're home free. The most recent applications of the principles of at-will employment involve newly hired employees terminated because of their social media posts. "While this might feel like discrimination or a violation of our First Amendment rights as Americans, firing an employee or new hire for putting their foot in their mouth via social media is completely legal," wrote attorney Lewis Massey in his firm's online newsletter in 2016. "Some might even argue that it is a justifiable consequence. Employers have the right to fire employees who do not represent their employee well."[53]

Labor attorneys Amy DelPo and Lisa Guerin strongly discourage employers from punishing employees for complaining online about company policies; they believe those criticisms are acceptable as long as they stick to the policies themselves and don't get into personal gripes about individual supervisors. "Employees have the legal right to talk to each other and try to improve or change their working conditions," they wrote in their 2017 book, *Dealing with Problem Employees*. "As long as the topic of discussion is workplace rules, conditions, terms (such as pay or hours), you can't discipline employees for this conduct."[54]

The authors cited two cases to support that point. One involved a collections agency employee who was unhappy about her transfer to another office, and the other was a veterinary technician who was denied a promotion. In both cases, the employees took their complaints to Facebook, and in both cases, their coworkers posted messages of support.

The employers fired the individuals at the center of the cases and threatened to reprimand their coworkers for supporting them, but in both cases, the National Labor Relations Board ordered their reinstatement and ruled that both the terminations and the threatened reprimand of their coworkers violated NLRB rules.[55]

"I think we will be hard-pressed to see an example of a private company getting into hot water for disciplining or firing an employee over a Facebook gaffe, unless, of course, there are other issues in the background," wrote attorney Venkat Balasubramani in a 2011 post to Technology and Marketing Blog.[56] While not absolutely required to be successful in defending itself against a wrongful termination lawsuit, Balasubramani wrote, a private employer can enhance its chances by having a social media policy in place. While Facebook is the main culprit, he wrote, employers should have more comprehensive policies that go beyond social media and also address all forms of digital communication, including email, blog entries, forum posts, tweets, and status updates.[57] The NLRB has called some companies' social media policies "problematic" because they attempt to ban all employee discussions that mention the company, even posts that are positive.

Human resources professional June D. Bell says the turning point came around 2010, when the National Labor Relations Board began fielding complaints from workers who had been disciplined or terminated for their online behavior. The NLRB responded by warning employers about social media policies that were vague and overbroad, tried to limit conversations about "concerted activities," or attempted to ban all social media mentions of a company, even those that were positive or promotional.[58]

Having a social media policy is not a foolproof way for a business to defend itself when terminating employees based on social media behavior. In a 2011 case in Wisconsin, the NLRB ruled that a restaurant's policy was overbroad because it attempted to prohibit all mentions of the restaurant—even those that were positive or promotional—on employees' social media accounts. That also included comments about pay, working hours, and tax paperwork that the NLRB considers protected speech (this case is discussed in more detail in the Chapter 3 section about restaurant employees).[59]

Employers often justify their monitoring of incoming and outgoing email traffic based on their ownership of the computer equipment and computer networks, and court rulings support their right to do so. Not only are employers trying to prevent the unauthorized release of company information, but they are also attempting to limit other forms of communication that may result in lawsuits involving libel, privacy, or sexual or racial harassment. In a recent survey conducted by the American Management Association, more than two-thirds of companies responded that they routinely monitor the email communication of their employees as well as monitor the websites they visit — both work-related and non-work-related. Experts in the fields of both law and technology point out that when individuals use their employers' computer equipment and Internet access to vent in cyberspace, their bulletin board postings and electronic mail postings are not as private as they might believe.

Depending on which survey you believe, between one-third and one-half of all private employers survey the internal and outgoing email of their employees. Most use automated programs that search for problematic keywords, while some large employers are monitoring employee email traffic and hiring outside consultants to develop systems for determining the origin of anonymous postings to industry bulletin boards. "If you work at a Fortune 500 company, chances are good your email has been reviewed at least once," says Joan Feldman, founder of the Seattle-based Computer Forensics Inc., which helps companies track their employees' illegal or unethical use of company-owned technology.[60]

According to Barry, when individuals get "called on the carpet" for information posted online, it's "less often a case of employers violating free-speech rights and more a case of employees being victims of their own bad judgment."[61] In a 2024 interview, Barry said the reason behind employers monitoring their employees on social media isn't necessarily because they are sensitive to criticism. "I assume they (employers) monitor less for criticism than for crazy—finding out who among the workforce is living the virulently racist or sexist or otherwise objectionable life off-work," Barry said.[62]

While some free-speech and privacy advocates claim that employer monitoring of email violates the rights of employees, recent news stories provide the best evidence of the dangers that companies face by not doing so. When federal investigators looking into allegations of financial wrongdoing at Enron in 2003 gained access to archived computer files, for example, they found pornography, racial comments, offensive jokes, and other material in employee email that would have exposed the company to lawsuits if it had been detected before the company dissolved.[63]

Despite the potential danger involved in not monitoring employee email, many companies are still reluctant to do so. One factor is the cost, which for companies with large numbers of employees may be substantial. Another factor is trust—employers simply prefer to trust their employees and respect their privacy. Many companies in this category wait until they have "probable cause" or other suspicions before snooping in email files.

One such "trust" incident occurred at the *Toledo Blade*, one of Ohio's largest daily newspapers, in 2006. Wanting to determine which staff member sent an anonymous email criticizing the newspaper's Pulitzer Prize entry to the organization administering the competition, the management hired a private investigator. Following preliminary evidence, the investigators confiscated the company-owned laptop computer of a reporter and used a computer forensics expert to analyze its hard drive. The newspaper fired the reporter, who had sent the anonymous email through his personal Yahoo account but using the company-owned laptop. Following the incident, however, the company reverted to its policy of not monitoring employee email except in extreme circumstances.[64]

While they discourage their employees from using the company's online access for shopping, dating, or participation in social media networking or fantasy sports leagues, some employers are reluctant to enforce outright bans as long as employees are doing these activities during lunch breaks or after working hours. But many employers believe that engaging in non-work online activities during working hours is a major drain on productivity. Even though their employees claim they would "never do that during working hours," research indicates that at least some of their peers do. One survey of Internet retailers found that two-thirds of their business occurs during business hours (9 a.m. to 5 p.m.), with a significant fall-off on the weekends.[65]

Court rulings have consistently found that because they are providing the technology, employers are free to conduct such monitoring, and employees do not have a legitimate claim that their privacy has been invaded. That ruling assumes, however, that employers are doing so for a legitimate purpose such as protecting company assets or preventing the transmission of material that is sexually or racially offensive, is harassing, or violates copyright law. Courts would be more sympathetic to the employee if he or she is able to prove that the monitoring is unrelated to legitimate purposes or is voyeuristic in nature.[66]

Only two states—Connecticut and Delaware—prohibit employers from watching employees' web activity or intercepting emails unless they provide advance notice of the monitoring. Many employers in those states have their employees sign documents acknowledging the employers' rights. In the other forty-eight states, employers may monitor employee communications except in cases in which their motives are voyeuristic in nature or their intent is to watch or disrupt union or collective bargaining activity.[67]

A 2014 decision by the National Labor Relations Board upheld an employer's right to monitor their employees' online activity in order to investigate or prevent the harassment of coworkers, defamation, or the disclosure of trade secrets.[68]

Despite the absence of state laws prohibiting them from doing so, employers should still resist the temptation, says Marc Rotenberg, executive director of the

Electronic Privacy Information Center. "Having the right to do it doesn't make it the right thing to do," Rotenberg said in an interview with the *Daily Record* in Kansas City, Kansas. "If you reason that since it's the employer's equipment, they have the right to monitor, does that mean there's no expectation of privacy in the employer's restrooms as well? I make that point only to underscore the fact that ownership alone doesn't resolve the privacy issue. I think that in personal communications, and even for use of the Internet, there should be some safeguards for employees' expectations of privacy."[69]

Two decades of court rulings generally back up employers: in 1993, two employees of the Nissan Motor Corp. sued the company for invading their privacy by monitoring their email communication, despite having signed a copy of the company's policy that prohibited using the system for non-work purposes. One of the employees claimed that she was humiliated when one of her sexually explicit emails was used in a training session as an example of inappropriate computer use. A California court found in favor of the company.[70]

In 1996, a former employee was unsuccessful in a wrongful termination suit against the Pillsbury Company. The court ruled that the company's right to prevent its computer system from being used for inappropriate and unprofessional comments outweighed the employee's privacy interests. The employee had been terminated for criticizing supervisors and coworkers[71] (this case is discussed in more detail in Chapter 3).

In 1999, the stock brokerage firm Salomon Smith Barney fired two executives after a routine check of internal communication discovered their use of the company's internal email system for transmitting sexually explicit material.[72]

Also, in 1999, the "zero tolerance" policy of Edward Jones & Company resulted in nineteen employees being terminated after creating or forwarding racist and sexist jokes and sexually explicit images.[73]

In 2011, courts in California and Georgia ruled in separate cases that employers did not violate the privacy rights of their employees by monitoring their personal email communication. In the California case, the court ruled that the employee's communication with her attorney was not protected by attorney-client privilege. In the Georgia case, the court ruled that an employer had a legitimate interest in monitoring an employee's email to determine if he was running an outside business on company time.[74]

In 2019, employees at the McKesson Corporation, a San Francisco-based supplier of medical equipment, discovered the company had been monitoring their email activity for years. They were upset, but under California law had no legal foundation on which to complain. The company justified the monitoring by explaining that by examining the employees' communication with each other as well as with customers and suppliers, it could determine how such interactions could be improved. It also wanted to discover why certain departments had higher employee turnover rates than others.[75]

"Employers are parsing those (online) interactions to learn who is influential, which teams are most productive, and who is a flight risk," wrote *Wall Street Journal* reporter Sarah Krouse in a 2019 article.[76] Despite companies having the law on their side, lawyers suggest that employers who choose to electronically monitor their online activity prevent problems by advising employees that monitoring may occur, requiring them to sign documents acknowledging that possibility, and issuing lists reminding employees of what forms of online activity are permissible and not permissible.

Is No Policy the Best Policy?

While many labor lawyers and human resources professionals endorse the concept of social media policies, that sentiment is not universal. SnackNation, a Culver City, California food-delivery service, is among many companies that prefer to trust their employees. "I'd like to think we hire adults," says one company manager in an interview with SHRM News. "We don't as a company have the time and bandwidth to monitor everyone's social media, and if you do crack down on someone, you become the cop and the bad guy."[77]

Technology journalist Tiffany Black suggests a blog policy should provide guidelines such as (1) not disclosing confidential business information, (2) providing a disclaimer that the views expressed are those of the author and not the company, (3) not including company logos or trademarks, and (4) not claiming nor implying that they are speaking on the company's behalf.[78]

"In the absence of reliable evidence that the employee is doing something really damaging to an employer's interests or violating substantial company policies, leave any password-protected social media site alone," advised attorney Brian Hall in a 2009 article of *Employer Law Report*. "If it is just a bunch of employees blowing off steam, it won't be the first time employees have gotten together somewhere to say something unflattering about the boss."[79]

Notes

1 Christine Rosen, "The Shaming Spiral: How Social Media Moralizes for Profit," *Commentary*, June 2015, pp. 45–8. See also: Peter D'Amato, "Nonprofit Worker Provokes Fury with Cemetery Photo," *London Daily Mail*, February 22, 2015.
2 Rosen, "The Shaming Spiral."
3 John D. Winer, "Can My Ten-Year-Old Tweet Get Me Fired?" *Legal News*, August 29, 2018. See also: Randy Bobbitt, *Exploring Communication Ethics* (New York: Taylor & Francis, 2020), p. 271.
4 Ibid.
5 The PGA of America is not to be confused with the PGA Tour. The PGA of America is a trade association comprised of golf instructors and administrators, most of whom are employed at golf courses and clubs; the PGA Tour is composed of golfers who compete in professional tournaments.
6 Ted Bishop, *Unfriended: The Power Brokers, Political Correctness, and Hypocrisy in Golf* (Stratford, CT: Classics of Golf Publishing, 2016), pp. 17–22.
7 Ibid., p. 225.
8 Ibid.
9 Christine Porath, *Mastering Civility: A Manifesto for the Workplace* (New York: Grand Central Publishing, 2016), p. 115.
10 Ibid., pp. 117–18.
11 Charles J. Muhl, "Workplace E-Mail and Internet Use: Employees and Employers Beware," *Monthly Labor Review*, February 2003, pp. 36–45.
12 Mark F. Kluger, interview with the author, January 2, 2024.
13 Ibid.
14 Patricia Graves, "Ask an Expert: Online Behavior," *SHRM News*, May 27, 2021.
15 Michael Corkery, "How a Dollar General Employee Went Viral on TikTok," *The New York Times*, April 18, 2022.
16 Lewis Massey, "Can I Get Fired Over a Tweet? What NOT to Say on Social Media," online newsletter of Massey, Watson & Hembree, April 13, 2016.
17 Samuel Greengard, interview with the author, January 3, 2024.
18 Daniel J. Solove, *The Future of Reputation: Gossip, Rumor, and Privacy on the Internet* (New Haven, CT: Yale University Press, 2007), p. 39.
19 Stephanie Armour, "Warning: Your Clever Little Blog Could Get You Fired," *USA Today*, June 14, 2005.
20 Ibid.
21 *Shepherd v. McGee*, 2013 U.S. Dist. LEXIS 159432 (2013).
22 Terry Collins, "TikTok Got Me Fired: The Pitfalls of Talking Work on Social Media," *USA Today*, July 19, 2022, p. 4-B.

23 Kashmir Hill, "East Stroudsburg University Professor Reinstated After Facebook Post About Hit Man," *Forbes Online*, March 17, 2011.
24 Tiffany Black, "How to Handle Employee Blogging," *Inc,* April 6, 2010.
25 Todd Bishop, "Microsoft Fires Employee Over Weblog," *Seattle Post-Intelligencer*, October 30, 2003. See also: Bruce Barry, *Speechless: The Erosion of Free Expression in the American Workplace* (San Francisco: Berrett-Koehler Publishers, 2007), p. 170.
26 "The Hill's Sex Diarist Reveals All," *The Washington Post*, May 24, 2004. See also: Anna Bahney, "Interns? Bloggers Need Not Apply," *The New York Times,* May 25, 2006, p. 1-A. April Witt, "Blog Interrupted," *The Washington Post*, August 15, 2004.
27 Black, "How to Handle Employee Blogging."
28 Greengard, "The Virtual Pen is Not Mightier Than the Ax," *Workplace Management*, March 1, 2005, pp. 74–6.
29 Eric Auchard, "Famed Microsoft Blogger Leaves for Startup," *Reuters News Service*, June 11, 2006.
30 Robert Scoble, "Correcting the Record about Microsoft," *Scobleizer*, June 10, 2006. See also: Auchard, "Famed Microsoft Blogger Leaves for Startup."
31 Amanda Lenhart and Susannah Fox, "Bloggers: A Portrait of the Internet's New Storytellers," *Pew Internet and American Life Project*, July 19, 2006.
32 Ibid.
33 Ibid.
34 Ibid.
35 June D. Bell, "Firing for Online Behavior," *SHRM News*, August 24, 2018.
36 Greengard, "The Virtual Pen Is Not Mightier Than the Ax."
37 Black, "How to Handle Employee Blogging."
38 Jennifer Jolly, "Grads, Clean Up That Social Media," *USA Today*, June 6, 2022, p. 3-B.
39 Jeff Marcu, "Website Exposes Your Life," *Gannett News Service Report*, July 30, 2011.
40 Ibid.
41 Alan Finder, "For Some, Online Persona Undermines a Resume," *The New York Times,* June 11, 2006, p. 1-A.
42 Ibid.
43 Ibid.
44 Jolly, "Grads, Clean Up That Social Media."
45 "Myemployersucks.com: Why You Need a Blogging Policy," *Virginia Legal News,* July 2005.
46 Ibid.
47 Bell, "Firing for Online Behavior."
48 Winer, "Can My Ten-Year-Old Tweet Get Me Fired?"

49 Lori Andrews, *I Know Who You Are and I Saw What You Did: Social Networks and the Death of Privacy* (New York: Free Press, 2012), p. 122.

50 Ibid.

51 Matt Gouras, "City Drops Request for Internet Passwords," *Associated Press Report*, June 19, 2009. See also: Doug Gross, "Facebook Speaks Out Against Employers Asking for Passwords," *CNN News*, March 23, 2012.

52 Solove, *The Future of Reputation*, p. 203.

53 Massey, "Can I Get Fired Over a Tweet?"

54 Amy DelPo and Lisa Guerin, *Dealing with Problem Employees: How to Manage Performance and Personality Issues in the Workplace* (Berkeley, CA: NOLO Press, 2017), p. 28.

55 Ibid., p. 72. See also: Venkat Balasubramani, "Do Employers Really Tread a Minefield by Firing Employees for Facebook Gaffes?" *Technology and Marketing Law Blog*, January 28, 2011.

56 Balasubramani, "Do Employers Really Tread a Minefield by Firing Employees for Facebook Gaffes?"

57 Ibid.

58 Bell, "Firing for Online Behavior."

59 NLRB Cases 34-CA-12915 and 34-CA-12926. See also: *Three-D v. National Labor Relations Board,* 629 F. App. 33 (2015). Venkat Balasubramani, "NLRB Invalidates Employer's Blogging Policy and Reverses Firing Based on Facebook Posts," *Technology and Marketing Law Blog*, September 27, 2014.

60 NLRB Cases 34-CA-12915 and 34-CA-12926. See also: *Three-D v. National Labor Relations Board,* 629 F. App. 33 (2015). Balasubramani, "NLRB Invalidates Employer's Blogging Policy and Reverses Firing Based on Facebook Posts."

61 Barry, *Speechless,* p. 67.

62 Barry, interview with the author.

63 Bobbitt, *Exploring Communication Ethics*, p. 250.

64 Ibid.

65 Hall Adams, Suzanne M. Scheuing, and Stacey A. Feely, "E-Mail Monitoring in the Workplace: The Good, the Bad, and the Ugly," *Defense Counsel Journal* 67, no. 1 (January 2000): pp. 32–46.

66 Patricia Wallace, *The Internet in the Workplace: How New Technology is Transforming Work* (New York: Cambridge University Press, 2004), pp. 244–5.

67 Stan Hill, "The Multilayered Minefield of Workplace E-Mail Monitoring," *Employment Relations Today* 42, no. 1 (Spring 2015): pp. 55–62.

68 Ibid.

69 Ibid.

70 Jane Pribek, "Employer Rights When Monitor E-Mail, Internet Use," *The Daily Record* (Kansas City, MO), February 20, 2006.
71 Adams, Scheuing, and Feely, "E-Mail Monitoring in the Workplace."
72 Ibid.
73 Ibid.
74 Jeffrey L. Seglin, "You've Got Mail. You're Being Watched," *The New York Times*, July 18, 1999.
75 Lisa Frye, "Reviewing Employee E-Mails: When You Should, When You Shouldn't," *SHRM News,* May 15, 2017.
76 Sarah Krouse, "The New Ways Your Boss is Spying on You," *The Wall Street Journal*, July 20–21, 2019, p. 1-B.
77 Ibid.
78 Bell, "Firing for Online Behavior."
79 Brian Hall, "Court Upholds Jury Verdict in Pietrylo v. Hillstone Restaurant Group," *Employer Law Report*, October 19, 2009.

3

Free Speech in Corporate America

Robust Discussion versus Office Harmony

Open Mouth, Insert Foot

In 2017, a Google engineer named James Damore went from obscurity to national fame after his internal memo was leaked to the press. The ten-page document stated that technology jobs were better in men's hands and that women were "better suited for jobs in artistic and social areas."[1] According to technology journalist Kelly Weill, Damore's assertions relied on "cherry-picked data and was built on a framework of misogynist tropes that flourish in right-wing conspiratorial scenes."[2]

The ideas in Damore's missive were quickly debunked by experts in both neuroscience and human resources. He had only a few defenders, most of them associated with conservative media organizations and think tanks. Citing the common expression, "I disagree with what you say, but I will defend to the death your right to say it,"[3] other observers said he had the right to say what he said, no matter how ignorant. In a similar tact, Google defended the firing by stating that if his opinion was published in a public forum, it would have been protected as free speech, but because it was first circulated internally and seen by thousands of female employees, it violated the company's zero-tolerance policy on harassment.

"Google ended up firing Damore, not because the company is some bastion of political correctness, but because most workplaces frown on it when employees mass-email their colleagues with rants about how a good chunk of them are physically incapable of competence," wrote Amanda Marcotte in her 2018 book, *Troll Nation.*

> People need to get along with their colleagues, which is hard to do when you know for a fact that your coworker is sitting there glowering with rage because

he thinks your job belongs to a man by biological right. Perhaps Google could have dealt with the problem by firing all the women instead, a solution that would have no doubt pleased Damore, but would have gotten the company in serious trouble with the EEOC.[4]

Recurring Themes

Although well-publicized, the Damore case was not the first time an employee of a private company ran afoul of management in matters of opinion. On the issue of private employers and the free-speech rights of their employees, case law in this area can be found as far back as the 1970s, when the Polaroid company fired an employee who was picketing outside its factory, charging that the company refused to close its operations in South Africa during the era of apartheid, even though many competitors had already done so.[5] During that same era, a psychiatric nurse was fired from her job at a Pennsylvania mental hospital after criticizing the management of the institution in a newspaper interview (this case is discussed later in this chapter).[6]

There have been long stretches of time during which there were few court cases involving employee free speech, but that does not necessarily mean those conflicts were not taking place. "Most situations don't end up in courts or newspapers; they stay inside the organization, under the sway of employer rules and policies, managerial whims, and an organization's culture," wrote Bruce Barry, professor of management at Vanderbilt University, in a 2007 book.[7] Barry adds that while the law changes slowly, employers can help the process by enacting employee-friendly free-speech policies that would provide for more robust employee discourse and, in the process improve morale in the workplace. "They could do it today," Barry wrote.[8]

Free-speech rights within the private workplace have been on the decline for the last decade for two reasons. First, mostly because of the growth of social media, employers are more sensitive to criticism that comes from within and more likely to reprimand or terminate employees for being the source of that criticism. The second reason is that the courts are giving them more latitude to do so.

One factor affecting the level of workplace speech that is allowed is the size of the organization. A larger organization might be more tolerant of free speech—even speech that is critical of the organization—simply because of the distance between management and labor and the lack of effect the speech has on productivity or the reputation of the company. In smaller organizations, however, management might allow employees to exercise their free-speech rights as long as the opinions expressed are consistent with the opinions of those who sign the paychecks.

As a general rule, private companies are not required by the First Amendment to extend free-speech rights to their employees, but many claim to do so for a variety of reasons:

1. *Seeking feedback on management performance.* A common topic of discussion in academic literature in the management field is whether such feedback should be solicited out in the open or anonymously. The reluctance of employees to publicly criticize their employers has led to the growth of websites where workers can post comments anonymously, whether still at the company or after moving on. One of the first such sites was Bitch Vault, which was created in 2000 by the founders of its parent company, Vault.com.[9]
2. *Encouraging "robust discussion" to generate ideas for better serving customers and creating new products.* High-tech is one field in which employers like open and unfettered discourse, whether through internal computer networks or around the water cooler. A few, however, seem to want it both ways. They believe in free speech when it is to their benefit, but not when it creates negative media coverage or internal discord.

   Bitch Vault was followed in 2008 by Glassdoor, which today is the largest website where employees can gripe about current and past employers, and a company's prospective employees can check out reviews.[10] The site started with posting only quantitative information such as salaries, but then expanded its scope to also cover more subjective content such as the treatment of minorities, opportunities for advancement, workplace culture, and work-life balance. A 2017 court ruling determined that Glassdoor would not be required to disclose the identity of users to employers but would be required to disclose their identity to law-enforcement personnel investigating crimes allegedly committed by companies.[11]

   "If employees are given a chance to speak up about things and they feel like they are being heard, they will also be more inclined to offer helpful suggestions and not just complain about negative things," wrote clinical psychologist and management consultant Rudy Nydegger in his 2018 book, *Clocking In: The Psychology of Work.* "However, when employees do complain or have negative comments, they should make sure they are talking about an issue about which something can be done; they could even try to make suggestions as to how things could be changed for the better. Even when their suggestions are not followed, when employees feel that they have been listened to and their ideas at least fairly considered, this does make a difference in how they feel and how motivated they will be to try to do a better job."[12]

Mark F. Kluger, an attorney and partner in the firm of Kluger Healey, LLC in Montclair, New Jersey, has been successful in persuading Glassdoor to remove negative posts about his clients, but after doing so twice he found himself blocked from the site. He knows that many large employers have someone monitor the site and respond to posts but questions the value of those responses. "I am not so sure those responses are effective, but they do make it clear that the employer is hearing the complaints," Kluger said in a 2024 interview. "So often those (negative) posts are written by former employees who have been terminated and are clearly ready to burn down the world. Job seekers may well dismiss those posts, as they are usually pretty transparent."[13]

In a 2016 article in *Harvard Business Review*, business professors James R. Detert and Ethan Burris provided three reasons for allowing employees to voice opinions openly instead of anonymously (such as on Glassdoor) or through an ombudsman. First, they wrote, taking an anonymous "suggestion box" approach to soliciting employee feedback sends the message that it's not safe for employees to take any other route. "The subtext is 'It's not safe to share your views openly in this organization, so we've created other channels to get the information we need,'" the authors wrote. The second reason revolves around paranoia. Detert and Burris cited a case involving a Fortune 500 company that solicited employee feedback online; the company found that many of the responses came from public libraries and coffee shops because they feared that if they used their home or office computers, their responses could be traced. The same employees expressed skepticism about talking to the company's ombudsman, simply asking "who pays his salary?" The third reason, Detert and Burris wrote, was that those employees making criticisms, no matter how constructive, seldom provided enough detail, making it difficult to address issues while protecting the identity of who raised them.[14]

One company well known for its transparency in soliciting feedback is Facebook. One example occurred in 2016, following public debate over the role of social media misinformation in that year's presidential election. Founder Mark Zuckerberg downplayed the criticism and announced there would be no changes to company policy leading up to the 2020 campaign. Facebook's own employees disagreed with the company's lack of action and publicly criticized their boss in an open letter signed by more than 250 workers at all levels of the company. "We strongly object to this policy as it stands," the employees wrote. "It doesn't protect voices, but instead allows politicians to weaponize our platform by targeting people who believe that content posted by political figures is trustworthy." To his credit, Zuckerberg did not discipline any of the employees who signed the letter, but he also did not reverse the policy.[15]

3. *Retention of current employees and recruitment of new ones.* According to management literature as well as mainstream media reports, companies with liberal free-speech policies will enjoy greater morale and productivity, leading to greater retention of employees, and will make the company more attractive to prospective employees.[16]

   A 2016 article in *Harvard Business Review* reported that while private employers don't have to allow the unfettered right of expression to their employees, many do so for the same reason they offer reasonable work hours and more generous vacation and leave policies: it increases morale and productivity and makes the company more attractive to potential hires.[17]

Other companies see little value in those ideas and instead prefer to maintain a tight grip on employee speech—internal and external, online and in-person—for a variety of valid reasons:

1. *Maintaining office harmony and preventing workplace disruption.* This issue is usually discussed in the context of social media, oftentimes because social media is seen by some company leaders to be a drag on productivity. Another term used in this discussion is "comfortable working environment."

2. *Adhering to laws regarding harassment, discrimination, and defamation.* Again, this issue is usually discussed in the context of social media, and new rules are often promulgated after it is too late. Expensive litigation, or the threat of litigation, is usually enough for company leaders to issue new rules regarding internal communication. When employees challenge their employers' policies, the National Labor Relations Board and the courts often scrutinize the intent behind the comments in question: employees making legitimate comments about workplace conditions such as working hours and pay are usually on safe ground, while they are not protected if their comments are based on personal grievances or are potentially defamatory. In addition, the NLRB and the courts consider the issue of "workplace disruption," but courts in different states often disagree on whether the burden should be on the employer to prove the speech was disruptive or on the employee to prove that it was not.
3. *Dealing with threats, real and perceived.* Closely related to the issues of "workplace disruption" and "harassment" is the issue of real or perceived threats. Courts give employers great latitude to discipline or terminate employees in cases in which hostile speech could be construed as threats. Many First Amendment cases turn on the difference between speech and conduct—the former constitutionally protected and the latter not—but in these cases, the concern is speech that might lead to *harmful* conduct. Cases in this chapter include an employer who allegedly threatened (in what he thought was a private email to his boss) to kill coworkers and two cases of emergency medical technicians who were terminated when their careless comments about their frustrations with uncooperative patients were considered a danger to patient safety.
4. *Avoiding competition.* Many states have laws that prohibit discrimination against employees based on their off-work activities, but allow exceptions if the employees' activities are in competition with the interests of the employer or are otherwise disruptive. For example, a company that manufactures T-shirts can prohibit its employees from designing T-shirts that are sold in the same stores.[18]
5. *Preserving company reputation and avoiding negative media coverage.* These concerns, sometimes well founded and sometimes not, are related to the potential loss of customers, or in the case of nonprofit organizations, loss of donors or potential donors (mostly in cases involving social media). In a 2018 case in Toledo, Ohio, for example,

a well-liked pastor was terminated when church elders discovered he believed the Earth was flat. Although he never incorporated such thoughts in his sermons, his bosses contended that his attendance at an annual Flat Earth Conference and his promotion of the theory on social media might cause outsiders to believe the church supported such ideas.[19]

Several cases in this chapter deal with how this concern applies to the matter of dress codes. Companies enforcing what some employees believe are draconian dress codes contend that adherence to the code (as well as other company policies) outweighs the value of personal expression. This view is very common in states with strong at-will laws. As illustrated in cases in this chapter involving employees wearing "Black Lives Matter" masks during the Covid-19 pandemic of 2020–1, courts typically back up employers as long as the rules are enforced fairly. A company would have less success defending itself in court, however, if it had a history of prohibiting "Black Lives Matter" masks but allowing those that read "Make America Great Again" (or vice-versa).

6. *Arbitrary application of the at-will principle.* In short, employers limit employee speech because the laws of their state say they can. In many cases, the reason behind the rules is based on sensitivity to criticism, even when such criticism has no tangible effects on reputation or sales.

Exceptions to such rules, codified in state and federal law, provide protection for (1) speech that is related to union activity and (2) speech related to good-faith whistleblowing.[20]

In addition, as outlined in the Introduction, even in states where "at-will" employment is standard, employers cannot dismiss employees solely because of their membership in classes protected by federal anti-discrimination laws.

Many states have laws that prohibit employers from making hiring or firing decisions based on an employee's political beliefs and behaviors, as long as those behaviors do not interrupt or interfere with the employer's business. An example of permissible action would be a car dealership telling an employee he or she cannot display political posters in an office or cubicle in view of customers. The rule would have to be content-neutral, however; an employer could not prohibit political materials of one party while allowing materials of another.

"Employees who exercise the right to free speech can face many potential difficulties at work," wrote English labor attorney Lucy Vickers in her 2002 book, *Freedom of Speech in Employment*. "Whatever the type of speech, and regardless of its subject matter, an employer may take advantage of the employment relationship to censure the speech with a work-based penalty. This may be because the employee's speech embarrasses or shames the employer, because it interferes with work, or merely because the employer disagrees with the sentiment expressed."[21]

7. *Inconsistency in the resolution of whistleblower claims.* In some cases, companies justify the termination of whistleblowing employees by claiming those employees should have followed an internal chain of command and reported issues to management before disclosing them to the media or government regulators. How the courts view that requirement is inconsistent: in some cases, they see value in the requirement and rule in favor of the company, but in others, they determine the chain-of-command idea is a suggestion rather than a binding rule and find in favor of the employee. In cases in which employees claim they did bring up issues internally first and the companies say they didn't, courts don't know whom to believe. Up until the 1980s, they tended to give the benefit of the doubt to the employer, but more recently they tend to give the benefit to the whistleblowing employee.
8. *Alleged double standards in cases involving journalists.* As illustrated by several cases later in this chapter, broadcasters—especially those in sports—have a history of speaking out on issues unrelated to the sports they cover. Employers often express disappointment (or sometimes outrage) at offensive comments made by on-air talent. But media critics have noticed an apparent double standard in how cases are addressed. Employees who were female, Black, or both were either fired or forced to resign after making political comments that outraged fans, while their counterparts who were male, white, or both got slaps on their wrists. In the only case in this chapter involving a print journalist, a white female reporter was fired after criticizing her newspaper on her blog.

Facebook, Twitter, Instagram, TikTok, and Other Ways to Waste Time at Work

As mentioned in previous chapters, social media has become an issue for many companies, as human resources personnel and company attorneys are concerned about employers' liability for defamatory comments made by employees who appear to be speaking on behalf of the company, whether intentional or not.

In December 2004, the manager of a local office of the Allstate insurance company in the Chicago suburb of Villa Park published an online essay critical of homosexuality. J. Matt Barber claimed to have based his opinion on deeply held religious and politically conservative beliefs, but it was later discovered that much of his discourse had been gleaned from materials published by conservative political groups and television and radio talk shows. Among his beliefs were claims that the gay lifestyle was at odds with "family values," same-sex marriage should not be legalized, and that "conversion therapy" programs had a positive track record in "saving" people from being gay and returning them to a "normal" lifestyle.[22]

When his supervisors learned about the posting, Barber was suspended, escorted from the building, and later fired. He sued Allstate in federal district court, claiming he was fired for his religious beliefs. He also asserted that he was dismissed in part for refusing to take part in the company's "diversity training" and in retaliation for reporting cases of sexual misconduct (affecting other employees, not himself) on a business trip.

Allstate countered that he was fired not for his beliefs, but for using company resources on company time for "personal journalism activities" in which he identified himself as an Allstate employee without the disclaimer that his opinions were solely his own and did not reflect the views of the company. Around the community of Chicago and nationwide, the case created battle lines between conservative religious and political groups calling for his reinstatement and pro-equality and pro-diversity interests saluting the company for taking a bold stand, even though Allstate insisted throughout the process that Barber's termination was based on his use of company resources to disseminate his opinions, not on the opinions themselves. After fourteen months of "he said/he said" debates inside and outside of the courtroom, Barber and Allstate settled the case, with terms not being disclosed.[23]

When Facebook and Twitter first became popular, policies regulating employees' use of social media were especially tough on younger workers. Careless tweets and postings caused the termination of a twenty-four-year-old employee of the Pittsburgh Pirates who criticized the team's personnel moves and a sixteen-year-old girl who complained about her job being "boring" without identifying her employer. A twenty-two-year-old job prospect at Cisco

Systems saw an employment offer withdrawn after she was caught bragging on Facebook about what her salary would be.[24]

In 2004, Rob Smith was fired from his supervisory job at the energy company Kerr-McGee after his superiors discovered his personal blog, which he made no attempt to make anonymous, on which he said "the N-word was sometimes deserved" and that the company's violence prevention seminars were unnecessary because he kept a three-foot piece of steel pipe behind his desk because "that's all he needed."[25]

That same year, a webpage designer for the startup social media platform Friendster was fired in 2004 over her blog, titled Troutgirl, in which she discussed the inner workings of the company. Joyce Park declined to take legal action against the company, realizing that she would not have a strong case because of California's at-will employment law. She did become somewhat of an industry martyr, however, claiming in media interviews that she didn't mention anything on her blog that was not already public knowledge and was neither given any warning nor the opportunity to remove her posts.[26]

In 2005, Mark Jen was fired during his first month on the job at Google after he posted information on his blog in which he disclosed information about the company's financial statements—meant to be discussed only internally—as well as yet-to-be-released products. He was told he was being terminated for violating the company's intellectual property and trade secret policy, but believing his disclosures did not affect stock prices and caused no real harm, he assumed the firing was because his supervisors and coworkers didn't like him personally. But because of the at-will nature of his job—common in industries and especially in California—Jen had little recourse.[27]

In his first few weeks working as an intern at the cable television network Comedy Central in 2005, Andrew McDonald was caught violating the first rule of the workplace: don't use your social media platforms to discuss the behind-the-scenes aspects of how the workplace functions, even if such revelations are not embarrassing or revealing company secrets.

McDonald got away with just a reprimand, and in exchange for the light sentence agreed to change the name of his blog from "I'm a Comedy Central Intern" to "I'm an Intern Working in New York" and pledged not to "reveal how the comedic sausage is made."[28]

Viacom, the network's parent company, then developed a more specific policy to deal with interns who joined the company subsequently. "Employees are discouraged from publicly discussing work-related matters, whether constituting confidential information or not, outside of appropriate work channels, including online chat rooms or blogs," the policy reads.[29]

In yet another example of privacy settings not working the way they were designed to, Peter Whitney lost his job at a Seattle brokerage firm owned by Wells Fargo Bank after blogging about his work. His superiors had been aware of the blog for months but said nothing to him about it. The end came when he complained about being asked to chip in for a birthday card for a manager he didn't like. Whitney admitted that while those comments and previous ones were unwise, his termination was unfair considering the company's lack of a social media policy.

"There needs to be clearer guidelines," he told *USA Today*. "Some people go to a bar and complain about co-workers, but I decided to do it online. Some people say I deserve what happened, but it was really harsh. It was unfair."[30]

In 2009, Virginia Rodriquez was an hourly employee at the Sam's Club discount warehouse store in San Diego when she was accused of violating the store's employee purchasing policy. The store manager accused her of having another employee mark down the price on an item so that Rodriquez could later purchase it. While suspended for that offense, Rodriquez learned that two coworkers called in sick so they could attend a party hosted by a third employee. Rodriquez did not attend the party herself but saw photos of the event on Facebook and posted her own comments, questioning the honesty of the employees who were allegedly sick.[31] While it's not clear if the other employees were disciplined, Rodriquez was terminated for violating the social media policy of Wal-Mart, the parent company of Sam's Club. The policy prohibits conduct that "adversely affects" their job performance or that of other associates.[32]

"You are more likely to resolve work-related complaints by speaking directly with your co-workers or by utilizing our Open Door Policy than by posting complaints to a social media outlet," the policy read. While employees are allowed to post complaints, the policy reads, they cannot post items that appear "unprofessional, insulting, embarrassing, untrue, or harmful."[33]

Rodriquez, whose court documents described her as a "Hispanic woman over 40," sued Wal-Mart in federal court, claiming that age and race discrimination played a bigger role in her termination than her social media comments or the original violation of policy regarding employee purchases. The court granted the company's motion for summary judgment, determining that she failed to prove her discrimination case and that the company's social media policy was reasonable.[34]

In 2009, Connor Riley had a job offer from Cisco Systems. After she tweeted that in considering the job offer, she had to decide whether the "fatty paycheck" would be worth the "long commute to San Jose and hating the work." She didn't have to decide: once Cisco managers saw the tweet, they rescinded the offer.[35]

In 2012 in South Carolina, Nate Fulmer and his wife Diana had a blog on which they railed against organized religion. Even though he did not identify his employer, his Christian conservative boss was offended and terminated him. An archaeologist by training, Fulmer went on to publish an online newsletter about his fieldwork in the state, titled the *Palmetto Brick Society*.[36]

That same year, Sarah Black was working as a private security guard in Tacoma, Washington, when she became angry at the string of tragedies across the country in which unarmed Black men were killed by white police officers. When a local police officer was shot, she called it "karma" in a profanity-laden Facebook post that also said she didn't "give a fuck about that police officer that got shot" and police needed to "quit fuckin with ppl."[37] That resulted in her firing and her recognition that because her employer was a private company, she had no recourse. But when it came to receiving unemployment benefits, she had more success in her claim than others terminated under similar circumstances. Under Washington law, terminated employees could be denied benefits if their discharge was based on on-the-job misconduct. But Black won her claim because (1) there was no nexus between her conduct and her work, (2) her employer had no social media policy in place, and (3) her Facebook postings were done on her own time and using her own computer.[38]

For a Halloween party in 2013—six months after three people were killed and hundreds injured in the Boston Marathon bombing—a twenty-two-year-old office employee in Michigan wore a costume that included running gear, a runner's number, bandages, and fake blood. Alicia Ann Lynch was fired from her job after photos of her in costume appeared on social media, and she received disturbing threats on those same platforms. Internet trolls found her parents' home address and threatened them as well. Lynch's apologies could not stop the threats and social media vitriol, forcing her to delete her social media presence and hide in her apartment for months.[39]

In the 2016 case of *Caplan v. L-Brands/Victoria's Secret LLC*, a federal district court ruled in favor of a retail store that fired an employee over Facebook posts in which she called Los Angeles Clippers owner Donald Sterling a racist and ridiculed the team's efforts to improve race relations in the community. Mindy Caplan had joined the company in 2001, and by 2014 had risen to become a district manager. Several times over those thirteen years, she had been approved for medical leave to attend to her own health issues and those of her son. When her Facebook posts came to the attention of the company's regional office, it terminated her.

Caplan claimed that her termination was in retaliation for missing time at work, even though her requests were approved by her managers and fell within the guidelines of the Family and Medical Leave Act. But the store's parent company successfully argued that her inflammatory posts, even though they were done on her own time and using her own computer, reflected poorly on the company because she mentioned her employer and included photographs of herself standing in front of one of the stores.[40]

In the 2003 case of *Intel Corporation v. Hamidi*, the central issue was whether a terminated employee was trespassing when he used the employer's email system to communicate with his former coworkers. Karoush Hamidi had been dismissed as a result of a dispute over whether injuries resulting from a 1992 car crash while on a company trip qualified him for disability leave. He immediately formed a support group for other former Intel employees who believed they were wrongly terminated for a variety of reasons, as well as those still with the company. Hamidi had retained a copy of an email list that allowed him to email former coworkers, and what followed was a series of rants about his own case as well as general complaints about working conditions and leave policies. He also used the list to recruit current employees to join the support group.[41]

Intel was successful in blocking some of the emails, but Hamidi found a way around that by using different computers. After Hamidi ignored the company's request to stop sending the emails, Intel went to state court, requesting it issue an injunction blocking further emails and claiming the unwanted communication constituted trespassing under California law. Hamidi's defense was based partly on his claim that he offered employees a way to opt out of receiving the emails, but that wasn't enough to dissuade the court from ruling in favor of the company. A state appeals court affirmed the decision, but the California Supreme Court reversed, determining that Hamidi's free-speech rights took priority over the company's trespassing claim. The court also pointed out that the emails could easily be ignored, did not disrupt the workplace, and did not harm the company's email system or hardware.[42]

In many cases, employees fired for their social media missives are told their dismissals were made on a content-neutral basis: not because of what they said, but because of the manner in which they said it, with profanity being a common culprit. One example was Chrysler's termination of its employee in charge of the corporate Twitter page, who meant to post a comment on his personal account but accidentally used the company account. "I find it ironic that Detroit is known as the #motor city and yet no one here knows how to fucking drive," his fateful comment read.[43]

Consequences for offensive comments on social media may also be felt by external spokespersons who are not official employees but whose comments or behavior still cast the company in a bad light. For more than a decade, comedian Gilbert Gottfried had been the voice of the AFLAC duck in the insurance giant's radio and television commercials. But in March 2011, shortly after a tsunami killed thousands of people in Japan, Gottfried tweeted more than a dozen jokes about the tragedy, including "Japan is really advanced. The people don't go to the beach. The beach comes to them." Gottfried was unaware that AFLAC did more than 75 percent of its business in Japan, and despite numerous apologies, he was fired.[44]

Politics, Flags, and Covid-19

The history of individuals getting in trouble for controversial political commentary (unrelated to their jobs) goes back to 1976, when American Civil Liberties Union regional director Charles Morgan Jr. was forced to resign over his *New York Times* quote in which he disparaged northern voters for opposing presidential candidate Jimmy Carter simply because he was a southerner. His offense? He did not go far enough in making it clear to the interviewer that the comments were his own and not meant to represent the official position of the ACLU.[45]

When Matthew Dixon, a machinist at Coburg Dairy in South Carolina, displayed a Confederate flag on his toolbox, which was his personal property, he was asked to remove the stickers following complaints from his coworkers. The year was 2000, and a proposal to remove the flag from the dome atop the state Capitol building was entangled with the presidential election campaign, which included an early primary in South Carolina. Another factor was a South Carolina law, in effect since 1962, that protected employees from being discharged from their jobs or tenants being evicted from rental homes based on their political beliefs.[46]

The company offered to provide Dixon with a new box so he could keep his personal toolbox at home, but he refused and was terminated. A federal district court decided in favor of the company, determining that while the symbol of the Confederate flag was protected by the First Amendment, Dixon did not have the right to bring it into a private workplace. The fact that his coworkers found it offensive was enough for the court to determine that it was disruptive.[47]

First Lady Michelle Obama had long been a target of criticism, but in 2016, two women lost their jobs after posting their vitriol on social media. On July 25, Obama gave a passionate and inspirational speech on the opening night of the Democratic National Convention in Philadelphia, telling the audience that her strategy for dealing with opponents was "when they go low, we go high."[48] The speech marked the beginning of the end for the first lady, as she and her presidential husband were entering the last six months of their time in office. But it marked the start of a nightmare for a mortgage officer in Ann Arbor, Michigan. Lisa Greenwood, a registered Republican and critic of the Obamas, responded to the complimentary traffic on Twitter that called the speech "historic" and "beautiful."[49]

"FLOTUS beautiful?" Greenwood posted. "Seriously, she is an ugly black bitch."[50] While the response on Twitter was hostile, the greeting she received at work the next day was even worse. Another Twitter user had traced her username and was able to identify her employer, Home Point Financial. Even though Greenwood quickly deleted the original post, she couldn't do anything about the responses, many of which mentioned the company by name. She was terminated by her employer, which also issued a statement that it "does not agree with nor condone her comments."[51]

Even though Home Point's reputation for dealing with a diverse customer base was neither positive nor negative, the case prompted a larger discussion about the overall mortgage industry and its allegedly discriminatory lending practices, as well as warnings about how an employee's conduct unrelated to work can still affect the employer's reputation.[52]

In the days following the election, disparaging remarks about the first lady caused the director of a nonprofit organization in West Virginia to lose her job. Pamela Taylor, the director of the Clay County Development Corporation, took to Facebook following a televised speech by incoming first lady Melania Trump and contrasted her appearance with that of the then first lady Michelle Obama. "It will be refreshing to have a classy, beautiful, dignified First Lady back in the White House," Taylor wrote. "I'm tired of seeing the ape in heels."[53]

After days of social media backlash and negative media coverage, Taylor apologized, and her employer, which provides services to low-income and elderly residents, placed her on administrative leave. She was scheduled to return to work on December 23, but when the officials in the state government became concerned about the organization's dependence on government funding and accusations of discrimination and harassment, they told the board that Taylor had to go. She was fired on Christmas Eve.[54]

Things got worse for Taylor in 2019 when she pleaded guilty to defrauding the Federal Emergency Management Agency out of $18,000 in relief funds following floods in West Virginia. She was sentenced to ten months in prison.[55]

In October 2017, Julie Briskman was out for a bike ride when she was pulled off the side of the road in suburban Virginia to allow President Donald Trump's lengthy motorcade to pass by. Unaware that a newspaper photographer was nearby, she directed the universal symbol for contempt—her right middle finger—at the presidential limousine. The resulting photograph was widely seen on social media, and not realizing it would be problematic, Briskman also posted it on her Facebook page.

She lost her job—fired or forced to resign, depending on whose version of the story is to be believed—at Akima LLC, a government contractor, which claimed her Facebook post violated the company's policy that prohibited "obscene" content on social media. Briskman claimed the company had violated her free-speech rights and believed her job loss was related to the company's stance that maintaining its relationship with the federal government was more important than her free-speech rights.

The following year, a federal court agreed, ruling that the at-will nature of her employment gave Akima the right to terminate her without explanation. "Freedom of speech does not equal freedom from consequences—private, social, or moral—for that speech," wrote attorney Elie Mystal in an online newsletter, *Above the Law*.[56]

The concern of many human resources officers is that workplace discussions about politics may quickly morph into teasing, then harassment, then bullying. The Society for Human Resources Management reports that prior to 2016, discussions of politics in the workplace were mostly civil in three years out of every four. But the 2016 presidential election and subsequent impeachment hearings marked the genesis of office discord in the area of political conflicts. "Political views are so entrenched," said Julie Moore, an employment attorney for Employment Practices Group, a Boston-area firm, in a 2020 interview with *SHRM News*. "I've never seen it so divisive as it is right now. I've seen people who've really had to avoid conversations (with co-workers) because their political views are so diametrically opposite. It leads to bullying in the workplace."[57]

Four years later, an SHRM study found that 26 percent of Americans report talking about politics at work on a regular basis (defined as 15 minutes or more per week). The study also found that 42 percent of employees had a "political disagreement" at work and 12 percent claimed to have been victims of bias based on their political opinions or affiliations.[58]

The article announcing the findings of that study also made five suggestions for human resources managers to incorporate into company policies: (1) hold training sessions about respect in the workplace, (2) have company leadership set the example, (3) remove news channels from televisions in break rooms and other common areas, (4) steer conversations in meetings away from politics, and (5) limit or ban visual displays in the office, including campaign buttons, posters, and stickers.[59]

"No federal statute protects private employees who want to express their political opinions at work," wrote Shari Lau in an earlier advisory from SHRM. "Therefore, when Joe Employee says he has the right to free speech at work, you can confidently tell him otherwise."[60]

During the 2004 presidential campaign, Glen Hillier lost his job at a West Virginia advertising and design company after attending a rally for incumbent President George W. Bush, for which he assumed attendance was mandatory. His offense? He attempted to ask Bush a difficult question about the war in Iraq. Others in the crowd shouted him down, so he never completed his question and Bush never attempted to answer. But after one of the company's clients reported the incident to an agency manager, Hillier was fired. He consulted with an attorney but was told he had no recourse.[61]

Labor attorneys who represent individuals suing employers or former employers acknowledge the difficulty in pursuing such cases because the First Amendment applies to the actions of government but not to those of private employers.[62] The only exceptions, points out human resources expert Johnny C. Taylor, would be if an employer were to terminate or discipline only employees of a certain religion, gender, or sexual orientation. Such actions would be illegal, even in states with strong at-will employment rules.[63]

After several years of criticism, Google announced in 2019 that it had issued new guidelines to its employees limiting the discussion of politics and other topics not related to work. It also replaced the volunteer employees monitoring internal message boards (for offensive content) with paid staffers. The company's internal network offered thousands of message boards ranging from social issues to sports, but in recent years some of the discourse went off-course and became either offensive or threatening. In addition to the paid monitors, the company added a feature that would allow users to flag content that violated the rules, just in case the monitors missed it. Specific content the company hopes to eliminate includes name-calling or blanket statements about groups or categories of people.

Part of the impetus for the policy was the 2017 controversy (discussed in more detail at the beginning of this chapter) in which Google fired an employee for an internal memo in which he stated that women were not as good as men in technical positions. While that was the reason given for the firing, the employee claimed he was fired for expressing conservative views in a political forum on the internal message boards.[64]

A 2005 article in *DePaul University Law Review* claimed that the terrorist attacks of September 11, 2001, gave employers the rationale to prohibit any speech from their employees that could be construed as unpatriotic or not supportive of the military.[65]

Prior to the terrorist attacks, American flags were often displayed in common areas of office buildings, and even in buildings housing diverse workforces, there were seldom complaints. But following September 11, many companies dealt with conflicts when individual employees displayed the flag in their cubicles or private offices, with the complaints often coming from employees from other nations. Those complaints diminished for a while but resurfaced during the presidency of Donald Trump, when the American flag became, for some white and politically conservative employees, a symbol of dislike for immigrants, including those working in neighboring cubicles. When the flag was accompanied by "Make America Great Again" hats or posters, it made the discord worse.

Flag controversies are not new. In 1991, Gonzalo Cotto was fired from his job at the Sikorsky Aircraft assembly factory in Connecticut after he refused to display an American flag at his workstation during a celebration to mark the end of the first Gulf War. The aircraft manufacturer was a government contractor, but that wasn't enough to provide First Amendment protection. The termination began an eight-year legal battle in the state court system, leading to a 1999 decision by the Connecticut Supreme Court that his rights were not violated and the company could fire him under the at-will principle.[66]

In 1992, William Niess was fired from his executive position with a Wisconsin company after he refused to donate to the Republican Party. Niess, a registered Democrat, had little recourse, his lawyer and the courts told him because state law protected him from punishment for what he did in the area of politics but could not protect him for what he didn't do.[67]

The 2010 Supreme Court case of *Citizens United v. Federal Elections Commission* is best known for allowing nearly unregulated corporate donations to political parties and candidates, but a lesser-known provision allows employers to communicate political information to employees and require employees to attend political rallies or other activities while on paid time. The latter rule applies to employees at all levels; prior to *Citizens United*, only managers could be required to attend.[68]

When President Donald Trump toured the new Shell Petrochemical Complex in Western Pennsylvania in August 2019, a crowd of mostly male workers wearing orange and yellow vests listened attentively—or at least pretended to. The local media found out later that those employees had two choices: either attend the event and act like they wanted to be there or skip the event and not be paid for the day. Employees at the complex typically worked fifty-six hours a week, with sixteen of those hours considered overtime. Those skipping the event—and few did—would lose about $700 each.[69]

Security procedures called for employees to show up early in the morning in order to pass through metal detectors and at the same time scan their employee identification cards. "No scan, no pay," they were told.[70] The workers were also told the morning schedule would include safety training and that the president would not take the stage until lunchtime. The event was billed as an official presidential event rather than a campaign rally, but once on stage, the president hit on familiar themes: support for unions, mocking of Democratic presidential candidates, and the negative consequences of him losing the next year's election (2020).

If the crowd appeared enthusiastic for the president's speech, it was because that was also part of the deal. Employees were told there could be no "yelling, shouting, protesting, or anything viewed as resistance," but it was not clear whether those rules came from the company or the union, Steamfitters Local 449. In its defense, a company spokesperson said the event "took place on a training day with a guest speaker who happened to be the president . . . we do these several times a year with various speakers."[71]

A union spokesperson added that workers were technically not "forced" to attend the event, as they had the right to stay home, because "this is America."[72] After the event, which ran past mid-afternoon, several employees told NBC News off-camera that they didn't like Trump and didn't want to attend the event, but they couldn't afford to forfeit a day's pay.[73]

In a 1996 case tangentially related to politics, a federal court ruled in favor of a school that was sued by a former employee who claimed he was a victim of discrimination and retaliation. His case was combined with those of two other employees, one who claimed he was denied a promotion based on his race and another who claimed she faced retaliation after filing a sexual harassment complaint against her supervisor. While the latter claims were unrelated to free-speech issues, the cases all carried racial overtones.

The defendant was Career Blazers Learning Center, a private vocational school in Washington, D.C. The chief plaintiff was admissions representative Charles Beckwith, who was told on October 12, 1995, that he had been selected as the school's new director of admissions, a promotion that came with a $3,000 salary increase. Four days later, before his promotion became effective, Beckwith took a day off to participate in the Million Man March, an event organized by controversial civil rights leader Louis Farrakhan.

When he returned to work the next day, he was told his promotion had been cancelled. Although he was never given a reason, he assumed that it was because of his participation in the march and other displays of advocacy for civil rights. He also claimed that he was placed under surveillance and wrongly accused of stealing school property. He resigned on November 20 and sued the school in federal district court. In what many observers called a hair-splitting exercise, the court determined that the march was a "national day of atonement for black men" and not a political protest, and therefore ruled that the former was not a protected free-speech activity, while the latter would have been.[74] The court cited a case from the previous year in which a court upheld the firing of a teacher in Kansas City, Missouri, because her complaints were not about the school's employment practices (a matter of public concern) but its educational practices (her personal complaint).[75] The court ruled against the other two employees because they failed to prove their discrimination and retaliation claims.[76]

Between 2020 and 2022, news reports documented a number of cases involving employees fired for criticizing the policies of their employers as well as other entities for their Covid-19 policies—for either not doing enough to address the pandemic or for doing too much.

In Bellingham, Washington, in March 2020, Mark Ling lost his job as an emergency room doctor after criticizing the hospital on Facebook about its Covid-19 procedures. Ling reported that the administration of PeaceHealth St. Joseph Medical Center did not effectively screen visitors, could not provide periodic testing for all employees, and was unable to provide protective equipment. Ling told the Associated Press that his concerns were based on his work in New York in the aftermath of the September 11, 2001, terrorist attacks. "I feel so overwhelmed," Ling said concerning the Covid-19 pandemic. "We're like a high school basketball team that's about to play an NBA team. The storm is coming, and I don't feel that we're prepared."[77]

That same month, nurses in Portland, Oregon, and Los Angeles were reprimanded for complaining about their respective hospital's slow response to the pandemic, the former in media interviews and the latter on Facebook. In the Los Angeles case, Jhonna Porter had complained about working long hours, an excess of staffing vacancies, and lack of protective equipment—all of which the hospital denied. Not only did the alleged misinformation harm public confidence in the hospital, administrators said, but in some cases violated patient privacy, as names and room numbers were disclosed.[78]

In another 2020 case tangentially related to the pandemic, a nurse was fired not for criticizing the hospital's Covid-19 procedures but for defending a colleague who did. Adam Witt was president of the local nurses' union when he told his manager that he was taking the following day off work to support a colleague at her disciplinary hearing. The manager at Jersey Shore University Medical Center asked him to take only a half day off due to the staff's increased workload. He took the whole day, prompting the hospital to terminate him the following week and circulate his photo around the hospital with a caption that read, "Mr. Witt is not allowed on property at JSUMC. If he is seen on property, please contact your supervisor immediately."[79]

Witt had also been critical of hospital procedures but believed he was spared from criticism because of his position with the union. But when the dispute arose over his time off, he believed it was used as an excuse to terminate him anyway. "It's not what they normally do in these cases," Witt told *The New York Times*. "You don't get 'wanted' posters."[80]

When stories about doctors and nurses terminated or disciplined for criticizing their employers in media interviews or on their own social media platforms make it into the mainstream press, the employers either decline to comment, citing "personnel matters," or claim the personnel actions were taken because of issues of attendance or competence.[81]

For one senior executive at Levi Strauss, the problem was not her company's Covid-19 policy but that of California public schools. And instead of opining that the state was not doing enough, she complained that it was doing too much. When California lagged behind other states in reopening schools, Jennifer Sey wrote on Twitter that school closures would "fall heaviest on disadvantaged kids in public schools, who need the safety and routine of school the most."[82]

When she made similar statements in media interviews, company leaders advised her to tone down her comments, as they contradicted the company's public support for the state's guidelines. She told a reporter from CNBC that CEO Chris Bergh pulled her aside at a company event and told her that she was on track to succeed him, but her public comments were getting in the way. "All I had to do was stop talking about the school thing," Sey said. "But it shouldn't be a condition of employment to 100 percent align with your company's views."[83]

Company leaders were also concerned that media outlets identified her as a Levi Strauss employee. Sey pushed back on that criticism, clarifying that she was speaking not as a company representative, but as "a mom of four public school kids."[84] She also pointed out the inconsistency in the company's position, as she was not criticized for publicly supporting Democratic presidential candidate Elizabeth Warren or expressing sadness over the deaths of Black citizens killed by white police officers.[85]

After two years of cautionary emails and meetings in the human resources office, Sey says she was asked to resign and offered a $1 million severance package. But it came with a catch: in exchange for accepting the buyout, she would have to sign a non-disclosure agreement. She declined the money and refused to sign the NDA. "I made the decision to leave on my own terms so I could speak freely," she told CNBC. "I feel the issues at stake here are not just kids, but free speech more broadly, and accepting a package to stay silent would fly in the face of that."[86]

Unfriendly Skies

In 2004, Ellen Simonetti was a flight attendant for Delta Airlines until she was fired for blogging about her job and posting semi-suggestive photographs. Her supervisor said her termination was based on "inappropriate photographs in a Delta uniform."[87]

Her almost-daily postings under the title "Diary of a Flight Attendant" had quickly become one of the most popular work-related blogs at the dawn of the blogging era. In her semi-anonymous blog, she called herself the "Queen of the Sky." Her entries covered a number of topics, including the positives and negatives of her job, relationships with her coworkers and passengers, and the challenges of dating while in a career that required constant travel.

She did not reveal her name or the identity of the airline, but her uniform and the occasional Delta logo in the background gave it away. With no union or contract protection and Georgia's at-will law standing in her way, she nevertheless filed a complaint with the Equal Employment Opportunity Commission (EEOC) and a lawsuit against the airline, complaining about sexual discrimination and unlawful termination. Both the EEOC complaint and civil lawsuit were based in part on the airline's history of not terminating or disciplining male flight attendants or pilots who blogged about their jobs. Simonetti claimed that her blog was part of her grief therapy she began after her mother died the previous year. "Now, my employer was telling me that the very thing that had gotten me through those tough times, my blog, could cost me my career."[88] For years after her termination, Simonetti continued her blog but re-named it "Diary of a Fired Flight Attendant."[89]

There were two ironies involved in the Simonetti case: the fact that Delta encouraged its employees to promote the company on their personal social media accounts, and the fact that Delta was frequently named one of the "Best Places to Work" by regional and national business publications. Barry has written extensively about the Simonetti case and sympathized with her, claiming that as one of the largest airlines in the world and the largest employer in the United States, the suggestion that its image "could suffer a negative effect because of an employee blog was far-fetched."[90]

The first well-publicized case involving free speech and an airline employee occurred in 1997 with the case of *Marsh v. Delta Airlines*, which began when a baggage handler at Denver's Stapleton Airport was fired after he wrote a letter to the editor of the *Denver Post*, criticizing his employer's decision to replace higher-paid regular employees with lower-paid contract workers.

Although he was not directly affected, Michael Marsh wrote that Delta had unnecessarily "put thousands of loyal employees and their families on hold or on the street."[91] Marsh had written previous letters, all critical of the airline, under a pseudonym. But after his December 16, 1994, letter was published under his own name, Marsh was first suspended without pay, and when he refused to apologize to the company, was asked to resign. He refused that as well and was then terminated for "conduct unbecoming a Delta employee."[92]

When he sued the airline, Marsh claimed his letters were protected as free speech, even though the airline was a private, rather than a public, employer. Delta countered that Marsh was terminated because his letter exacerbated tensions between permanent and temporary workers in an already volatile work environment. The airline's attorneys added that Marsh composed and photocopied his letter on company time and was therefore not protected by Colorado's wrongful discharge statute, which was intended to protect "off-the-job privacy."[93]

A federal district court ruled in favor of the airline, based on its published policy that called for employees to be "loyal to Delta in his public communication" and because there was no matter of public safety involved, Marsh did not qualify for whistleblower protection.[94]

In 2008, Virgin Atlantic Airlines fired thirteen flight attendants after the company's management found Facebook postings that referred to some passengers as being "chavs"—a British slang term for young people who are unsophisticated or poorly dressed—and joked about the airline's maintenance issues. Some comments met the legal definition for libel, such as identifying one aircraft for which the "engines had been replaced four times in one year," when no such repair had taken place.[95] A spokesman for the airline told the British media that the employees "brought the company into disrepute and insulted some of our passengers" and that "Virgin Atlantic staff are known for their world-class customer service and there is no place in our business for anyone who behaves otherwise."[96]

In 2016, United Airlines suspended a pilot who posted threatening remarks about Democratic presidential candidate Hillary Clinton. The pilot was also a member of the West Virginia Legislature, and while he was criticized by his constituents and colleagues, his political career remained intact (this case is discussed in more detail in Chapter 4). In another case tangentially related to the 2016 presidential election campaign, Southwest Airlines flight attendant Charlene Carter found herself out of work shortly after questioning her union president's participation in the Women's March that took place in Washington, D.C., the day after President Donald Trump was inaugurated in January 2017.

One of the themes of the march was support for abortion rights, and Carter, who opposed abortion based on her religious beliefs, sent the union leader five private social media messages that included links to videos showing images of aborted fetuses. She also posted messages on her own Facebook page calling for the union leader to be removed from office. After she was terminated by Southwest, she sued the airline and the union, claiming the termination violated her rights of free speech and religious expression. Because her Facebook posts also criticized union officials for using union funds to attend the rally and for getting release time from work, the case became entangled with National Labor Relations Board rules that protect union members when they oppose union policy.

Carter had more luck in her case than Simonetti. The court found that the airline and union had violated her constitutional rights and ordered her reinstated.[97]

On October 29, 2021, a Southwest Airlines pilot used his aircraft's public address system to take a somewhat vulgar shot at President Joe Biden during a flight from Houston to Albuquerque, New Mexico. He closed his "welcome aboard" message with the anti-Biden expression, "Let's Go Brandon," widely known in political circles as a euphemism for "fuck Joe Biden." Associated Press reporter Colleen Long was on board, and that kicked off media coverage of the incident. Another passenger recorded the comments and the audible "gasps" that could be heard from the passengers—and posted the audio on TikTok. Harvard University Professor Juliette Kayyem told a CNN reporter that the pilot should be fired on the grounds that he was too mentally unbalanced to fly a plane. The airline apologized publicly for the incident, yet declined to say if the pilot faced any consequences.[98]

Service with a Scowl

In 2009, server Jon-Barrett Ingels served actress Jane Adams a bowl of soup and a cup of lemonade at Barney's Greengrass Café in Beverly Hills, California.

Unable to pay the $13.44 bill, Adams simply walked out. That prompted Ingels to post about the dine-and-dash incident on Twitter. Adams's agent returned to the café the next day to pay the tab but didn't include a tip, which produced another tweet from Ingels. Adams returned about a month later to tip the server, but by that time Ingels had already been fired because of the tweets.[99]

That's just one case from the restaurant world, where servers and other employees often find themselves in trouble after posting social media comments on everything from uniform design to working hours to customers who under-tip or don't tip at all. In the majority of termination cases, employees either don't challenge their employers in court, or if they do, they lose—mostly because they're working under "at-will" rules.

In 2009, an employee at California Pizza Kitchen was fired for using Twitter to complain about new employee uniforms.[100] In 2011, North Carolina server Ashley Johnson was fired from her job at Brixx Pizzeria after complaining on social media about specific customers who left only a $5 tip after tying up one of her tables for three hours. She did not identify the customers but did mention the name of the pizzeria, prompting management to fire her for violating the restaurant's social media policy.[101]

That same year in Wisconsin, the Triple Play Sports Bar and Grille fired two employees for their Facebook activity but ran afoul of National Labor Relations Board policy. Jillian Sanzone and Vincent Spinella had good working relationships with their managers at the restaurant and even used their own Facebook accounts to promote the establishment. But after another employee, Jamie LaFrance, left the restaurant, she used her Facebook page to accuse managers of poor payroll practices that resulted in shorting employees on salary and making errors on their tax paperwork. Sanzone added her own comments in agreement and called one manager an "asshole." Spinella did not add any commentary but pressed the "like" button. The next day, Sanzone and Spinella were fired for violating the restaurant's social media policy.[102]

The NLRB reviewed the case and found the restaurant's policy problematic because it included "inappropriate discussions about the company, management, and/or coworkers."[103] NLRB guidelines specify that online discussions related to pay, scheduling, safety, or other workplace conditions are considered "concerted" and treated the same as if they took place in-person in a break room or off-property. Instead, the guidelines say, punishable acts are those that are defamatory or represent verifiable workplace disruption. The NLRB also objected to the employee being fired for pressing the "like" button.[104] Triple Play's parent company sued the NLRB in federal court, claiming it had overstepped its boundaries in interfering with its employment practices, but the court found that the NLRB's actions were appropriate.[105]

In 2014, a Texas Roadhouse server in Findlay, Ohio, was fired after complaining on Facebook about bad tippers. Kirsten Kelly wrote that "if you come into a restaurant and spend $50 or more, you should be able to tip appropriately for that."[106] In another post, she called an unidentified customer an "asshole." After one of her Facebook friends showed the posts to the restaurant's manager, Kelly was fired. A corporate officer from Texas Roadhouse stated that the language she used was "never okay in any venue" and the overall tone of Kelly's posts violated the company's "Respect for Others" policy that covers both face-to-face conversations and social media activities. The policy also prohibits employees from mentioning the company—positively or negatively—in any venue.[107]

The most notable conflict involving restaurant workers making its way into the court system was *Pietrylo v. Hillstone Restaurant Group*. The case began when two employees created a MySpace page that they used to air their grievances against their employer in a password-protected environment and invited other employees (but not managers) to join. However, one manager learned about the site from an employee and alerted another manager, and the two coerced the employee into giving up her password. The managers fired the employee who had created the site, claiming they were not offended by the criticisms posted on the site but only by the profane language, saying it "violated the restaurant's 'core values.'"[108]

The key issue at trial was whether the employee was coerced into giving the managers her password information. The employee testified that she felt coerced to surrender her password and feared that she would have been terminated if she had not complied. There was no evidence that she gave up the password willingly, and the court believed her account of the events, upholding the lower court's verdict in favor of the employees.[109]

Two Standards for the Fourth Estate

One irony involved in some of these cases is that a few of the private employers that punish employees for speaking out on public issues and controversies are those you least expect: media organizations. ESPN, for example, has a history of firing or reprimanding employees who use their work-related social media accounts to sound off on controversial issues, including alleged racism in sports.

One noteworthy case in this category involved Jemele Hill, a Black female commentator for ESPN, who tweeted in 2017 that "Donald Trump is a white supremacist who has largely surrounded himself with other white supremacists."[110] She also called for fans to boycott the Dallas Cowboys to protest owner Jerry Jones's stance on players kneeling during the national anthem.[111]

Her comments were not scrutinized by her employer, but the blowback in political circles and on social media was immediate. The first comments came from Trump himself, who demanded (but did not get) a public apology, and White House Press Secretary Sarah Huckabee Sanders, who recommended she be fired.[112]

Meanwhile, social media pundits told her to "stick to sports," but after the mini-controversy dragged on, the mostly anonymous posts became more threatening. After she left the network—it was never clear whether she was fired or resigned—similar vitriol followed her as she began a new career as a freelance magazine journalist. After the U.S. Supreme Court issued its 2022 abortion ruling, she cited her own personal abortion story in an article in *The Atlantic*, drawing more threats and harassment online.[113]

In 2022, another female ESPN broadcaster was demoted after making comments critical of the company's Covid-19 vaccine mandate. Sage Steele had used her podcast, unrelated to her primary role at ESPN, to comment on sports, and because she stayed away from controversial topics, the network had no objection to that work. But when she criticized the company for requiring its employees to be vaccinated, she was required to apologize to her podcast subscribers and was given less glamorous assignments on ESPN. Steele, who identifies as biracial, filed suit against the network, claiming not only a violation of her free-speech rights but that the company was inconsistent in dealing with similar issues involving her coworkers who were male and white.[114] The two parties reached an undisclosed financial settlement in 2023, after which Steele left the network.

ESPN broadcaster Samantha Ponder was not reprimanded by her employer but caught flak from network viewers over her 2023 on-air criticisms of LGBTQ causes and support for Riley Gaines, a University of Kentucky swimmer who became an opponent of transgender athletes competing in women's sports. Ponder's public position even resulted in rebuke from other female journalists, including *USA Today* sports columnist Nancy Armour. Instead of worrying about what she called a "minuscule number of transgender women participating in sports," Armour wrote that Ponder should instead use her platform for exposing other issues in women's college and professional sports, including the failure of the National Collegiate Athletic Association and U.S. Department of Education to enforce Title IX, a 1972 law dealing with equity in women's college sports. The controversy came five years after Jemele Hill left the network and less than a year after the Steele case. ESPN declined to answer media inquiries as to whether Ponder's comments violated the network's social media policy or why Ponder was treated differently than Hill and Steele.[115]

Media ethicists were quick to point out how severely the three women (two of them Black) were treated differently from their male and white counterparts who drew similar negative attention to the network.

Two examples occurred in 2023, when ESPN commentator Pat McAfee made a controversial comment on Twitter regarding Michigan State University's new football uniforms, and colleague Ryan Clark admitted he made a "bad joke" about Miami Dolphins quarterback Tua Tagovailoa. Then, early in 2024, McAfee was criticized by some fans—but not reprimanded by the network—for giving New York Jets quarterback Aaron Rodgers a platform for making controversial and non-football-related comments (this case is discussed in more detail in Chapter 9). *USA Today* columnist Mike Freeman pointed out the double standard between the treatments of Hill and McAfee. "ESPN had its ear to the ground, listening carefully to right-wing news sources, ran scared, and failed Hill," he wrote. "In other words, ESPN catered to the right by suspending Hill and are catering to the right again by no more forcefully rebuking Rodgers."[116]

In the first McAfee case, Michigan State's neon-green uniforms had already been heavily criticized on various social media platforms, but McAfee took it too far when he tweeted that Larry Nassar, a former MSU-connected physician convicted in 2018 of sexually assaulting female gymnasts who came to him for treatment, "was in on the design team."[117] It was never clear what connection he was trying to make between Nassar and the unpopular uniforms, but women's rights advocates and other observers noticed that unlike Hill and Steele (female and Black) who were forced out, McAfee (male and white) kept his job and received no rebuke from the network after he issued a "weak apology."[118]

Clark, who played for three National Football League teams during a twelve-year career, was hired by ESPN in 2015 and joined a long roster of former players who got paid for criticizing active ones. Clark said he observed the injury-prone Tagovailoa during training camp and described him as overweight and out-of-shape. "He looks like he's been skipping the gym and might be spending too much time at the tattoo parlor," Clark said. "When at the dinner table, he was not eating what the nutritionist advised."[119]

There was no discussion, at least not publicly, implying that Clark was treated differently from Hill and Steele because he was male. Instead, network representatives said they were disappointed in Clark's comments, but he would not be reprimanded because his comments were directly related to the sport he was covering—unlike Hill and Steele, whose comments were about political and social issues. Instead of hearing from his superiors at the network, his rebuke came from Tagovailoa, Dolphins Coach Mike McDaniel, and commentators on social media. In a newspaper interview the day after Clark's comments, Tagovailoa said he "would appreciate it if he (Clark) kept my name out of his mouth."[120]

Two rare examples of male sportscasters being vilified for expressing controversial political opinions are ESPN commentator Stephen A. Smith and NBC football analyst Tony Dungy.

Smith has developed a reputation for outspokenness during his nearly two decades with the network. Although often criticized by viewers on social media, he has faced no discipline from the network. His most controversial comments include suggestions that women are partially to blame for domestic violence, that teams' decisions to play or not play certain players are based too often on skin color, and speculating that some players' poor performances on the football field or basketball courts were because of drug use—comments which are potentially libelous.[121]

Dungy is a former Super Bowl-winning head coach and member of the Professional Football Hall of Fame. During his time coaching the Tampa Bay Buccaneers and Indianapolis Colts, Dungy was known not only for his coaching success but also for translating his Christian faith into community service, both for him and his players. But after he transitioned into the broadcast booth, first for ESPN and then NBC Sports, he developed a foot-in-mouth tendency to say the wrong things to the wrong audiences at the wrong times.

He made frequent off-camera comments critical of same-sex marriage that were reported in the media, and when confronted about their veracity, he made no effort to deny or explain them. His reputation took another hit in 2014 when he commented on the St. Louis Rams' drafting of Michael Sam, the league's first openly gay player. "I wouldn't have taken him," Dungy told NBC News. "Not because I don't believe Michael Sam should have a chance to play, but I wouldn't want to deal with all of it. It's not going to be totally smooth. Things will happen. There will be too many distractions."[122] In another tweet from 2020, Dungy wrote that being "LGBTQ is a lifestyle," a sentiment that suggested being queer is a choice.[123]

In early 2023, Dungy shared an already debunked myth to his nearly 950,000 Twitter followers, claiming that public schools were providing litter boxes for students who identify as cats. His tweet was in response to an article regarding a Mississippi state bill that would mandate menstrual products in boys' bathrooms. In response to media inquiries, an NBC Sports spokesperson stated, "NBC Sports does not support or condone the views expressed in the tweet and we have made that clear to Tony. Our company has long and proudly supported LGBTQ+ rights and works hard to ensure that all of our employees are seen, acknowledged, recognized and respected."[124]

One Black television reporter found himself out of work, albeit temporarily, after criticizing the National Football League in general—and Commissioner Roger Goodell specifically—for the league's lack of diversity among coaches, team executives, and at the league's New York headquarters. In September 2023, Jim Trotter was told his contract with the NFL Network, a league-controlled media outlet, would not be renewed. The news did not come as a surprise to Trotter, who had been critical of the league's diversity efforts for more than a year and, prior to that, critical of individual team owners.

"The NFL has claimed it wants to be held accountable regarding diversity, equity, and inclusion," Trotter said in a statement released by his attorneys. "I tried to do so, and it cost me my job."[125] The NFL said its decision not to renew Trotter's contract was driven by budget constraints. "We take his concerns seriously, but strongly dispute his specific allegations, particularly those made against his dedicated colleagues at NFL Media," a spokesperson told *The New York Times*.[126]

Trotter was quickly hired by *The Athletic*, a sports-oriented online news service owned by *The New York Times*. Late in 2023, he filed a lawsuit against the NFL, claiming his dismissal was in retaliation for his comments.[127]

The phenomenon of broadcasters getting in trouble for their comments on social media is not limited to those who work in sports. Veteran CBS humorist Andy Rooney, whose commentary at the end of the long-running news program

60 Minutes earned him the title of "America's favorite curmudgeon," caught the ire of the Black community because of comments he made in a 1990 interview with Chris Bull of *The Advocate*, the country's leading publication for the gay audience. Rooney was quoted as saying that "blacks have watered down their genes because the less intelligent ones have the most children . . . they drop out of school early, do drugs, and get pregnant."[128]

Rooney denied the quote and said his actual comments mirrored those made in an earlier interview with the *New York Post*, in which he said that "school dropouts are having the most children, and the people who got all the way through college are having the least."[129] With no audio or videotape to settle the issue, CBS management believed *The Advocate*'s version of the quote and suspended Rooney for three months without pay. Rooney believed the publication intentionally misquoted him in retaliation for his earlier on-air comments opposing gay marriage.[130]

In 2016, Pittsburgh television anchor Wendy Bell lost her job at WTAE-TV after posting on Facebook her take on a story which she had reported two weeks earlier. A backyard party in the suburb of Wilkinsburg was marred by a shooting that killed five of the participants, including a pregnant woman. "You needn't be a criminal profiler to draw a mental sketch of the killers who broke so many hearts," she wrote. "They are young black men, likely in their teens or early 20s. They have multiple siblings from multiple fathers and their mothers work multiple jobs. These boys have been in the system before. They've grown up here. They know the police."[131] After she was terminated, general manager Charles Wolferitz addressed viewers on air, apologizing for the comments and saying "Ms. Bell show an egregious lack of judgment."[132] The station's parent company, Hearst Broadcasting, added in its statement that Bell's comments were "inconsistent with the company's ethics and journalistic standards."[133]

Bell then apologized on Facebook, saying, "I now understand that some of the words I chose were insensitive and could be viewed as racist. I regret offending anyone. I'm truly sorry."[134] In a subsequent interview with the Associated Press, she backtracked slightly, saying she didn't get a "fair shake" and argued that viewers' focus should be on "African Americans being killed by other African Americans."[135]

Even those comments drew criticism nationwide, with media ethicists and scholars in the field of race relations saying she was "clueless about race" and needed to be held accountable. Locally, opinions were mixed, with leaders of the African American community applauding her ouster, while a smattering of viewers came to her defense, calling it an unjust termination based on political correctness.[136]

It wasn't the first time Bell had to apologize for racially insensitive comments. In 2010, following a segment on using sunscreen to prevent skin cancer, Bell turned to her Black co-anchor and said, "I want to use whatever you're using."[137]

Bell eventually landed a job as a political host at WKDA radio in Pittsburgh but quickly found herself in trouble again. She was reprimanded and later terminated for passing along misinformation about the coronavirus pandemic and criticizing local businesses for mandating masks for their employees, which caused numerous advertisers to cancel their accounts with the station. She landed at KJAS Radio, also in Pittsburgh, where she was terminated after five months for suggesting that park rangers should shoot Native Americans who were protesting President Trump's visit to Mount Rushmore.[138]

Rachel Mosteller, a twenty-five-year-old reporter for the *Durham Herald-Sun* in North Carolina, learned that not identifying yourself, your employer, nor the coworkers you're blogging about is not enough to protect you from employer wrath. Writing under the pseudonym "Sarcastic Journalist" in 2005, Mosteller mocked the newspaper's awards program as "stupid little awards that are supposed to boost company morale . . . they put your name on some piece of paper and bring you chocolate and balloons."[139]

Mosteller was unaware that her editors knew about her blog and were monitoring it. Most of her posts were benign, but when she concluded that missive with, "two people in the newsroom just got awards FOR DOING THEIR JOB," they decided she had crossed the line. She was fired the next day.[140]

Not even those who forecast the weather are safe from criticism. But in the case of Chris Cloninger, chief meteorologist at a television station in Iowa, the consequences came not from station management but from the station's viewers. Cloninger found himself the target of public vitriol for simply telling the truth about the connection between global climate change and the last decade's uptick in cases of more intense hurricanes, flash floods, and wildfires.

Cloninger had been chief meteorologist at KCCI-TV for only two years, but had already established himself as a credible source of weather information and a popular figure in Des Moines and the surrounding community. However, political conservatives in the area turned against him when he began talking about the science behind cases of extreme weather.

"I just started connecting the dots between extreme weather and climate change, and then the volume of pushback started to increase dramatically," Cloninger told the Associated Press.[141]

What began as skepticism quickly morphed into criticisms, accusations that he was a "liberal conspiracy theorist" and "Biden puppet," and eventually reached the level of death threats.[142] One email said that conservatives were threatening him as payback for how liberals treated Judge Brett Kavanaugh during his Supreme Court confirmation hearings in 2018.[143]

Edward Maibach, director of the Center for Climate Change Communication at George Mason University, told AP that nationwide, television station managers are discouraging weather forecasters from talking about climate change because of the fear of viewer vitriol. Maibach said the trend began with the 2006 case of Heidi Cullen, a Weather Channel reporter, who faced sexist and harassing comments from viewers after covering the issue.[144]

"Science is under attack in this country," added Chitra Kumar, a spokesperson for the Union of Concerned Scientists. "It's part of a larger trend. It's really unacceptable from our perspective that anyone should have to fear for their lives for merely stating the facts."[145]

Cloninger reported struggling with post-traumatic stress disorder (PTSD) as a result of the harassment, and fearing for the safety of his family, he announced his resignation.[146]

It's Not a Problem Until It's a Problem

In 2008, a worker at Lincoln Financial Field in Philadelphia was fired after a profanity-laden Facebook rant in which he criticized the local National Football League team, the Philadelphia Eagles, for releasing his favorite player, defensive back Brian Dawkins, who was later signed by the Denver Broncos. "I'm fucking devastated," Dan Leone wrote on Facebook. "Damn Eagles R retarded."[147] Leone deleted the post and apologized to the team and stadium management for his comments, but that wasn't enough to retain his job. In the team's defense, a spokesperson said that Leone was not fired for his comments critical of the team, but because he used profanity to express them.[148]

"I shouldn't have put it up there," Leone told ESPN. "I was ticked off, and I let my emotions go, but I didn't mean to offend any one person or target a specific individual. I was just upset that we lost such a great guy. Dawkins was one of my favorite players. I made a mistake."[149]

When the Broncos visited Philadelphia the following season, Dawkins was made aware of Leone's firing and sent him two tickets for that game. While that perk didn't compensate Leone for his job loss, he did admit to having learned a lesson as a result. "If you know your boss is online, or anyone close to your boss is online, don't be making comments that can be detrimental to your employment," he told ESPN.[150]

In 2008, New England Patriots cheerleader Caitlin Davis lost her spot on the squad after old photos from her Facebook page showed her at a Halloween party where she posed with a passed-out man whose clothing showed swastikas, anti-Semitic remarks, and profanity.[151]

In 2010, a Pittsburgh Pirates mascot was fired for using social media to criticize team management over personnel moves.[152]

In 2011, entering the online debate over gay marriage resulted in negative consequences for sports agent Todd Reynolds and his friend, freelance television writer Damian Goddard. After New York Ranger forward Sean Avery recorded a public service announcement in support of a proposed state law that would protect gay-marriage rights, Reynolds (not Avery's agent) tweeted his opposition. "Very sad to read Avery's misguided support of same-gender 'marriage,'" his tweet read. "Legal or not, it will always be wrong."[153]

Goddard quickly joined the fray, retweeting what Reynolds wrote and adding, "I completely and whole-heartedly support Todd Reynolds and his support for the traditional and true meaning of marriage." While Reynolds lost clients, the consequences for Goddard were more severe: he was fired by Rogers Sportsnet—the Canadian equivalent of ESPN—and had difficulty finding work afterward.[154]

Unions in the Private Sector

Section 7 of the National Labor Relations Act states that "employees shall have the right to self-organization, to form, join, or assist labor organizations, to bargain collectively through representatives of their own choosing, and to engage in other concerted activities for the purpose of collective bargaining or other mutual aid or protection."[155] The NLRA is grounded partially in the First Amendment's assembly clause; it states that citizens have the right to "peaceably assemble," but over the legal history of the country, that clause has been interpreted to include the "right of association"—the right to join political parties, civil groups, or labor unions.[156] The NLRA requires that company management remain neutral when employees debate or vote on union formation.[157]

In 1947, the NLRA was modified by the Taft-Hartley Act, named after its sponsors, Senator Robert Taft of Ohio and Congressman Fred A. Hartley of New Jersey. It effectively took away some unionization rights provided by the NLRA and gave employers the right to campaign against unionization. One critic of the new law was New York Senator Robert F. Wagner, author of the original NLRA, who said, "the talk of restoring free speech to the employer is a polite way of re-introducing employer interference, economic retaliation, and other insidious means of discouraging union membership and union activity."[158] When the law is challenged, the courts have ruled that employers can attempt to persuade employees to vote against the union as long as their tactics are not coercive.[159]

In the 1940 case of *Thornhill v. Alabama*, the U.S. Supreme Court upheld the right of union members to form picket lines, regardless of whether they were on company property or public property that was adjacent. The court based its ruling primarily on the First Amendment right of free speech, but it also cited the Fourteenth Amendment's equal protection clause. Because different states had different levels of protection for picketers, the court held, a more uniform approach was needed so that the protection applied regardless of which state the company was located in. In subsequent cases, the Court upheld the precedent but carved out specific exceptions that would permit employers to sue picketers for defamatory claims on picket signs and allow states or local authorities to punish picketers for blocking traffic or otherwise disturbing the peace.[160]

Union organizers have recently discovered a new communications medium to reach potential members: TikTok. According to a 2022 article in *The Progressive*, one example took place at Amazon, where a union campaign titled "People Over Prime Pledge" denounced the company for its anti-union tactics. While using traditional face-to-face recruiting methods as well, the newly formed Amazon Labor Union found the company's mostly young workforce responded more effectively to the social media approach, with TikTok videos at the forefront.[161]

Dress Codes Matter

For much of 2020, employees at Whole Foods stores across the country were required to wear masks due to the Covid-19 pandemic. But the company's dress code specified that the masks should bear the company's logo or no messages at all. Three employees at stores in different parts of the country chose to wear "Black Lives Matter" masks, which the company claimed violated its dress code. All three were terminated after repeated warnings.

Haley Evans of Marlton, New Jersey; Savannah Kinzer of Cambridge, Massachusetts; and Christopher Michno of Berkeley, California, sued the company in federal district court in Boston, the closest venue for Kinzer, the lead plaintiff. The former employees claimed their dismissal violated their First Amendment rights and was racially discriminatory because they saw other employees wearing masks that were also inconsistent with the dress code. The company countered that it had been lax in enforcing the code prior to the controversy, but once it did begin enforcement, it did so fairly. The company also claimed that Kinzer's dismissal was based in part on job performance and not solely on the dress code issue.[162]

After eighteen months of preliminary hearings and discovery proceedings, Judge Allison Burroughs dismissed the case, agreeing with the company's claim that it had "legitimate business explanations" for the dismissals. "This ruling is not about the importance of the Black Lives Matter message, the value of the plaintiff's advocacy in wearing the masks, the valor of their speaking out against what they perceived to be discrimination in their workplace, or the quality of Whole Foods' decision-making," she wrote.[163]

Whole Foods, which had just been acquired by the online retailer Amazon, issued a statement that claimed the company "remained dedicated to ensuring our team members feel safe and free from discrimination and retaliation at Whole Foods Market."[164] The following year, a circuit court of appeals denied the plaintiff's appeal.[165] Rather than continue to press their case through the federal court system, the plaintiffs went to the National Labor Relations Board, which ruled in favor of Whole Foods in December 2023, stating that the company's dress code did not violate the plaintiffs' First Amendment rights because their masks were addressing a matter unrelated to their workplace conditions.[166] That ruling was similar to one made by a different NLRB panel the previous year. Employees at a Home Depot store in Minnesota were fired for refusing to remove

"Black Lives Matter" pins from their orange aprons. Administrative law judge Paul Bogas ruled that the BLM messaging "lacked an objective, and sufficiently direct, relationship to terms or conditions of employment."[167] Their case took on special significance because it occurred in the Minneapolis suburb of New Brighton, about 12 miles from where George Floyd died two years earlier.[168]

In a similar case resolved in 2023, an NLRB administrative judge made the opposite ruling in a case involving Fred Meyer Stores, a supermarket chain with most of its locations in the Pacific Northwest. In that case, the NLRB ruled in favor of employees who were fired for wearing BLM masks and pins because the items were issued by their union, the United Food and Commercial Workers International Local 21, and were thereby protected as a "concerted activity" related to workplace conditions.[169]

The three "Black Lives Matter" cases are consistent with previous cases—dating back more than a half-century—dealing with dress codes. Long before employees began to write or post problematic content on social media, an important form of expression was found in the clothing they chose.

The courts have generally decided in favor of employers on dress code issues. Under the "at-will" principle, employers may dismiss employees for repeated dress code violations without having to explain or defend the code—even if the rules are outdated or draconian. However, employers can strengthen their cases if they can provide a rationale, such as public perception (for sales representatives and other meet-the-public roles) or safety (for employees working around machinery, etc.).

In 1972, the National Labor Relations Board ruled in favor of Michigan Bell Telephone Company when it prohibited employees from wearing sweatshirts bearing the slogan "Ma Bell is a Cheap Mother." A simpler statement against management or in favor of the union would have been protected, the NLRB clarified, but the statement in question could be banned because it was "borderline obscene."[170]

Employers may even find court backing in cases where rules are somewhat discriminatory. In a 1975 case, for example, a federal court ruled in favor of a company that required male employees to wear neckties, while female employees faced no such requirement. When male employees claimed the policy was discriminatory, the court agreed with the company's assertion that customers had different expectations for male and female sales representatives, and the company could base its rules on those expectations.[171]

In 2011, a Green Bay Packers fan working at a car dealership in Oak Lawn, Illinois, was fired for wearing a Packers tie at the time when the company was involved in a promotional campaign with the Chicago Bears. Instead of suing to reclaim his job, John Stone decided to take his talent for sales to a competing dealership, where the publicity surrounding the case prompted customers to show up asking "for the Packers guy."[172]

Whistleblowing and the Case of the Two-Dollar Screwdriver

In 1977, Ray Palmateer was a machinist at International Harvester's manufacturing plant in East Moline, Illinois. When he reported to local police that a coworker had stolen a screwdriver valued at $2, the company fired him based on the at-will principle and the fact that Palmateer should have first reported the theft to his supervisor. The following year, he filed suit against the company, at first claiming "retaliatory discharge" but then amending the suit to add the claim of emotional distress, stating that he was "intimidated, harassed, and humiliated" by managers and coworkers as a result of his whistleblowing.[173]

A Rock Island County Court dismissed both claims, citing the "at-will" provision in Illinois law and agreeing with the company's claim that Palmateer did not follow the chain of command in reporting the alleged theft. Palmateer appealed his case to the Illinois circuit court of appeals, which issued a split decision, ruling in his favor on the discharge claim but against him on the claim of emotional distress.[174]

"If you think voicing your political opinions is dangerous, try talking about your own company," wrote attorney Lewis Maltby in his 2009 book, *Can They Do That? Taking Back Our Fundamental Rights in the Workplace.* "One of the most common reasons people are fired is because they reveal improper conduct by the employer. Corporations consider whistleblowers traitors and will go to any length to get rid of them. Even reporting abuse within the company can get you fired."[175] Lewis's book lists a number of examples in which employees "stuck their necks out" in reporting problems within the company, followed the correct internal procedures rather than taking the information to the media or government regulators, and in the process likely saved lives and saved their companies millions of dollars. But instead of being praised, they were labeled "boat-rockers" and terminated.

The history of private-sector whistleblowing dates back to 1971 when a commercial bus driver in California became so frustrated with the mechanical condition of the company's vehicles that he took his concerns to a local television station. He claimed to have first told his superiors of the problems but got no response. After the segment aired, the driver was fired based on the company's "loyalty rule," which prohibited employees from using "words or acts of hostility to the company, its officers, agents, or employees, its services, equipment or its condition, or criticisms of the company to anyone others than superior officers."[176]

While state officials sympathized with his plight, none was in a position to help. The office of the California attorney general said the loyalty rule was unfair but it was unable to overturn the decision. The state's Public Utility Commission said it was concerned about the public safety issue involved, but it also lacked the authority to help the terminated employee. Only pressure from the drivers' union and the television station that aired the original story resulted in the driver being reinstated.[177]

The 1974 case of *Geary v. U.S. Steel* began when George Geary, who had been selling the company's products for fourteen years, went to his superiors with his concerns that some of the company's products had not been adequately tested and posed a safety risk to customers. His concerns were ignored, and he was labeled a "boat-rocker." He eventually took his concerns higher up the organizational chart to a vice president, where he was certain he would find a sympathetic ear. He did—somewhat. The company eventually fixed the problem, likely saving lives and saving his employer millions of dollars, but instead of receiving praise from management, he received a termination notice.

Geary took his case to state court, and he eventually found himself before the Supreme Court of Pennsylvania. There he found three sympathetic ears, but that wasn't enough. The court ruled 4-3 in favor of the company, determining that the "at-will" nature of his employment was the primary factor in its decision and that it was not the role of the court to judge the merits of his concerns.[178]

In a case involving external whistleblowing that came too late to save lives, two engineers at Morton Thiokol, the company that manufactured the booster rockets that helped lift the space shuttle into Earth orbit, expressed concerns that cold temperatures in Florida might endanger the January 28, 1986, launch of *Challenger*. They claimed they spent six hours on the telephone the night before the launch explaining their concerns to company managers, but their concerns were ignored, and the company gave the National Aeronautics and Space Administration (NASA) the green light to launch. The engineers' concerns turned out to be genuine, and critical parts of the booster rockets failed during the launch, causing a massive explosion that killed the seven astronauts of the company to anyone other than superior officers.

One of the engineers, Roger Boisjoly, was called to testify before a presidential commission, and he spilled the beans about the tragedy that could have been avoided. Morton Thiokol retaliated by transferring him to what he called the "worst location in the company" and looked the other way as coworkers harassed him on a daily basis. Only the company's dependence on government contracts (for NASA and other agencies) prevented his firing. Eventually, Boisjoly tired of the harassment and left the company.[179]

At the height of the Covid-19 pandemic in 2020, the owner of a dog day-care center in Boise, Idaho, dismissed the complaints of two employees who were concerned about their exposure to a third employee who remained at work after suffering from Covid symptoms. Kayla Martin, owner of the House of Hounds, told the employees to go home, but after they left the building, she removed their names from the list of staff on the company website and cancelled their subsequent work shifts. When the two employees applied for unemployment benefits, Martin opposed their application and told the Idaho Department of Labor that the two women "quit." The two ex-employees sued Martin under the state's whistleblowing law and its anti-retaliation provision. Martin was forced to pay the plaintiffs $25,000 each, and the financial strain prompted her to sell the business.[180]

The Truth About Fiction

Even speaking out in the form of fiction can get an employee in trouble with his or her employer. The first known case in this category began in the 1970s when a chemical engineer executed an unusual twist on corporate whistleblowing.

Louis McIntire and his wife self-published a novel about employees of a fictional Logan Chemical Company, which looked suspiciously like McIntire's real employer, the DuPont Company. In the novel, characters complained about the company's failure to compensate employees when appropriating their inventions, its refusal to recognize unions, and other workplace injustices.

DuPont officials were not pleased with the novel, of which less than 2,000 copies were sold or given away.

After being terminated, McIntire sued the company for $20 million, claiming the company violated his First Amendment rights and blacklisted him among his prospective employers. The court denied the First Amendment claim based on DuPont's status as a private employer but did find in his favor on the blacklisting claim.[181]

In the early days of blogging, Cameron Barrett, an information technology specialist in Michigan, liked to write short stories in his off-work hours. His employer was not identified in his work, but the sexual and violent nature of his writings offended his boss, who fired him.[182]

Health-Care Cases: Matters of Public Concern versus Workplace Disruption

Long before the Covid-19 pandemic prompted health-care workers to complain about their working conditions, nurses and other hospital employees were sounding alarms about the quality of patient care at their institutions.

In the 1973 case of *Rafferty v. Philadelphia Psychiatric Center* (discussed in more detail in Chapter 1), a nurse at a state-run psychiatric hospital in Philadelphia was quoted in a newspaper story about staff conduct and the quality of patient care at the facility. The court found in her favor, partly because the employer was a public entity.[183]

The Rafferty case is an anomaly in the fifty-year history of health-care professionals and nonprofit executives at odds with employers over free-speech issues. Rafferty won partly because her employer was a quasi-governmental agency and partly because the court recognized her comments were a matter of public concern. In cases involving private employers, individuals challenging them have little chance of winning in court. Factors working against health-care professionals and nonprofit executives include the employers' claims of workplace disruption, the courts' determination that the comments were related more to personal grievances than to public issues or legitimate efforts at whistleblowing, and their comments taking the form of legitimate threats rather than simple workplace frustration.

Fifteen years after Rafferty's legal win in Pennsylvania, another nurse publicly commenting on the quality of patient care met with a different fate, mostly because the hospital at which she was employed was private rather than public. In *Jones v. Memorial Hospital*, the nurse was unsuccessful in her claim that the hospital violated her First Amendment rights when it fired her after a local newspaper published her letter to the editor. Pamela Sue Jones's letter claimed the staff prolonged the lives of terminally ill patients and denied them the right to "die with dignity."[184] She sued the hospital but had a different outcome than Rafferty, largely because her case involved a private employer rather than a government one. Jones's attorneys claimed the hospital held a number of government contracts and that qualified it as a public employer under the concept of "state action," but the court did not equate that relationship as the same as that between a private contractor that held contracts with branches of the military.[185]

In 1994, the case of an obstetrics nurse at a public hospital in Pennsylvania had a similar outcome, even though she was employed by a public hospital. In what she thought were private conversations, Cheryl Churchill complained to her coworkers about the hospital's procedure of dealing with staff shortages by filling gaps with lesser-qualified employees from other departments. Churchill believed the policy jeopardized patient care. One of the coworkers who was part of the discussion reported it to hospital management, saying that Churchill's remarks were personal in nature and dealt more with the competency of specific individuals rather than the general policy. Churchill was terminated, based on the hospital administrator's belief that her comments disrupted the workplace by discouraging employees from accepting voluntary transfers among departments.[186]

Churchill sued in federal district court, losing at the trial court level but prevailing at the circuit court of appeals. The hospital appealed to the U.S. Supreme Court, which remanded the case to the lower court to be retried.[187] There's no record of a second trial taking place, leading scholars to believe the two parties likely reached an out-of-court settlement, with the details not being disclosed.

The ruling in favor of the hospital took many legal scholars by surprise, as her comments about the quality of obstetrics care at a public hospital met the definition of "matters of public concern."[188] Justice John Paul Stevens, one of two justices siding with the nurse, began his dissent with, "This is a free country."[189]

In another case of a health-care employee being fired for complaining about workplace conditions that did not rise to the level of whistleblowing, a nuclear medicine technician at a hospital in Independence, Kansas, was terminated for Facebook posts that claimed she was paid for hours she did not work, questioned the credentials and skills of her coworkers, and hinted that her boss had "creepy hands."[190] Mercy Health System's human resources department questioned Sara DeBord to determine the validity of her complaints and whether a harassment investigation of her supervisor was warranted.

The department found no basis for her complaints about her own pay or the skills of her coworkers and determined that posting comments to Facebook about her boss's "creepy hands" was not the company's preferred method for making harassment complaints. The department also questioned why she took so long to lodge her complaint; she claimed the behavior began in 2004, but she did not mention it until 2009. DeBord was terminated for "disruption, inappropriate behavior, and dishonesty."[191] She sued the company, claiming gender discrimination and retaliation for having filed the harassment complaint. A federal district court ruled against DeBord on all counts, agreeing with the hospital's rationale for the termination. It also agreed with the hospital's position that she had not only used the wrong channels to complain about harassment but had waited too long to do so.[192]

Threats

On December 17, 2008, a cardiac nurse at Memorial Hospital in Colorado Springs, Colorado, was late driving to work when she crossed paths with a police officer who stopped her for speeding on Interstate 25. Officer Duaine Peters wrote Miriam Leverington a ticket, and according to court records, the conversation then became "less than cordial." According to Peters, Leverington told him that she "hoped to never have him as a patient."[193] Peters followed through on his warning the next day, reporting the interaction to the hospital. That prompted a meeting involving three executives within the hospital's human resources department, who agreed that Leverington should be terminated.

In August 2009, Leverington sued Peters and the City of Colorado Springs, which ran not only the police department for which Peters worked but also Memorial Hospital. A federal district court found no basis for her First Amendment claim, determining that her free-speech rights did not cover threats, whether overt or subliminal. The court also noted that Leverington failed to meet any of the criteria established by the Pickering-Connick Test, as her comments did not address a matter of public concern and the hospital's interests in terminating her outweighed her free-speech rights. Later that year, a federal appeals court affirmed the lower court's ruling.[194]

In 2011, Bernadet Guevarra worked as a nurse at Seton Medical Center in Daly City, California, when she complained on Facebook about a recent pay cut and having to work on her birthday, wedding anniversary, and Mother's Day. She also posted that she wanted to curse patients with a "lifetime of pain and suffering," and wished she could "smash them down and pound them into unconsciousness."[195]

The case took two turns much different from the other cases described in this and later chapters. First, instead of just terminating Guevarra, hospital employees also reported the incident to the police, as her comments were considered threats rather than just workplace complaints. Second, instead of just suing the hospital for wrongful termination, Guevarra also filed a complaint against the hospital for opposing her application for unemployment benefits, which was denied by the California Unemployment Insurance Appeals Board.

There were no legal consequences for her threats, but she lost both her wrongful termination case against the hospital and her demand for unemployment benefits. A state court ruled that her termination was justified, determining that her complaints about her working schedule and other conditions were based on personal grievances rather than legitimate whistleblowing. An administrative law judge ruled against her on the unemployment claim, agreeing with the hospital's argument that her threats made the case different from a simple case of termination based on workplace complaints.[196]

The Desert View Care Center in Buhl, Idaho, provides another example of dealing with outspoken employees by adding the insult of denying them unemployment benefits to the injury of firing them. In 2013, nurse Joseph Talbot posted his job frustrations on Facebook, asking followers, "Ever have one of those days where you'd like to slap the every-loving bat snot out of a patient who is being a jerk just because they can?"[197] The management of DVCC, a skilled nursing and rehabilitation center, terminated him based on its social media policy, which prohibited "slanderous, vulgar, obscene, intimidating, threatening, or other 'bullying' behavior electronically."[198] Talbot had been on the job for less than six months but claimed his comments were "expressing frustration and venting."[199] He sued for wrongful termination in state court but lost, as the court sided with DVCC's contention that Talbot's comments had gone beyond workplace complaints and constituted a threat to patient safety. The state then added to Talbot's problems by denying him unemployment benefits based on the nature of his comments.[200]

In 2012, two emergency medical technicians learned, as Leverington, Guevarra, and Talbot did, that making off-hand remarks that could be construed as threats—even when made sarcastically—were not related to "matters of public concern" and were not protected by the First Amendment.

Janis Roberts and Robert Sumien were employees of Careflite, an air-ambulance company serving the Dallas-Fort Worth metropolitan area. They were dismissed for posting comments to Facebook about their frustrations with specific patients. Roberts said in one post that she had an uncooperative patient that she "wanted to slap," and Sumien commented that one of his patients deserved a "boot to the head."[201]

Both sued Careflite, claiming that even though it was a private company, it held a quasi-public position in the community because it operated under contracts with several municipalities in the area; therefore, their comments carried First Amendment protection.

The cases were tried separately and were based on different claims that went beyond the free-speech issue. Roberts claimed that the company had violated her privacy by reading her posts and that she didn't understand how Facebook's privacy settings worked, while Sumien claimed his comments were expressions of "workplace frustration."[202]

Despite the different approaches, the cases produced similar and predictable outcomes: state courts found that the company was justified in firing the employees based on the threatening nature of their posts, and neither Roberts's "invasion of privacy" claim nor Sumien's "commenting on workplace conditions" had any merit.[203]

Docs vs. Glocks

In several southern states, conservative legislatures have attempted to take away the free-speech rights of physicians with one slate of laws that would have prevented them from speaking and others that would have required them to speak in cases in which they didn't want to.

One example of the former occurred in 2011 when the Florida Legislature passed a controversial law that prohibited physicians from asking patients whether they owned firearms. The law, nicknamed "Docs vs. Glocks," was patterned after similar ones in other states, where medical associations claimed the practice of asking patients to voluntarily disclose the information and then providing them with gun-safety information was aimed at preventing deaths—especially of children—by accident and suicide. Gun-rights advocates complained that the questions violated their privacy, even though the medical associations repeatedly clarified that answering such questions was voluntary. In Florida and most other states, courts found the laws unconstitutional because they violated the physicians' First Amendment rights.[204]

While that law would have *limited* what doctors could ask, other proposed laws—also unsuccessful—would have *required* them to speak. In Florida and several other states, legislatures attempted to pass laws that would have required doctors to counsel patients seeking abortion services on the alternative of carrying their pregnancies to term and then offering the babies for adoption. Citing numerous cases in the category of "compelled speech"—meaning the government cannot force anyone to participate in speech to which they object—the courts also found those proposed laws unconstitutional.[205]

Notes

1 Amanda Marcotte, *Troll Nation* (New York: Skyhorse Publishing, 2018), pp. 17–18.
2 Kelly Weill, *Off the Edge: Flat Earthers, Conspiracy Culture, and Why Some People Will Believe Anything* (Chapel Hill, NC: Algonquin Books of Chapel Hill, 2002), p. 135.
3 This quote is attributed to English writer Evelyn Beatrice Hall as well as the French philosopher Voltaire.
4 Marcotte, *Troll Nation*, pp. 17–18.
5 Alan F. Westin and Stephan Salisbury, eds., *Individual Rights in the Corporation* (New York: Pantheon Books, 1980), p. 140.
6 *Rafferty v. Philadelphia Psychiatric Center*, 356 F. Supp. 500 (1973).
7 Bruce Barry, *Speechless: The Erosion of Free Expression in the American Workplace* (San Francisco: Berrett-Koehler Publishers, 2007), p. 191.
8 Ibid.

9 Janelle Brown, "Bitch, Bitch, Bitch," *Salon*, February 1, 2001.

10 "Employees Rate Their Employers, CEOs on Glassdoor," *Associated Press Report*, March 29, 2013.

11 *United States v. Glassdoor, Inc.* (in re: grand jury subpoena, case 16-03-217 (2017). See also: Lindsay Huber, "Court Requires Glassdoor to Reveal Identities of Anonymous Users," *The American Genius*, November 15, 2017.

12 Rudy Nydegger, *Clocking In: The Psychology of Work* (Santa Barbara, CA: Greenwood Publishing, 2018), p. 62.

13 Mark F. Kluger, interview with the author, January 2, 2014.

14 James R. Detert and Ethan Burris, "Can Your Employees Really Speak Freely?" *Harvard Business Review*, January–February 2016, pp. 80–7.

15 Marcotte, *Troll Nation*, p. 14. See also: Laura Forman, "Facebook's Politics Aren't Aging Well," *The Wall Street Journal*, June 30, 2020, p. 11-B.

16 Kelley Holland, "How Office Politics and Real Politics Can Mix," *The New York Times*, October 8, 2006. See also: Matt Krupnick, "Tenure Limits Drive Away Professors," *USA Today*, January 9, 2024, p. 1-A. Susan Milligan, "How Should HR Handle Politics in the Workplace?" *SHRM News*, February 26, 2020.

17 Eric Reid and Lakshmi Ramarajan, "Managing the High-Intensity Workplace," *Harvard Business Review*, June 2016, pp. 85–90.

18 Barry, *Speechless*, p. 116.

19 Weill, *Off the Edge*, pp. 125–6.

20 Barry, *Speechless*, p. 101.

21 Lucy Vickers, *Freedom of Speech and Employment* (New York: Oxford University Press, 2002), p. 2.

22 Barry, *Speechless*, p. 140.

23 Ibid., pp. 140–1.

24 Ibid., pp. 79–80.

25 Ibid., p. 168.

26 Stefanie Olsen, "Managers Tell an Employee She Stepped Over the Line, The Latest Warning Shot for Workers Who Blog," *CNET News*, August 31, 2004. See also: Stephanie Armour, "Warning: Your Clever Little Blog Could Get You Fired," *USA Today*, June 14, 2005.

27 Evan Hansen, "Google Blogger: I Was Fired," *The New York Times*, February 11, 2005.

28 Anna Bahney, "Interns? Bloggers Need Not Apply," *The New York Times*, May 2006, p. 1-A.

29 Ibid.

30 Armour, "Warning: Your Clever Little Blog Could Get You Fired."

31 *Rodriquez v. Wal-Mart*, 2013 U.S. App. 19345 (2013). See also: Venkat Balasubramani, "Court Upholds Doocing for Snarky Facebook Post," *Technology and Marketing Law Blog*, September 21, 2013.

32 *Rodriquez v. Wal-Mart*. See also: Balasubramani, "Court Upholds Doocing for Snarky Facebook Post."
33 Ibid.
34 Ibid.
35 Natalie Umansky, "10 Outrageous Tweets That Got People Fired," *Oddee.com*, February 21, 2014.
36 Lewis Maltby, *Can They Do That? Retaking Our Fundamental Rights in the Workplace* (New York: Penguin Group, 2009), p. 11
37 *Puget Sound Security Patrol v. Washington Department of Employment Security*, Case No. 70738-8-1 (2014). See also: Balasubramani, "Employee Terminated for Ill-Advised Facebook Post Gets Unemployment Benefits," *Technology and Marketing Law Blog*, January 6, 2015.
38 Ibid.
39 Umansky, "10 Outrageous Tweets That Got People Fired."
40 *Caplan v. L-Brands/Victoria's Secret LLC*, 210 F. Supp. 3d 744 (2016).
41 *Intel Corporation v. Hamidi*, 30 Cal. 4th 1342 (2003).
42 Ibid.
43 Lewis Massey, "Can I Get Fired Over a Tweet? What NOT to Say on Social Media," *Online Newsletter of Massey, Watson & Hembree*, April 13, 2016.
44 Kashmir Hill, "Tweets That Will Get You Fired," *Forbes Online*, March 17, 2011.
45 Robert Ellis Smith, *Workrights* (New York: E.P. Dutton, Inc., 1983), p. 85.
46 South Carolina Code Annotated, 16-17-560.
47 Barry, *Speechless*, p. 120.
48 Beth Dalbey, "Racist Tweet About Michelle Obama Gets Mortgage Lender Fired," *The Patch*, July 28, 2016.
49 Ibid.
50 Ibid.
51 Ibid.
52 Ibid.
53 Samantha Cooney, "West Virginia Official Who Called Michelle Obama an 'Ape in Heels' Loses Her Job," *Time*, December 28, 2016.
54 Ibid.
55 Ashley May, "Woman Who Wrote Racist 'Ape' Post Defrauded FEMA," *USA Today*, February 18, 2019.
56 Elie Mystal, "Biker Who Flipped Off Trump Loses Wrongful Termination Case," *Above the Law*, July 2, 2018. See also: Debra Cassens Weiss, "Judge Tosses Wrongful Termination Claim by Woman Forced to Resign After Flipping Off Trump," *ABA Journal*, July 2, 2018.
57 Milligan, "How Should HR Handle Politics in the Workplace?"
58 Ibid.

59 Ibid.

60 Shari Lau, "Shari's Solutions: Can We Prohibit Political Discussions at Work in This Heated Election Season?" *SHRM News*, June 1, 2016.

61 Maltby, *Can They Do That?*, pp. 5–6.

62 Johnny C. Taylor, "Off-Work Politics May Hurt Your Job," *USA Today*, July 10, 2018, p. 5-B. See also: Jena McGregor, "Can Your Off-Hours Political Activism Get You in Trouble at Work?" *The Washington Post*, May 31, 2017.

63 Taylor, "Off-Work Politics May Hurt Your Job."

64 Sarah E. Needleman and Katherine Bindley, "Google Reins in Politics at Work," *The Wall Street Journal*, August 24–25, 2019, p. 1-A.

65 Wines, William A. and Terence J. Lau, "Can You Hear Me Now? Corporate Censorship and Its Troubling Implications for the First Amendment," *DePaul Law Review* 55, no. 1 (Fall 2005): pp. 119–67.

66 Bruce Barry, "The Cringing and the Craven: Freedom of Expression in, Around, and Beyond the Workplace," *Business Ethics Quarterly* 17, no. 2 (2007): pp. 263–96.

67 Maltby, *Can They Do That?*, p. 13.

68 Lau, "Shari's Solutions."

69 Nicole Einbinder, "Shell Workers in Pennsylvania Were Told to Either Attend Trump Event or Not Get Paid," *Business Insider*, August 17, 2019.

70 Ibid.

71 Ibid.

72 Ibid.

73 Shannon Pettypiece and Allan Smith, "Shell Workers Would Have Lost Pay if They Missed Trump Speech at Plant," *NBC News*, August 18, 2019.

74 *Beckwith v. Career Blazers Learning Center*, 946 F. Supp. 1035 (1996).

75 *Evans v. Kansas City, Missouri School District*, 65 F. 3d 98 (1995).

76 Ibid.

77 Gene Johnson, "Doctor Loses Job After Criticizing Hospital's Virus Response," *Associated Press Report*, March 28, 2020.

78 Noam Schreiber and Brian M. Rosenthal, "Nurses and Doctors Speaking Out on Safety Now Risk Their Jobs," *The New York Times*, April 9, 2020.

79 Ibid.

80 Ibid.

81 Ibid.

82 Susan Caminiti, "Former Levi Strauss Executive Jennifer Sey on Decision to Leave Company Over Covid 'Free Speech' Controversy," *CNBC Workforce Wire*, February 17, 2022.

83 Ibid.

84 Ibid.

85 Ibid.
86 Ibid.
87 Christine Negroni, "Fired Flight Attendant Finds Blogs Can Backfire," *The Washington Post*, November 16, 2004.
88 "Perspective: I Was Fired for Blogging," *CNET News.com*, December 16, 2004. See also: Barry, *Speechless*, p. 169.
89 Negroni, "Fired Flight Attendant Finds Blogs Can Backfire."
90 Barry, *Speechless*, p. 170.
91 Keith Fink, *Free Speech in the Workplace* (San Diego: Cognella Press, 2013), pp. 220–7.
92 Ibid.
93 Ibid.
94 *Marsh v. Delta Airlines*, 952 F. Supp. 1458 (1997). See also: Fink, *Free Speech in the Workplace*, pp. 220–7.
95 Dalia Fahmy, "More Workers Getting Fired Over Social Media Rants," *ABC News*, March 2, 2010.
96 Ibid.
97 Leah Sheppard, "Airline Employee Wins Verdict Over Anti-Abortion Speech," *SHRM News*, August 3, 2022.
98 Rich Lowery, "The Life of Brandon," *USA Today*, November 8, 2021, p. 8-C. See also: Susan Rowan Kelleher, "Southwest Apologizes for Pilot's Trumpy 'Let's Go Brandon' Sign-Off," *Forbes*, October 31, 2021.
99 Umansky, "10 Outrageous Tweets That Got People Fired."
100 Ibid.
101 Kaitlin Madden, "12 Ways to Get Fired for Facebook," *CareerBuilder.com*, date unknown.
102 NLRB Cases 34-CA-12915 and 34-CA-12926. See also: *Three-D v. National Labor Relations Board*, 629 F. App. 33 (2015). Venkat Balasubramani, "NLRB Invalidates Employer's Blogging Policy and Reverses Firing Based on Facebook Posts," *Technology and Marketing Law Blog*, September 27, 2014.
103 Ibid.
104 Ibid.
105 Ibid.
106 Geoff Herbert, "Texas Roadhouse Waitress Fired After Complaining About Bad Tips on Facebook," *Syracuse.com*, July 3, 2014.
107 Ibid.
108 *Pietrylo v. Hillstone Restaurant Group*, DJN 06-5754 (2009).
109 Ibid. See also: Brian Hall, "Court Upholds Jury Verdict in Pietrylo v. Hillstone Restaurant Group," *Employer Law Report*, October 19, 2009.

110 Marcotte, *Troll Nation*, p. 19.

111 Mike Freeman, "Hill's Insight on ESPN is Illuminating," *USA Today*, January 14, 2024, p. 4-C.

112 Ibid.

113 Steve Gardner, "Jemele Hill Reveals Why She Had an Abortion at 26," *USA Today,* June 30. 2022, p. 5-C.

114 Tom Schad, "Sage Steele Sues ESPN Over Free Speech," *USA Today,* April 29, 2022, p. 3-C.

115 Nancy Armour, "ESPN Personality Uses Social Media Posts as Weapon," *USA Today,* May 30, 2023, p. 8-C.

116 Freeman, "Hill's Insight on ESPN is Illuminating."

117 Jenna Malinowski, "ESPN's McAfee Apologizes, Defends His Post," *USA Today*, August 2, 2023, p. 7-C.

118 Ibid.

119 Safid Dean, "Ryan Clark Apologizes to Tagovailoa After 'Bad Joke,'" *USA Today*, August 25, 2023, p. 2-C.

120 Ibid.

121 "ESPN's Stephen A. Smith Suggests Racism in Chip Kelly's Roster Moves," *Pro Football Talk*, March 9, 2015. Drew Gregory, "Stephen A. Smith is Never Satisfied," *GQ*, December 11, 2019. Nina Mandell, "Stephen A. Smith Won't be on ESPN for a Week After Controversial Comments," *USA Today*, July 29, 2014.

122 Matt Lavietes, "Tony Dungy's anti-LGBTQ History Gets Renewed Attention After Controversial Tweet," *NBC News*, January 25, 2023.

123 Ibid.

124 Ibid.

125 Ken Belson and Katherine Rosman, "NFL Reporter Files Racial Discrimination Claim Against League After Dismissal," *The New York Times*, September 12, 2023.

126 Ibid.

127 Ibid.

128 Nat Hentoff, *Free Speech for Me—But Not for Thee* (New York: HarperCollins, 1992), pp. 298–302.

129 Ibid.

130 Ibid.

131 Daniel Victor, "Pittsburgh TV Anchor Fired After Racial Facebook Post," *The New York Times*, March 31, 2016.

132 Ibid.

133 Ibid.

134 Ibid.

135 Ibid.

136 Ibid.
137 Ibid.
138 Ryan Deto, "Wendy Bell Is Off the Pittsburgh Airwaves Again," *Pittsburgh City Paper*, May 10, 2021.
139 Amy Joyce, "Free Expression Can Be Costly When Bloggers Bad-Mouth Jobs," *The Washington Post*, February 11, 2005, p. 1-A.
140 Ibid.
141 Hannah Fingerhut, Heather Hollingsworth, and Summer Ballentine, "Meteorologists Under Threat for Climate Change Coverage," *Associated Press Report*, July 8, 2023.
142 Ibid.
143 Ibid.
144 Ibid.
145 Ibid.
146 Eric Lagatta, "An Iowa Meteorologist's Climate Change Coverage Led to a Death Threat," *USA Today*, June 22, 2023.
147 "Dawkins Giving ex-Eagles Worker Tickets," *ESPN.com*, April 4, 2009.
148 Ibid.
149 Ibid.
150 Ibid.
151 Madden, "12 Ways to Get Fired for Facebook."
152 Ibid.
153 Massey, "Can I Get Fired Over a Tweet?"
154 Ibid.
155 National Labor Relations Act, 29 U.S.C. 157. See also: Barry, *Speechless*, p. 101.
156 Barry, *Speechless*, p. 102.
157 Ali M. Raza and A. Janell Anderson, *Labor Relations and the Law* (Upper Saddle River, NJ: Prentice-Hall, 1996), p. 179.
158 Kate E. Andrias, "A Robust Public Debate: Realizing Free Speech in Workplace Representation Elections," *Yale Law Journal* 112 (2003): pp. 24–9.
159 Barry, *Speechless*, p. 104.
160 *Thornhill v. Alabama*, 310 U.S. 88 (1940). See also: Charles O. Gregory and Harold Katz, *Labor and the Law* (New York: W.W. Norton & Company, 1979), pp. 296–8.
161 Sarah Jaffe, "Labor Rising," *The Progressive*, October/November 2022, p. 26.
162 *Kinzer et al. v. Whole Foods*, U.S. District Court-Massachusetts, Case 20-11358. See also: Allen Smith, "Court Upholds Discipline of Workers Wearing Black Lives Matter Masks," *SHRM News*, February 9, 2021, and Jonathan Stempel, "Judge Dismisses Whole Foods Workers' Lawsuit Over 'Black Lives Matter' Masks," *Reuters*, January 23, 2023.

163 Ibid.

164 Ibid.

165 Ibid.

166 Ibid.

167 Ibid.

168 Josh Eidelson, "Home Depot Wins Ruling Rejecting Right to Wear BLM at Work," *Bloomberg News Report,* June 10, 2022. See also: Ayana Archie, "Judge Dismisses an Ex-Home Depot Employee's Case About Not Wearing BLM on Uniforms," *National Public Radio*, June 13, 2022.

169 Ibid.

170 Leah Shepherd, "Whole Foods Ban on Black Lives Matter Logo Is Lawful, NLRB Judge Rules," *SHRM News,* December 21, 2023. See also: Paul Roberts, "Feds Say Fred Meyer Broke the Law by Banning BLM Buttons at Work," *Seattle Times,* September 21, 2021.

171 William B. Gould IV, *A Primer on American Labor Law* (Cambridge, MA: The MIT Press, 1986), p. 97.

172 Fink, *Free Speech in the Workplace*, p. 47. See also: "Illinois Salesman Fired for Packers Tie Gets New Job," *Rockford Register Star*, January 25, 2011.

173 *Palmateer v. International Harvester*, 85 Ill Appl. 2d 124 (1981).

174 Ibid.

175 Maltby, *Can They Do That?*, pp. 7–8.

176 David W. Ewing, *Freedom Inside the Organization: Bringing Civil Liberties to the Workplace* (New York: E.P. Dutton, 1977), p. 99. See also: Ewing, "Employee Rights: Taking the Gag Off," *Civil Liberties Review*, Fall 1974, p. 56.

177 Ibid.

178 *Geary v. U.S. Steel*, 319 A2d 174 (1974). See also: Maltby, *Can They Do That?*, pp. 7–8 and pp. 219–20.

179 Maltby, *Can They Do That?*, p. 8.

180 Angela Palermo, "Judge Orders Boise Dog Day-Care Business, Ex-Owner to Pay Workers Fired Over Covid-19," *The Idaho Statesman*, October 4, 2023.

181 Ewing, *Freedom Inside the Organization*, p. 7.

182 Maltby, *Can They Do That?*, p. 11.

183 *Rafferty v. Philadelphia Psychiatric Center*, 356 F. Supp. 500 (1973).

184 *Jones v. Memorial Hospital*, 746 S.W. 2d 891 (1988).

185 Ibid.

186 *Waters v. Churchill*, 511 U.S. 661 (1994). See also: Cynthia L. Estlund, "Free Speech and Due Process in the Workplace," *Indiana Law Journal* 71, no. 1 (Winter 1995): pp. 101–51.

187 Estlund, "Free Speech and Due Process in the Workplace."

188 Lawrence Rosenthal, "Permissible Content Discrimination Under the First Amendment: The Strange Case of the Public Employee," *Hastings Constitutional Law Quarterly* 25, no. 4 (Summer 1998): pp. 528–84.

189 *Waters v. Churchill*. See also: Rosenthal, "Permissible Content Discrimination Under the First Amendment."

190 *DeBord v. Mercy Health System of Kansas*, 737 F. 3d 642 (2013). See also: Venkat Balasubramani, "Facebook Complaints About Boss's 'Creepy Hands' Can't Salvage Retaliation/Harassment Complaints," *Technology and Marketing Law Blog*, December 11, 2013.

191 Ibid.

192 Ibid.

193 *Leverington v. City of Colorado Springs*, 643 F. 3d 719 (2011).

194 Ibid.

195 *Guevarra v. Seton Medical Center*, 2013 BL 333932 (2013). See also: Venkat Balasubramani, "Nurse Properly Fired and Denied Unemployment Due to Facebook Rant," *Technology and Marketing Law Blog*, January 13, 2014.

196 Ibid.

197 *Talbot v. Desert View Care Center*, Idaho State Court, Opinion 61 (2014). See also: Eric Goldman, "More Proof That Facebook Isn't the Place to Bitch About Your Job," *Technology and Marketing Law Blog*, June 21, 2014.

198 Ibid.

199 Ibid.

200 Ibid.

201 *Roberts v. Careflite*, 2012 Tex. App. LEXIS 8371 (2012). *Sumien v. Careflite*, Tex. App. No. 02-12-00039-CV (2012). See also: Venkat Balasubramani, "Texas Court of Appeals Rejects Privacy Claims Based on Facebook Firing," *Technology and Marketing Law Blog*, October 10, 2012.

202 Ibid.

203 Ibid.

204 Catherine Rampbell, "Americans and the 'F' Bomb," *The Washington Post,* February 23, 2017.

205 The issue of "compelled speech" was first addressed in the Supreme Court case of *Wooley v. Maynard* 430 U.S. 705 (1977) and has been debated in several cases since.

4

Free Speech for Governmental Employees

Public Concern versus Personal Grievances

Prosecutors and Petitions

In 1980, Sheila Myers was an assistant district attorney in New Orleans when she circulated a petition among her coworkers about office morale, policies regarding case assignments and office transfers, confidence in their supervisors, and whether they felt pressured to work on political campaigns. Myers's circulation of the survey was partly prompted by her upcoming transfer to another office.[1] One of her aims was to generate support for forming an employee grievance procedure, which her boss, District Attorney Harry Connick Sr. (father of the famous entertainer), felt was unnecessary. Myers refused to cease her campaign, and when Connick let her go, she sued in federal district court, claiming violation of her First Amendment rights. She found little support in the court system, which determined that her actions were not protected because they were based more on a personal grievance than genuine public interest.

When the case reached the U.S. Supreme Court, the justices ruled in favor of Connick, deciding not only that her actions were unrelated to public concern but had the potential to disrupt the workplace.

Some legal scholars pointed out the inconsistency in the court's ruling: Myers's petition drive was based on concern over office morale and workplace relationships, but when she took her case to the courts, she was told that her firing was justifiable because her actions had the potential to affect office morale and workplace relationships.[2] Myers argued that the questionnaire was a form of free speech, but as with cases discussed in Chapter 3, the Court ruled it was based more on personal grievances and did not rise to the level of public concern.

In another case involving government lawyers, a deputy district attorney for Los Angeles County suspected that local sheriff's deputies may have falsified information when applying for a search warrant related to a retail theft operation. After Richard Ceballos gathered enough information to confirm his suspicions, he communicated it to his superiors and urged them to drop the case. Not only did they decline, but the defendant's attorneys subpoenaed him to testify in court to support their motion to dismiss the case. That motion was successful, which meant Ceballos, who did not qualify for whistleblower protection under state or federal law because he never took his suspicions to anyone outside the office, was now anathema in his own workplace. He was transferred to another office and assigned to lesser cases.

Ceballos sued in federal district court and lost, but the circuit court of appeals reversed on First Amendment grounds. The U.S. Supreme Court reversed again and ruled in favor of the district attorney's office, determining that despite his honorable intentions, Ceballos was simply carrying out his work duties when he wrote his memo, and his speech was therefore not of public concern and not eligible for First Amendment protection.[3]

Recurring Themes

In terms of precedents, the Connick case is often paired with *Pickering v. Board of Education*, a 1968 case in which the Supreme Court ruled that a local school board could not punish or limit the speech of a teacher who wrote a letter to a local newspaper criticizing the administration of the school system. That ruling was based partly on the metaphorical distance between the teacher and the school board; because board members were not his direct supervisors nor individuals he worked with on a daily basis, the board's claim that his comments were disruptive had no merit[4] (this case is discussed in more detail in Chapter 7).

As a result of the *Pickering* and *Connick* cases, the courts developed a simple two-prong test to evaluate employees' free-speech claims, simply called the Pickering-Connick Test. First, the courts decide whether an employee's speech is related to a matter of concern; and second, if the employee's right to expression outweighs the employer's right to limit speech (usually in the interest of maintaining employee morale or preventing disruption, or in the case of law-enforcement agencies, maintaining public trust and confidence). If an employee is successful with both of those claims, he or she must then prove that his or her speech is the sole reason for the employer's action. In other words, if an employer claims that an employee is being terminated for other reasons at the time the speech takes place, the employer might be successful in the case. If the employee is successful in meeting all three steps, the employer would then be given the opportunity to show that its action was non-discriminatory and that the policy applies to all employees equally.

One of the rare cases in which the law could not help an employee involved one who was fired for complaining to an acquaintance, who was also a state senator, about her relationship with her supervisor. The New Hampshire Supreme Court ruled that her complaints were not protected by the law because they were personal in nature. The court also cited a state law that prohibited state employees from speaking with legislators without authorization.[5]

Only two factors support free speech for government employees:

Protection of good-faith whistleblowers. In addition to free-speech protection under the U.S. Constitution, many states have their own laws protecting the expression of state employees. One example is found in New Hampshire, where a law called the Public Employee Freedom of Expression Act has been at the core of numerous suits filed by state, county, and city employees. Almost immediately after the law was enacted in 1979, successful cases were brought by a county tax assessor who was fired after speaking to a reporter about the city's tax policy and a state prison employee who was fired for publicly criticizing conditions at the facility.

Because of First Amendment considerations involving religious speech, the courts have set a high bar for government agencies attempting to limit such expression by employees and are often skeptical of claims that such expression is disruptive. Those cases are difficult, but not impossible, and agencies can strengthen their claims if they invoke the establishment clause and can successfully argue that allowing the expression creates the appearance that the agency is promoting one type of political or religious expression over others.[6]

1. *First Amendment considerations.* Courts have ruled that public employees cannot be disciplined or discharged for the purpose of curtailing or penalizing the exercise of the right of free expression or association when those government actions are applied arbitrarily or inconsistently, as in cases in which some employees have free speech rights and their counterparts in the same agencies do not.[7] However, two 1973 Supreme Court rulings have determined that government employees can see their rights limited by law.[8]

Despite the overarching freedoms afforded to public employees under the First Amendment, government agencies often attempt to regulate speech for a variety of reasons, many of them similar to those claimed by their private-sector counterparts:

2. *Maintaining workplace harmony and efficiency of services.* In 1964, an Internal Revenue Service agent named Wayne Kennedy was reassigned to the Office of Economic Opportunity, a federal government agency with a field office in Chicago, where he oversaw the awarding of federal grants to nonprofit organizations working in the field of job training and economic development. After being transferred to another office in Indiana, he noticed that some of the organizations receiving grants in his new service area were poorly run and not financially responsible. He recommended those organizations consider replacing some board members, and those suggestions violated the agency's policy of staying out of the internal affairs of grant recipients. He also accused a colleague of violating treaties between the government and Native American tribes in the Midwest.[9]

   He was suspended for sixty days, prompting him to sue his employer on First Amendment grounds. He also accused the government of violating the Lloyd-LaFollette Act of 1912, a law designed to protect the due-process rights of public employees and considered a forerunner of the Whistleblower Protection Act of 1989. He lost at the district court level but was successful in his appeal to the circuit court. The U.S. Supreme Court reversed again, determining that Kennedy's speech disrupted the "efficiency of services" provided by the agency.[10]

   Another example occurred in 2007 when employees of the U.S. Department of Agriculture were reprimanded and threatened with termination after speaking with the press about morale problems within the department. Across the country, other government employees at the local and county levels have been disciplined or terminated following media interviews in which they criticized the performance of city and county leaders. Another rationale sometimes offered is the need for "efficient delivery of government services."
3. *Public perception and trust.* This is especially common in cases involving local governments. Mayors, county administrators, and school superintendents lack the legal authority to limit the speech of elected members of city councils, county commissions, or school boards.

Concerned about how government agencies and personnel are perceived by the public, local leaders often ask elected officers to voluntarily comply with rules of decorum so constituents see them as "acting like adults."

Many governmental bodies have codes of ethics that are cited in cases involving free speech, but adherence to them is voluntary; other than public scrutiny or the threat of not being re-elected, it is difficult to hold elected officials accountable for their offensive speech.

The rationale for limiting speech in these cases is to avoid drawing unwanted attention to the city or county government or school system, including cases in which employees are "talking out of school"—either on social media or in unauthorized media interviews—and making controversial comments inconsistent with established policy. In cases involving social media, employees including their job titles or the names or logos of the agencies they work for may cause some audience members to erroneously believe they are speaking for their agencies.

In a 2020 article in *University of Illinois Law Review Online*, labor attorneys Andrew Melzer and Whittney Barth provided guidelines for government employees desiring to participate in public debate, whether on social media or in public protests. First, they say, employees should not mention the agency they work for on social media platforms nor display work-related logos on their clothing when attending a public rally or protest. Second, if participating in a media interview during which the interviewer knows where the individual works, the individual should emphasize to the interviewer that the opinions being expressed are personal rather than an official position of the agency.[11]

"If you are a public employee, you can generally speak your mind away from work on issues that have nothing to do with your job or your workplace without risking reprisal," wrote Bruce Barry, professor of management at Vanderbilt University, in his 2007 book, *Speechless: The Erosion of Free Expression in the American Workplace.* "Assuming your message is wholly unrelated to work, you can publish an article, make a speech, call a radio show, or write the great American novel without fearing for your job. And you can even accept payment for your efforts."[12] In one rare case, the Supreme Court ruled in favor of federal employees terminated for accepting compensation for public speaking, determining that their free-speech rights outweighed concerns over appearance of impropriety, but it left the door open to support employers in future cases in which a conflict of interest could be established.[13]

Closely related to the issue of government officials being asked to "act like adults" is the expectation that they will remain "above the fray." One example is found in the case of judges being admonished when they exhibit odd behavior or make controversial statements while presiding over a trial—sometimes in open court and sometimes outside of the courtroom. Although such cases are covered under rules of judicial conduct rather than the First Amendment, the lines between the two worlds sometimes blur. Two examples of this issue are found later in this chapter.

4. *Avoiding the appearance of endorsing religious or political viewpoints.* Several cases discussed in this chapter deal with religious or political expression that takes place in individual workplaces such as cubicles and private offices. Courts do not consider the difference between a "cubicle" and an "office" as much as they consider whether that workspace is open to visitors. An employee who seldom has visitors in his or her office has more leeway in political and religious displays than one who sees visitors on a regular basis. Two cases discussed in Chapter 6 involve law-enforcement officers who wore crosses on their uniforms or displayed political bumper stickers on their private vehicles; because those displays were very public, the courts allowed employers to prohibit the messages on the grounds that they imply an endorsement of those religious or political views.

   Another free-speech issue to be covered in this chapter is the Hatch Act, a 1940 law that prohibits employees of the government from using their platforms to engage in political activity.

5. *Political considerations.* This chapter includes the discussion of a case in which a state's governor suspended a local district attorney over a matter in which the latter's speech was clearly protected under the First Amendment—simply because it was inconsistent with his own political position. Many of the state's journalists and citizens considered the governor's actions more of a political vendetta than a legitimate exercise of executive authority.

6. *Maintaining national security.* Many federal government employees are required, as a condition of employment, to agree in writing that they will submit all writings—including those with only tangential connections

to their work—to their supervisors for "security review" prior to publication. As illustrated by three cases involving Central Intelligence Agency operatives, the government cited the concern over national security in dramatically editing "tell-all" books. Those cases are described later in this chapter.

7. *Dismissing cases involving personal grievances that are not matters of public concern.* This is a recurring theme in many cases in this chapter, especially those involving complaints that employees may believe constitute good-faith whistleblowing, but their supervisors (and the courts) consider personal gripes.

Disorder in the Court

Two examples of government employees—specifically judges—needing to be "above the fray" occurred in 2023.

The first took place in the aftermath of the trial of Nikolas Cruz, who was being prosecuted for killing fourteen students and three teachers at the Marjorie Stoneman Douglas High School in Parkland, Florida, in 2018. Five years later, as the trial neared its conclusion, Judge Elizabeth Scherer violated several rules of judicial conduct in media interviews when she chastised one of Cruz's court-appointed lawyers and wrongly accused another attorney of threatening her children.

Florida's Judicial Qualifications Commission investigated the judge's comments and recommended she be reprimanded, stating that "during this unique and lengthy case, Judge Scherer allowed her emotions to overcome her judgment."[14] The Florida Supreme Court reviewed and confirmed the recommendation of the commission.

Later that year, a more bizarre case involved a judge in Oklahoma who met a more serious fate for her courtroom behavior. Courtroom cameras showed Lincoln County District Judge Traci Soderstrom checking Facebook and exchanging more than 500 texts with a female bailiff. The case over which she was presiding involved a man charged with manslaughter in the death of his girlfriend's two-year-old son.

An investigation found that the judge's texts included comments about a "bulge" in the prosecutor's pants and her admiration for the defense attorney, asking, "Am I allowed to applaud for her?" She also wrote that she admired the looks of a police officer who testified, saying, "He's so pretty. I could look at him all day."[15]

More problematic were her texts calling the child's mother "a liar" following her testimony and indicating she had already decided that the defendant was innocent. "They just couldn't accept that a mom could kill their kid, so they went after the next person available," Soderstrom wrote in one text.[16]

Oklahoma Supreme Court chief judge John Kane IV referred the case to the Oklahoma Council on Judicial Complaints, which launched an investigation. Kane later revealed that Soderstrom told the council that she was texting about things that probably could have waited "instead of recognizing that these types of communications should never be made at all." When Soderstrom heard that remark, she replied to the council, "Oh, that's funny. Now let's move on."[17]

The council voted to suspend Soderstrom from her position, with the final decision on her status pending as of early 2024.[18]

Barry's comment about "receiving compensation" is not an afterthought. In 1978, Congress passed the Ethics in Government Act, which prohibited federal employees from accepting payment for making speeches or writing articles, regardless of the topic and whether it was related to their work.

In 1995, the law was challenged by employees of the U.S. Treasury, where several employees had made paid speeches and written magazine and newsletter articles on a variety of topics unrelated to their work.

There was no evidence that such payments affected the judgment or work performance of the employees, but they were nonetheless reprimanded and told to stop.[19] Instead, the employees chose to challenge the law with the help from their union, filing suit in federal district court. When the Supreme Court finally ruled on the matter in 1995, it determined that the employees' First Amendment right of free speech outweighed the government's interest in avoiding the appearance of impropriety.[20]

In writing for the majority, Justice John Paul Stevens cited the example of Walt Whitman, who he claimed might not have become a great poet if the law was in place and he was unable to publish his poetry while serving as an Army clerk and nurse before and during the Civil War.[21] Justices on both sides, however, agreed that such activity could be banned if a conflict of interest could be proven.

"If government employees didn't have any free speech rights, America might well be a much quieter place," attorney Randy Kozel wrote in a 2005 article in *Northwestern University Law Review*. "But tying public employers' hands by denying them the ability to restrict employee speech could take a massive toll on government efficiency—a toll that we would all end up paying with our tax dollars."[22] Kozel points out that the government performs two functions: as a sovereign entity that provides services and controls people's lives and as an employer who hires and compensates individuals who carry out the first function. He argues that in the former role it should not censor speech, but in the second role, it may and should.

Kozel explained that prior to the 1967 case of *Keyishian v. Board of Regents* and the 1968 case of *Pickering v. Board of Education*—cases involving the free-speech rights of college professors and K–12 school teachers, respectively—public employees were treated the same as private employees (these cases are discussed in more detail in Chapters 7 and 8, respectively). "The public employee had no right to object to conditions placed upon the terms of employment—including those which restricted the exercise of constitutional rights," Kozel wrote.[23] In making that point, Kozel quoted Oliver Wendell Holmes, while a justice on the Supreme Court of Massachusetts, who wrote an opinion on an 1892 case which limited the rights of a police officer to talk about local politics while on his beat. "He may have the constitutional right to talk politics," Holmes wrote. "But he has no constitutional right to be a policeman."[24] In short, Kozel paraphrased Holmes, claiming that when a public employee accepts a job, he or she agrees to keep opinions to themselves. "If you were a public employee and wanted to keep your job, your best bet was to button your lip," he wrote.[25]

In the same article, Kozel suggested a return to what he called the "Holmesian model"—a system that would no longer recognize a difference between public and private employees in terms of free-speech protection. Both types of employees, as a condition of employment, forfeit their free-speech rights (this proposal is discussed in more detail in the Conclusion).

Politics and Patronage

As far back as the early 1800s, there was concern over government employees who were "on the clock" overtly taking part in political campaigns—including those in which their bosses were the candidates. In 1801, newly inaugurated President Thomas Jefferson opined that the political involvement of government employees should be limited to voting and should not include active campaigning.[26] Laws were passed later in the nineteenth century to prohibit government employees from donating money to political campaigns for fear that those donations could have been coerced or made with the expectation that a promotion or more prestigious job would be given in return.

There was no serious attempt to restrict political involvement by government officials until 1930, when the federal government successfully prosecuted Harry M. Wurzbach, a member of the U.S. House of Representatives representing Texas, for soliciting campaign donations from federal employees, which violated the Federal Corrupt Practices Act. A federal court dismissed the charges, citing First Amendment concerns and other legal issues. The U.S. Supreme Court eventually reviewed the case and remanded it back to the lower court to be retried, but before a second trial could be scheduled, Wurzbach died, leaving the issue unsettled.[27]

In 1939, Congress passed the Hatch Act, named after its primary sponsor, Senator Carl Hatch of New Mexico. In short, the law prohibited federal government employees from taking part in campaigns, and the following year the law was expanded to include state and local government employees whose work involved federal programs. The law was more effective than previous attempts because it laid out specific examples of what was and was not permitted: employees could contribute to campaigns but not collect money from others, they could attend rallies but not organize them, and they could sign nominating petitions but not circulate them.[28]

Two challenges to the Hatch Act—in 1947 and 1973—were based on First Amendment grounds and resulted in the Supreme Court upholding the law, ruling that the desire to maintain the integrity of elections outweighed any free-speech concerns.[29] In both cases, dissenting justices wrote that despite its good intentions, the law violated the spirit of the First Amendment and should not be used to limit the free speech of government employees unless it could be proven that the political activity impaired the employees' or their coworkers' performance of their duties.[30] In 1993, the law was amended to apply only to employees on "company time" and would no longer apply to what they did in their non-working hours.

In 1998, a federal court ruled against the wives of two Oklahoma Highway Patrol officers who wanted to display political yard signs, which violated a departmental policy prohibiting political activity (this case is discussed in more detail in Chapter 6).

While a government employee has a constitutional right to speak out on matters of public concern, he or she does not have a constitutional right to engage in political campaign activity if that activity is prohibited by either state or federal law.[31]

One important consideration is whether the employee identifies himself or herself as an employee of the government agency, either by saying so in a media interview or a social media posting, or by wearing a company logo or including the logo on a website. "If you're out there waving around the federal agency that you work for, or wearing a T-shirt, that's a problem because it looks like the government is supporting what you're saying," said labor attorney Kelly Dobbs Bunting in a 2023 article in SHRM News. "Don't drive the truck with the logo on it when you attend a rally."[32]

While public employers cannot regulate political debate in the workplace, they can get involved if the speech or conduct crosses the line into fighting words, intimidation, harassment, or threats. But where do we draw that line? In a 1971 U.S. Supreme Court case, Justice John Marshall Harlan commented that "one man's vulgarity is another man's lyric."[33] In today's workplace, what one person believes to be humor or harmless fun may be considered by others to be something more onerous.

Candidates for federal office are not allowed to promise jobs or other benefits in exchange for political support or to threaten to take away jobs or other benefits if someone does not engage in political activity. It is also a crime for federal offices to solicit contributions from federal employees or for federal employees to make voluntary contributions to federal candidates.[34]

In the 2016 case of *Williams v. McKee*, a federal court ruled that a county sheriff's interest in maintaining the appearance of political neutrality outweighed the First Amendment right of one of his employees to display a bumper sticker on his truck that insulted one political party more than it conveyed a political viewpoint[35] (this case is covered in more detail in Chapter 6).

While private employers are prohibited from discriminating against current or potential employees based on race, sex, sexual orientation, age, marital status, or disability, the same cannot be said about political associations or activity. Therefore, non-government employers may refuse to hire a person who indicates on a resume or social media platform their affiliation with progressive causes such as Black Lives Matter or the American Civil Liberties Union, or conservative causes such as Moms for Liberty or the American Legion.

With government employers, the general rule that prohibits them from most forms of discrimination does not always apply. Elected representatives at the federal, state, and local levels are free to hire only those employees who are members of the same political party, but only if those jobs are high-level positions that involve policymaking. Federal agencies are allowed to scrutinize a person's political background or affiliations for jobs associated with national security.[36]

The term "patronage" refers to the centuries-old tradition of newly elected political candidates rewarding their supporters with jobs. Newly elected presidents, for example, often appoint major campaign donors to ambassadorships. In local and state offices, newly elected public officials fill open positions with those of the same party, while often purging their staffs of those belonging to other parties.

That system of patronage, often called "cronyism," was virtually unchallenged until 1970, when Richard J. Elrod was elected sheriff in Cook County, Illinois. One of his first moves was to dismiss four employees appointed by his Republican predecessor and replace them with Democrats. John Burns was the lead plaintiff in the case, which began in federal district court, where his case was dismissed based on the court's recognition that patronage had long been a traditional part of the employee selection and retention process. Burns and his former colleagues took their case to the circuit court of appeals, which reversed the findings of the lower court and ruled in their favor. Elrod appealed to the U.S. Supreme Court, which upheld the ruling of the circuit court in 1976, basing its decision mostly on the fact that the employees who sued were in lower-level, non-policymaking positions.[37]

In writing the majority opinion, Justice William Brennan opined that "patronage dismissals severely restrict political belief and association, which constitute the core of those activities protected by the First Amendment, and government may not, without seriously inhibiting First Amendment rights, force a public employee to relinquish his right to political association as the price of holding a public job."[38]

Four years later, in *Branti v. Finkel*, the Court similarly sided with two assistant public defenders in Rockland County, New York, who were dismissed because of their political affiliation. Aaron Finkel and Alan Tabakman were registered Republicans, and their boss, Peter Branti Jr., was a Democrat who had been recently appointed to the job by the county legislature. Determining that the plaintiffs had been satisfactorily performing their jobs and the sole reason for their termination was their political affiliation, a federal district court ruled in their favor and ordered them reinstated. The case followed a different path compared to *Elrod v. Burns* but ended in the same result: because the terminated employees were not in policymaking positions, their dismissal violated their rights to political beliefs and affiliation under the First and Fourteenth Amendments.[39]

In that case, the Supreme Court determined that government officials may not discharge public employees for refusing to support a political party or its candidates, unless political affiliation is a "reasonably appropriate requirement for the job in question."[40]

Conversely, in subsequent cases, the Court has ruled that employees in high-ranking, policymaking positions could be hired and fired based on their political affiliations.[41]

Some bizarre examples have happened recently. In Santa Rosa County, Florida, in 2023, one county commissioner refused to go along with his colleagues in approving the hiring of a county official for a non-partisan position because she was a registered Democrat and he felt the county should "only hire republicans."[42] Everyone else on the board agreed that Shana Alford was highly qualified for the unpaid position on the Marine Advisory Board, but her candidacy was nearly derailed by the lone holdout, Republican James Calkins. He was previously known for his opposition to abortion and support for gun rights—two issues not within the county commission's purview. He told his colleagues he had researched Shana Alford's background and was concerned about her membership in the "most evil party in this country."[43]

Other commissioners, even Republicans, came to Alford's defense based on her strong credentials and repeated the fact that the position was non-partisan. Commissioner Ray Eddington interrupted Calkins's diatribe to say that "saying a party is evil goes against the American system . . . this system works because we have opposing ideas. We need two parties for the system to work."[44] Chairman Colton Wright added that Calkins's comments show "how misguided and out of touch (he) is with the citizens of Santa Rosa County."[45] Even the chair of the local Republican Party chastised Calkins, saying his remark "has no place in a civil society."[46] Alford's appointment was confirmed by the commission by a 4-1 vote. After the meeting, Calkins doubled down on his position when speaking to local media. "I will not vote for a democrat to be appointed to any board in Santa Rosa County," Calkins said. "We have a lot of republicans qualified to serve in this position and I will absolutely not vote for a democrat."[47]

The Santa Rosa County Democratic Executive Committee encouraged citizens to file complaints against Calkins with the Florida Ethics Commission, but the FEC dismissed all twenty it received.[48]

State and Local Governments

In 2017, Beth Sweet was a customer service representative for the town of Bargersville, Indiana, where her primary job was to assist citizens with their utility payments and investigate problems with billing and related matters. Jim Parsetich, one of the town's wealthy residents, fell behind on his payments and was at risk of having his services disconnected. Supervisor Steve Longstreet, Parsetich's friend and real-estate business partner, decided to give him more time to catch up, saying that it was part of the city's new "customer-friendly" policy and that their business relationship was not a factor.[49] That didn't sit well with Sweet, who nonetheless turned off Parsetich's utilities. If she had kept the details of the disagreement to herself, she might have gotten off with just a reprimand, but when she continued to discuss the situation with coworkers, despite Longstreet's insistence that she drop her complaint, he fired her early in 2018.

That began a lengthy "he said/she said" scenario within the grievance procedure available to city employees. Longstreet said Sweet was fired not for the Parsetich situation, but for a history of poor performance evaluations dating back to 2012. One specific issue was a billing error (for which Sweet was responsible) that cost the city more than $1,000. Sweet believed her dismissal was based solely on retaliation for the Parsetich matter.[50]

After her grievance was denied, Sweet took the case to federal court, but the case never made it to trial. The city of Bargersville asked for and received summary judgment, with the court ruling that Sweet had failed to prove her retaliation claim. While it gave some merit to Sweet's First Amendment argument, it was insufficient to override Longstreet's claim that her dismissal was based on job performance. The circuit court of appeals eventually agreed with the trial court's finding.[51]

Across the country, state and local government employees have not fared well when reprimanded or terminated for venting about their working conditions in media interviews or on social media platforms. The reasons for their lack of legal success are varied, but in many cases, courts determine that their unhappiness is based on personal grievances rather than legitimate whistleblowing, and their free-speech rights are overshadowed by the government's need to maintain efficiency in government services.

In a 2013 case in Massachusetts, for example, a state official learned the hard way that Facebook was not an appropriate venue for venting about job frustrations. Tyson Lynch was a state official responsible for hearing the cases of individuals challenging requirements related to the state's sex-offender registry. He had been frustrated with his job for more than five years and, over that time period, vented on Facebook with comments about hearings that ran too long, individuals who spoke Spanish, attorneys who were not prepared to argue their cases, and other state officials who wrote reports using the Arial font. He also referred to those appearing before him as "pervs."[52]

When an individual identified in court documents as John Doe appealed the requirement that he register as a level 3 sex offender, his case was heard by Lynch, who ruled against him. Doe's attorney learned of Lynch's Facebook history and used it to successfully appeal his client's case. The court determined that his Facebook record tainted Lynch's credibility to make important decisions that would affect people's lives. Unlike Sweet (whose case occurred four years later), however, he received only a reprimand but eventually left government service and followed another career path.[53]

Cases involving religious expression in the workplace often appear to be hair-splitting exercises, such as in the cases of Monte Tucker, a computer analyst who worked in the California Department of Education, and Daniel Berry, a social worker in Tehama County, California. Tucker had a private office where he was visited by few coworkers and no one from the public, whereas Berry frequently saw clients in his office. In his 1996 case, Tucker was successful when he challenged an office policy prohibiting the display of religious materials in the workplace, with the court determining that because no members of the public visited his office, there was not an establishment-clause issue.[54] A decade later, a different court made the opposite ruling in Berry's case, determining that visitors could get the impression that the county agency for which he worked endorsed or was aligned with a particular religious viewpoint, which was clearly an establishment clause violation.[55]

Even government officials who are elected rather than appointed are vulnerable to having their free-speech rights curtailed. Shortly after the Supreme Court ruled to overturn *Roe v. Wade*—the 1973 decision that legalized abortion—numerous states enacted or proposed abortion bans, with those in Bible Belt states such as Texas, Alabama, and Florida being the most restrictive. Around the same time, those states also enacted or proposed laws restricting gender-altering surgery or hormone treatments for minors. Andrew Warren, the twice-elected state attorney in Hillsborough County, Florida, announced that he would not prosecute women seeking abortions, doctors performing abortions, nor doctors treating transgender teenagers. That infuriated Governor Ron DeSantis, who publicly admonished Warren and suspended him from his duties.

"Five minutes after receiving the email about my suspension, I was escorted out of my office by an armed deputy," Warren told a reporter from *The Atlantic*. "I didn't even have time to get my house keys from my desk."[56]

Warren immediately sued the governor, based on the absence of any clause in the state constitution that allowed one elected official to suspend another. The other important distinction is that DeSantis suspended an official not for what he did or did not do, but for what he said he would not do. In January 2023, a federal judge ruled that DeSantis had violated Warren's First Amendment rights and rights granted by the Florida Constitution, but he lacked the authority to reinstate him.[57] As of early 2024, the case had not yet been resolved, and Warren has filed paperwork to run for the office in the November 2024 election.

In September 2023, an elections director in Cochise County, Arizona, resigned after only five months on the job, partly because he continued to push widely debunked claims of voter fraud in the 2020 presidential election. Bob Bartelsmeyer gave no reason for his leaving, but local media suspected he was forced out of the job because he had embarrassed the community in national media interviews. In his resignation letter, he told county officials he was returning to his previous job as elections supervisor in La Paz County, California.[58]

In 2010, high school students in Pleasant Plains, Arkansas, began a campaign to wear purple as a way to bring awareness to the issue of teen suicide and honor their classmates who had taken their own lives. Clint McCance, vice president of the Midland School District, never said anything during public meetings to indicate his beliefs on gay issues but questioned on his personal Facebook page why students "wanted (him) to wear purple because five queers killed themselves . . . the only way I'm wearing it for them is if they all commit suicide. I can't believe we've gotten this stupid. We are honoring the fact that they sinned and killed themselves because of their sin."[59]

In subsequent postings, McCance downplayed the problem of teen bullying, used the terms "queer" and "fag," said he would disown his own children if he found out they were gay, and stated that he enjoys "the fact that gay people give each other AIDS and die."[60]

Despite the conservative political climate in the community, the incident caused an uproar. McCance couldn't be fired because his position was elected rather than appointed, but that didn't stop the local and national critics from getting involved.

After complaints from parents and protests from local and national LGBTQ advocacy groups, McCance publicly apologized. "I'm sorry I've hurt people with my comments," McCance told the local media. "I'm sorry I made those ignorant comments and hurt people on a broad spectrum."[61] McCance said that in addition to media scrutiny, he received an outpouring of criticism over his comments, including "thousands of phone calls, hate mails, people threatening to kill my family and me."[62]

McCance then resigned to avoid bringing unwanted negative attention to the school district. McCance said in media interviews that he sent his family out of the state because of fears for their safety and installed a security system at their home.

In 2023, a school board member in Idaho met a similar fate after making comments on the opposite end of the political spectrum. Shiva Rajbhandari, an eighteen-year-old high school senior serving as the student representative on the Boise School District Board of Trustees, publicly opposed Governor Brad Little for his opposition to gender-affirming care for transgender youth. "Fuck you," Rajbhandari wrote on Twitter, "I pray you live a long life so you can bear witness to the pain you've unleashed on Idaho's children and families today. When you die, though, I'm pissing on your grave."[63]

After several days of public and private criticism, Rajbhandari issued an apology through the board's communications office. "I'm sure everyone has seen my profane tweet on my personal account toward the governor," his statement said:

> To our patrons, I'm sorry. I'm sorry that I communicated in a way that was crude and cruel and violated your trust in me. To our students, I'm sorry. I'm sorry that during a time of crisis, I failed to act as a role model for all of you and that I failed to represent the articulate, unrelenting, and kind people that I know all of you to be. And to our board, I'm sorry. I'm sorry that my actions reflected poorly on each of your characters and values.[64]

Despite the apology, the board was unforgiving and demanded Rajbhandari's resignation, which was submitted the following day. The following week, in an interview with the *Idaho Statesman*, Rajbhandari said that he did not offend anyone but was "unapologetic in my commitment in solidarity with the LGBTQ community" and against the governor's action.[65]

In other cases, however, free-speech rights prevailed—without the necessity of court trials—even in cases in which the "act like adults" rule was rejected.

In Milton, Florida, in 2023, a series of volatile social exchanges took place between city council members and constituents, and then between council members and each other. That prompted Mayor Heather Lindsay to suggest amending the city charter to limit social media activity among both elected and appointed city officials.

The city already had policies in place to regulate social media usage among lower-level employees, but Lindsay's plan would have taken those same rules and applied them to higher-level employees as well as city council members. The policies would require those officials to "uphold the values of the city of Milton: civility, honor, and respect for all people, which should include how we conduct ourselves on social media."[66]

The mayor said limiting council members' social media discourse was necessary because they were "unable to police themselves," but local residents labeled the mayor's idea as "socialist" and "communist." The wife of a county commissioner who had been at the center of another unrelated free-speech controversy added that "you're in a very dangerous place when you're trying to control freedom of speech."[67]

The dustup started when council member Jeff Snow addressed a building industry group and said that several of his colleagues "never should have been elected."[68] That set off a series of exchanges that began with criticisms of Snow's remarks and expanded to include other examples of the city government's dirty laundry. Lindsay's proposal was defeated 8-0, with many of the votes coming from the council members criticized by the mayor.[69]

Making ignorant comments on the floor of houses of government is not limited to national political leaders. After watching the Women's March, a January 21, 2017, event that followed the previous day's inauguration of President Donald Trump, a Republican lawmaker in Atlantic County, New Jersey, asked on the floor of the state legislature if those women were "going to be home in time to cook dinner."[70] Commenting on the same event, Carlsbad, New Mexico City Councilor J. R. Doporto wrote on Facebook that the women should "stop their bitching" and "have the right to be slapped."[71] Another local official in Rhode

Island tweeted, "definitely a guy came up with the idea for the march as a way to get the wives outta the house."[72]

Dress codes for employees of local governments are rare, and challenges to those codes are even rarer. In a 2003 case in Kentucky, a public library had a policy prohibiting clothing or ornaments that conveyed messages on clothing that were "religious, political, or offensive," but that rule was invalidated by a federal district court after an employee who had been fired for wearing a simple cross pendant successfully sued. The court ruled that her accessory "could not possibly be interpreted by a reasonable observer as government endorsement of religion."[73]

Government Contractors

Free-speech protections for government employees extend to employees of private companies who work on government contracts, but it doesn't always result in favorable outcomes for the plaintiffs. In the early 1970s, for example, an employee of the Avco Corporation was fired after publishing an article in a labor newsletter that was critical of his company's management. Had Michael Holodnak been working for any other private employer, he would not have had a valid legal claim. But because Avco manufactured helicopter engines on government property and under Department of Defense contracts, it was treated as a government employer when Holodnak took his case to federal court.[74]

Holodnak was unsuccessful in his case, however. The court ruled that Avco was functioning as a "state actor," but nevertheless ruled against Holodnak, siding with the company's claim that his writings were defamatory and disruptive.

In subsequent cases, plaintiffs in similar situations have also found little success. In a 1996 case, an employee of a private prison contractor in California sued his employer, claiming that he was fired for reporting problems with how other employees were being trained for their work at the prison. Jon L. George was first hired as a custodian, but then enrolled in a training program to become a corrections officer. As a result of taking the course, George observed safety and security issues that he mentioned in class. The company called his comments "false and defamatory" and terminated him. When he sued, claiming the company was a "state actor" that violated his First Amendment rights, a federal district court found in favor of his employer.[75]

In both the *Holodnak* and *George* cases, the terminated employees argued that entering into government contracts to perform work customarily performed by government agencies meant the otherwise private employers were functioning as state actors. In *Holodnak*, the court agreed with the "state actor" claim but ruled against the terminated employee for other reasons. In *George*, a different court determined that while the operation of a prison was usually a state function, the training of employees was not. The plaintiffs' attorneys in the two unsuccessful cases described the proceedings as "hair-splitting exercises."

In the 1988 case of *Jones v. Memorial Hospital*, a Texas court ruled that a hospital violated the free-speech rights when it fired Pamela Sue Jones, a nurse who complained about the quality of patient care at the hospital. That hospital was technically a private entity but was treated as a public agency in court because it held a number of government contracts[76] (this case is discussed in more detail in Chapter 3).

In some cases, private companies feel obligated to limit the rights of their employees to comment on political issues because they are dependent on government contracts and see themselves as quasi-governmental employers. One example took place in 2017 when a Virginia woman was shown on social media giving the "middle finger" to the passing motorcade of President Donald Trump. She was fired by her employer, a government contractor.[77]

Two years later, when Trump was launching his reelection campaign, employees at a construction site in Pennsylvania were told they were expected—but not required—to attend an on-site speech by President Donald Trump. Planning for the event went beyond the usual security procedures, with many of the details dictated by White House staff. Journalists speculated that the willingness of the company to go along with the plan was based on its status as a defense contractor.[78] Both the "middle finger" and "mandatory attendance" cases are discussed in more detail in Chapter 3.

I Didn't Really Mean What I Said

"Rhetorical hyperbole" is a widely accepted reason for excusing an individual's outrageous utterances when they become the subject of a defamation lawsuit. The rationale is that the person didn't really mean what he or she said or that his or her comments were so exaggerated or outrageous that no "reasonable person" would take them seriously. While the term has a long history in defamation cases, it seldom works to excuse a politician's outrageous statements about other politicians or anyone else. In 2016, a state lawmaker in West Virginia and an aide to a state tax official in California learned that lesson when they made online postings that included derogatory words and images regarding Democratic presidential candidate Hillary Clinton.

In West Virginia, State Delegate Mike Folk tweeted that Clinton should be "tried for treason, murder, and crimes against the U.S. Constitution, then hung on the mall in Washington, D.C."[79] State Delegate Mike Folk's comments were based on the ongoing investigation of Clinton for her use of a private email server to conduct business as Secretary of State.[80]

The state's Democrats and even some of Folk's Republican colleagues denounced his comments, prompting him to walk them back by labeling them "hyperbole" and telling the media that he still wanted to see Clinton held accountable, but didn't want her executed. "I could have said that a little better," Folk told the media. "I regret the tone and the second part of that tweet. The biggest misconception is that for some reason, everybody thinks I made a death threat, which I did not. Clearly it was not that."[81]

While Folk's semi-apology was good enough to keep him out of long-term trouble with his colleagues and constituents, it wasn't good enough for his full-time employer. Being a state delegate in West Virginia is just a part-time job, and he depended on his job as a pilot for United Airlines for the majority of his livelihood. As a result of public outrage over the tweet, United suspended him pending its own investigation.[82]

After the controversy subsided, Folk was reinstated by United and was re-elected to the House of Delegates that November. In 2018, he ran unsuccessfully for a seat in the West Virginia Senate. In 2020, he challenged incumbent Governor Jim Justice but received only 199 votes out of a statewide total of 784,000.[83]

Also in 2016, an aide to a member of the California Board of Equalization tweeted an image of a hangman holding a noose. The caption underneath read, "I'm Ready for Hillary."[84] The following day, Nathan Miller resigned. "This was not political satire. That is a threat," said Howard Katz, the chairman of the Riverside County Democratic Party, in a media interview.[85]

In Maine in 2023, a state employee responsible for regulating the state's gambling industry was suspended for a week without pay after tweeting derogatory comments about women and supporting a white nationalist group. Milt

Champion used his personal account to make the comments, which came at the worst possible time for him and his agency, which was overseeing the rollout of new sports betting regulations. The comment about women—which suggested they should be called "bitches" rather than "ladies"—was clearly unrelated to his work, but his support of a white nationalist group was tangentially related to local Native American tribes, which were working on the sports betting platforms as well as expansion of the state's casino industry.[86]

Pre-Publication Agreements

Many federal government agencies require employees to sign pre-publication agreements that mandate them to submit manuscripts for any books based on their experiences for government approval (and usually censorship). Significant cases involving pre-publication agreements are *United States v. Marchetti* (1972) and *Snepp v. United States* (1980).

The Marchetti case involved Victor Marchetti, a Central Intelligence Agency operative who wrote a book titled *The CIA and the Cult of Intelligence*[87] in which he chronicled his experiences in South America. The CIA enforced a pre-publication agreement that he had signed when he joined the agency. The agreement did not bar him from writing a book, but it required that the manuscript be submitted to CIA officials in advance so it could be cleared.

Marchetti accepted the requirement at first and submitted his manuscript for review. The CIA made 339 deletions, which represented almost 20 percent of the manuscript. Marchetti claimed that even though he signed the agreement, deleting 20 percent of his manuscript would constitute prior restraint and violate his First Amendment rights.[88]

Before going to court, Marchetti and his lawyer met with CIA officials, who agreed to drop 171 of the objections, reducing the proportion of deleted material from 20 percent to about 10 percent. Marchetti still was not satisfied and took his claim to federal district court and eventually the U.S. Supreme Court, but the high court upheld the remaining deletions and ruled that pre-publication agreements are a justifiable form of prior restraint. The book appeared in its abridged form, and in each place where material had been deleted, the publisher printed the word "DELETED" in capital letters.[89]

Eight years later, in *Snepp v. United States,* the Supreme Court made a similar ruling on pre-publication agreements. Plaintiff Frank Snepp was a former CIA analyst who had worked in Southeast Asia and was one of the last Americans to be airlifted from Saigon before the North Vietnamese took over in 1975. After Snepp returned to the United States, he resigned from the CIA and wrote a book titled *Decent Interval*[90] in which he was critical of the agency's operations during the war.

Like Marchetti, Snepp claimed that the pre-publication agreement he had signed was a violation of his First Amendment rights and that once the CIA censors removed anything objectionable, there would not be anything left worth publishing. This case also went to the Supreme Court, which ruled again that pre-publication agreements for government employees were constitutional. By the time the court made its ruling, Snepp's book had already been published. Instead of attempting to recall the book, the court required that Snepp surrender all of his royalties to the CIA—more of a punitive payment than a compensatory one. The court paid some attention to the First Amendment values of the case, but decided the issue based largely on the principles of contract law, determining that Snepp had signed away his First Amendment rights when he agreed to the provision in his CIA contract.[91]

A few years after the Snepp case, President Ronald Reagan failed in his attempt to apply the pre-publication rule to current employees. His executive order was determined to be unenforceable because under contract law, the rule could only be applied as a condition of employment at the time of hiring and could not be applied retroactively.

The issue of pre-publication agreements surfaced again in 2005 when twenty-three-year CIA veteran Gary Berntsen published his book, *Jawbreaker*, which detailed his experiences in Afghanistan.[92] He submitted the manuscript to the agency's publication review board, which he later accused of "dragging its feet" and causing him to miss his publisher's deadline for completing his work. He was also angered when the board instructed him to delete details of military operations in Afghanistan that had already been reported in books written by authors who were not CIA agents. In his court case, he asked to be allowed to include in future editions those details that had been deleted from the 2005 edition. An unabridged version was released in 2006.[93]

Notes

1 Randy J. Kozel, "Reconceptualizing Public Employee Speech," *Northwestern University Law Review* 99, no. 3 (Spring 2005): pp. 1007–51.

2 Lewis Maltby, *Can They Do That? Retaking Our Fundamental Rights in the Workplace* (New York: Penguin Group, 2009), pp. 14–15.
3 Bruce Barry, *Speechless: The Erosion of Free Expression in the American Workplace* (San Francisco: Berrett-Koehler Publishers, 2007), pp. 82–3.
4 Henry Cohen, *Freedom of Speech and Press: Exceptions to the First Amendment* (New York: Nova Science Publishers, Inc., 2008), p. 49.
5 Randy Bobbitt, *The View From Under the Bus: A Case Study in Media Influence, Public Opinion, and Moral Outrage* (Pensacola, FL: Windchase Bay Publishing, 2020), pp. 90–1.
6 Barry, *Speechless*, p. 153.
7 Alvin L. Goldman, *Labor Law and Industrial Relations in the United States of America* (Washington, DC: The Bureau of National Affairs, Inc., 1983), p. 83.
8 *U.S. Civil Service Commission v. National Association of Letter Carriers* (413 U.S. 548) and *Broadrick v. Oklahoma* (413 U.S. 601). See also: Goldman, *Labor Law and Industrial Relations in the United States of America*, p. 84.
9 *Arnett v. Kennedy*, 416 U.S. 134 (1974).
10 Ibid.
11 Andrew Melzer and Whittney Barth, "Whether Employees Can Be Fired for Participating in Peaceful Protests," *University of Illinois Law Review Online*, Fall 2020, pp. 221–34.
12 Barry, *Speechless*, p. 93.
13 *United States v. National Treasury Employees Union*, 513 U.S. 454 (1995).
14 Jessica Schladebeck, "Commission: Parkland Judge Should be Reprimanded for Conduct During Nikolas Cruz Trial," *New York Daily News,* June 6, 2023.
15 Nolan Clay, "Investigation Says Oklahoma Judge Checked Facebook, Texted About Prosecutor's Genitals During Murder Trial," *USA Today*, October 12, 2023.
16 Ibid.
17 Ibid.
18 Ibid.
19 *United States v. National Treasury Employees Union*. See also: Barry, *Speechless*, p. 92.
20 Ibid.
21 Kozel, "Reconceptualizing Public Employee Speech," pp. 1007–51.
22 Ibid.
23 Ibid. See also: *Keyishian v. Board of Regents,* 233 F. Supp. 752 (1965) and *Pickering v. Board of Education,* 391 U.S. 563 (1968).
24 *McAuliffe v. Mayor of New Bedford*, 29 N.E. 517 (1892).
25 Kozel, "Reconceptualizing Public Employee Speech."
26 Barry, *Speechless*, p. 90.

27 *United States v. Wurzbach*, 280 U.S. 396 (1930).

28 Barry, *Speechless*, p. 91.

29 *United Public Workers v. Mitchell* 330 U.S. 75 (1947) and *U.S. Civil Service Commission v. National Association of Letter Carriers* 413 U.S. 548 (1973).

30 Barry, *Speechless*, p. 91.

31 Ibid.

32 Leah Shepherd, "How to Handle Political Speech in the Workplace," *SHRM News*, June 12, 2023.

33 *Cohen v. California*, 403 U.S. 14 (1971).

34 Darien A. McWhirter, *Your Rights at Work* (New York: John Wiley & Sons, 1989), pp. 130–1.

35 *Williams v. McKee*, 655 Fed. App. 677 (2016).

36 *American Bar Association Guide to Workplace Law* (New York: Random House, 1977), pp. 131–2.

37 *Elrod v. Burns*, 427 U.S. 347 (1976).

38 Ibid.

39 *Branti v. Finkel*, 445 U.S. 507 (1980).

40 Ibid. See also: McWhirter, *Your Rights at Work*, p. 132.

41 Tom McLaughlin, "Santa Rosa Commissioner Rails for Democratic-less Government; His Own Party Says He Went Too Far," *Pensacola News Journal*, May 31, 2023, p. 1-A.

42 Ibid.

43 Ibid.

44 Ibid.

45 Ibid.

46 Ibid.

47 Ibid.

48 Ibid.

49 Roger Archille, "First Amendment Does Not Protect Employee's Criticism of Supervisor," *SHRM News*, January 26, 2022.

50 Ibid.

51 Ibid.

52 *Doe v. Sex Offender Registry Board*, 11-P-1700 (Mass. Appeals Court (2013). See also: Eric Goldman, "Facebook Rant Against 'Arial' Font Helps Reverse Sex Offender Determination," *Technology and Marketing Law Blog*, November 26, 2013.

53 Ibid.

54 *Tucker v. State of California Department of Education*, 97 F3d 1204 (1996). See also: Barry, *Speechless*, pp. 151–3.

55 *Berry v. Department of Social Services*, 447 F. 3d 642 (2006). See also: Barry, *Speechless*, pp. 152–3.
56 Helen Lewis, "The Magic Kingdom of Ron DeSantis," *The Atlantic,* May 2023, pp. 41–50.
57 Ibid.
58 "Arizona County Elections Leader Promoted Voter Fraud Conspiracies Resigns," *Associated Press Report*, September 19, 2023.
59 "Arkansas School Board Member Officially Resigns Over Anti-Gay Post," *CNN.com*, November 1, 2010. See also: Lori Andrews, *I Know Who You Are and I Saw What You Did: Social Networks and the Death of Privacy* (New York: Free Press, 2011), p. 84.
60 "Arkansas School Board Member Officially Resigns Over Anti-Gay Post."
61 Ibid.
62 Ibid.
63 Rachel Roberts, "Boise Trustee Apologizes, Accepts Penalties for Profane Tweet Directed at Idaho Governor," *Idaho Statesman*, April 10, 2023.
64 Ibid.
65 Tom McLaughlin, "City Social Media Policy Rejected," *Pensacola News Journal,* May 12, 2023, p. 1-A.
66 Ibid.
67 Ibid.
68 Ibid.
69 Ibid.
70 Amanda Marcotte, *Troll Nation* (New York: Skyhorse Publishing, 2018), p. 33.
71 Ibid., p. 34.
72 Ibid., p. 35.
73 *Draper v. Logan County Public Library*, 403 F. Supp. 2d 608 (2003). See also: Barry, *Speechless*, pp. 153–4.
74 *Holodnak v. Avco Corporation*, 514 F. 2d 285 (1975).
75 *George v. Pacific-CSC Work Furlough*, 91 F. 3d 1227 (1996).
76 McWhirter, *Your Rights at Work*, p. 133.
77 Mark Moore, "Woman Fired After Giving Trump's Motorcade the Finger," *New York Post*, October 6, 2017.
78 Charisse Jones, "Can Your Supervisor Force You to Attend Speech by Politician?" *USA Today*, August 23, 2019, p. 2-B.
79 "United Airlines Suspends Pilot Who's a W.Va. Lawmaker Over Hillary Clinton Execution Tweet," *The Columbus Dispatch*, July 19, 2016.
80 Ibid.

81 Lori Kersey, "WV Delegate Calls for Clinton to be Executed," *Charleston Gazette-Mail,* July 16, 2016. See also: "United Airlines Suspends Pilot Who's a W.Va. Lawmaker Over Hillary Clinton Execution Tweet."

82 "United Airlines Suspends Pilot Who's a W.Va. Lawmaker Over Hillary Clinton Execution Tweet."

83 Ballotpedia report on the 2020 gubernatorial election in West Virginia.

84 Jim Miller, "Tax Official's Aide Quits Over 'Hangman' Tweet on Clinton," *The Sacramento Bee*, August 4, 2016.

85 Ibid.

86 Philip Conneller, "Maine Chief Gambling Regulator Suspended for Offensive Treats," *Casino.org*, May 24, 2023.

87 Victor Marchetti, *The CIA and the Cult of Intelligence (*New York: Alfred A. Knopf, 1974).

88 *United States v. Marchetti*, 466 F.2d 1309 (1972).

89 Ibid.

90 Frank Snepp, *Decent Interval (*New York: Random House, 1977).

91 *Snepp v. United States*, 444 U.S. 507 (1980).

92 Gary Berntsen, *Jawbreaker (*New York: Crown Publishing, 2005).

93 Dana Priest, "Suing Over the CIA's Red Pen; Retired Operative Says Agency Unfairly Edited His Book," *The Washington Post,* October 9, 2006, p. A-15.

5

Free Speech in the Military

Personal Expression versus the Doctrine of Military Necessity

The Philadelphia Fifteen

On June 16, 2023, a solemn ceremony was held in the Pentagon's Hall of Heroes, which drew hundreds of Pentagon employees as well as Franklin Parker, assistant secretary of the Navy. The guests of honor were seventy-two-year-old Larry Ponder and other descendants of fifteen African American sailors who lost their lives in naval service during the Second World War or died in their retirement years. The ceremony was part of the Navy's attempt to apologize to the family members for how their ancestors were treated more than eighty years earlier.

In the fall of 1940—a year before the Navy was devastated by the Japanese attack on Pearl Harbor—Ponder's father, John Ponder, was among a group of fifteen Black sailors assigned to a submarine named the *U.S.S. Philadelphia*. Later known as the "Philadelphia Fifteen," they submitted a letter to the editor of a Black civilian newspaper in which they complained about how they were mistreated by white officers and peers. The letter claimed that Naval recruiters had promised them training opportunities and assignments that would lead to advancement, but instead they functioned as waiters and housekeepers. The letter also recommended that Black parents discourage their children from enlisting in the military.[1] "We take it upon ourselves to write this letter, regardless of any action the naval authorities may take or whatever the consequences might be," the letter stated. "We only know that it could not possibly surpass the mental cruelty inflicted upon us on this ship."[2] While the newspaper had a limited circulation, the letter caught the attention of Navy leadership, who ordered the men arrested and discharged from the military.

The expansion of the Second World War in the Pacific caused the issue to be lost, but for those who survived the war, the humiliation extended well into their retirement years. Larry Ponder told *The New York Times* that his father, who died in 1997, was one of the military's first "whistleblowers" and was guilty of nothing more than calling attention to racial discrimination. "All they did was inform the general public about them being mistreated," Ponder said. "They tried to do what was right through the chain of command but it didn't go anywhere, so they wrote that letter."[3] In addition to issuing the public apology, the Navy posthumously changed the status of the sailors' discharges from "undesirable" to "honorable."[4]

Recurring Themes

In a 1993 episode of the television drama *Law & Order*, lawyers in the New York district attorney's office were frustrated by their efforts to bring to justice a murder suspect that was already being prosecuted by a military court. By the end of the episode, the district attorney's office won, and the defendant was tried in a civilian court.[5]

In the real world, jurisdictional disputes between civilian and military courts are not resolved as easily. In general, the majority of cases involving the armed forces—both criminal cases and those concerning free speech—are decided in military courts. And unlike the Philadelphia Fifteen case, conflicts seldom take eight decades to resolve.

As many cases in this chapter illustrate, the concept of "free speech" is applied quite differently in the military as opposed to civilian settings. The reasons behind those tendencies, backed up by decades of court rulings, are similar and overlapping. In the case of the military, superiors claim they need to regulate the speech of subordinates to keep internal order and discipline and maintain the appearance of political neutrality. The military's use of the term "order and discipline" is analogous to civilian employers' use of the term "workplace disruption." In the military, however, the bar for proving the need to maintain order and discipline is lower than a civilian employer's need to prove workplace disruption.

Employment attorney Mark F. Kluger says the concerns of military leaders are no different from those of private employers. "Although some lawyers and legal scholars may disagree, most legal doctrine is not about fairness," Kluger says:

> Private sector employers have a similar rationale for ensuring uniformity in the manner in which employees communicate about the organization. That rationale, while perhaps less noble than that of the uniformed services, is still about survival. Public attacks against an employer from within can lead to its loss of reputation, which can lead to a loss of customers, which can lead to a loss of jobs and ultimately the loss of the business. Employers have a protectable interest in their reputation. Ensuring that their employees don't destroy that interest through negative social media attacks is part of an employer's fiduciary duty.[6]

Because the armed forces are sworn to uphold the values of freedom, especially free speech, they attempt to provide avenues for expression that do not compromise their mission, with the following caveats:

1. *Protecting free speech (up to a point).* In most matters unrelated to "order and discipline" or national security, military personnel enjoy many of the freedoms enjoyed by their civilian counterparts. Some of these freedoms are codified into written regulations, including rules that allow for the distribution of mainstream news publications on military bases as long as they do not demonstrate support for an enemy government, encourage illegal behavior by military personnel, or advocate the overthrow of the federal government. In addition, Article 10, Section 1034 of the U.S. Code protects the right of military personnel to communicate with government officials such as the president or members of Congress as long as those communications do not constitute threats or compromise national security. When communicating with the media, military personnel are encouraged to do so out of uniform and clarify that opinions offered are their own and do not represent an official opinion of the armed forces.[7]

   In the civilian world, the standard for limiting political speech has evolved from "clear and present danger" to "incitement."[8] In military cases, the standard is much lower and is aimed at speech that "interferes with or prevents the orderly accomplishment of the mission or presents a clear danger to loyalty, discipline, mission, or morale of the troops."[9]

2. *Recognizing the difference between speech and conduct.* Much like other applications of free-speech law, in cases involving individuals employed by the military and law enforcement, employers and courts struggle with the fuzzy dividing line between speech and conduct. Simply expressing support for or opposition to a political candidate is considered speech (although not necessarily protected), while participating in a riot at the U.S. Capitol building when your candidate loses is conduct, and is clearly unprotected. That difference has been at the heart of several recent cases involving military personnel expressing support for and participating in the activities of extremist groups.

Despite those theoretical safeguards, support for the free-speech rights of military personnel is still not as stringent as it is for their civilian counterparts, for a number of reasons:

1. *The Doctrine of Military Necessity.* Decades of court rulings have supported the principle that military service is a "unique environment" that requires men and women who work within it to forfeit some of the freedoms their civilian counterparts enjoy. This contrast is easily seen in cases involving free speech. In civilian workplaces, the most common phrase used is "avoiding workplace disruption," but in military workplaces, the equivalent terms are "maintaining order and discipline" and "maintaining unit cohesion and morale." An article in *Free Speech Today*, a Georgetown Law School publication, stated that, "For many soldiers and civilian onlookers, these restrictions constitute a necessary and justifiable trade-off, as soldiers' ability to express themselves is secondary to the national security they were hired to defend."[10]
2. *Civilian courts' deference to military courts.* From the founding of the country through the late 1950s, the Supreme Court repeatedly declined to review cases involving military personnel challenging their working conditions or disciplinary outcomes, stating that it had neither the authority nor interest in second-guessing decisions made by military courts. When Congress enacted the Uniform Code of Military Justice, it included an appeals process that is similar to the federal court system in that it consists of two levels: each branch of the military has its own appeals court (analogous to the circuit courts of appeal), and the Department of Defense offers the overarching Court of Military

Appeals (analogous to the U.S. Supreme Court). Specific to free-speech issues, military personnel have access to the Inspector General Complaints Resolution program, although the focus of the program is to protect whistleblowers. The program is grounded in Article 10 of the United States Code and includes an anti-retaliation provision similar to federal whistleblowing laws. Unlike federal laws applied to civilian whistleblowers, however, the military equivalent protects only criticisms that go through official channels; information disclosed to the media is not protected.[11]

Some legal scholars believe the establishment of the military appeals process gives the U.S. Supreme Court even more reason to continue its "hands-off" approach. It wasn't until 1953, in a case in which two servicemen challenged their court-martials, that the Supreme Court agreed to judicial oversight of military courts and procedures. In that case, as it remains today, the Court's concern is that military personnel are afforded the same due-process rights as civilians.[12]

"Although individuals in the military may have the same claims against the government as have civilians, the (civilian) courts exercise more restraint towards the military than other government entities, both out of institutional respect and also due to the courts' unfamiliarity with the military," wrote law professor Linda Sugin in a 1967 article in *New York University Law Review*.[13] That argument is strongest in cases involving purely military matters that have no parallel in the civilian world. In a 1953 case, for example, the Supreme Court declined to review a case charging unfairness in military promotions.[14]

In a 1962 lecture at the New York University Law School, Chief Justice Earl Warren told students and faculty that "our citizens in uniform may not be stripped of basic rights simply because they have doffed their civilian clothes."[15] Warren did, however, note that under the doctrine of military necessity, also known as the "Orloff Rule" from *Orloff v. Willoughby* (1953), the military can implement its regulations largely outside the purview of judicial review, because the Court's attitude had historically been "hands off."[16]

"It is indisputable that the tradition of our country, from the time of the revolution until now, has supported the military establishment's broad power to deal with its own personnel," Warren said, adding, "The most obvious reason is that Courts are ill-equipped to determine the impact upon discipline that any particular intrusion upon military authority might have."[17]

One example of civilian courts showing deference to military culture occurred in *Goldman v. Weinberger* (1986). In that case, the U.S. Supreme Court ruled that the Air Force could prohibit an Orthodox Jew from wearing a yarmulke in order to maintain uniformity in its dress code. The Court determined that the military's interest in maintaining a cohesive, homogeneous community outweighed an individual's right to wear clothing that represented one's religious observance. Rather than evaluating the military's claim that uniform appearance is essential to its functioning, the Court deferred to the military's judgment[18] (the case is discussed later in this chapter).

In cases involving free speech and related issues, some legal scholars believe this rule of deference should apply only to wartime and not peacetime, but this view is not universally accepted.[19]

3. *Maintaining order and discipline*. As mentioned earlier, this is the military equivalent of a civilian workplace's need to "maintain workplace harmony" and "minimize disruption." Other terms used in these cases include "unit cohesion" and "internal morale."

   "Military personnel inhabit a more tightly regulated sphere of freedoms than their civilian counterparts," wrote a contributor to *Free Speech News*, a Georgetown Law School newsletter.

   "When civilians recite the oath to become a soldier, many of their constitutional rights—including freedom of expression—are restricted."[20] The Georgetown article compared the military rules to a bit of dialogue in the 1995 film *Crimson Tide*, when the submarine commander portrayed by Denzel Washington told his crew that "we're here to preserve democracy—not to practice it."[21]

   In the majority opinion in a 1974 case, Associate Justice William Rehnquist wrote that the different standards are necessary because the military is a "specialized society" separate from the civilian world. "While members of the military are not excluded from the protection granted by the First Amendment, the different character of the military community and of the military mission requires a different application of those protections," Rehnquist wrote. "The fundamental necessity for obedience, and the consequent necessity for imposition of discipline, may render permissible within the military that which would be constitutionally impermissible outside it."[22]

One Pentagon official speaking on the value of "maintaining order and discipline" added that "the military is OK with the idea of free speech but not OK with bullshit . . . and it tends to use the latter term as a noun, verb, adjective, and adverb."[23]

Lawyer Porn

Article 10, Chapter 47 of the U.S. Code, better known as the Uniform Code of Military Justice, is a 756-page tome that underwent nineteen days of debate before being passed by Congress and signed into law by President Harry Truman in 1950. Modern-day attorneys who specialize in UCMJ cases call it "lawyer porn" due to its dense and bureaucratic language.[24] It was passed partly in response to issues arising from American participation in the Second World War and was intended to move military law away from a model of "absolute commander control" and toward a more balanced system more closely resembling the civilian legal arena.[25]

Over the first 175 years of the military's existence, each branch of the military had its own rules of conduct, carrying titles such as the "Army Articles of War" and the "Articles for Government of the Navy," but their enforcement was inconsistent. One of the purposes of the UCMJ was to provide consistency in the language (hence the use of the term "uniform").[26]

Early cases tried under the UCMJ resulted in two principles: first, that appellants must exhaust all possible remedies within the military system before taking their cases to the civilian appeals system; and second, that once in the civilian system, appellants cannot make extraordinary efforts to find courts they believe would be the most sympathetic (what the civilian system refers to as "venue shopping").[27]

There are nine articles within Part X of the UCMJ that involve free speech:

- Article 82 prohibits the solicitation of other military personnel that encourages them to desert or commit acts of misbehavior.
- Article 88 prohibits military personnel from using "contemptuous speech" against the president, vice president, members of Congress, the Secretary of Defense, or any state governor or legislature.

- Article 89 prohibits "disrespect toward superior officers."
- Article 90 prohibits "willingly disobeying a lawful command of his superior officer."
- Article 91 prohibits "insubordinate conduct toward non-commissioned officers."
- Article 92 punishes "failure to obey an order."
- Article 117 prohibits "provoking or reproachful words or gestures."
- Articles 133 and 134 are catch-all rules that prohibit "conduct unbecoming an officer and a gentleman" and "disorders and neglects to the prejudice of good order and discipline."

When it was debated in the U.S. Senate, there was bipartisan skepticism about the necessity of Article 88, with opposition coming from Democrats Estes Kefauver of Tennessee and Wayne Morse of Oregon and Republican Leverett Saltonstall of Massachusetts. Kefauver questioned why Congress should be "immune from criticism," and Morse added that "criticism from people in uniform is a good thing."[28] Saltonstall at first said the article "might be too restrictive," but then added, "I hate to see a fellow called out on Saturday night and say everything against his government, and then on Monday morning he appears in uniform with a great smile on his face and squared-up shoulders."[29]

In a 1968 article in *Harvard Law Review*, military law attorney John G. Kester also questioned the necessity of the article, claiming that many of those charged with that offense were nothing more than "noisy drunks and habitual gripers and blowhards."[30]

Today, Article 88 remains one of the most controversial articles and the most difficult to enforce. In a case similar to those involving Central Intelligence Agency operatives (discussed in Chapter 4), a lieutenant colonel in the Army wrote a book about the Korean War and, based on Air Force regulations, submitted it to the appropriate authorities for security review. The review took more than a year, and when author Melvin Vorhees received the results, he thought many of the Air Force's concerns—mostly the passages critical of General Douglas McArthur—were unfounded. When he published the book through Simon and Schuster without making the required deletions, he was dismissed from the Air Force.

In 1954, the newly formed Court of Military Appeals upheld his conviction based on the "Doctrine of Military Necessity." Addressing the issue of alleged falsity in Vorhees's account of McArthur's conduct of the war, the CMA determined that "it matters little whether the published comments were true or false because the effect on the public would be the same, and the cause would be weakened."[31]

Another notable case occurred during the Vietnam War when Second Lieutenant Henry Howe participated in an anti-war protest outside Fort Bragg Army Base in Texas. Howe was off-duty and wearing civilian clothes, but photographs of him carrying a sign calling President Lyndon Johnson a "fascist" were enough to lead to a general court-martial under Article 88. He was found guilty, sentenced to hard labor, and discharged from the Army. The court based its ruling partly on Howe's position as an officer and determined that soldiers "could hardly be expected to willfully and cheerfully respond to the orders of the appellant where the latter has publicly manifested such disloyalty and contempt to his own superiors."[32] Responding to Howe's claim that his comments on his sign amounted to "political hyperbole," the court ruled that concept applied to civilian cases but not to those involving military personnel.[33]

In 2019, the Supreme Court denied hearing an appeal of the case of *Larrabee v. United States*, which let stand a lower court's ruling that retired service members could be court-martialed for crimes committed after they left the service.[34]

Later that year, one of the most famous retired military men in the country found himself facing a possible Article 88 violation. General James Mattis, retired from the Marine Corps since 2013 and ten months removed from his service as Secretary of Defense, was an invited speaker at the Al Smith Memorial Foundation Dinner in New York City. In an atmosphere in which all of the speakers were expected to satirize public people and events, Mattis chose to target President Trump, the man who appointed him to his former job. Making fun of Trump having avoided the draft because of bone spurs in his feet, Mattis quipped, "I earned my spurs on the battlefield . . . Donald Trump earned his spurs in a letter from his doctor."[35]

The following year, Mattis granted an interview with *The Atlantic* and used the opportunity to criticize the president in a more serious tone. "Donald Trump is the first president in my lifetime who does not try to unite the American people—does not even pretend to try," he told the reporter. "Instead he tried to divide us. We are witnessing the consequences of three years of this deliberate effort. We are witnessing the consequences of three years without mature leadership."[36]

According to a 2021 article in the *Harvard National Security Journal*, Mattis was not alone in his criticism. For more than a year, several retired Army generals and Navy admirals had publicly rebuked the president for his comments about the military and use of the service personnel for photo-ops.[37] Among them was retired Admiral William McRaven, who published an op-ed in *The Washington Post* that blasted Trump for his treatment of the media and said he would "consider it an honor to stand alongside those who have spoken up against the Trump presidency."[38]

Supporters of the president, including some members of Congress, called for an investigation into those public criticisms and contended that those former military personnel should be stripped of their security clearances and retirement benefits and prosecuted under Article 88.[39] While a formal legal decision was never reached, some legal scholars concluded that the comments made by Mattis and the other retired leaders were "professionally inappropriate" but not punishable under the UCMJ.[40]

Disrespect for the office and the officeholder was also a problem for Trump's predecessor. During the presidency of Barack Obama (2009–17), the military sought to punish its active-duty members who were critical of the president either in media interviews, television talk shows, or in their own social media activity.[41]

Obama's approval ratings among military personnel were low, although in line with those of Bill Clinton, the previous Democrat to hold the office. While service members admired Obama for his role in killing terrorist leader Osama bin Laden, many disagreed with his overall record on fighting terrorism, the repeal of the "Don't Ask Don't Tell" policies on gays in the military, and long-term military budget cuts.[42]

In 2012, for example, a Marine based at Camp Pendleton in California was told to take down his Facebook page on which he criticized Obama. Gary Stein had problems with the repeal of "Don't Ask, Don't Tell" as well as the president's overhaul of the health-care system, known formally as the Affordable Care Act and informally as "Obamacare." On the page, he also pledged not to follow any "unlawful orders" the president issued. "Just because I'm a Marine doesn't mean I don't have free speech or can't say my personal opinion about the president or other public official just like anybody else," Stein said. "The Constitution trumps everything else."[43] The Marine Corps didn't agree, however. Faced with charges that he violated Article 88 of the UCMJ and specific Marine Corps rules regarding social media, Stein agreed to delete his Facebook page and faced no further discipline.[44]

Article 88 was also an issue for Trump's successor. In 2022, Marine Lt. Col. Stuart Scheller, Jr. was prosecuted under Article 88 for using social media to criticize President Joe Biden and military leadership during the U.S. withdrawal from Afghanistan in 2021.[45] The seventeen-year veteran was based at Camp Lejeune in North Carolina, but had previous deployments in Afghanistan, pleaded guilty, and agreed to leave the Marine Corps without the formality of the discharge process. But he said publicly, "I did what I did because I thought it was in the best long-term interest of the Marine Corps. Going forward, I am still demanding accountability."[46] Corps officials responded that "proper channels are in place for Marines to raise concerns about accountability via their chains of command, and criticizing leadership on social media is not an acceptable substitute for this."[47]

Experts in military law applauded Scheller for "owning" his comments but condemned him for making his disagreement with military leaders and the president public. "Scheller may disagree strongly with his government's policy, but he has no right to undermine that policy by publicly criticizing it while holding a commission on active duty," wrote Thomas R. Beall, a retired Navy captain, in the *U.S. Naval Institute News*. "He had other options, including resigning his commission and running for Congress. From that political platform he could have expressed his views and even influenced military policy with which he disagrees."[48]

As of early 2024, Scheller has not run for public office but did publish a book based on his opinions, titled *Crisis of Command: How We Lost Trust and Confidence in America's Generals and Politicians*[49] and launched a website "aimed at sparking a dialogue on military leadership and accountability."[50]

Article 88 is often paired with either Article 133 (banning "conduct prejudicial to good order and discipline in the Armed Forces") or Article 134 (addressing "conduct unbecoming an officer and a gentleman"). These regulations have been used to restrict political expression as well as other activities. Also, under the code, military personnel can be severely punished—including dismissal, forfeiture of pay, and imprisonment—for participating in rallies that criticize war efforts, even if they are off duty and dressed as civilians, an issue addressed in *United States v. Howe* (1967).[51]

Article 88 applies only to officers and not enlisted men, based on the belief that officers speak from a position of authority and their comments reflect on the military more than those of enlisted men. "It is difficult for the public to disassociate the speaker from his position in the military," wrote Indiana Law School Professor Edward F. Sherman in a 1971 article in *Hastings Law Journal*. "On the other hand, very few would mistake a second lieutenant or enlisted man as speaking for the Army."[52]

One of the most controversial military-based cases to come to the Supreme Court began in 1981 when a clinical psychologist, who was also an ordained rabbi, was assigned to an Air Force hospital at March Air Force Reserve Base in southern California. S. Simcha Goldman customarily wore a yarmulke, a traditional Jewish head covering, while doing his work. Nothing was said while he was at the hospital, but when he testified as a defense witness at a court martial, the prosecutor cited military regulations and complained to Goldman's commanding officer, who then ordered him to refrain from wearing the yarmulke at work. Goldman sued and, unable to reach a satisfactory outcome in the military justice system, eventually took his case to the civilian court system. He claimed the military dress code violated the free exercise clause of the First Amendment, but surprisingly, the court ruled 5-4 in favor of the Department of Defense. Writing for the majority, Justice William Rehnquist stated that the dress code was evenly applied and non-discriminatory because it banned all head coverings (worn indoors) and not just yarmulkes.[53] In addition, Rehnquist repeated a viewpoint he first stated in a 1974 case (*Parker v. Levy*) when he called the military a "specialized society" entitled to enforce rules that might be viewed as inappropriate in a civilian setting.[54]

Justice Sandra Day O'Connor was among the four dissenting votes, writing that the DOD failed to meet its burden in explaining the harm that would come from granting Goldman an exemption to the dress code.[55] While the fairness of military dress codes is only tangential to the issue of free speech, the case serves as another example of civilian courts being reluctant to second-guess decisions made in military courts.[56]

During the Vietnam War era, several military speech restrictions were unsuccessfully challenged for overbreadth under the First Amendment. In *Parker v. Levy* (1974), for example, an officer was convicted by court-martial for criticizing the military for its role in Vietnam. Howard Levy was a recent medical school graduate who sought to continue his medical training in the Army and was stationed at Fort Jackson in South Carolina. He became disenchanted with his situation and made his feelings public, encouraging young Black soldiers to refuse to go to Vietnam and calling U.S. Special Forces the "murderers of women and children."[57] He was charged with violating three articles of the UCMJ: 90 ("willingly disobeying a lawful command of his superior officer"), 133 ("conduct unbecoming an officer and a gentleman"), and 134 ("disorders and neglects to the prejudice of good order and discipline"). His free-speech case, based on his claim that the articles under which he was prosecuted were overbroad, was unsuccessful, as the Supreme Court ruled that the First Amendment "can be applied differently in the military context because of its distinctive character and purpose."[58]

Following Vietnam, the attention of military and civilian courts turned to politics. In *Greer v. Spock* (1976) and *Brown v. Glines* (1980), the Court upheld other military regulations that restricted or prohibited service personnel or civilians from distributing political materials or organizing political events on military bases without the permission of base commanders. The *Greer* case involved supporters of 1972 presidential candidate Benjamin Spock, a nationally known pediatrician running on the People's Party ticket, whose major issue was opposition to the Vietnam War. Their request to stage a rally and distribute literature was denied, prompting them to sue in federal district court on First Amendment grounds.

When the case reached the Supreme Court, it ruled that the function of military bases was to train personnel and maintain military readiness rather than serving as a forum for political discussions and that a base commander's need to maintain order and discipline outweighed the free-speech rights of outsiders. In his concurring opinion, Chief Justice Warren Burger wrote that "permitting political campaigning on military bases cuts against a 200-year tradition of keeping the military separate from public affairs."[59]

The court also rejected two other claims: (1) that because the military bases were open to members of the public who wanted to visit base museums or other areas, they should similarly be open for political events; and (2) that political speech should have been treated the same as the distribution of magazines and newspapers, which had traditionally been allowed.[60]

The *Brown* case involved Albert Glines, a captain in the Air Force Reserves, who distributed petitions on public property outside of Travis Air Force Base in California. The petitions protested grooming standards for Air Force personnel, and Glines intended to send them to members of Congress and the Secretary of Defense. Nothing was said at first, but when Glines visited Anderson Air Force

Base in Guam and left behind copies of the petition with a colleague, the two were charged with distributing materials without seeking the permission of the base commander. When Glines returned to Travis, he was reassigned to a less prestigious unit, prompting him to sue the base commander in federal district court.

Glines claimed his communication fell within the scope of Article 10, Section 1034 of the U.S. Code, which protected the rights of service personnel to communicate with members of Congress. The trial court and appeals court ruled in his favor, but the U.S. Supreme Court reversed, issuing a hair-splitting ruling that said members of the military may, under Section 1034, communicate with members of Congress with single-signature letters, but may not gather multiple signatures on petitions without permission from their base commanders.[61]

Going to Extremes

Concerns over monitoring what military members do on their own time and out of uniform raise First Amendment concerns: how much of their involvement is conduct, which can be limited, and speech, which cannot (or at least not as much). The U.S. military has struggled for decades to enforce rules prohibiting active-duty members from joining the Ku Klux Klan and other groups espousing white supremacy. A 2019 survey by *Military Times* found that one-third of all active-duty troops said they had "personally witnessed" examples of white nationalism or ideological-driven racism within their ranks."[62]

In the 2008 case of *United States v. Wilcox*, an appeals court ruled against an Army private first class who was charged with violating Article 134 (prohibiting "disorders and neglects to the prejudice of good order and discipline"). Jeremy Wilcox, an Army paratrooper based at Malmstrom Air Force Base in Montana, created an America OnLine (AOL) profile, both for dating purposes and for posting online content promoting white supremacy. One of the women responding to his profile was working undercover for the Army's Criminal Investigative Division. She communicated with Wilcox to gather information on his views and then reported him to his superiors and provided them with transcripts of their conversations. Wilcox was charged with violating Article 134, based on the content of their conversations and his attendance at a Ku Klux Klan rally, which he first denied and later admitted. The Army later added the charge of violating Article 92 based on its allegation that Wilcox had ignored his commanding officer's order to cease trying to recruit other personnel to militant and white supremacist causes. An Army trial court found Wilcox guilty of violating Article 134 (upheld on appeal) but acquitted him of violating Article 92.[63]

That same year, Coast Guard storekeeper Chad Blair, stationed in Massachusetts, was charged with and pleaded guilty to using military computers to access Stormfront, a white supremacist website, and posting flyers on military property to recruit other personnel to white supremacist causes.[64]

Long before the January 6, 2021, attack on the U.S. Capitol, civil rights lawyer Morris Dees wrote to Caspar Weinberger, the Secretary of Defense under President Ronald Reagan, warning him of the large numbers of active-duty military members who were affiliated with the Ku Klux Klan and other white supremacist groups. The 1985 letter was accompanied by photographs of military personnel, including Marines based at Camp Lejeune in North Carolina, participating in KKK rallies.

"It is simply intolerable that members of the U.S. armed forces, sworn to uphold and defend the Constitution of the United States, be allowed to hold membership in an organization which seeks to overthrow the government by violent means," wrote Dees, founder of the Southern Poverty Law Center.[65]

In his 1991 autobiography, Dees recalled recognizing the difficulty in balancing the free-speech rights of military personnel with the rights of the military to maintain order and discipline. That tightrope-walking act is still an issue today.[66] Richard Cohen, Dees's colleague at the SPLC, reviewed his letter and assured him that despite the potential First Amendment conflicts, he was on solid legal ground.[67]

Although it is unknown if it was prompted by Dees's letter, the Federal Bureau of Investigation eventually began monitoring the participation of military personnel in extremist groups and assembling information on attendance at group meetings, gang participation, tattoos, and other symbols.[68]

A few months following the January 6, 2021, incident, news reports found that the crowd that attacked the Capitol included active duty and retired military. Secretary of Defense Lloyd Austin launched an investigation that resulted in a number of proposals, including (1) screening recruits for possible extremist views by asking questions about affiliations and tattoos, (2) creating an investigative unit to weed out extremists, and (3) educating veterans about the dangers of extremist groups that might try to recruit them.[69]

In the two years that followed, journalists who cover the Pentagon and defense-related issues pressed Austin for updates on his proposal, but learned only that the Pentagon had revised its policies and now bans "engaging in electronic and cyber activities regarding extremist activities—including posting, liking, sharing, retweeting, or otherwise distributing content—when such action is taken with the intent to promote or otherwise endorse extremist activities."[70] Early in 2024, the Pentagon released a heavily redacted version of the report, which found that military personnel suspected of being part of extremist groups or plotting to overthrow the government represented a "tiny fraction" of the more than 2 million Americans in uniform.[71]

The underlying themes mentioned in the summary included references to "the need to continue to monitor the trend" and "the need to recognize the difference between speech and conduct," with the former being protected by the First Amendment and the latter unprotected.[72]

Partly as a result of the FBI and Pentagon studies, the country's service academies began including "loyalty to the Constitution" as part of the curriculum and revising their graduation oaths to include that same concept. Some legal scholars see that as another awkward conduct versus speech case, as the rhetoric of extremist groups may lead to conduct that violates the Constitution, but attempts to limit free speech may also do so.[73]

Going Social

Tangentially related to the issue of membership in extremist groups are rules regarding access to social media. In 2009, the U.S. Marine Corps officially banned access to MySpace, Facebook, and Twitter. The rationale for the rule was that the use of social media by members of the military made them more vulnerable than the civilian population to identity theft and may result in intelligence or other confidential information being compromised. In addition, the use of social media might allow foreign powers to recruit military members to act as spies or pass along classified information.[74]

Other branches of the military did not follow suit, based partly on the complaints of inconsistency that might arise if they banned personnel from accessing social media platforms while still using those platforms as recruiting tools. For military personnel serving overseas, there are rules banning the posting of information or photographs that would provide valuable information to enemies, but most personnel stationed in the United States have unfettered access to social media.

Joseph L. Jordan, a Killeen, Texas-based civilian attorney specializing in defending military personnel in court-martials, says the common-sense rule of "think before you post" applies more to military personnel than it does to the general population. "Military members are free to express themselves on social media based on their First Amendment rights," Jordan wrote on his website. "However, anything they post, share, like, or comment on is still subject to the UCMJ and basic rules of service member conduct. This means talking negatively about or being disrespectful toward a superior officer is not allowed. Officials recommend that 'if you wouldn't say it in formation to your leader's face, don't say it online.'"[75]

Whistleblowing in the Military

Two decades after the Philadelphia Fifteen penned their life-changing letter, A. Ernest Fitzgerald became a better-known whistleblower. He had left a successful career on the business side of the aeronautics industry to accept a civilian job at the Pentagon as deputy for management systems for the Air Force. Part of his job was to watch for cost overruns and make sure the Pentagon's share of the taxpayer pie was well spent.

His downfall was that he did his job too well. In short, he found that for the military, waste and overspending were standard operating procedures. Fitzgerald learned that the military's habit of overspending and not attempting to curtail cost overruns began during the Second World War and continued through the Eisenhower and Kennedy administrations. Some degree of waste had to be tolerated, he was told, in order to keep things humming during the Cold War, even when it "created a climate in which scoundrels could flourish."[76]

He focused his attention on the C-5A transport plane, the aircraft for which the production was always behind schedule and always over budget—two problems that only he seemed to notice. He took his concerns first to his superiors and then their superiors, and then testified to a Senate subcommittee about what he called "bureaucratic bungling, chiseling, waste, collusion, and fraud" on the part of defense contractors who built the plane.[77]

As a result of his testimony, Fitzgerald got support from a bipartisan assortment of senators that included Democrats opposed to increases in the Pentagon budget and Republicans who were tolerant of spending increases but skeptical about cost overruns. Chief among his supporters was Senator William Proxmire, a Democrat representing Wisconsin. He even got support from two unlikely individuals—President Richard Nixon and Defense Secretary Melvin Laird. Media coverage of the story included a historical nugget: as a senator in 1951, Nixon had introduced Senate Resolution 1390, a proposal to protect whistleblowers in the Pentagon.

While Fitzgerald was testifying on Capitol Hill and doing media interviews, Department of Defense officials called in the Office of Special Investigations (OSI) to look into his private life in hopes of finding something that might discredit his testimony. After investigators found nothing of interest and with the process of terminating an employee taking too long, his superiors found a quicker way to silence him: they eliminated his position (ironically, the reason he was given for eliminating the position was to reduce costs). But the effect was the same: Fitzgerald was silenced, albeit temporarily.

In the end, Nixon and other administration officials dropped their support when polling told them it might be an issue for his 1972 reelection campaign. That left Fitzgerald with nothing but the prospect of suing the government in federal court—not an easy thing to do for a civilian employee working at the Pentagon. Fitzgerald was eventually reinstated to his job and turned his story into a tell-all book, *The High Priests of Waste*.[78]

In a case with numerous similarities to *Pickering v. Board of Education* (discussed in Chapter 7) but taking place one year earlier, a federal district court ruled in favor of a Navy mechanic who received an honorable discharge after writing a letter to Fred Korth, the secretary of the Navy. Joseph Swaaley, who worked at the Brooklyn Naval Shipyards in New York, accused his superiors of demonstrating favoritism in promotions and hinted that decision-makers were taking bribes. "You do not get a promotion because you deserve it, you must pay for it," he wrote.[79] The Navy based Swaaley's punishment on the alleged falsity of his claims, while Swaaley based his appeal on his First Amendment right to "petition the government for the redress of grievances."[80]

The court never addressed the petition claim but ruled that his comments were protected under the Supreme Court's 1964 *New York Times v. Sullivan* ruling that established the "actual malice" standard for defamation cases involving public figures and large organizations.[81]

The problem faced by military whistleblowers extends to those on the periphery of military service, such as those in other branches of the government that support the military tangentially. One example was Mark Davis, a retired Air Force colonel who functioned as chief prosecutor for terrorism suspects held at Guantanamo Bay in Cuba and had gone on to work for the Congressional Research Service, a function of the Library of Congress. Davis's job was to use his knowledge of military procedures and culture, as well as access to LOC materials, to brief members of the Senate and House of Representatives on issues related to national security.

But he also publicly criticized the process of terrorism prosecutions that took place after his retirement, which caused him to lose his job at the LOC. He sued for reinstatement, claiming a violation of his First Amendment rights, but a federal district court ruled against him.[82]

Another example took place at Veterans' Administration hospitals across the country shortly after the turn of the century when media stories proliferated about long wait times and inefficiency in healthcare provided to veterans. Many of the employees who provided the evidence to journalists found themselves terminated or demoted. That included Dr. Jacqueline Brecht, a urologist working at a VA clinic in Alaska, who was suspended in 2014 after publicly revealing the practice of making waiting times appear shorter by listing phantom appointments and marking those patients as no-shows.[83]

Notes

1 John Ismay, "The Final Fight for Black Sailors Known as the 'Philadelphia 15,'" *The New York Times*, June 16, 2023.

2 Ibid.

3 Ibid.

4 Mark F. Kluger, interview with the author, January 2, 2024.

5 "Conduct Unbecoming," *Law & Order*, Season 3, Episode 17. Original air date March 10, 1993.

6 Danielle Johnson, "Watch What You Say—Don't Violate the UCMJ," *305th Air Mobility Wing Newsletter*, May 4, 2007.

7 Ibid.

8 *Schenck v. United States,* 249 U.S. 47 (1919) and *Brandenburg v. Ohio*, 395 U.S. 444 (1969).

9 *United States v. Wilcox*, 66 M. J. 442 (2008). See also: "Free Speech and Social Media Issues Affecting Military Members," Air Force JAG publication, date unknown.
10 Jaime Moore-Carrillo, "Guns and Gags: How the Military Can Unduly Curb the Free Speech Rights of Soldiers," *Free Speech Today*, date unknown.
11 Johnson, "Watch What You Say."
12 *Burns v. Wilson,* 346 U.S. 137 (1953). See also: Earl Warren, "The Bill of Rights and the Military," Address at New York University Law School, given February 1, 1962; later reprinted in *United States Air Force JAG Bulletin*, May–June 1962, pp. 6–21.
13 Linda Sugin, "First Amendment Rights of Military Personnel: Denying Rights to Those Who Defend Them," *New York University Law Review* 62 (October 1967): pp. 855–89.
14 *Orloff v. Willoughby*, 345 U.S. 83 (1953). See also: Sugin, "First Amendment Rights of Military Personnel."
15 Warren, "The Bill of Rights and the Military." See also: *Orloff v. Willoughby.*
16 Warren, "The Bill of Rights and the Military."
17 *Goldman v. Weinberger*, 106 S. Ct. 1310 (1986).
18 Sugin, "First Amendment Rights of Military Personnel." See also: *Goldman v. Weinberger.*
19 Moore-Carrillo, "Guns and Gags."
20 Ibid.
21 Ibid.
22 *Parker v. Levy*, 417 U.S. 733 (1974).
23 Mark Sheffield, "Fifty Years of the UCMJ," *Independent News* (Pensacola, FL), May 6, 2000.
24 Ibid.
25 Edmund Morgan, "The Background of the Uniform Code of Military Justice," *Vanderbilt Law Review* 6 (1953): pp. 169–85. See also: Pavin S. Krishnamurthy and Javier Perez, "Contemptuous Speech: Rethinking the Balance Between Good Order and Discipline and the Free Speech Rights of Retired Military Officers," *Harvard National Security Journal* 12 (2021): pp. 288–328.
26 Krishnamurthy and Perez, "Contemptuous Speech." See also: Edward F. Sherman, "The Military Courts and Servicemen's First Amendment Rights," *Hastings Law Journal* 22 (January 1971): pp. 325–73.
27 Sherman, "The Military Courts and Servicemen's First Amendment Rights."
28 John G. Kester, "Soldiers Who Insult the President: An Uneasy Look at Article 88 of the Uniform Code of Military Justice," *Harvard Law Review* 81 (June 1968): pp. 1697–769.
29 Ibid.
30 Ibid.

31 *United States v. Vorhees*, 4 U.S.C.M.A. 509 (1954). See also: Sherman, "The Military Courts and Servicemen's First Amendment Rights."

32 *U.S. v. Howe*, 37 C.M.R. 555 (1967). See also: Sherman, "The Military Courts and Servicemen's First Amendment Rights."

33 *U.S. v. Howe*. See also: Sherman, "The Military Courts and Servicemen's First Amendment Rights."

34 *Larrabee v. United States*, 139 U.S. 1164 (2019).

35 Tom McElroy, "Mattis Laughs at Trump at Charity Gala," *Associated Press Report*, October 17, 2019. See also: Krishnamurthy and Perez, "Contemptuous Speech."

36 Jeffrey Goldberg, "James Mattis Denounces Trump, Describes Him as a Threat to Democracy," *The Atlantic*, June 3, 2020. See also: Krishnamurthy and Perez, "Contemptuous Speech."

37 Krishnamurthy and Perez, "Contemptuous Speech."

38 William H. McRaven, "Revoke My Security Clearance Too, Mr. President," *The Washington Post*, August 16, 2018. See also: Krishnamurthy and Perez, "Contemptuous Speech."

39 Krishnamurthy and Perez, "Contemptuous Speech."

40 Ibid.

41 Kenneth T. Walsh, "Military Members Hold Negative View of Obama," *U.S. News and World Report*, January 9, 2017.

42 Ibid.

43 "Marine's Obama Criticism Tests Free Speech Rules," *CNN.com*, March 8, 2012.

44 Ibid.

45 Thomas R. Beall, "Morality, Duty, and Military Ethics: The Case of Lieutenant Colonel Scheller," *U.S. Naval Institute News*, December 2021.

46 Ibid.

47 Ibid.

48 Ibid.

49 Stuart Scheller, *Crisis of Command: How We Lost Trust and Confidence in America's Generals and Politicians* (New York: Knox Press, 2022).

50 Todd South, "Marine Vet Tells His Side of the Story in New Book," *Marine Times*, October 31, 2022.

51 *U.S. v. Howe*, 37 C.M.R. (1967).

52 Sherman, "The Military Courts and Servicemen's First Amendment Rights."

53 *Goldman v. Weinberger*.

54 *Parker v. Levy*. See also: *Goldman v. Weinberger*.

55 *Goldman v. Weinberger*.

56 C. Thomas Dienes, "When the First Amendment is Not Preferred: The Military and Other 'Special Contexts,'" *University of Cincinnati Law Review* 56 (1988): pp. 779–842.

57 *Parker v. Levy*. See also: Daniel J. Imwinkelried and Donald N. Zillman, "An Evolution in the First Amendment: Overbreadth Analysis and Free Speech Within the Military Community," *Texas Law Review* 42 (1975): pp. 52–70.

58 *Greer v. Spock*, 424 U.S. 828 (1976). See also: Sugin, "First Amendment Rights of Military Personnel."

59 *Greer v. Spock*.

60 *Brown v. Glines*, 444 U.S. 348 (1980).

61 Ibid.

62 Kali Holloway, "White Nationalist Hate Is Infiltrating Our Police," *The Nation*, November 15, 2022.

63 *United States v. Wilcox*, 66 M.J. 442 (2008).

64 *United States v. Blair*, Case CGCMG 0229 (2008).

65 Morris Dees and Steve Fiffer, *A Season for Justice* (New York: Simon & Schuster, 1991), pp. 269–70.

66 Ibid.

67 Ibid., p. 270.

68 Will Carless, "Extremism in Military Still Goes Unchecked," *USA Today*, July 28, 2023, p. 1-A.

69 Ibid.

70 Ibid.

71 Gary Fields, "Military Academies Focus on Loyalty to the Constitution," *Associated Press Report*, January 21, 2024.

72 Carless, "Pentagon Extremism Report Is Finally Out," *USA Today*, December 28, 2023, p. 2-A.

73 Fields, "Military Academies Focus on Loyalty to the Constitution."

74 Noah Shachtman, "Marines Ban Twitter, MySpace, Facebook," *Wired*, August 3, 2009.

75 Law firm of Joseph L. Jordan website (www.jordanucmjlaw.com).

76 Kenneth Walters, "Your Employees' Right to Blow the Whistle," *Harvard Business Review*, July–August 1975, pp. 26–34 and 161–3.

77 Ibid.

78 Ernest Fitzgerald, *The High Priests of Waste* (New York: Norton Press, 1972).

79 "Fired U.S. Employee Wins Plea," *United Press International Report*, May 19, 1967.

80 *Swaaley v. United States*, 376 F. 2d 857 (1967).

81 Ibid. See also: *New York Times v. Sullivan*, 376 U.S. 255 (1964).

82 David K. Shipler, *Freedom of Speech: Mightier Than the Sword* (New York: Alfred A. Knopf, 2015), p. 15.

83 Eric Lichtblau, "V.A. Punished Critics on Staff, Doctors Assert," *The New York Times*, June 15, 2014.

6

Free Speech for First Responders

Personal Expression versus Public Confidence

Walking the Beat

In 1892, John J. McAuliffe was a police officer in the tiny hamlet of New Bedford, Massachusetts, when he began to make extemporaneous speeches, while walking his beat, that supported the opponent of the incumbent mayor in an upcoming election. If he had stopped with simple conversation, it might have gone unnoticed, but the case became more complicated when he began soliciting donations on behalf of candidates and causes. The police chief and mayor ordered him to stop, but he refused, resulting in his termination. He sued, claiming the mayor violated his First Amendment rights. The case eventually made its way to the Massachusetts Supreme Court, where Justice Oliver Wendell Holmes (a future U.S. Supreme Court justice who later became a free-speech advocate) quipped that the plaintiff "had a constitutional right to talk politics, but did not have a constitutional right to be a police officer."[1]

The McAuliffe case remained the standard precedent in cases involving the free-speech rights of law-enforcement officers for nearly a century. It was not until the 1990s that state and federal courts began ruling in favor of law-enforcement officers in about half the cases, and three decades later that split remains in effect. The deciding factors include where and when the communication took place and whether it was clear to the listener if the officer was speaking as a private citizen or government employee.

Recurring Themes

Placing this chapter on free-speech issues for law-enforcement personnel and first responders immediately following the one on free-speech issues in the military is not a coincidence. That placement is because of one important factor they have in common. It's not because they are both male-oriented and often include a macho image and culture. It's because, while technically part of the government, branches of the military and law-enforcement agencies at all levels employ people who do not benefit from the same free-speech rights as their counterparts in other areas of government.

In law-enforcement circles, superiors limiting the speech of their subordinates often cite the need to maintain workplace civility as well as to present a positive and non-controversial image to the public being served. This chapter includes several cases of law-enforcement officers prohibited from displaying political buttons or religious symbols on their uniforms or political yard signs in front of their homes. Much like in the military, the rationale is the need to maintain an image void of any symbols that might imply the agency for which the officers work is endorsing a political or religious viewpoint.

Some themes governing how free-speech cases in law enforcement are decided include:

1. *Free-speech concerns outweigh concerns over discipline and morale.* While the military hierarchy emphasizes the need to maintain "order and discipline" and maintain "political neutrality," those same values apply to law-enforcement agencies. When challenged in court, however, rules limiting free speech for those public servants do not hold up as often as they do in cases involving the military. Over the last half-century, there have been at least five cases involving employees fired for simply criticizing department policy or making other controversial statements, and in all five cases, those employees were reinstated by the courts.
2. *Disallowance for personal grievances.* Much like the cases discussed in Chapter 4, whistleblowing provisions and other rules regarding free speech in law-enforcement circles require that such behavior be disallowed if it is based on personal grievances rather than constructive comments on public policy. Several examples involving law-enforcement personnel are included in this chapter.

3. *Maintaining political and religious neutrality.* As it does with members of the military, this rule prohibits law-enforcement officers from wearing political messages on their uniforms or displaying them in their offices or cubicles. In some jurisdictions, law-enforcement officers are prohibited from displaying political bumper stickers on their personal vehicles (if parked on department property) or yard signs in front of their private residences.

   One parallel to the "political neutrality" issue concerns the First Amendment's establishment clause, as in the case of a police officer wearing a cross on his uniform; the concern of his supervisors was that the presence of the cross might be perceived as the police department's endorsement of a religious viewpoint. That case is discussed later in this chapter.
4. *Maintaining public trust.* The issue of public trust is a concern in cases where law-enforcement officers show poor judgment on their social media pages and publicly available YouTube videos. Many of those cases, discussed later in this chapter, involve either sexual content or expressions of racial supremacy. The latter is especially problematic when law-enforcement officers make social media comments about racial issues in their off-duty hours and then serve a racially diverse population while at work.

   Closely related to the issue of officers making racially insensitive remarks on social media is that of officers' membership in extremist groups spreading white supremacy content online.
5. *Concerns over public access to call records.* In cases involving the use of cellular telephones and similar devices by law-enforcement officers, administrators are concerned that the content of their communications may be subject to public records requests and may compromise the integrity of ongoing investigations or litigation.
6. *Concern for witness credibility.* One lesser-used justification for limiting the speech rights of law-enforcement officers is the concern that when officers are called to testify in the criminal trials of those they arrested, defense lawyers may use the material posted on their blogs or other social media platforms to challenge their credibility.

Free Speech and Internal Morale

In the 1980s, Baltimore police officer Robert Berger was also a part-time musician performing in local taverns wearing blackface and doing an Al Jolson impersonation. The police department asked him to stop, contending his performance showed racial insensitivity, but he claimed the department's requests violated his First Amendment rights. A federal appeals court agreed, determining that Berger's right of artistic expression outweighed the police department's interests in maintaining the image of the department or preventing his coworkers from being offended.[2]

The 1987 case of *Rankin v. McPherson* began six years earlier with an assassination attempt on then president Ronald Reagan. Ardith McPherson, a nineteen-year-old clerk in the county constable's office in Harris County, Texas, heard the news on the radio and told her coworkers, "If they go for him again, I hope they get him."[3] Another employee was upset by the remark and told Constable Harold Rankin, who fired McPherson. She sued the constable in federal district court, which led to a decision in favor of Rankin, who argued that McPherson's termination was necessary to "maintain morale, efficiency, and discipline in the workplace."[4]

A circuit court of appeals reversed that decision, determining that McPherson's low position on the organizational chart meant her comment carried little weight, and the fact that it was heard by only a few coworkers negated Rankin's claim.[5]

Rankin appealed the case to the Supreme Court, claiming that the firing of McPherson was based on the fact that the comment demonstrated that "she was not a suitable employee to have in a law enforcement agency."[6]

The Supreme Court affirmed the ruling of the circuit court, ruling 5-4 that McPherson's free-speech rights outweighed Rankin's concerns and that her comments were related more to her disapproval of the president's policies than a direct threat to his safety. One of the dissenting justices was Antonin Scalia, a Reagan appointee, who wrote that McPherson's comments appeared to "support the idea of assassination" and that "no law enforcement agency is required by the First Amendment to permit one of its employees to 'ride with the cops and cheer for the robbers.'"[7]

Policy, Performance, and Personal Grievance

Between 1951 and 1973, four Supreme Court cases upheld the First Amendment rights of first responders to publicly criticize their supervisors for their job performance.

The case of *City of St. Petersburg v. Pfeiffer* began late in 1949 when firefighter Frank Pfeiffer told his coworkers that he had little confidence in the fire chief's ability to manage the department. When the city suspended him for ninety days, he sued in state court and won, prompting the city to appeal. After eighteen months of litigation, the Florida Supreme Court agreed with the lower court, determining that "civil service cannot be expected to compel personal admiration of one's superiors."[8]

The 1970 case of *Muller v. Conlisk* began when a police officer in Chicago reported to his supervisors the problem of his coworkers appropriating for their own use stolen items recovered as part of their work. When his supervisors failed to act, he took his concerns to a local television station, which interviewed him and not only reported his concerns, but quoted him as saying the failure to follow up on his concerns was part of a "cover-up."[9]

He was quickly terminated for making "derogatory comments reflecting on the image or reputation of the Chicago Police Department." A federal court ruled that he should be reinstated on the grounds that the rule about making "derogatory comments" was "constitutionally overbroad."[10]

That same year, in *Brukiewa v. Police Commissioner of Baltimore*, a state court in Maryland ruled in favor of a police officer who criticized departmental leadership in an interview with a local television news station. Eugene Brukiewa was a highly decorated officer and highly regarded by his peers and superiors—until he became president of the local police union. He wrote a fourteen-page position paper that was circulated within the department and among the local media. When he and another police officer participated in a June 19, 1968, television interview, they blasted Police Commissioner Donald Pomerleau for his restructuring of the department, claiming that it was a "criminal waste of money" and endangered the lives of officers.[11]

Pomerleau suspended Brukiewa for violating the rules and regulations of the police department, based on "conduct unbecoming a member of the Baltimore Police Department and prejudicial to and tending to undermine good order, efficiency, or discipline of the department."[12] Citing the *Pickering* case (discussed in Chapter 7), the Maryland Court of Appeals negated the suspension, determining that none of the comments Brukiewa made in the position paper or in the television interview were false or defamatory and that the First Amendment "protected outspoken policemen despite their paramilitary status."[13]

In the 1973 case of *Dendor v. Board of Fire and Police Commissioners,* a firefighter in the Chicago suburb of Northbrook, Illinois, was terminated after saying in public meetings that the town's fire marshal "did not know how to manage the department" and predicted that his lack of direction would "end in disaster." The department justified the firing of Raymond Dendor because his continued presence "would be seriously detrimental to the discipline, morale, and efficiency of the Fire Department."[14] When Dendor sued, he was reinstated when the court found that the city failed to prove any disruption had taken place or might take place and that its claim did not "justify the impairment of free speech."[15]

There were no notable cases of rank-and-file police officers and firefighters getting in trouble for nearly three decades after the *Dendor* case. The trend of these individuals winning their cases ended in 2009, with a case of a police officer's online conduct creating problems for his real-life job.

In Brooklyn, New York, a police officer posted comments on his MySpace page about his theories on how to deal with suspects, many of them inconsistent with acceptable police practice. Vaughn Ettienne, an eighteen-year police veteran, was described by his friends and police colleagues as "polite and thoughtful," but the forty-four-year-old bodybuilder became profane and confrontational when he mused online about the current state of law enforcement. Commenting on arrest scenes from reality television shows and videos on YouTube, Ettienne said that police should never strike suspects in handcuffs, but instead do so before the handcuffs are on. "If you were going to hit a cuffed suspect, at least get your money's worth," he wrote.[16]

Ettienne never received more than light reprimands for his online commentary and was never ordered to stop posting or delete any posts. "I'm not saying it was the best of things to do in retrospect," he told *The New York Times*. "You want to run your mouth with the best of them . . . stupidity on the Internet is there for everyone to see for all times in perpetuity. That's the case for me. There were hundreds of comments I made that were positive."[17]

The comments that caused the most problems for Ettienne were ones in which he described himself as "devious" and compared himself to the character of a police officer portrayed by Denzel Washington in the 2001 film, *Training Day.* [18]

When a man whom Ettienne arrested on suspicion of stealing a motorcycle while carrying a loaded gun went on trial, his defense attorney introduced the officer's online rantings to portray him as a "rogue cop" and cited Ettienne's Facebook admission that he was "watching Training Day to brush up on police procedure."[19] The attorney accused Ettienne and his partner of planting the gun on his client, beating him, and breaking three of his ribs.[20]

"You have your Internet persona, and you have what you actually do on the street," Ettienne told local media after the suspect was acquitted. "What you say on the Internet is all bravado talk, like what you say in a locker room . . . he (the suspect's attorney) tied his defense to the story in the movie. It was a masterful piece of fantasy, but it was one that the jury bought."[21] After the case, Ettienne continued to make online comments about law-enforcement issues but pledged to do so anonymously.[22]

That same year, Maria Gresham was a police officer in Atlanta when she made what she thought was a routine arrest of a fraud and identity theft suspect after he tried to pass a fraudulent check at an electronics store. She was unaware that the suspect, Jeriel Scrubb, was the nephew of Barbara Floyd, a senior officer in the police department. When Gresham and Scrubb arrived at the police station for processing, Floyd took over the case and arranged for Scrubb to be released.

The following week, Gresham described the incident on Facebook and questioned the ethics of what happened. "Who would like to hear the story of how I arrested a forgery perp at Best Buy?" the post read. "Only to find out later he was the nephew of an Atlanta Police Investigator who stuck her ass in my case and obstructed it. Who thinks this is unethical?"[23]

In January 2010, Gresham received a written reprimand for violating the Atlanta Police Department's policy—applied to social media or any other venue—that prohibited employees from criticizing coworkers or the department except through official channels. Nothing else was said about the issue until 2012, when Gresham was denied a promotion, which she felt she deserved. She sued the city of Atlanta for violation of her First Amendment rights and retaliation.

A federal court denied both claims, based mostly on its determination that her comments were based on personal grievance rather than public interest and its agreement that the department's policy was reasonable.[24]

On May 1, 2012, a Pearl, Mississippi police officer named Mike Walter was killed in the line of duty. A few days later, hundreds of his coworkers in Pearl and officers from surrounding counties who had never met him attended his funeral. That would have been the end of the story if it had not been for what happened with officers in Greenville, a town 123 miles away. They were not allowed to attend the event, being told by Chief Freddie Cannon that budgetary considerations would not allow officers time off or the use of departmental vehicles to get there.

That didn't sit well with Susan Graziosi, a twenty-five-year veteran of the Greenville Police Department, and she said so in an open letter to Mayor Chuck Jordan that was published on the city's Facebook page. "This is totally unacceptable," she wrote. "Mr. Mayor, can we please get a leader that understands that a department sends officers to a funeral of an officer killed in the line of duty?"[25]

The GPD terminated her, claiming she had no right to criticize the police chief's budgetary decision. When she sued the city, she claimed that (1) she was speaking not as a city employee but as a private citizen, and (2) her comments dealt with a matter of public concern, which under the *Pickering* standard would have provided First Amendment protection. The trial court ruled against her on both factors, noting that her letter used the terms "we" and "our" in reference to the police department too many times for her comments to be construed as her own.[26]

The court agreed with GPD's determination that because she was not exposing waste or fraud in the budget, but rather her personal disagreement with a budgetary decision, it could not be considered a matter of public concern.

The court then cited a familiar theme: the city's interest in maintaining public confidence in its police department outweighed Graziosi's right to inform the public of her disagreement with the decision. In short, the court drew a fine line between a person discussing a "matter of public concern" and a "personal rant." Specifically, the court pointed to Graziosi's suggestion that the police chief needed to "get the hell out of the way."[27]

A few hours after pro-Trump rioters stormed the U.S. Capitol on January 6, 2021, a civilian public information officer for the Franklin County Sheriff's Office used his personal Facebook page to criticize the response of the Capitol Police in failing to curtail the violence.

"Law enforcement freely letting mobs storm the Capitol Building, not stopping domestic terrorists from desecrating the House and Senate Chambers, and even taking selfies with the Trumpies," wrote Marc Gofstein, who was also a candidate for Columbus City Council. "If this was a BLM (Black Lives Matter) protest, we'd be seeing tanks and mass casualties. White privilege at its worst."[28]

The next morning, Gofstein was called into a meeting with Sheriff Dallas Baldwin and Chief Deputy Rick Minerd and given a choice: resign or be fired. Gofstein chose to resign, ending his four-year stint with the sheriff's office. But it didn't stop him from commenting on the events. "I completely stand by what I posted and what the world saw," he wrote in his next Facebook post. "The officers at the Capitol failed to do their jobs and instead, let the mob rule. The raw emotion of what happened inspired me to comment, and I will never apologize for that."[29]

Gofstein did issue a semi-apology, however, for the difficult position in which he put his boss. The sheriff, however, told other employees and the local media that Gofstein clearly violated the department's social media policy, and for that, there could be no forgiveness. "Our policy prohibits off-duty social media comments that would negatively affect the office, damage morale, or hurt our ability to protect the Franklin County families who count on us," the sheriff's official statement read. Gofstein's posts were especially harmful, the sheriff added, as his responsibilities included working with the local media, and his comments might harm his credibility.[30]

In 2021, Shaina Kirkland was a patrol officer with the police department in Maryville, a suburb of Knoxville, Tennessee. However, she had previously worked for the Blount County Sheriff's Office, where she had an adversarial relationship with Sheriff James Berrong, resulting in her being banned from attending BCSO training events. After moving to the city police department, she launched a social media attack against Berrong, suggesting that she was banned from training because he assumed she did not vote for him. After ignoring several warnings to stop posting, Kirkland was terminated by the city of Maryville. A federal district court ruled in December 2022 that the police department's interests in maintaining a good working relationship with the sheriff's department outweighed Kirkland's free-speech rights.[31] That decision was upheld on appeal by a circuit court.[32]

In a similar case in Florida the following year, a sheriff's deputy was fired for criticizing his supervisor, the county sheriff, for reorganizing the agency. Frank Williams had just returned to duty after a three-month hiatus during which he recovered after being shot in the line of duty. Williams wrote on his Facebook page that Sheriff Clovis Watson's plans for the Alachua County Sheriff's Office were "disruptive and unnecessary" and compared the sheriff's lack of rapport with deputies to a "domestic violence relationship."[33] An internal affairs investigation found that Williams's post violated the department's social media policy as it "undermined the public respect and detracts from the mission of the ACSO."[34]

Political Neutrality

A bizarre case involving the free speech of law-enforcement personnel began with an election for county sheriff in a rural community in Oklahoma in 1996. Paula Horstkoetter and Kimberly Dean invited Les Morton, a candidate for Woodward County Sheriff, to place campaign signs in their yards. The problem was that their husbands were officers in the Oklahoma Highway Patrol, and the department's policy forbade employees from being involved in political campaigns, which included the display of yard signs.[35]

The OHP's insistence that the women remove the signs began a two-year legal battle that hinged on one critical issue: While the policy clearly applied to the employees, could it extend far enough to include spouses? It also resulted in a Catch-22 conundrum: If the wives took responsibility for the signs, the OHP could not punish their husbands; but if they claimed that in court, they could not win a lawsuit because the threat of harm (in this case, termination) applied only to their husbands.[36]

The Horstkoetter home was owned jointly by the husband and wife, while the Dean home was owned solely by the husband. The men's supervisors claimed, and the trial court agreed, that ownership of the homes did not matter, as the public would not know those details. A federal district court dismissed the women's cases, agreeing with the OHP's claim that maintaining the perception of political neutrality was more important than the free speech rights of their officers—or their spouses.[37]

In 1998, a federal appeals court affirmed the ruling of the lower court.[38]

In June 2011, a citizen in Delta, Colorado, noticed a provocative bumper sticker on a truck parked in front of the Work Release Facility of the Delta County Jail. The citizen felt the sticker, which read, "Still Voting Democrat? You're Stuck on Stupid," insulted him based on his political beliefs. He complained to Sheriff Fred McKee and asked if he agreed with the sentiment of the sticker.[39]

McKee traced the ownership of the truck to Michael Williams, a detention officer who had worked in that building for less than a year, and asked him to remove the sticker or park in a place where the political statement would not be associated with the county.

Williams continued to park in front of the building but agreed to cover the sticker with tape each day before coming to work. That plan worked for two months, but one day he forgot, prompting the same citizen to complain again. After a few more incidents in which Williams came to work with the sticker uncovered and McKee told him to cover it, Williams requested a leave of absence, citing work-related stress that had been made worse by the conflict over the sticker. Instead of granting Williams leave, McKee terminated him.

Two years later, Williams was hired as a property appraiser with Delta County. Within a few months, he began talking to his new coworkers about his plans to sue the sheriff over his dismissal. As his case proceeded through its preliminary phases, those coworkers complained to Tax Assessor Debbie Griffith that Williams was "over-sharing" information about the suit.[40]

Citing "workplace disruption," Griffith terminated Williams, prompting him to file a second suit against Delta County, claiming both firings violated his First Amendment rights. The county asked the court for summary judgment in both cases. On the matter of the bumper sticker, the county claimed the sheriff's interest in maintaining the appearance of political neutrality outweighed Williams's right to free speech. The court agreed and added that a bumper sticker simply supporting or opposing a political candidate or party would have qualified for First Amendment protection, but one which called opponents "stupid" did not.[41] In the case against Griffith, the county claimed the assessor was within her rights in terminating Williams based on the "workplace disruption principle," and the court agreed with that position as well.[42]

The general rule that law-enforcement agencies can limit the free speech of their employees based on the need for political neutrality is not absolute, however. Two cases decided nearly three decades apart illustrate this possibility.

In a 1994 case in Leavenworth, Kansas, three members of the city's police force were successful in a lawsuit against their department after two of them were reprimanded for violating a policy prohibiting them from participating in political activities, even if that participation took place in their off-duty hours. A third employee, a non-uniformed civilian, did not participate in any political activities but joined the suit, claiming that the policy created a "chilling effect" that would have prevented her from doing so if she chose to in the future.[43]

Officers Gregory Ruff and Russell Wood were closely following the city commission's consideration of bringing the city under the state's Public Employer-Employee Relations Act, a move that would have enhanced employees' benefit packages and made it easier for their unions to bargain with the state. Wood was president of the Fraternal Order of Police and advocated for the city to adopt PEERA. Following a commission meeting at which it was rejected, he spoke to a reporter from a local newspaper and announced his support for two candidates planning to seek election to the commission that fall and who were promising to take a second look at PEERA. The following week, Ruff and Wood designed an FOP-funded advertisement that appeared in two local newspapers—one daily and one weekly—that supported the two candidates and explained the benefits of PEERA.

Citing a policy that prohibited city employees from being involved in politics, Police Chief Lemoine Doehring placed letters of reprimand in both officers' personnel files and suspended them pending an internal affairs investigation. That process found that even though Ruff and Wood did the work on their own time and used their own computer equipment, their activity was still prohibited because it caused disruption within the department and created the appearance that all members of the police force agreed with their support of the candidates.[44]

Ruff and Wood sued the city of Leavenworth in federal district court, which led to a lengthy and highly detailed ruling. The first two-thirds of the written document created the appearance of supporting the police department, as it hit on familiar themes, including maintaining trust with the public and avoiding the appearance of political partisanship. It even cited Justice Oliver Wendell Holmes's quote from an 1892 Massachusetts Supreme Court case in which he wrote that a police officer "may have a constitutional right to talk politics, but has no constitutional right to be a policeman."[45] It also determined that "the city has a strong interest in ensuring that its employees 'enforce the law without bias or favoritism' for or against any political party or group" and that the city "has a right to ensure that the administration and enforcement of the law not be, nor even appear to be, influenced or affect by political associations employees attempt to foster."[46]

But in its final pages, the ruling took an unexpected turn and pointed out that "an employee does not abandon his or her First Amendment rights simply by agreeing to work for a public entity."[47] The court found the city's policy "unconstitutionally overbroad and vague" in that it failed to adequately define the behaviors that it sought to prohibit. One of its concerns was that while the current case was based on good intentions, future police chiefs and other city leaders might use the policy arbitrarily and for less admirable reasons. The court also agreed with the position of the third plaintiff, evidence custodian Linda Sanders, who claimed the policy would cause her to "think twice" about expressing her own political views.[48]

Twenty-seven years later and two states to the south, a similar case unfolded in El Paso, Texas, when a county sheriff was unable to defend himself in a lawsuit filed by a deputy who allegedly supported the sheriff's opponent for reelection.

The plaintiff was Keith Duda, a deputy in the El Paso County Sheriff's Office, who was heard asking coworkers whether they planned to vote for the incumbent sheriff, Bill Elder, in his 2018 reelection campaign. Duda did not wear campaign buttons nor display yard signs in support of Elder's opponent, but the sheriff knew Duda had often criticized him and other EPSO administrators while on duty. Duda was then identified as a source for a newspaper article describing sexual harassment within the department and cases in which officers who participated in off-duty political activities were punished or not punished based on which candidates they supported.[49]

Duda was terminated based on both the leaking of information to the press and his involvement in political activities. When Duda sued for wrongful termination and retaliation, the court ruled in his favor based on three factors: the sheriff could not establish that Duda's political activity disrupted the workplace or affected department morale, the sheriff's actions were based more on self-interest than a genuine concern for the image of the department, and while department policy did prohibit political activity, it was not enforced in a neutral manner.[50]

Religious Neutrality

In 2001, a police officer in Arlington, Texas, was fired for refusing to remove a gold cross pin from his uniform, which violated the department's uniform policy. Before his termination, his superiors offered him two alternatives for expressing his Christian beliefs on his uniform: wearing it underneath his shirt collar or wearing instead a ring or bracelet expressing the same beliefs. They also offered to transfer George Daniels to an office job where he would have little public contact and could wear whatever he wanted with his civilian attire. He refused all the alternatives and sued for reinstatement, claiming his termination amounted to discrimination based on his religious beliefs. The department was able to successfully defend itself based on a history of consistently enforcing the rule against all infractions—religious or political. If the department had allowed some political or religious viewpoints to be expressed while not allowing others, Daniels would have had a much stronger case.[51] In hearing the case, the court found itself trying to resolve a conflict between two clauses of the First Amendment: the free exercise clause, which prohibits the government from limiting religious expression, and the establishment clause, which prohibits the government from siding with one religion's viewpoint over another. In the end, the court based its ruling partly on the latter, stating that "visibly wearing a cross pin—religious speech that receives great protection in civilian life—takes on an entirely different cast when viewed in the context of a police uniform."[52]

The case was mirrored closely in 2006 in the Trevor Keezor/Home Depot case (discussed in more detail in the Introduction). In that case, the court did not have to deal with the establishment clause because Home Depot was a private, not a public, employer.[53] But it reached a similar conclusion on the matter of free exercise because the company had a track record of banning all religious and political expressions and did not discriminate against any.

Questionable Judgments

In 2000, a San Diego police officer was fired after his supervisors discovered that he was selling videotapes online showing himself stripping out of his police uniform and masturbating. His supervisors also did not like his email address, Code3stud@aol.com. They gave him the opportunity to delete the online listings, and after he refused to do so, they terminated him.

The officer sued in federal district court and lost, then won at the ninth circuit court of appeals. That court determined that the content of the tapes was explicit but not obscene, did not disrupt the workplace, did not use police department computers (although the court did note the use of a uniform), and was a frivolous expression not related to a personal grievance.[54] The U.S. Supreme Court overturned and ruled in favor of the police department, determining that the officer's conduct was not related to a matter of "public concern" and that its decision "was not even close call."[55]

Two decades later, an officer with the Minneapolis Police Department met a similar fate over a similar side job. An unnamed female officer was earning extra money through OnlyFans, a website that allows amateur filmmakers to produce and star in their own soft-core pornographic videos and charge subscribers for access. Unlike Roe, who was turned in by other officers, the Minneapolis officer's extracurricular activity came to light during a traffic stop when the offending motorist turned out to be a subscriber who recognized her.

The MPD launched an investigation but admitted that with no social media policy in place, it would base its inquiry on an off-duty employment policy that prohibited officers from "working in any business that is not compatible with police work."[56] A spokesperson for Minneapolis Mayor Jacob Frey told the media, "If all we're talking about is some naked pictures behind a paywall, the mayor has no problem, but the (police) chief will determine if there are any policy violations."[57] As of early 2024, there had been no announcement of the results of the investigation, and it was not publicly disclosed if any of the videos identified the woman as a police officer.[58]

In South Carolina in 2010, firefighter and paramedic Jason Brown entertained his colleagues and the surrounding community with an animated video, posted on Facebook, that spoofed the work of the fire department and local hospital. Brown eventually received a termination letter that accused him of "displaying poor judgment in producing a derogatory video . . . the video has created an embarrassing situation for this department, our public image and the cooperative relationship we enjoy with the medical center."[59] Pointing out the video did not identify the fire department or the hospital, Brown appealed his termination to county authorities but lost.[60]

That same year, a police dispatcher in West Allis, Wisconsin, was fired after twenty-one years on the job for posting on her Facebook page that she was "addicted to Vicodin, Adderall, marijuana, and absinthe."[61] Dana Kuchler had worked at the police department for twenty-one years and insisted her posts were a joke. After she tested negative for any foreign substances, her union, the American Federation of State, County, and Municipal Employees, appealed the case and got the punishment changed to a thirty-day suspension. An attorney for the union said Kuchler's Facebook comment was "clearly off-duty, not related to her job, and interpreted to be humorous."[62]

City officials admitted there was no social media policy in effect at the time but claimed that allowing her to continue in her police dispatch job would "mock the mission of the department because dispatchers deal with the public, which must trust a dispatcher's judgment."[63]

Racial Rants

In January 2013, the fire chief in Howard County, Maryland, was at home watching television when a story aired about a proposal to ban certain types of firearms. Kevin Buker then went to his Facebook page and posted, "Let's all kill someone with a liberal . . . then maybe we can get them outlawed too. Think of the satisfaction of beating a liberal to death with another liberal. It's almost poetic."[64]

A few minutes later, a volunteer paramedic in the county named Mark Grutzmacher replied to the post with, "but was it an 'assault liberal'? Gotta pick a fat one, those are the 'high capacity' ones. Oh, and pick a black one, those are more scary. Sorry, had to perfect on a cool idea."[65]

Two months earlier, the department had announced a social media policy that prohibited employees from "posting any statements, endorsements, or other speech, information, images, or personnel matters that could be interpreted to represent or undermine the views or positions of the department."[66] A related policy, announced a month later, was aimed at "ensuring members of the Department maintain the highest level of integrity and ethical conduct both on and off duty."[67]

When other employees of the department complained about the posts, Buker and Grutzmacher were told to delete the posts and desist from any further commentary. That started a series of Facebook posts involving Buker, Grutzmacher, and other employees of the fire department and other county agencies about the fairness of the social media policy and whether it represented too much "political correctness."[68]

Claiming the comments "had racial overtones and was insensitive and derogatory in nature" and demonstrated "repeated insolence and insubordination,"[69] the fire department notified Buker of his termination on February 25. Buker then filed suit in federal district court, claiming the department violated his First Amendment rights to "speak on matters of public concern."[70] The court granted summary judgment to the department, determining that Buker's posts were based on personal opinions and not matters of public interest and had the potential to disrupt the operation of the department.[71] The court also found the department's social media policies were reasonable and the department's need to maintain public trust outweighed Buker's free-speech rights. On appeal, the circuit court of appeals affirmed the decision of the lower court.[72]

In 2012, against the backdrop of a presidential election campaign and a national discussion about the Confederate Battle Flag, the deputy police chief at Clayton State University in suburban Atlanta posted to Facebook an image of the flag and the phrase, "Time for a Second Revolution."[73] Rex Duke, a veteran law-enforcement officer with more than thirty years of experience, claimed he used privacy settings on the account and, having second thoughts about the appropriateness of his post, deleted it in less than an hour. By that time, the post had already caught the attention of a local television station, which broadcast a brief story about the issue. That brought it to the attention of Police Chief Bobby Hamil, CSU administrators, and the public. Backed up by the administration and public outrage, Hamil demoted Duke in rank, cut his salary, and reassigned him to a less desirable shift.

Duke sued Hamil and the university in federal district court, claiming that he had posted the image on his own time and using his home computer, and that by taking disciplinary action the university had violated his free-speech rights.[74]

The court saw it differently, however. While the court acknowledged that Duke's role as a public employee gave him more First Amendment protections than a private employee; those rights were outweighed by the university's need to "maintain internal order and public trust." The court also noted that even though CSU had no social media policy, the court agreed with its claim that its employees "should not espouse political beliefs in public."[75]

Free-speech scholars use the case to illustrate the dangers of social media posts regardless of one's employment status and that public employees should not assume the First Amendment will protect them.[76]

In 2020, a Denver police officer was fired for an Instagram photo showing him and two fellow officers wearing riot gear, accompanied by a caption that read, "Let's start a riot."[77]

The same year, a police officer in Fulton, New York, lost his job after tweeting—less than a month after the death of George Floyd at the hands of police in Minneapolis—that "Black lives only matter to black people when they are killed by a white person."[78]

A 2023 case in Oregon demonstrated that the prohibition against police officers using social media to disparage minority groups extends well past retirement and transition into other fields of work. Dean Sawyer, who worked as a Newport police officer for three decades before being elected mayor in 2018, resigned from that office when seven years of Facebook posts—some of them dating back to his years on the police force—came to light. In those posts, he made comments and passed along memes ridiculing African Americans, women, gays, transgender persons, immigrants, and non-English speakers.[79]

The posts were supposed to be limited to current and former police officers who had formed a group called "LEO Only," but his comments somehow became public. That drew criticism from other city officials and local and national advocacy groups for the LGBTQ community.[80]

In Minneapolis, a veteran police officer learned that old emails can lead to problems, especially when they are racist in nature and become public at a time when the department for which one works is already in the national spotlight. Following the 2020 murder of George Floyd by a Minneapolis officer, the Minnesota Department of Human Rights launched an investigation into the police department's troubled history in race relations. The probe uncovered an email chain from 2012 in which several officers passed around racially offensive messages and photos.[81]

Only one officer included in the chain was still with the force: a veteran homicide detective named Aimee Linson. She claimed to not remember forwarding the message, but an interim police chief placed her on paid leave for more than a year while a separate investigation focused on her. When a permanent chief was named early in 2023, he decided that a written reprimand, not termination, was the appropriate punishment.[82]

That didn't sit well with local civil rights leaders, who were even more discouraged when Linson was promoted to chief of the homicide unit in November of that year.[83]

Not a New Problem

Across the country, law-enforcement agencies have long struggled with an increase in the number of officers whose off-the-clock participation in activities sponsored by or linked to white supremacy or other extremist positions, much of it taking place in online forums. Many go beyond the middle-of-the-road forums such as Facebook, Twitter, Instagram, and Telegram, and into more dangerous forums such as 8-Chan.

Law-enforcement agencies are enacting policies to prohibit such involvement, but as in cases involving members of the military, agencies must balance their officers' rights of free speech and freedom of association with not only the reality of problems but the public perception of potential problems.

"These reforms, while well-intentioned, leave unaddressed an especially harmful form of bias, which remains entrenched within law enforcement: explicit racism," wrote attorney Michael German on the website of the Brennan Center for Justice at New York University's Law School:

> Explicit racism in law enforcement takes many forms, from membership or affiliation with violent white supremacist or far-right militant groups, to engaging in racially discriminatory behavior toward the public or law enforcement colleagues, to making racist remarks and sharing them on social media. While it is widely acknowledged that racist officers subsist within police departments around the country, federal, state, and local governments are doing far too little to proactively identify them, report their behavior to prosecutors who might unwittingly rely on their testimony in criminal cases, or protect the diverse communities they are sworn to serve.[84]

Adds Georgetown University Law Professor Vida B. Johnson: "The system can never achieve its purported goal of fairness while white supremacists continue to hide within police departments."[85] When cases go to court, judges must balance the officers' First Amendment rights with the need of their departments for "order, loyalty, morale, and harmony."[86]

The problem is nothing new. A 2006 report from the Federal Bureau of Investigation warned of a new tide of "White Supremacist Infiltration of Law Enforcement." The report found that hate groups have long found police departments to be "fertile recruiting grounds."[87]

In 2019, the Center for Investigative Reporting found that more than 400 former or retired police officers were participating in online discussion groups with titles such as "Ban the NAACP" and "The White Privilege Club."[88]

The Brennan Center reports that between 2000 and 2020, law-enforcement officers were linked to problematic groups in at least fourteen states, with online commentary showing racist, sexist, and nativist viewpoints. Such activity is known to law-enforcement administrations but results in discipline only when it becomes public and/or violates the department's anti-discrimination or social media policies. In the rare cases that officers are terminated, the result is lengthy litigation that exposes a department's "dirty laundry" and reflects poorly on all law-enforcement agencies.[89]

Then came January 6, 2021.

Media reports indicated that at least nineteen defendants charged with rioting at the Capitol building that day were current or former police officers, along with more than eighty members of the military.[90]

In 2022, the Anti-Defamation League announced it had identified more than 370 current police officers and more than 100 active-duty military members on the membership rolls of the Oath Keepers, a white supremacist group partly responsible for the Capitol riot.[91]

Push Comes to Shove

When law-enforcement officers use their department-issued cellular phones, those call records are subject to public records laws, which could embarrass their employers.

In 2001, for example, Jeff Quon was an officer with the police department in Ontario, California, and a member of its Special Weapons and Tactics (SWAT) team. After several months in which Quon and other officers exceeded the limits for messages sent on their department-issued texting devices—agreed upon by the police department and the company that provided the service—administrators investigated in order to determine if the limits were too low or if the officers were using their devices for unauthorized personal use. Police Chief Lloyd Scharf learned that many of the messages sent by Quon and another officer were personal in nature, and some were sexually explicit.[92]

Neither officer was disciplined, but instead was told to discontinue using their devices for personal matters. However, because they were embarrassed when the contents of their messages became public, they sued the city of Ontario, claiming that the investigation violated their Fourth Amendment right to privacy. They also claimed that the OPD's service provider, Arch Wireless, violated the Stored Communications Act of 1986 by providing transcripts of the officers' communication to the police chief.[93]

The district court found in favor of the police department, but a circuit court of appeals reversed, determining that Scharf had less intrusive means by which to evaluate the usage of the devices and did not need to request the transcripts from Arch Wireless. The city appealed the case to the U.S. Supreme Court, which reversed in 2010, ruling that the officers had no expectation of privacy, the police chief's actions were reasonable, and the Fourth Amendment did not protect sexually explicit material.[94]

In 1996, two Reno, Nevada, police officers became the subject of an internal affairs investigation after supervisors learned they had used their department-issued devices to send text messages to each other that were deemed "inappropriate" under department policy, even though the specific contents of the messages were never disclosed. When the devices were issued several years earlier, officers were told their communications would be stored on the department's server so they could be periodically reviewed to check on potential violations of department policy or in response to public information requests. The department also warned officers that they had no expectation of privacy and that the system could not be used to criticize department policy or take part in any behavior that violated the department's non-discrimination policies.[95]

But when they were notified of the investigation, John Bohack and Jon Catalono claimed the storage of the information and the review of it by their superiors violated the federal wiretapping laws and compromised their privacy. They asked for and received a temporary restraining order stopping the investigation and barring the public release of their messages. Another judge then vacated the order and allowed the investigation to continue.[96]

When the employees sued the department, a federal district court ruled against them, determining the department's action did not violate wiretapping laws nor compromise their privacy. In addition, the court ruled that the storage of communication was necessary because it might be needed to comply with public information requests, and periodic review of officers' text messages was necessary in order to prevent inappropriate usage of the equipment.[97]

Witness Credibility

Two cases involving not law-enforcement personnel per se, but professionals who work with them, raised the issue of whether government agencies had the right to regulate the speech of their employees when it called their credibility into question and jeopardized their ability to provide court testimony. In both cases, employers argued that their need to protect the credibility of the office and its employees who testified in court cases outweighed the employees' free-speech rights.

In 2012, Jennifer Shepherd was a caseworker for Child Protective Services, a division of the Oregon Department of Human Services. Frustrated by visits to homes in which she encountered parents who owned luxury cars and expensive televisions while also collecting welfare and food stamps, she vented on her Facebook page with a list of eight rules for parents that covered topics such as eligibility for public assistance, forced sterilization for parents who had too many children, and what should happen to parents who abuse or neglect their children. When the list came to the attention of her supervisors, she was placed on administrative leave and eventually terminated.[98]

Shepherd sued DHS, claiming that she used privacy settings to limit the reach of her postings, her comments were "satire," and the termination violated her First Amendment rights. The state countered that Shepherd's postings jeopardized pending court cases because defense lawyers could easily challenge her credibility as a witness.[99]

DHS was able to defend the firing, convincing the court that even though her supervisors understood the frustrations of her particular job, she chose the wrong venue in which to vent about them. And the ease with which Shepherd's coworkers and superiors could easily find her postings negated her claim about privacy settings. The court also determined her termination did not violate the First Amendment because her comments were job related and not made as a private citizen.[100]

Four years later, a veteran criminologist with the Iowa Department of Public Safety was fired after making racially offensive comments on her Facebook page. Commenting on a case in Dallas in which five police officers were murdered by a Black suspect, Amy Pollpeter said the "Black Lives Matter" movement was misguided and that she no longer felt safe around Black people. "The cops in Dallas never shot a black person, yet the Black Lives Matter movement seems to think it's OK to remain silent about what one of their people did," she wrote on July 8, 2016. "Yes, not every black person is going to shoot me because I look at them wrong, or because I happen to be wearing a DCI (Department of Criminal Investigation) shirt that day, but I know that there is a stronger chance that they will today than they would have 5 years ago."[101] Her comments came just a few days after she posted similar comments to the Facebook page of local television station KCCI in advance of a Black Lives Matter rally. "If there weren't so many of you trying to kill cops, maybe there wouldn't be cops who have to fear for their lives at a basic traffic stop," she wrote.[102]

As a result of both sets of comments, Pollpeter was placed on administrative leave on July 12, then terminated on July 26. Much like in the Shepherd case, the core issue was one of public trust and credibility as an expert witness.[103]

In defending the termination, IDPS cited its own social media policy that stated that employees were "free to express themselves on their own time and using non-state resources" but warned that "action could be taken against the employee if the expression affects his or her credibility as a witness for the state."[104]

Gary Licht, Pollpeter's supervisor, denounced the posts in an interview with *The Des Moines Register*. "They're offensive and do not reflect my thoughts or actions," he told the paper.[105]

IDPS Commissioner Roxann Ryan added that it has a "strong commitment to integrity, impartiality, and professionalism in every aspect of our work. We have adopted these policies in order to ensure that the public has trust in all that we do, and our policies reflect the high standards that we maintain."[106]

Rather than face long odds in a wrongful termination suit, Pollpeter opted not to contest the firing and instead filed for unemployment benefits. After drawing more than $3,800 over the next two months, an administrative law judge ruled her ineligible and ordered her to repay the money because her Facebook posts amounted to "work-related misconduct."[107]

I Might Be Wrong, But I Doubt It

In 2023, a St. Louis police officer found himself in speech-related news stories twice—first for speaking, and then for not speaking.

Earlier in the year, Roger Murphey, a twenty-eight-year veteran of SLPD, was reprimanded for inflammatory comments in his Facebook posts and media interviews. His favorite target was District Attorney Kim Gardner, whom he accused of "making St. Louis a more dangerous city" by encouraging cash bail, preferring rehabilitation over punishment, and declining to prosecute nonviolent crimes such as shoplifting.[108]

The community's racial wounds had still not healed from the 2014 case in the suburb of Ferguson, in which an unarmed Black man was killed by white police officers. Murphey blamed the turmoil on "black thugs" and accused

Black politicians and civil rights leaders of "always casting the violence in racial terms."[109]

Those posts drew the ire of the local NAACP and other civil rights groups, who felt that Murphey's comments were at best insensitive and at worst symptomatic of a larger race problem in the St. Louis area. As a result, Murphey's name was placed on local district attorney Gardner's "exclusion list," a roster of police officers whose requests for search warrants would receive extra scrutiny because of past problems.[110]

When Murphey was called to testify in murder trials and other serious cases in which he was the arresting officer, he refused to appear as a form of protest against being on the list and because of what he called the prosecutor's "soft-on-crime" agenda.[111] He acknowledged that his failure to appear would jeopardize cases and allow the guilty to go free, but he told local media that opposing the idea of the list was more important. He also told the media that if subpoenaed, he would appear in court but refuse to answer questions, even if it meant being charged with contempt of court. He claimed that if he testified in court, defense attorneys would use his place on the list to impugn his credibility, but criminal justice experts with no direct connection to the case said his failure to cooperate not only harmed the integrity of the cases but also called into question the police department's commitment to justice.[112]

Notes

1 *McAuliffe v. Mayor of New Bedford*, 29 N.E. 517 (1892).

2 *Berger and Barhight v. Battaglia*, 779 F. 2d 992 (1985). See also: Bruce Barry, *Speechless: The Erosion of Free Expression in the American Workplace* (San Francisco: Berrett-Koehler Publishers, 2007), p. 14.

3 *Rankin v. McPherson,* 483 U.S. 378 (1987). See also: Randy J. Kozel, "Reconceptualizing Public Employee Speech," *Northwestern University Law Review* 99, no. 3 (Spring 2005): pp. 1007–51.
Kozel, "Reconceptualizing Public Employee Speech." See also: Barry, *Speechless*, p. 14.

4 *Rankin v. McPherson.* See also: Kozel, "Reconceptualizing Public Employee Speech."

5 Ibid.

6 Ibid.

7 Ibid.

8 *City of St. Petersburg v. Pfeiffer*, 52 So. 2d 796 (1951).
9 *Mueller v. Conlisk*, 429 F. 2d 900 (1970).
10 Ibid.
11 *Brukiewa v. Police Commissioner of Baltimore*, 263 A.2d 210 (1970) See also: "The Law: Dissent Through the Courts," *Time*, April 27, 1970.
12 Ibid.
13 Ibid.
14 *Dendor v. Board of Fire and Police Commissioners*, 197 N.E. 2d 316 (1973).
15 Ibid.
16 Jim Dwyer, "The Officer Who Posted Too Much on MySpace," *The New York Times*, March 10, 2009.
17 Ibid.
18 Ibid.
19 Ibid.
20 Ibid.
21 Ibid.
22 Ibid.
23 *Gresham v. City of Atlanta*, 2013 U.S. App LEXIS 20961 (2013). See also: Venkat Balasubramani, "Police Officer's Facebook Venting Isn't Protected by the First Amendment," *Technology and Marketing Law Blog*, October 21, 2013.
24 Ibid.
25 *Graziosi v. City of Greenville*, No. 13-60900 (2015). See also: Venkat Balasubramani, "Police Officer's Facebook Post Criticizing Chief's Budget Decision Justified Termination," *Technology and Marketing Law Blog*, January 13, 2015.
26 Ibid.
27 Ibid.
28 Randy Ludlow, "Sheriff's Official Told to Quit Over Facebook Comments Critical of Police in Capitol Riot," *The Columbus Dispatch*, January 8, 2021.
29 Ibid.
30 Ibid.
31 *Kirkland v. City of Maryville*, No. 21-5569 (2022). See also: David L. Hudson, "Federal Appeals Court Rules Against Former Police Officer Fired for Facebook Post," *First Amendment News*, December 26, 2022.
32 Ibid.
33 Ryan Wyatt Turbeville, "Sergeant Fired for Criticizing Alachua County Sheriff, Lawsuit Filed," *WCJB-TV*, March 15, 2023.
34 Ibid.
35 *Horstkoetter v. Oklahoma Department of Public Safety*, 159 F. 3d 1265 (1998)
36 Ibid.

37 Ibid.
38 Ibid.
39 *Williams v. McKee*, 655 Fed. App. 677 (2016).
40 Ibid.
41 Ibid.
42 Ibid.
43 *Ruff v. City of Leavenworth, Kansas*, 858 F. Supp. 1546 (1994).
44 Ibid.
45 *McAuliffe v. Mayor of New Bedford.*
46 *Ruff v. City of Leavenworth, Kansas.*
47 Ibid.
48 Ibid.
49 *Duda v. Elder*, No. 20-1416 (2021). See also: Roger S. Achille, "First Amendment Protects Against Viewpoint Discrimination," *SHRM News,* October 13, 2021.
50 *Duda v. Elder.*
51 *Daniels v. City of Arlington*, 246 F. 3d 500 (2001). See also: Barry, *Speechless*, pp. 150–3.
52 Ibid.
53 "Home Depot Employee Claims He Was Fired Over 'One Nation Under God' Pin," *New York Daily News,* October 28, 2009.
54 *San Diego v. Roe* 543 U.S. 77 (2004). See also: Barry, *Speechless*, pp. 82–3.
55 Ibid.
56 Nicholas McEntyre, "Cop Recognized as OnlyFans Model by Subscriber She Pulled Over," *New York Post*, October 5, 2023.
57 Ibid.
58 Ibid.
59 Lori Andrews, *I Know Who You Are and I Saw What You Did: Social Networks and the Death of Privacy* (New York: Free Press, 2011), pp. 75–6.
60 Ibid.
61 Kaitlin Madden, "12 Ways to Get Fired for Facebook," *CareerBuilder.com*, date unknown.
62 Ibid.
63 Ibid.
64 *Kevin Patrick Buker v. Howard County Chief William Goddard III*, Case 1:13-CV-03046-MJG (2017). See also: Leah Shepherd, "How to Handle Political Speech in the Workplace," *SHRM News,* June 12, 2023.
65 Ibid.
66 Ibid.
67 Ibid.

68 Ibid.
69 Ibid.
70 Ibid.
71 Ibid.
72 Ibid.
73 *Duke v. Hamil*, 1:13-CV-01663 (2014). See also: Venkat Balasubramani, "Demoting Police Officer for Posting Confederate Flag to Facebook Isn't First Amendment Violation," *Technology and Marketing Law Blog*, February 11, 2014.
74 Ibid.
75 Ibid.
76 Ibid.
77 Andrew Dalton, "Ill-Considered Posts Lead to Lost Jobs," *Associated Press Report*, June 7, 2020.
78 Ibid.
79 "Mayor of Coastal Oregon City Resigns Over Posts in Police Facebook Group," *Associated Press Report*, July 10, 2023.
80 Ibid.
81 "Minneapolis Police Lieutenant Disciplined Over Racist Email Promoted to Homicide Unit Leader," *Associated Press Report*, November 9, 2023.
82 Ibid.
83 Ibid.
84 Michael German, "Hidden in Plain Sight: Racism, White Supremacy, and Far-Right Militancy in Law Enforcement," *Brennan Center for Justice Report*, August 27, 2020.
85 Ibid.
86 Ibid.
87 Kali Holloway, "White Nationalist Hate is Infiltrating Our Police," *The Nation*, November 15, 2022.
88 Ibid.
89 German, "Hidden in Plain Sight."
90 Holloway, "White Nationalist Hate is Infiltrating Our Police."
91 Ibid.
92 *Ontario v. Quon*, 560 U.S. 746 (2010).
93 Ibid.
94 Ibid.
95 *Bohach v. City of Reno*, 932 F. Supp. 1232 (1996).
96 Ibid.
97 *Bohach v. City of Reno.* See also: Charles J. Muhl, "Workplace E-Mail and Internet Use: Employees and Employers Beware," *Monthly Labor Review*, February 2003, pp. 36–45.

98 *Shepherd v. McGee*, 2013 U.S. Dist. LEXIS 159432 (2013).
99 Ibid.
100 Ibid.
101 Jason Clayworth, "Iowa Employee Fired for 'Offensive' Facebook Posts," *The Des Moines Register*, July 27, 2016.
102 Ibid.
103 Ibid.
104 Ibid.
105 Ibid.
106 Ibid.
107 "Judge: Iowa Analyst Fired Over Racist Posts Must Pay Back Benefits," *Times-Republican*, October 21, 2016.
108 Jeremy Kohler and Ryan Krull, "A Detective Sabotaged His Own Cases Because He Didn't Like the Prosecutor," *ProPublica,* October 10, 2023.
109 Ibid.
110 Ibid.
111 Ibid.
112 Ibid.

7

Free Speech for K–12 Educators

Political Participation versus Political and Legal Considerations

Letter-Writing as a Subversive Activity

In 1964, Marvin Pickering was a high school teacher in Illinois who was concerned by a proposed tax increase aimed at generating additional funding for public schools—with an emphasis on athletic facilities. Pickering's view was that the school district should spend less money on athletics and more on English, history, math, social sciences, and the arts. He expressed those sentiments in a letter to the editor of his local newspaper, the *Lockport Herald*.

Even though the term "whistleblowing" was not in wide usage at the time, he wrote the letter in that spirit, as it pointed out the district's unauthorized usage of funds from the sale of public bonds to finance a new athletic stadium. His letter criticized the district for creating a "totalitarian atmosphere" and lying to the public about the sources of athletic funding.[1]

The school board did not appreciate his criticisms and terminated him, describing his letter as "detrimental to the efficient operation and administration of the schools of the district."[2] After being terminated, Pickering took his case to the Illinois court system, which denied his claim based on the district's assertion that Pickering did not bring his complaints to the school board first—a claim that was never determined.

Pickering had more success at the U.S. Supreme Court, which determined that teachers do not "relinquish their First Amendment rights they would otherwise enjoy as citizens to comment on matters of public interest."[3] The Court also ruled that Pickering's letter did not defame individual employees nor take any action that disrupted the workplace.[4]

In its landmark decision, the Court reversed the lower court rulings and determined that his letter expressed his own opinion, and while tangentially related to his job, it was protected by the First Amendment. "Free and open debate is vital to informed decision-making by the electorate," the Court ruled. "Teachers are, as a class, the members of a community most likely to have informed and definite opinions as to how funds allotted to the operation of the school should be spent. Accordingly, it is essential that they be able to speak out freely and ask questions without fear of retaliatory dismissal."[5] The Court found that his violation of the "unwritten rule" about "going through channels" was an act of carelessness rather than recklessness; he had the right to comment on matters of public concern even though he skirted some school district rules in the process.[6]

"The question of whether a school system requires additional funds is a matter of legitimate public concern," the Court ruled. "On such a question, free and open debate is vital to informed decision-making by the electorate."[7]

Recurring Themes

For more than a half-century, the *Pickering* case has been the gold standard for determining the extent to which teachers—and in some cases other public employees—may criticize their employers without punishment or retribution (see the discussion of the "Pickering-Connick Test" in Chapter 4). As in that case, when teachers or other government employees pursue wrongful termination cases, they must establish that they were speaking as private citizens and not in their official roles and that their comments did not represent the official position of the school, school board, or other public entity.

In two cases in the 1970s—*Mt. Healthy City School District v. Doyle* and *Givhan v. Western Line Consolidated School District*—the Supreme Court ruled in favor of teachers who publicly criticized their respective school boards, in part because they followed the correct steps in bringing their concerns to school administrators first.

There are only two categories of cases in which teachers have fared well in defending their free-speech rights:

1. *Alerting officials to legal or ethical wrongdoing.* In a handful of whistleblowing cases described later in this chapter, courts ruled in favor

of teachers—even in cases in which they did not go through proper channels—determining the severity of their whistleblowing claims (usually related to a school's discriminatory conduct or failure to adhere to the law) outweighed the need for formality and that "going through channels" was a suggestion and not a legal requirement.

2. *Shifting attitudes toward religious expression.* In one of the most controversial cases of the last decade (not counting abortion and affirmative-action cases), the Supreme Court in 2022 ruled in favor of a football coach who was fired for leading his team in prayer following games, in violation of school district policy heavily influenced by school-prayer rulings of the 1960s (this case is discussed at the end of this chapter). Advocates of keeping religion out of public schools are concerned that the shifting of public opinion on the school-prayer issue and the current makeup of the Supreme Court might result in more decisions supporting religious expression in the near future.

   Fortunately for most teachers, the *Pickering, Mt. Healthy,* and *Givhan* cases are not outliers. Except for the cases of *Bernasconi v. Tempe Elementary School District* (1977) and *Wales v. Board of Education* (1997) (discussed later in this chapter), public school teachers who call attention to problems in their districts—either through writing letters to their school boards or disclosing information in media interviews—have been backed up by the courts.

While K–12 educators have a successful track record of winning wrongful termination cases involving their free-speech rights, there are still multiple hurdles to overcome:

1. *Higher authorities' reluctance to second-guess decisions made by lower authorities.* The courts and state education boards often defer to local school boards on personnel decisions, and those school boards in turn defer to school principals and other administrators. These decisions are made even in cases in which the terminated employee appears to have a stronger case "on paper."
2. *Skepticism of whistleblowers.* As many of the cases in this chapter illustrate, terminated whistleblowers in K–12 education typically fare poorly (with rare exceptions, as described earlier) when appealing their wrongful termination cases. County school boards and state departments of education offer due-process procedures in the form of internal appeals

committees, but those bodies usually look at appealing employees as "guilty until proven innocent" and maintain the default position that such terminations are justifiable. The most common justification given is that the whistleblower did not follow the internal chain of command before taking the issue public.

3. *Maintaining the trust of parents and the general public.* As several of the cases in this chapter demonstrate, school principals and sometimes school boards often respond in a "knee-jerk" fashion when parents complain about the expression of teachers, especially in the age of social media. In some cases, school boards respond to public criticism of teachers with accusations that their comments reflected poorly upon the school or, in some cases, the teaching profession. In cases involving school teachers criticized for outside-the-classroom activities involving drinking or sexual activity (as communicated through social media), the courts have ruled in favor of school districts, determining that maintaining the trust of parents and the reputation of the school outweighed the teachers' free-speech rights.

   Public perception was at the heart of a four-year conflict involving a high school teacher in Duval County, Florida, who was terminated for refusing to remove a "Black Lives Matter" flag from the wall in her classroom. Amy Donofrio began displaying the flag in 2020, shortly after the school had changed its name from Robert E. Lee High School to Riverside High School. School district officials had cautioned teachers to "remain neutral" in discussions of the name change, Covid-19 policies, and the presidential election.[8] When Donofrio refused to remove the flag, school officials fired her based on their determination that the public might not distinguish between her personal speech and that of the school district.

   In 2024, an administrative judge awarded her $300,000 and reinstated her teaching license, but also ruled that she would be ineligible to teach again in Duval County.[9]

The Only Thing We Learn From History is That We Don't Learn From History

In the years leading up to the Civil War, school boards frequently dismissed teachers they suspected of having abolitionist views. "The safest bet was for teachers to avoid the slavery issue and every other controversial question," wrote civil libertarian

Jonathan Zimmerman in his 2021 book, *Free Speech and Why You Should Give a Damn.* In the following century, Zimmerman wrote, teachers continued to be scrutinized for belonging to any political groups or speaking publicly about their opposition to the world wars. But those same school boards showed their own political bias by disciplining or dismissing teachers who held liberal views while not doing so in cases in which they held conservative views, such as those who criticized President Franklin D. Roosevelt's New Deal programs.[10]

The concern over political beliefs dates back to the 1940s, when K–12 educators and college professors were subject to "loyalty oaths" as well as inquiries into their personal lives and beliefs. Those believed to be homosexual or overly concerned with the rights of manual laborers or disadvantaged persons were suspected of having communist connections.

Airing Our Dirty Laundry

In a 1969 case remarkably similar to *Pickering*, a public-school teacher in Seward, Alaska, held private conversations with other teachers to gather support to remove the school superintendent from his position. When he found little concurrence, he wrote an open letter to the school board that was published in the local newspaper. "We are unable to get rid of the superintendent, so let's get rid of the school board," James A. Watts wrote.[11]

The school board voted to terminate Watts because his letter "brought the teaching profession into public disgrace or disrespect," and cited a relevant section of state law.[12] A state superior court upheld the firing, as did the Alaska Supreme Court.

Watts then took his case to the U.S. Supreme Court, claiming his firing violated his First Amendment right to free speech and his Fourteenth Amendment right to equal protection, claiming he was denied the rights enjoyed by non-teachers. Before he could get a court date, the Alaska Legislature amended its code, partly in response to the *Pickering* case, to remove the clause upon which the school board had based the termination. The Supreme Court, citing *Pickering*, voted 8-1 to send the case back to the state trial court, which reversed its original ruling.[13]

The *Pickering* and *Watts* cases introduced an era of whistleblowing in K–12 education, as many teachers were successful when challenging their working conditions and school policies. A few years after *Watts*, for example, a school teacher in Arkansas with more than twenty-five years' experience was faced with the non-renewal of her contract after expressing concerns over a broken water fountain in her classroom and the health impact of an incinerator next to the school's playground. She was already in trouble with the school board after helping students write letters asking for changes in the school's lunch menu, but when she took the school district to court, she won reinstatement and back pay.[14]

In the 1977 case of *Mt. Healthy City Board of Education v. Doyle*, the Supreme Court ruled that a school district in Ohio was wrong when it declined to renew the contract of a teacher who had been critical of school policies, including comments to a local radio station about the school's teacher dress code.[15]

Two years later, the Supreme Court's support of free speech was extended to include conversations taking place behind closed doors. In *Givhan v. Western Line Consolidated School District*, the Court ruled that a teacher could not be fired for criticizing school policies as racially discriminatory in a private meeting with her principal. Bessie B. Givens was fired after accusing school administrators of racially discriminatory practices and sued the school district in federal district court. The Court noted that the teacher acted in good faith by limiting her comments to private conversations but did not address the question of whether her comments would have received similar protection if they had been aired publicly.[16]

In a 1980 case, a federal judge ruled in favor of a teacher in Mississippi who criticized the school superintendent in a television interview, suggesting that he be "put on one of those long midnight trains to Georgia."[17]

The 1982 case of *Anderson v. Central Point School District No. 6* began when a teacher-coach at an Oregon high school penned a letter to the school board complaining about how the athletic departments at his school and other schools were managed. The school board told Jerry Anderson that his letter violated board policy—mostly because he didn't bring his concerns to his supervisor first—as well as Oregon Administrative Rules and the National Education Association Committee on Professional Ethics Code. At the board's direction, School Superintendent Rod Groshong informed Anderson that "it is my considered opinion that athletics at Crater High School are not benefited with you as a member of the coaching ranks. Hereafter, you will not be assigned a coaching role in School District 6."[18]

Anderson kept his teaching job but considered the cancellation of his coaching duties a violation of his First Amendment rights. He sued the school district, and the following year a federal district court ruled in his favor, determining that the rule about "going through channels" was a suggestion and not a requirement. The court based its ruling largely on the *Pickering* case, which dealt with a similar set of facts.[19]

In the 1987 case of *Southside Public Schools v. Hill*, a federal court ruled that a school district in Arkansas violated the First Amendment rights of elementary school teachers when it terminated them for simply reporting that the school district was out of compliance with federal disability laws by denying students the accommodations necessary for them to succeed.[20]

Two of the rare cases in which whistleblowers were unsuccessful in legal claims against their employers took place in Arizona in 1977 and Illinois in 1997. In *Bernasconi v. Tempe Elementary School District*, an appeals court made a hair-splitting ruling in a case in which a guidance counselor claimed she was transferred to a different school in retaliation for pointing out problems with how students were being tested. Socorro Hernandez Bernasconi claimed students whose primary languages were either Spanish or from Native American tribes were at a disadvantage when being tested in English, and when they performed poorly, they were transferred to classes for mentally retarded students. Bernasconi, who identified as Mexican-American, was transferred to another school where students were from more affluent families and were more academically successful. She felt unchallenged in her new job and sought to be returned to her original school, alleging her transfer was a form of discrimination based on her nationality as well as in retaliation for her whistleblowing. The court ruled against her discrimination claim, and even though it agreed with her whistleblowing claim, it declined to order her transfer back to her original school. The court based that ruling on the fact that a transfer was not a serious punishment because it was not the same as termination.[21]

In the 1997 case of *Wales v. Board of Education*, a public-school teacher in Illinois wrote a memo to the principal and superintendent complaining about her school's disciplinary process, claiming she was hired to "serve as a teacher, not a guard in a detention center."[22] When she was terminated, the school district claimed it was because of her negative performance evaluations rather than her whistleblowing. A federal district court accepted that claim and sided with the school district, determining that "matching a person's skills to the job at hand is a difficult yet vital task for any employer, and the First Amendment does not require defendants to retain someone they believed was not best for the children."[23]

In a case that stretched the definition of "whistleblowing," a high school English teacher in Fort Worth, Texas, was fired near the end of the 2018–19 school year after sending tweets to then president Donald Trump asking him to "rid the school" of the children of undocumented immigrants.[24] Georgia Clark had taught in the district for more than two decades and was employed at Carter-Riverside High School at the time of her controversial posts.

On May 17, 2019, Clark tweeted,

> Mr. President, Fort Worth Independent School District is loaded with illegal students from Mexico. Carter-Riverside High School has been taken over by them. Drug dealers are on our campus and nothing was done to them when drug dogs found the evidence. I contacted the feds here in Fort Worth a few months ago and the person I spoke with did not want to help me or even listen to me. The campus police officer spends his time texting on his cell phone and doing the bidding of Jennifer Orona, the Hispanic assistant principal who protects certain students from criminal prosecution. There is fraud being committed by Orona and how the Special Education Department on our campus is being run. FWISD knows about this and turns a blind eye to it. I need protection from recrimination should I report to the authorities but I do not know where to turn. I contacted the Texas Education Agency and then my teacher organization. Texas will not protect whistleblowers. The Mexicans refuse to honor our flag.[25]

Concerned parents informed the school district on May 29, prompting the superintendent to place Clark on administrative leave. After six weeks of negative media coverage, the school board met to hear the concerns of parents, then voted to terminate her contract. After her dismissal, she claimed that she believed her tweets were private communication between herself and the president, and her lawyer contended the comments were protected as free speech because they were related to a matter of public concern. Her Twitter account was later deleted. County administrators, however, cited the school district's notoriety of having the largest Hispanic population in the country and that her comments were unacceptable.

The Texas Education Agency appointed a committee to look into the case, and after a six-month investigation, ordered the school district to reinstate her with back pay. The agency found that the tweeting incident was not Clark's first conflict with her school's administration. During the 2013–14 school year, she was reprimanded for referring to her classroom as "Little Mexico," and that incident, little-known prior to the investigation, became part of the larger story.[26]

The district appealed the ruling, claiming that Clark's comments served to intimidate students and hamper their learning, while also causing concern for the students' parents. It also pointed to a standard clause in the teachers' contracts in which they agree not to publicly criticize the school district or make other public statements of a disruptive nature.

"We stand by our decision because we firmly believe this is in the best interests of all students," said Kent P. Scribner, superintendent of the Fort Worth Independent School District.[27]

The committee concluded that Clark's tweets were "free speech" because they were her "statements of a citizen on a matter of public concern protected by the U.S. Constitution; the evidence was not sufficient to show that the tweets caused a substantial and continuing disruption to the efficient functioning of the district, and her interest in free speech outweighed the district's interest in the efficient provision of public services."[28]

The school district's appeal was successful in the short term. In 2021, the TEA reversed its earlier decision, which allowed the school district to move forward with the termination.[29] Clark then took the case to the state district court for Travis County, which upheld the termination. Although the court agreed with Clark's claim that she did not waive her rights of free speech by signing her contract, the justices cited the *Pickering* case and determined that her comments, while related to a matter of public concern, were not related to her specific duties. The court also determined that decisions to hire and fire teachers should be made at the local level and not by state officials.[30] In 2023, a state appeals court in Austin reviewed the case and confirmed the decision of the district court that Clark's termination was lawful.[31]

While the trend of teachers complaining about their workplace conditions has waned since the Covid-19 pandemic, experts don't believe there is a connection. However, they have noticed that between 2020 and 2023, K–12 teachers still have the same complaints—low pay, overcrowded classrooms, and disrespectful students—but they keep those thoughts to themselves, according to the 2022 Merrimack College Teachers Survey. One exception is an Ohio teacher who quit his job in Ohio because of low pay and created a TikTok video to explain why he was taking a higher-paying job as a Walmart store manager. Sethy Gabriel told viewers that he "loved teaching" but could make $20,000 more at Walmart while working forty-five hours a week instead of sixty.[32]

The issue of educators publicly complaining about workplace conditions is not limited to classroom teachers. In 2021, for example, a controversy took place on a high school football field in California, but it was during a graduation exercise rather than an athletic competition. Instead of commending the graduating class or sending them off with words of encouragement, the school's principal, Ben Nakamura, used his allotted time on the dais to run down a list of grievances about the school board's management style. Because of Covid-19 measures, the senior class had been divided into three groups, and Nakamura's incident happened at the first session. He was barred from the two afternoon sessions and was formally fired the next day.[33]

Taking One for the Team

In 1958, a year after a school in Little Rock, Arkansas was ordered to be desegregated by the federal government, the state legislature in Arkansas held a special session to address the future school districting. The debate eventually morphed into a discussion of public-school teachers who were in favor of integrating schools or held membership in civil rights groups. Certain that those teachers must have been under "sinister outside influences"—perhaps communists—the legislature enacted a law that required teachers to sign affidavits at the beginning of each school year listing the groups to which they belonged or donated money.[34]

B. T. Shelton, an African American teacher, twenty-five-year veteran of the school district, and member of the National Association for the Advancement of Colored People, refused to comply with the law and was terminated. The local NAACP chapter represented Shelton in his suit against the school district. The same federal district court that had previously overturned a state law prohibiting public employees from joining the NAACP surprisingly upheld the state law regarding signing the affidavits.

Shelton appealed the case to the U.S. Supreme Court, which ruled the affidavit law violated the First Amendment right of assembly, which in similar cases had been expanded to include the right of association. In its majority opinion, the court determined that requiring teachers to disclose their group memberships "could have no possible bearing" on their ability to teach. Justice Potter Stewart wrote that "forcing a teacher to list every conceivable kind of associational ties—social, professional, political, advocational, or religious—constituted a comprehensive interference with associational freedom."[35]

In dissent, Justice Felix Frankfurter wrote that the state had a valid interest in such information, as "teachers might participate in so many organizations as to interfere with their work," and Justice John Marshall Harlan wrote that it was up to the state, not the courts, to determine "where the line should be drawn between a permissible inquiry and an overbroad inquiry."[36]

Matters of Judgment, or the Lack of It

When twenty-four-year-old high school teacher Ashley Payne returned from her summer vacation in Europe in 2009, she thought nothing of posting photographs of the trip on her Facebook page. Her photos included shots of her drinking wine and beer in cafes in Italy, Spain, and Ireland, and one photo included the word "bitch" on a banner in one of the bars—a reference to an Irish bar trivia game called "Bitch Bingo." Her employer, the Barrow County School System in Georgia, had a rule prohibiting teachers from "unacceptable online activities."[37] Payne believed her privacy settings would limit access to her friends and would not be available to students or their parents.

But in late August, only a few weeks into the new school year, Payne was called into her principal's office and confronted with the visual evidence. An email that her principal said came from a "concerned anonymous parent" prompted the inquiry.[38]

Citing the school system's policy, the principal gave her two choices—suspension or resignation. Payne chose the latter, but a few months later filed a lawsuit against the school system, claiming that the principal had violated a state law dealing with the due process that must be provided to teachers before they could be dismissed. Payne and her attorney asked for reinstatement to her position, back pay for the time she spent out of the classroom, and reimbursement for her legal fees.

Payne later learned that the anonymous email did not come from a parent, but from another unidentified person. She based her legal complaint partially on that detail and partially on the fact that she had conformed with the school board's policy that prohibited teachers from communicating with their students using social networking sites. But the school board contended that regardless of the privacy settings, Payne's Facebook page "promoted alcohol use" and "contained profanity."[39]

"Yes, I put it on the Internet, so you can make that argument," Payne told CBS News in a February 2011 interview. "But it sort of feels like the same thing as if I had put the pictures in a shoebox in my house and someone came in and took them and showed one of them to the principal."[40]

Her attorney, Richard Storrs, added, "It would be like I went to a restaurant and saw my daughter's teacher sitting there with her husband having a glass with some kind of liquid. Is that frowned upon by the school board? Is that illegal? Is that improper? Of course not. It's the same situation in this case."[41]

A Barrow County court ruled against Payne in 2011, and a state appeals court upheld that ruling. Today, Payne is an administrator for the Georgia Department of Education.[42]

A similar case occurred in Idaho in the fall of 2013 when a high school teacher and basketball coach in Pocatello, Idaho, posted photos from her family reunion on Facebook. One of Laraine Cook's photos showed her in a swimsuit in an embrace with boyfriend Tom Harrison, who was a teacher and football coach at the same school. In one of the photos, Harrison's hand is on Cook's breast.

Unlike Payne, Cook made no effort to keep her students from seeing the photos, as many students were among her "Facebook friends." It took three months for the photos to come to the attention of school administrators, who terminated Cook for "posting a picture of a sexual nature on a social media website."[43] Harrison, meanwhile, received a simple written reprimand.

Cook appealed to the school district's grievance panel, claiming that she removed the photos once she learned of the complaints, that the school district could not prove any substantial disruption to the operation of the school, and that the social media policy under which she was terminated was vague.

As a result of her appeal, the panel overturned the termination and ruled that Cook deserved only a reprimand. She returned to teaching and coaching the following school year.[44]

In cases involving personal conduct or the expression of opinions that did not rise to the level of whistleblowing, Cook's successful case is an outlier. Most K–12 educators who engaged in conduct that embarrassed their schools or raised the concerns of parents or school board members had little success in attempting to regain their jobs after termination.

The 2003 case of *Melzer v. Board of Education*, for example, began when a high school teacher in New York City was fired because of his membership in a controversial organization. Peter Melzer, who taught at the Bronx High School for Science, was a highly credentialed teacher and winner of numerous teaching awards, but when his membership in the North American Man/Boy Love Association (NAMBLA) became public knowledge, parents of students at the school complained to the school board, which terminated him. While just belonging to the group was problematic enough, what was more troublesome was Melzer's public support for eliminating laws prohibiting sexual activity between adults and children. Melzer's advocacy took the form of letters to legislators as well as media interviews.[45]

Melzer was on a one-year sabbatical when the discussion of his termination took place at a school district meeting. When enough of his coworkers joined parents in expressing their concerns to the school board, it informed Melzer that he could not return.

Melzer sued for wrongful termination and violation of his First Amendment right of association but lost at the trial court and appellate levels. While not specifically spelled out in their rulings, legal scholars writing about the case surmise that while the courts recognized that Melzer was commenting on a matter of public concern, that was overshadowed by the potential for disruption to the operation of the school.[46]

When the case reached the U.S. Supreme Court, it also ruled against him, determining that the firing was justified. Even though there was no evidence that Melzer had harmed any students, the court affirmed the school board's prerogative to terminate him because the controversy—during which parents threatened to withdraw their children from the school—had the potential to disrupt the operation of the school. The Court also denied the claim of Melzer's attorneys that lower courts had validated the school board's decision based on "the heckler's veto," a term used to describe deciding public policy based on who has the loudest voice.[47]

In 2010, a high school math teacher in Cohasset, Massachusetts, learned that Facebook was not the best place to vent about her job and the students in her classes. Tired of missing workdays because of catching illnesses from students, and weary of having to deal with their parents over grades and other issues, June Talvitie-Siple posted comments calling the students "germ bags" and their parents "snobby" and "arrogant."[48]

Two parents saw the postings and complained to the district superintendent, resulting in Talvitie-Siple being asked to resign. Talvitie-Siple said she did not understand how privacy settings worked and had no idea parents would be reading her posts, which were intended for her friends and family. "I made a stupid mistake, and it may have cost me my career," she told ABC News.[49]

In January 2013, Colorado high school math teacher Carly McKinney was fired after a local television station aired a story that showed messages from her Twitter account. One Monday post indicated that she spent the previous weekend "naked, wet, and stoned," and it was accompanied by photos of her half-dressed. Another post read, "Watching a drug bust go down in the parking lot. It's funny 'cuz I have weed in my car in the staff parking lot." In yet another tweet, she claimed to grade papers while high.[50]

School administrators placed her on paid leave while they investigated the veracity of the report, then fired her despite protests from her students and her insistence that she created the Twitter page as a parody.[51]

In 2022, a teacher in Crown Point, Indiana, took it a step further, telling one of her students that she had a "kill list" of students and school staff. Twenty-five-year-old Angelica Carrasquillo was teaching fifth grade at St. Stanislaus Catholic School when her frustrations with the job boiled over. Her threat to "kill those on the list and then herself" was reported to local police, who escorted her from the building and charged her with felony intimidation. She pleaded guilty and was sentenced to thirty months' probation. She was also ordered to undergo mental-health treatment and was barred from working in any school or day-care center.[52]

In 2023, an educator in Missouri found a clever way to deal with low teacher pay and student loan debt: signing up for OnlyFans, a website that allows amateur filmmakers to produce and star in their own soft-core pornographic videos and charge subscribers for access. Brianna Coppage was a twenty-eight-year-old teacher at St. Clair High School in Franklin County when her side job became public knowledge. School board officials could not cite a specific policy that would have prohibited her activity, saying only that it was "inappropriate."[53] She was placed on paid administrative leave shortly after the school year began in September, and instead of waiting to be terminated, she resigned. In subsequent media interviews, she claimed to have made nearly $1 million in her first three months on OnlyFans, about twenty-four times her annual teacher salary.[54]

School Prayer Revisited

In 2015, an assistant football coach at Bremerton High School in Washington was fired for quietly praying at mid-field at the conclusion of each game. Joe Kennedy was sometimes joined by players and sometimes not. Worried that some players might feel pressured by Kennedy or their peers, and therefore the act might be violating the letter (or at least the spirit) of a 1962 Supreme Court ruling[55] prohibiting school prayer, administrators asked him to stop. When he refused, the school board stepped in and terminated him.

Backed by the conservative Christian organization First Liberty Institute, Kennedy sued the school district, setting off a seven-year legal battle that ended up in the U.S. Supreme Court. Along the way, Kennedy's case generated public support from President Donald Trump, several conservative political organizations and media outlets, and a number of high-profile college coaches, including former Florida State University coach Bobby Bowden.

In one of its final decisions announced at the end of the 2021–2 term, the court sided with Kennedy and ordered that he be reinstated. In its 6-3 decision, the majority wrote that despite the public venue, Kennedy's actions were a private matter, were not coercive, and did not amount to a school district endorsement of Christianity.[56]

After the ruling, Kennedy and the school district reached an undisclosed financial settlement, but the coach said he was so emotionally drained by the ordeal that he would not coach during the 2022–3 season. He returned at the beginning of the 2023 season but resigned after one game, citing the need to care for an ailing family member.[57]

Notes

1 David W. Ewing, *Freedom Inside the Organization: Bringing Civil Liberties to the Workplace* (New York: E.P. Dutton, 1977), pp. 104–5.

2 *Pickering v. Board of Education*, 391 U.S. 563 (1968). See also: Randy J. Kozel, "Reconceptualizing Public Employee Speech," *Northwestern University Law Review* 99, no. 3 (Spring 2005): pp. 1007–51.

3 *Pickering v. Board of Education.* See also: Alan F. Westin and Stephan Salisbury, eds., *Individual Rights in the Corporation* (New York: Pantheon Books, 1980), p. 105.
4 Ibid.
5 *Pickering v. Board of Education.* See also: Darien A. McWhirter, *Your Rights at Work* (New York: John Wiley & Sons, 1989), pp. 125–6.
6 Bruce Barry, *Speechless: The Erosion of Free Expression in the American Workplace* (San Francisco: Berrett-Koehler Publishers, 2007), p. 71.
7 *Pickering v. Board of Education.* See also: Kenneth Walters, "Your Employees' Right to Blow the Whistle," *Harvard Business Review,* July–August 1975, pp. 26–34 and 161–3.
8 Steve Patterson, "Reprimand Settles Former Duval Teacher Amy Donofrio's Fight Over Black Lives Matter Flag," *Florida Times-Union,* June 14, 2024.
9 Ibid.
10 Jonathan Zimmerman, *Free Speech and Why You Should Give a Damn (*Buffalo, NY: New Idea Press, 2021). pp. 61–2.
11 *Watts v. Seward School Board*, 454 P. 2d 732 (1969). *Watts v. Seward School Board,* 381 U.S. 126 (1965).
12 Ibid.
13 Ibid.
14 *Downs v. Conway School District*, 329 F. Supp. 338 (1971). See also: Ewing, *Freedom Inside the Organization*, pp. 105–6; Walters, "Your Employees' Right to Blow the Whistle."
15 *Mt. Healthy City School District Board of Education v. Doyle*, 429 U.S. 274 (1977). See also: Lawrence Rosenthal, "Permissible Content Discrimination Under the First Amendment: The Strange Case of the Public Employee," *Hastings Constitutional Law Quarterly* 25, no. 4 (Summer 1998): pp. 528–84.
16 *Givhan v. Western Line Consolidated School District,* 439 U.S. 410 (1979). See also: Rosenthal, "Permissible Content Discrimination Under the First Amendment." Charles O. Gregory and Harold A. Katz, *Labor and the Law* (New York: W.W Norton & Company, 1979), p. 605.
17 McWhirter, *Your Rights at Work*, p. 127.
18 *Anderson v. Central Point School Dist. No. 6,* 554 F. Supp. 600 (1982).
19 Ibid.
20 *Southside Public Schools v. Hill*, 827 F. 2d 270 (1987). See also: McWhirter, *Your Rights at Work*, p. 128.
21 *Bernasconi v. Tempe Elementary School District,* 548 F. 2d 857 (1977).
22 *Wales v. Board of Education*, 120 F. 3d 82 (1997).
23 Ibid.

24 Mihir Zaveri, "Teacher Fired Over Tweets Wins Appeal to Texas Agency," *The New York Times*, December 1, 2019, p. 23-A.
25 Ibid.
26 Ibid.
27 Ibid.
28 Ibid.
29 *Clark v. Fort Worth Independent School District*, Case No. 03-21-00275-CV (Tex. App. Jan. 25, 2023).
30 Ibid.
31 Ibid.
32 Adam Piore, "Teachers Put to the Test," *Reader's Digest*, September 2023, pp. 62–71. See also: Shira LiBartov, "Teacher Turned Walmart Worker Says He Earns $20K More 'Not Using His Degree,'" *Newsweek*, July 19, 2022.
33 Laura S. Diaz and Cassie Dickman, "I Was Kicked Out: Ousted California Principal Escorted Off Campus After Graduation," *USA Today*, May 29, 2021.
34 *Shelton v. Tucker*, 364 U.S. 479 (1960).
35 Ibid.
36 Ibid.
37 "Did the Internet Kill Privacy?" *CBS Sunday Morning*, February 13, 2011.
38 Ibid.
39 Ibid.
40 Ibid.
41 Ibid.
42 Ibid.
43 Jake McGowan, "Teacher's Semi-Racy Facebook Photo Doesn't Justify Firing," *Technology and Marketing Law Blog*, February 2, 2014.
44 Ibid.
45 Kozel, "Reconceptualizing Public Employee Speech."
46 Ibid.
47 Ibid.
48 Ki Mae Heussner and Dalia Fahmy, "Teacher Loses Job After Commenting About Students, Parents on Facebook," *ABC News*, August 19, 2010.
49 Ibid.
50 Natalie Umansky, "10 Outrageous Tweets That Got People Fired," *Oddee.com*, February 21, 2014.
51 Ibid.
52 "Indiana Teacher with 'Kill List' of Students, Staff Sentenced to 2½ Years on Probation," *Associated Press Report*, August 7, 2023.
53 Emily Deletter, "Former Missouri Teacher Who Created OnlyFans Account Says She Has Made Nearly $1 Million," *USA Today*, November 7, 2023.

54 Ibid.
55 *Engel v. Vitale*, 370 U.S. 421 (1962).
56 *Kennedy v. Bremerton School District*, Case 21-418 (2022).
57 Natalie Neysa Alund and Jeff Graham, “Football Coach Fired for Praying on Field Resigns After One Game,” *USA Today*, September 8, 2023, p. 6-A.

8

Free Speech for College Educators

Academic Freedom versus Political and Legal Considerations

The Edge of the Envelope

Around the beachside community of Wilmington, North Carolina, Mike Adams was known for a number of attributes. The fifty-five-year-old professor of criminology at the University of North Carolina Wilmington was a born-again Christian, conservative political commentator, critic of political correctness and liberal ideology, a skeptic of Covid-19 masking and vaccination protocols, and in the last year of his life, a stubborn litigant in federal court. His popularity among his students was mixed, depending on who was commenting. One of his former department chairs joked that if there was a survey to determine the most popular and least popular professors in the criminology department, Adams would have likely won in both categories.[1]

He was also an avid gun collector. On a sweltering day in July 2020, Adams used one of his prized possessions to end his own life. His suicide shocked his former colleagues and the community surrounding UNCW. Three weeks earlier, Adams had won a legal battle against the university, agreeing to clean out his desk in exchange for a financial settlement that could have easily funded an early retirement.

Adams began teaching at UNCW in 1993, and the relationship between him and the administration was adversarial almost from the beginning. It hit a low point a week following the September 11, 2001, terrorist attacks, when Adams launched an online vendetta against a Muslim student who sent an email to university students and faculty blaming the attacks on the "American ruling elite that carried out violent enterprises around the world."[2]

The student's missive invited recipients to forward it to others, and Adams responded with his own university-wide email, saying he would forward the student's message but added that the First Amendment protects her speech, just as it has "protected bigoted, unintelligent, and immature speech for many years."[3]

The student complained that the response was defamatory. While she opted not to file a lawsuit to that effect, she was successful in prompting school administrators to open an investigation of Adams, in which they demanded and got access to all of his emails. While many of Adams's colleagues had defended him when his previous tirades were limited to criticizing the university in general terms, they drew the line at what they saw as a direct and personal attack against a student.

When Adams was denied a promotion in 2007, the arguments on both sides were predictable: Adams claimed his treatment by the university was based solely on his religious views and conservative stance on state and national political issues, while the university claimed his research productivity was substandard. Instead of using his non-teaching hours to produce scholarship that could be presented at academic conferences, Adams spent that time writing books with titles such as *Welcome to the Ivory Tower of Babel*[4] and *Feminists Say the Darndest Things: A Politically Incorrect Professor Confronts "Womyn" on Campus.*[5] Those titles earned him plenty of interviews on Fox News, talk radio, and other conservative media outlets, but because they were produced by "fringe" publishers, they did little to enhance the university's efforts to expand its reputation for scholarship.

His lawsuit failed at the trial court level, but in 2011 an appeals court reversed that decision and remanded the case back to the trial court. It took another three years to resolve the case, with the university agreeing to pay Adams $700,000, which included his attorney's fees and the salary he lost while his promotion was on hold. Although the legal drama took seven years, his victory and promotion to full professor were also considered a win for academic freedom.[6]

Between 2014 and 2020, Adams continued to thumb his nose at the UNCW administration and even other criminology professors across the country who circulated a petition suggesting that the university fire him. According to higher education watchdog groups, Adams became more and more defensive, using social media to mock students who were gay, lesbian, and transgender, as well as those involved in social causes such as Black Lives Matter.[7] He also published his final book, titled *Letters to a Young Progressive: How to Avoid Wasting Your Life Protesting Things You Don't Understand.*[8]

As pressure on the university continued to mount, the administration offered him another financial settlement in exchange for his early retirement. The $504,000 payout was again based on attorneys' fees, lost salary, and retirement benefits.[9] The school denied that it had done anything wrong, instead claiming that the financial settlement was an expedient way of parting company with Adams and "moving on."[10]

Rather than keeping a low profile, Adams continued to push the free-speech envelope until the end. During the Covid-19 pandemic, as his career at UNCW wound down, he used media interviews and his own social media platforms to compare North Carolina Governor Roy Cooper's mask mandates for the state's university campuses to how masters treated their slaves three centuries earlier. "Massa Cooper, let my people go," he wrote on Twitter. "Instead of shutting down entire universities, we should just shut down non-essential majors, like Women's Studies."[11]

Recurring Themes

Controversies such as those involving Mike Adams and UNCW have their roots in the work of a professional organization more than a century old. In 1915, the newly formed American Association of University Professors issued guidelines aimed at protecting its members, whether tenured or not, when they spoke out on controversial issues, regardless of whether those comments were part of classroom instruction, research activity, media interviews, or any other venue. The guidelines were updated in 1940 and 1967, with the latter version being expanded to include the rights of students and coining the term "academic freedom." When combined with a university's own faculty union protection, the guidelines have been effective in doing what they were designed to do, even though the courts have no legal obligation to enforce them.[12]

The issue of professors and administrators speaking out on public issues goes back to 1949, when the president of Fairmont State University was investigated by the West Virginia Board of Education after challenging the view of the American Legion that equated liberalism with communism. Having found nothing in her background to indicate she was a member of the Communist Party or held communist viewpoints, the board fired her anyway—because she was an atheist.[13]

That case kicked off a "terror campaign" against "left-leaning" professors who were suspected of having communist connections simply because they were liberal. Directed to do so by their boards of trustees in the 1950s, Ivy League schools purged their faculties of anyone suspected of being communists—whether proven or not—with little due process or opportunity to appeal. Yale University President Charles Seymour told the media that "there will be no witch-hunts at Yale, because there will be no witches."[14]

Concern over such matters waxed and waned for the next thirty years, hitting its peak again during the Vietnam era, when college professors who spoke out against the U.S. involvement in Southeast Asia, whether inside or outside the classroom, were subject to suspension, dismissal, and harassment from outside parties and politicians.[15] An English instructor at the State University of New York, for example, refused to answer administrators' questions about his political beliefs and alleged membership in the Communist Party. When his lawsuit went to the Supreme Court in 1967, the justices agreed with the instructor's contention that his political beliefs had no effect on his teaching ability and the inquiries violated his First Amendment right of association.[16]

While some state governments were still requiring professors to take anti-communist "loyalty oaths" as late as 2006, the concern today has broadened from "communist connections" to worries that professors are "indoctrinating" students and pushing a "woke agenda."[17] Much of the criticism results from faculty and administrators promoting ideas such as racial harmony, equal rights for the LGBTQ community, and conservatives' favorite target: programs promoting diversity, equity, and inclusion. In some states, the abbreviation "DEI" has become a "dirty word."[18] Today, several state legislatures have attempted to limit the speech of liberal professors by eliminating the tenure system.[19]

Given the idealistic way that colleges and universities address free speech, there are three overarching principles that guide decisions:

1. *First Amendment considerations*. College campuses have been called "First Amendment institutions" because of their importance within a civil society, or as civil rights attorney Paul Horowitz called them, "places where ideas begin."[20] Civil liberties attorney Jonathan Zimmerman, in his 2016 book, *Campus Politics: What Everyone Needs to Know*, added that a university's major role is "creating knowledge, which requires continuous testing, discussion, and analysis."[21] In a promotional video Walter Cronkite taped for the University of Texas, the veteran broadcaster said, "what starts here changes the world."[22]

While private universities are not required to respect the same First Amendment values as public institutions, many do so to some degree. As cases in this chapter illustrate, even conservative, faith-based private universities espouse the values of free speech but apply limits.

2. *Academic freedom*. In its early years, the concept of "academic freedom" applied mostly to conversations that took place in the classroom and the laboratory, or wherever a professor conducted his research. More recently, organizations such as AAUP have expanded the concept to cover social media commentary and other non-teaching and non-research forms of expression. That may include an educator's criticisms of the policies of their institutions as well as those of local, state, and federal governments, whether those criticisms are stated in-person, in media interviews, or on social media. Because the case law regarding research and classroom teaching would be overwhelming—and deserving of a separate volume—this book will not attempt to cover it (except for the three paragraphs to follow). Instead, this chapter will focus solely on the speech of professors (and in a few cases, administrators) that is unrelated to research and teaching, with most of it taking place in media interviews and social media activity.

   One factor that brings together both forms of speech—research/teaching and unrelated expression—is the changing nature of tenure. In Wisconsin, Texas, and Florida, state legislatures are either eliminating or limiting tenure for new hires while trying to do so retroactively for professors already tenured. While governors and legislators admit their rationale is to eliminate liberal "indoctrination" of students by professors teaching the "wrong" ideas, the concern is that it may also limit professors' roles in speaking out on social issues. University leaders in those states worry that may cause the loss of existing faculty while making their schools less attractive to job candidates.[23]

   What academic freedom may or may not cover—depending on whom you ask—are comments made outside of the classroom and outside of the professor's area of expertise. Can a professor of English literature be scrutinized for publicly criticizing a politician's position on abortion? Can a biology professor criticize the state legislature for its tax policy?

   "Academic freedom" does apply to some of those cases, however, based on popular definitions of the term. Princeton University Professor Keith Whittington, for example, defines academic freedom as "a specialized application of general free-speech principles, and incorporates an important set of both rights and duties that should be respected by the campus community."[24] Those rights and duties, Whittington added, "are designed to foster the productive exchange of ideas, the careful scrutinizing of claims, and the development of expertise needed both to teach students and to convey what has been learned to a broader world."[25] It is important, therefore, that professors be evaluated based "on the performance of their professional responsibilities and not on their privately held opinions."[26]

3. *The Pickering precedent*. Even though the *Pickering* case (discussed in Chapter 7) involved a high school teacher, the precedent is used in cases involving college professors. Courts ruled that professors have the right to criticize university policy (or broader public policy) when they do so as private citizens and not in their role as university employees.

While those concepts represent the idealistic (some might say utopian) view of free speech, university presidents and other administrators must make decisions based on practicality and real-world factors:

1. *Campus harmony and reputation.* Much like the military, colleges and universities are theoretically not allowed to interfere with the speech rights of their employees but often do so in the interest of preserving campus harmony and the elusive "comfortable learning environment." The latter phrase is an extension of DEI programs and their goal of helping schools attract and retain minority students, especially in cases in which an institution's track record in that area is not good.

   More than any other type of employer, universities are often guilty of knee-jerk reactions when employees make public comments that cast the institution in a negative light. Administrators claim their concern is not only the offense taken by students and other employees but also that audiences critical to the success of the school—public officials and donors—might believe such comments are endorsed by or represent the official position of the university.
2. *Political and legal considerations.* As several cases in this chapter illustrate, when professors make controversial comments—via traditional media, social media, or other venues—university administrators must balance their free-speech rights against the concerns of politicians, alumni, and donors.

Another factor is Title IX, a 1972 law dealing with sex discrimination in higher education. Several cases in this chapter deal with the legal issues raised by professors' comments regarding women on their campuses.

3. *The chilling effect.* While tenured professors have more leeway in their speech outside of the classroom, instructors without tenure—including those in non-tenure-track positions as well as adjuncts and graduate teaching assistants—are largely unprotected, as their employment is considered "at-will"[27] (defined in the Introduction). While theoretically covered by academic freedom even without tenure, many educators have learned that life is easier if they don't speak out on controversial issues. As many state legislatures are considering revising tenure procedures or doing away with the process altogether, that further clouds the issue.[28]

Leonard M. Niehoff, a civil rights attorney and adjunct professor at the University of Michigan Law School, once told the audience at a professional conference that "the first rule of communication on a college campus is that for every action, there is an equal and opposite over-reaction."[29]

The chilling effect is especially significant for faculty members, tenured and untenured, whose political beliefs lean conservative. Political commentator Kirsten Powers has been studying alleged bias against other conservatives in all aspects of society, including the college campus, for more than a decade. In her 2015 book, *The Silencing*, she claimed to have interviewed numerous conservative professors who told her "chilling accounts of intimidation, harassment, discrimination, denial of tenure, and more," but they did not want to be quoted in her book because they were fearful of being alienated from their liberal colleagues who hold their academic and professional futures in their hands.[30]

The problem even extends to university presidents, who are often reluctant to speak out on controversial issues such as international affairs, support for outspoken faculty members, or the school's diversity, equity, and inclusion (DEI) initiatives for fear of offending state officials or trustees they report to, or influential alumni or donors.[31]

Political Affiliations and Activities

Faculty members' rights of political affiliation were upheld in two Supreme Court cases dating back to the Cold War. The issue was not whether or not the college educators were actually members of the Communist Party, but their refusal to sign documents certifying they were not. In the 1952 case of *Wieman v. Updegraff,* faculty members at the Oklahoma Agricultural and Mechanical College were terminated because they missed—most likely intentionally—the deadline to sign the documents. After they were denied employment, they sued the state of Oklahoma and were reinstated. Although the Court drew a distinction between simply refusing to sign the documents and actual public statements declaring allegiance to the Communist Party or advocating violence against the U.S. government, it did leave the door open to allowing state governments to enforce loyalty oaths in the future.[32]

Fifteen years later, it closed the door for good, ruling in a similar case in New York that such laws were unconstitutional. The case of *Keyishian v. Board of Regents* began when faculty at the University of Buffalo, which had just shifted from a private university to part of New York's State University System, challenged a state law that required them to sign documents certifying they were not, and never had been, members of the Communist Party. Harry Keyishian, three other faculty members, and a librarian refused to sign the documents and were terminated. When the five men were fired, they sued the university system, but a federal district court refused to hear the case[33] and a circuit court of appeals ruled in favor of the state university system.

When the case reached the U.S. Supreme Court in 1967, the justices ruled 5-4 that Keyishian and his colleagues did not forfeit their First Amendment rights to political opinions and affiliation when they became state employees.[34] The four justices in the minority wrote separate dissenting opinions in which they claimed the case was not about free speech or association, but rather membership in an organization advocating the overthrow of the American government. There was no discussion of that potential in the oral or written arguments, even though the law under which they were terminated used the terms "treasonable or seditious utterances" in describing the state's opposition to the Communist Party.[35]

The rulings in the *Wieman* and *Keyishian* cases overruled the precedent set by the 1952 case of *Adler v. Board of Education of the City of New York*, which was argued at the beginning of the Cold War and national paranoia over the spread of Communism in Europe.[36] In that case, the Court upheld a similar New York law that required K–12 public-school teachers to sign the anti-Communist Party document.[37]

Taking part in the January 6, 2021, riots at the U.S. Capitol caused problems for police officers and active-duty military personnel, but it also ended the twenty-year teaching career of an adjunct professor at St. Vincent College in Pennsylvania. During the siege, Rick Saccone posted on Facebook, "We are storming the Capitol. Our vanguard has broken through the barricades. We will save this nation. Are you with me?"[38]

In addition to teaching courses in international relations and global terrorism at SVC, Saccone also served in the Pennsylvania House of Representatives from 2011 to 2019. Once SVC officials heard of the posts and investigated, Saccone deleted them.

That wasn't enough to save his job at the conservative Catholic school; he resigned rather than waiting to be fired. College President Paul R. Taylor told local media that SVC

> teaches the importance of the sanctity of human life, the rule of law, civil discourse, free speech and civil engagement, and we strongly condemn the extreme actions of violence and destruction that were on display at our nation's capital . . . we believe that all individuals have the right to an opinion, but when beliefs and opinions devolve into illegal and violent activities, there will be no tolerance.[39]

Stirring the Pot

Around the country, nearly every university has one of "those" professors who go by various monikers, the most common of which are the "loose cannons." They fall into two camps. The first is populated by individuals who make one-time outrageous comments that draw attention to themselves and their institutions; they could put an end to the controversies by simply apologizing or "walking back" their comments, but they refuse to do so on the grounds of stubbornness or resistance to what they view as "political correctness."

The other category consists of faculty members like Mike Adams who engage in long-running conflicts with their colleagues, their department chairs, administrators at their university, local and state officials, and the communities that surround their institutions. In most cases, these feuds begin after the faculty member earns tenure, which makes it harder for the institution to get rid of them. The debate follows a typical pattern: the university accuses the faculty member of engaging in discriminatory or harassing behavior (which could get around the tenure issue) or neglecting his or her teaching duties while engaging in issues outside of their fields of expertise. Conversely, the faculty members accuse their institutions of violating their First Amendment rights of free speech and/or discriminating against them because of their religious or political views.

Professors often look at their comments on controversial issues as examples of free speech or extensions of their research agendas, but few realize those comments expose them and their institutions to public criticism and legislative scrutiny. "An off-hand social-media post can trigger a highly orchestrated and widespread digital attacks from organized activists across the country," wrote Peter F. Lake, professor of law at Stetson University, in a 2022 op-ed in *The Chronicle of Higher Education*. "The law is unlikely ever to make a priority of protecting academics, but in the coming decades we will probably see more regulation of proper digital behavior. Until then, professors will continue to be the victims of coordinated attacks."[40]

Lake's op-ed made a number of recommendations for university administrations, all of them in the area of supporting faculty when they come under fire. "Administrators must make it clear to faculty members that their institution will protect basic freedoms of expression," Lake wrote. "An institution will face reputational harm and consequences from faculty-rights organizations for throwing someone under the bus in an effort to quell a controversy."[41]

One of those "loose cannons" was Donald Silva, an English professor at the University of New Hampshire in the 1990s. Throughout his career at UNH, he had faced criticism from students and colleagues for using an abundance of sexual metaphors in his lectures. Those comments were largely protected under the principle of academic freedom, but when he told a magazine interviewer that sex between faculty and students might "occasionally be beneficial to students," administrators decided those comments were unprotected. He was suspended and ordered to seek counseling at his own expense. He declined, and instead sued UNH in federal court, which ruled in his favor and ordered the university to reinstate him.[42]

Many universities are tempted to discipline or terminate employees in order to appease corporate sponsors that donate money to support the university's research efforts or athletic programs. "The First Amendment means little when university administrators and university professors engage in *self-censorship* to appease corporate interests," wrote professors William A. Wines and Terence J. Lau in a 2005 article in *DePaul University Law Review*. "Because the loss of employment is so damaging, the expectation that they will be fired for expressing their opinions could have a serious chilling effect on individuals' free speech."[43]

The terrorist attacks of September 11, 2001, sparked a series of controversies affecting faculty across the country. One example involved Richard Berthold, a history professor at the University of New Mexico, who told his class on that morning—while the drama was playing out on television—that "anyone who can blow up the Pentagon gets my vote."[44] Berthold was suspended without pay for the following semester, despite issuing an apology directly to the university administration and the local and national media. "It was stupid thing to say," he told a reporter for *The Nation*. "I deserve a lot of the shit that's been dumped on me. However, the First Amendment should protect even jackasses. A lot of my hate mail says, 'You commie,' which is ironic, given that I'm pretty conservative on most social issues."[45]

A mathematics professor at the City University of New York later said after the attacks that "the ultimate responsibility lies with the rulers of this country, the capitalist ruling class."[46]

In 2006, Kevin Barrett, a lecturer in the history department at the University of Wisconsin, had a different take on September 11. He was part of an online group of conspiracy theorists that believed, among other things, that the attacks were carried out by the U.S. government as a pretext to going to war in the Middle East. Students, faculty, alumni, and university donors were nearly unanimous in calling for Barrett to be fired. Even though Barrett was not protected by tenure and there was no evidence that he included such ideas in the content of his teaching (although he said this to students outside the classroom), university administrators cited "academic freedom" and "the free exchange of ideas" as grounds for retaining him. They allowed him to teach a course on Islamic history the following semester, but only if he agreed to balance his theories with more mainstream content. The provost also warned him that when he spoke to the media about his theories, he could identify himself as a UW faculty member but must also indicate that his beliefs were his own and did not represent those of the university.[47]

The provost's lukewarm support for Barrett didn't stop outsiders from escalating their calls for his dismissal. Those calls came from the Wisconsin chapter of the Anti-Defamation League, the UW Board of Regents, and a bipartisan group of state legislators.

Political commentator Stanley Fish, himself a former university administrator, wrote in a *New York Times* op-ed following the Barrett case that "academic freedom gives a professor the right to study what he wants and to talk about provocative ideas in the classroom, it doesn't give him the right to recruit students to a political agenda."[48] Barrett eventually left the university on his own terms to begin a second career in the conspiracy theory business as a conservative radio talk show host and publisher of a newsletter titled *False Flag News*.

In Pennsylvania in 2010, a professor at East Stroudsburg University was suspended for a month and forced to undergo a psychological evaluation after posting comments on Facebook about wanting to kill her students. "Does anyone know where I can find a very discrete hitman?" Gloria Gadsden wrote. "Yes, it's been that kind of day."[49] A month later, she posted, "Had a good day today . . . Didn't want to kill even one student. Now Friday was a different story."[50]

Gadsden didn't realize Facebook had changed its privacy settings, so what she thought were private and facetious comments to a handful of friends became public and were taken seriously, prompting a university spokesperson to tell the local media that, "given the climate of security concerns in academia, the university has an obligation to take all threats seriously and act accordingly."[51]

Aided by the Foundation for Individual Rights in Education, Gadsden was reinstated after completing her psychiatric evaluation.

While Mike Adams was locked in a multi-year feud with the administration at UNCW, a professor with a similar name was locked in a battle with the administration at Marquette University in Wisconsin. John McAdams was a tenured associate professor of political science and well known as a conservative voice on campus. During the fall semester of 2014, a graduate teaching assistant in the Philosophy Department refused to allow a student with political leanings similar to those of McAdams to speak in class about his opposition to gay marriage. Cheryl Abbate called his position "homophobic" because "everyone agrees on this."[52] That started a mini-controversy on campus, but it expanded in scope when McAdams used his personal blog to criticize Abbate by name, saying she was negligent and unprofessional in not allowing the student to speak.[53]

Without a hearing or other procedure of due process required by faculty contracts, the administration suspended McAdams from teaching. Marquette President Michael Lovell told him that he could be reinstated, but only if he issued a public apology to Abbate. He refused, prompting Lovell to suspend him indefinitely and order him off campus. In his written notice, McAdams was told the suspension was based on the blog post that constituted "dishonorable, irresponsible, or incompetent conduct that significantly reduced his value to the university."[54]

The American Association of University Professors (AAUP) wrote to Lovell and informed him that the suspension violated AAUP guidelines regarding due process.[55]

After Christmas break, with McAdams still barred from campus, Lovell began the process of termination but first referred the matter to a Faculty Hearing Committee. After nearly a year of investigation and debate, the FHC recommended against termination but told Lovell he would be justified in suspending McAdams for two semesters without pay.

Lovell once again offered McAdams the opportunity to return ahead of schedule if he issued a written apology to the university and Abbate, but he refused again and was effectively fired. McAdams took his case to state court, claiming a violation of his rights of academic freedom and due process. A trial court granted the university summary judgment, determining that even though the school "skipped a few steps of due process" at the beginning, once the case went to the FHC it was back on solid ground. The court upheld the firing, which sent the case to the Wisconsin Supreme Court. That court reversed the ruling of the trial court, determining that McAdams's online behavior, while inappropriate, did not reflect "on his unfitness to serve, taking into account his entire record as a teacher and scholar."[56] It also found that the Faculty Hearing Committee's recommendation was not legally binding, and in the end, the Court put more emphasis on the AAUP guidelines than the findings of the FHC or other administrative policies.[57]

In 2014, a political science professor was offered a position at the University of Illinois but saw the offer withdrawn after he posted on Twitter his anti-Semitic comments about the bombing of settlements in Gaza. Steven Salaita, who gave up a tenured position at Virginia Polytechnic University, claimed his comments were "taken out of context" and that he was strongly opposed to all forms of racism.[58] But that wasn't enough for Illinois president Robert Easter, who told a reporter for *The New York Times* that, "Professor Salaita's approach indicates he would be incapable of fostering a classroom environment where conflicting opinions would be given equal consideration."[59] The president later clarified that the withdrawal of the offer was based not on the content of his statements, but rather the tone with which they were made.

Senior Joshua Cooper had collected 1,300 student signatures on a petition opposing Salaita's hiring, and numerous alumni had threatened to stop their annual donations to the university if Salaita's hiring went forward.

Following his loss of the job in Illinois, Salaita was hired to teach at the American University in Beirut, Lebanon.[60]

One of the unwritten rules of academic freedom is that it includes the dichotomy found in many First Amendment cases that draws a distinction between conduct and speech. "They (professors) can't do anything they want, but they can—in theory—say anything they want," wrote Zimmerman in *Campus Politics*.[61]

The conduct versus speech dichotomy was a critical part of the case of a Florida Atlantic University professor who made national headlines in 2013. James Tracy, a professor of media history, claimed on social media and in media interviews that the December 2012 murders of twenty students and six employees at Sandy Hook Elementary School in Connecticut were a hoax—that killed no one—carried out by hired actors and staged by the federal government to generate support for gun-control legislation.

The following April, Tracy floated his theory that the bombing at the Boston Marathon that killed three spectators and injured hundreds of others was actually a "mass casualty drill" in which no one died. The university distanced itself from Tracy's conspiracy theories, which were posted on his personal blog and not the FAU website. "Florida Atlantic University does not agree with Mr. Tracy's views or opinions," the university clarified in its own public statement. "His editorialized postings do not reflect the positions of the university or its leaders. The university stands with the rest of the country in our support of the victims of these two tragedies."[62]

More recently, he has suggested the government staged news stories such as murders in San Bernardino, California; Charleston, South Carolina; and the Navy Yard in Washington, D.C.[63]

In early 2016, FAU fired Tracy, claiming his behavior was outrageous enough for his tenure to be revoked. The university claimed the dismissal was not related to his bizarre theories, but was based instead on him contacting parents of Sandy Hook children killed in the tragedy and accusing them of taking part in the conspiracy. After the parents of Noah Pozner, a six-year-old killed at Sandy Hook, asked Tracy to remove their son's photograph from his blog, Tracy responded with a demand that the parents provide proof that Noah ever lived and that they were his biological parents.[64]

In September 2022, as Queen Elizabeth II was on her deathbed in Aberdeenshire, Scotland, a university professor was creating a monarchy-related controversy 3,700 miles away in Pittsburgh, Pennsylvania. Uju Anya, who had taught linguistics and second-language acquisition at Carnegie Mellon University for only a year, tweeted that "I heard the chief monarch of a thieving, raping genocidal empire is finally dying . . . may her pain be excruciating."[65] Anya explained that her comments about the queen and the United Kingdom were based on a history of alleged violence against the people of her home country of Nigeria, including her own ancestors, during that nation's civil war in the 1960s.[66]

Within hours, her tweet was removed for violating a Twitter rule that prohibited comments wishing harm upon others, prompting her to post a follow-up. "If anyone expects me to express anything but disdain for the monarch who supervised a government that sponsored the genocide that massacred half my family and the consequences of which those alive today are still trying to overcome, you can keep wishing on a star," she tweeted.[67] Later, speaking to NBC News, she added, "I take deep offense at the notion that the oppressed and survivors of violence have to somehow be deferential or respectful when their oppressors die."[68]

The administration of CMU stated publicly that while they supported Anya's right to free speech, her comments were solely her own. "We do not condone the offensive and objectionable messages posted by Uju Anya today on her personal social media account," the statement read. "Free expression is core to the mission of higher education, however, the views she shared absolutely do not represent the values of the institution, nor the standards of discourse we seek to foster."[69]

The week after her controversial tweets, Anya doubled down on her comments on a podcast titled "This Week in White Supremacy." The hosts expected she might back away from the controversy, but instead she added, "I said what I fucking said."[70]

In Louisiana in 2023, the election of a conservative Republican governor rekindled a two-year feud between him and the chairman of the Department of Journalism at the state's flagship university.

As attorney general, Jeff Landry railed against the state's university system and what he perceived as its "woke agenda," threatening to revamp the tenure system and get rid of "liberal professors and ideology."[71] That caused Robert Mann, a veteran journalism professor and department chair at Louisiana State University, to become one of Landry's most outspoken critics. When Mann publicly criticized Landry's anti-mask and anti-vaccine positions during the Covid-19 pandemic, Landry reportedly asked LSU President William F. Tate to discipline or fire him. Tate declined to do so, issuing a public statement that neither condemned nor supported Mann but noted that LSU was "committed to free and open scholarship and the freedom to debate ideas and principles without interference."[72]

That kept Mann safely in place for a few years, but when Landry became governor-elect in October 2023, Mann began planning his exit strategy. He announced his pre-emptive resignation three months before the governor's scheduled inauguration. "The person who will be governor in January has already asked LSU to fire me," Mann wrote on X (formerly Twitter).[73] "I have no confidence the leadership of this university would protect the Manship School (of Mass Communication) against a governor's efforts to punish me and other faculty members."[74] In a subsequent interview with *The Daily Beast*, Mann described himself as "an irritant" to conservative officials like Landry and added, "I have done that because I have tenure, because I'm protected under the First Amendment. . . . But this is not going to be a governor who I think has any respect for that."[75]

Make Getting Fired Great Again

The election of Donald Trump in 2016 seems to have brought out the worst in social media vitriol on the part of short-term or part-time faculty not protected by tenure or faculty unions.

In 2017, a professor at a private university in Florida was fired after blaming the deaths and destruction caused by Hurricane Harvey in Texas as payback for that state having awarded its electoral votes to Trump. Kenneth Storey, a visiting professor of sociology at the University of Tampa, made the comments on his personal Twitter account. "I don't believe in instant karma but this kinda feels like it for Texas," he wrote. "Hopefully this will help them realize the GOP doesn't care about them."[76]

Storey apologized on his account the next day, but the university fired him shortly thereafter and issued a statement which clarified that his comments did not "reflect UT's community views or values . . . as Floridians, we are well aware of the destruction and suffering associated with tropical weather. Our thoughts and prayers are with all impacted by Hurricane Harvey."[77]

That same year, Fresno State University history instructor Lars Maischak was suspended, but later reinstated, after posting on Twitter that in order to save democracy, "Trump must hang. The sooner and the higher, the better."[78] The tweet resulted in Maischak receiving not only a notice of suspension from the university but also a visit from the U.S. Secret Service, which investigates all threats against the president, no matter how flippant.

Maischak deleted his Twitter account and claimed to have only twenty-eight followers but nevertheless apologized through media interviews. "I ask forgiveness of those who felt threatened or offended by my tweets," he said:

> My statements each represent the end point of a dark train of thought triggered by my despair over the actions of the present U.S. government. I never expected them to be read by anyone but a close circle of acquaintances who would know to place them in context. To treat Twitter as of no more consequence than a journal was a poor decision. In this spirit, I am prepared to take full responsibility for my statements.[79]

Anti-Trump rhetoric considered threatening also led Rutgers University adjunct professor Kevin Allred to lose two New Jersey teaching jobs. Shortly after Trump was elected in November 2016, Allred tweeted a number of anti-Trump comments that went largely unnoticed. However, a tweet in which he asked the question, "Will the Second Amendment be as cool when I buy a gun and start shooting at random white people or no?" was problematic.[80] After that tweet drew negative attention to the university, the administration cancelled his contract to teach two courses in gender and sexuality the following semester. He prepared to move on to Montclair State University, but shortly before the fall semester began in 2017, he tweeted that "this is such a fucking joke . . . someone should just shoot Trump."[81]

That got him another pink slip from the university as well as a visit from the Secret Service. Unlike Maischak, Allred refused to apologize and claimed his comments were not a direct threat, but rather an example of "rhetorical hyperbole" that was no different from the type of rhetoric that Trump used.[82]

In a bizarre twist, MSU issued a statement claiming it had never employed Allred or offered him a position, even though he provided documentation that he had been scheduled to teach that fall, had submitted syllabi, and notified the campus bookstore of his assigned textbooks. Ari Cohn, a lawyer with the Foundation for Individual Rights in Education, said it was "unconstitutional for a public university to take away someone's job for protected speech and that

Allred's tweets were well within the legal definitions of protected speech." Cohn added that professors "have been making incendiary remarks for decades" and "just because social media make those remarks more visible doesn't mean college leaders have any less of an obligation to defend free expression."[83]

The Dangerous Territories of Race and Sex

In his 2000 novel, *The Human Stain*, Pulitzer Prize-winning author Philip Roth tells the story of Coleman Silk, a professor of classics at a fictional private university in New England, who runs afoul of the administration after inadvertently referring to two students missing from class as "spooks." Silk was simply joking about their frequent absenteeism and was unaware that they were Black, but that wasn't enough for his superiors, who responded to student oversensitivity and their own "white guilt" by terminating the tenured professor, who was already close to retirement.

In media interviews, Roth disclosed that he based the novel and its protagonist on the real-life story of Melvin Tumin, a professor of sociology at Princeton University, who faced a similar ordeal that nearly ended his thirty-year career.[84]

The fictional Silk (who, much like Tumin, ironically was later exposed as a light-skinned Black man who passed for white for much of his life) was an obvious victim of "campus correctness" who did not deserve his fate. Other professors, who many critics believe were far more deserving of termination, eventually met that fate, but it took much longer—and required a series of incidents rather than a single one—to justify their firings.

In 1991, Michael Levin was a Jewish professor of philosophy at City College of New York who claimed in a magazine article that Blacks have been less successful in school than whites—not because of racial bias but because "the average black is significantly less intelligent than the average white."[85] The CCNY Faculty Senate passed a resolution condemning Levin's comment, and students, faculty, and staff circulated petitions calling for his firing. While CCNY administrators declined to terminate Levin, they did add more sections of the introductory philosophy course—for which Levin had previously been the only instructor—so students could take the class with a different professor. When Levin sued the college, he claimed the college violated his free-speech rights by passing the resolution, humiliated him by the creation of alternate course sections, and failed to protect him after he experienced death threats and had small fires lit outside his office.[86] The court ruled in his favor on all three claims.

At the University of Michigan in 2014 and 2015, a sociology doctoral student caused controversy by posting on Twitter a number of comments considered racist by her colleagues and students, including "white college males are the 'problem population' in America," "every year during MLK week I commit myself to not spending a dime in white-owned businesses," and "can we just call St. Patrick's Day the white people's Kwanzaa that it is?"[87]

But the controversy surrounding Saida Grundy was not enough to discourage Boston University from hiring her for her first full-time teaching job in 2015. Virginia Sapiro, the dean of the BU College of Arts and Sciences, defended the hire. "Universities are not opposed to controversy," Sapiro told a reporter for *The Boston Globe*. "Education requires that people be able to communicate with each other and listen and tolerate people communicating."[88]

In the days leading up to Halloween in 2015, administrators, faculty, and students at Yale University were caught up in a controversy regarding costumes deemed to be "insensitive or inappropriate."[89]

The dustup began when the school's Intercultural Affairs Committee sent an email to the student body discouraging the display of insensitive costumes that played on stereotypes.

One of the first to take notice was Erika Christakis, a lecturer and administrator of Silliman College, a residential unit within Yale. After she sent her own residents a response questioning the institution's "exercise of implied control over its students,"[90] students accused her of overreacting and staged a protest outside her office. They also attempted to have Christakis and her husband, also a Yale employee, censured and evicted from their home on campus. The administration stopped short of meeting the demands of the protestors, but twelve other administrators echoed the sentiments of the original memo in a memo of their own, which drew the attention of critics across the country and portrayed the incident as yet another example of political correctness affecting university campuses. "It is remarkable that these administrators took the time to compose, circulate, and co-sign a letter advising adult students on how to dress for Halloween, a cause that misguided campus activists mistake for a social-justice priority," wrote education reporter Conor Friedersdorf in a column in *The Atlantic*.[91]

At the end of the fall semester, Christakis resigned from her teaching position but retained her administrative duties at Yale.[92]

Sometimes administrators get in trouble for what amounts to simple misunderstandings. In 2015, for example, an administrator at Claremont McKenna College in California was forced to resign after a five-word clause in an email meant to provide encouragement to a struggling student was misconstrued. The student belonged to a minority group underrepresented on campus and had written to Mary Spellman expressing thoughts of "not fitting in." Spellman wrote back that she empathized with the student and others who "did not fit the CMC profile." The student took offense and spread the word around campus through official and unofficial channels, prompting student protests and Spellman's ouster.[93]

In 2020, Princeton University fired tenured professor Joshua Katz for having a sexual relationship with a student fifteen years earlier, but he complained that the affair was a smokescreen for the real reason he was fired: his criticism of the Black Justice League, a student group he labeled a "terrorist organization."[94]

The conflict had its roots in the campus protests that followed the murder of George Floyd in 2020, when hundreds of faculty members and graduate students drafted a letter to the university's administration, making dozens of suggestions to improve race relations at the school.

There was little public criticism of the letter, but Katz, a professor of classics and linguistics, found himself in trouble by questioning the practicality of the ideas being proposed. He agreed with many of the concepts but called others unethical and dangerous, such as making race a criterion in hiring and investigating and disciplining faculty for conducting research deemed to be racist.

Katz's criticism took the form of a letter to *Quillette,* an Australian-based online journal that focuses on science, technology, news, politics, and popular culture. As a corollary to his criticism of the proposal, he said the now-defunct Black Justice League had "made life miserable for the many (including Black students) who did not agree with its members' demands."[95] Students and alumni wanted Katz fired, and four of his departmental colleagues added their own opposition on the university's website. Fortunately for Katz, the final disposition of his case fell to President Christopher Eisgruber, a constitutional scholar and champion of free speech. Although he told the campus newspaper that he objected to Katz's "false description" of the group, he decided Katz's comments were protected as free speech and rejected demands for an investigation.[96]

Among college professors using social media platforms, the most prolific are those teaching at law schools, as they opine on everything from the latest Supreme Court rulings to what's happening at their local courthouses.

Amy Wax, a law professor at the University of Pennsylvania, caused a controversy with her 2019 comments about race as a speaker at a political conference sponsored by the Edmund Burke Foundation, a conservative think tank. Wax told the assembled crowd that she embraced "cultural distance nationalism, meaning in effect taking the position that our country will be better off with more whites and fewer non-whites."[97]

That dustup was not the first time Wax was scrutinized for her public comments. In a 2017 op-ed *in The Philadelphia Inquirer*, Wax and a coauthor wrote about the decline in "bourgeois values" such as hard work, self-discipline, traditional marriage, and respect for authority and said those principles were weakened by unemployment, single mothers having children, and college students lacking basic skills.[98]

The controversy prompted by those comments was fairly mild, but it became more intense when she told the student newspaper that "everyone wants to go to countries ruled by white Europeans."[99] A month later, Wax spoke on a conservative podcast and alerted listeners to the "inconvenient fact" that she could not recall "a black student graduating in the top quarter of the class and rarely, rarely in the top half" and claimed that students working on the school's *Law Review* were there only because of a "diversity mandate."[100] Law School Dean Theodore Ruger pushed back on those comments, claiming that black students often graduated near the top of their classes and denied there was a diversity mandate for the *Law Review* staff.[101]

Those comments prompted a petition circulated among Penn students, which generated more than 4,000 signatures and condemned her statements. An open letter expressing the same sentiments was signed by thirty-three faculty members in the law school. Spokespersons for Black Lives Matter and other civil rights advocacy groups called for her firing.[102]

Ruger told critics that because of her status as a tenured professor and the rules of due process, Wax could not be easily dismissed, but he did alter her teaching schedule to remove her as an instructor of first-year law classes.

Before attending Columbia University Law School, Wax was a physician, practicing neurology in Brooklyn for five years, but there is no mention in the media coverage of her comments that she based any of them on her medical background.

When classes at Georgetown University Law Center switched to Zoom meetings during the Covid-19 pandemic in the 2020–1 academic year, the format seemed to work well for adjunct professors Sandra Sellers and David Batson until they forgot to turn off the camera and microphone at the end of one session. Sellers began a forty-second rant about the quality of Black students at Georgetown and said she believed they passed their classes only because of grade inflation. Batson made no such comments but was seen nodding as though he agreed. When one student shared a recording of the incident online, Law Center Dean Bill Treanor called Sellers' comments "abhorrent and reprehensible" and referred the case to the center's Office of Institutional Diversity, Equity & Affirmative Action.[103]

The university's Black Law Students Association posted a letter to the administration calling for Sellers to be terminated and urging the law school to audit the grades and student evaluations in her past classes. The video revealed not only Ms. Sellers's "true beliefs about Black students," the letter stated, "it is also illustrative of the conscious and unconscious bias systematically present in law school grading at Georgetown Law and in law school classrooms nationwide."[104] Following the investigation, Sellers was terminated and Batson was placed on unpaid administrative leave; he later resigned.

"I would never do anything to intentionally hurt my students or Georgetown Law and wish I could take back my words," Sellers wrote in her resignation letter that she shared with *The New York Times*. "Regardless of my intent, I have done irreparable harm and I am truly sorry for this."[105]

In 2022, Ilya Shapiro quit his job at Georgetown University Law School before teaching his first class. His offense was tweeting an opinion on President Biden's intention to nominate Ketanji Brown Jackson for a seat on the U.S. Supreme Court. Shapiro had stated publicly that Sri Srinivasan, the chief judge for the circuit court of appeals for the District of Columbia, would be a better choice. Critics said his tweet carried racist overtones, as it concerned a male of Indian descent losing out to whom Shapiro felt was a lesser-qualified Black woman. It was actually the second time Srinivasan had been on the short list; in 2013 he was runner-up to Merrick Garland, who was nominated by President Obama.

"Alas, he (Srinivasan) didn't fit into the latest intersectionality hierarchy, so we'll get a lesser black woman," Shapiro tweeted. Those last three words were the focus of the controversy, even after Shapiro deleted the tweet. Law School Dean William Treanor said the language was "appalling" and was "at odds with everything we stand for at Georgetown Law."[106]

Shapiro was suspended with pay pending an investigation, and after four months the university reinstated him. He celebrated that decision at first, but changed his outlook when he read a report from the university's diversity office that warned that any similar remarks in the future would likely create a "hostile environment based on race, gender, and sex."[107]

Saying that the warning consisted of a "slow-motion firing," Shapiro resigned. "It took a little time to go through the report and see and understand that I was being put in an untenable situation," Shapiro told *The Chronicle of Higher Education*. "I'm not prepared to live and work under that kind of sword of Damocles, and I'm certainly not prepared to walk on eggshells to try to avoid any sort of inadvertent offense."[108]

If Mike Adams had a female counterpart in the area of free speech and academic freedom controversies, it might be Laura Kipnis, a film studies professor at Northwestern University.

While Adams was a conservative and Kipnis a liberal feminist, they shared one thing: disdain for perceived government overreach, even when those efforts were well-intentioned. For Adams, his favorite target was mask and vaccine mandates; for Kipnis, it was the government's zeal for prosecuting sexual assault cases without due process or the presumption of innocence for the accused.[109]

In 2015, Kipnis came under fire after publishing an article in which she claimed there was a "sexual paranoia" on America's college campuses and specifically described the issue of sexual relationships between professors and students as misunderstood. "When I was in college, hooking up with professors was more or less part of the curriculum," wrote Kipnis, whose own education took place at small private institutions during the sexual revolution of the 1970s and 1980s.[110]

Kipnis insisted that she was not saying that sexual assault was not an important issue, but rather that there was a "rush to judgment" that bypassed due process and the innocent-until-proven-guilty provision of American law. "In the post-Title IX landscape, sexual panic rules and slippery slopes abound," she wrote. "Gropers become rapists and accusers become survivors."[111] Accused students, she added, were eighteen-year-olds labeled as sex offenders for life, even if eventually found not guilty.[112]

Two Northwestern students filed Title IX complaints against her, and hundreds of other students signed petitions calling for her termination. She was called before an investigative panel, for which she was not told the nature of her offense ahead of time, was not allowed to bring an attorney, and was not allowed to record the session. Even after the panel decided to recommend against sanctions, it issued a gag order that prohibited her from discussing the proceedings with the media or anyone else.[113]

The gag order was lifted in time for Kipnis to write a follow-up column in *The Chronicle of Higher Education* titled "My Title IX Inquisition."[114] Meanwhile, the university provided its account of the proceedings in a brief statement by Alan Cubbage, the school's vice president for university relations. "Northwestern University is firmly committed to both academic freedom and to free speech, but it is also required to investigate and respond to allegations made by complainants that particular actions or statements might violate Title IX," Cubbage said in a statement released by his office. "Northwestern is confident that its policies and procedures comport with the law and were followed here."[115]

In 2021, a conservative professor in Montana was forced to resign for posting comments on his blog that had little to do with his field of computer science. While Rob Smith disparaged women, Muslims, and gays, he caught the most flak for his comments about older men dating younger women. "If you are at your peak, seek a woman in hers," he told his male followers. "This means you should be dating women who are as close to 18 as you can get."[116]

For women, his advice was that instead of pursuing college degrees, they should focus on "spouse selection," and he cautioned them that their "physical attractiveness is their most valuable asset in finding a husband. This value peaks from 16 to 18, fades slowly until 25, then starts fading quickly. Your pool of potential husbands shrinks significantly with every year past 18."[117]

After his blog entries came to the attention of the student newspaper, *The Montana Kaimin*, they set off a semester-long controversy highlighted by hundreds of students marching to the administration building and a "Fire Rob Smith" social media campaign.

UM President Seth Bodnar told the media that he was "disgusted by (Smith's) homophobic and misogynistic views . . . building a culture of respect, empowerment, and equity is foundational to our mission."[118]

In 2022, a social work professor at Calvin University in Grand Rapids, Michigan, learned that having a stellar record for teaching, scholarship, and community service wasn't enough to earn tenure when your employer is a private institution affiliated with the Christian Reformed Church (CRC). Joseph Kuilema was on a fast track to academic stardom, but his relationship with the administration began to sour as he approached his tenure decision date in 2018. Kuilema was told that while his application was solid on the surface, the school's Professional Status Committee had recommended against tenure based on his violation of the "Covenant for Faculty Members." Specifically, Kuilema was an advocate for the school's LGBTQ students and had spoken out in support of gay marriage, which conflicted with the official, scripture-based position of the university and CRC. He had also commented on Facebook that despite his rocky relationship with the administration, he expected to be tenured.[119]

It turned out that Kuilema was only partly wrong. While the board of trustees denied him tenure, it recommended that his employment continue on a series of non-tenure-track, two-year contracts that could be renewable in perpetuity. He settled for the "half a loaf" alternative to tenure rather than taking his talents to the job market.

That might have been the end of the story if not for his response to an invitation from a former student that he received in the spring of 2021. Would he officiate the ceremony when she married her female partner? He agreed to do so without hesitation, knowing it was risky but believing what he did outside of his academic role was none of the university's business.

Two months after the ceremony, Kuilema had just agreed to his second two-year contract when word of his role in the wedding reached the university's provost, who nixed the contract and told him that his fourteen-year career at Calvin was over.[120]

Much like it did for sports commentator Samantha Ponder (see Chapter 3), speaking out in defense of women's sports against the perceived threat of transgender athletes has meant consequences for coaches. At Oberlin College, a small private school in Ohio, lacrosse coach Kim Russell was reprimanded not for making social media comments, but for simply reposting comments made by a friend concerning the issue. The dominoes started to fall early in 2022 when University of Pennsylvania swimmer Lia Thomas became the first transgender athlete to win an NCAA championship. University of Virginia swimmer Emma Weyant finished second, and while she did not complain herself, thousands of

Instagram users posted messages supporting her cause. Russell recognized a friend's post and reposted it without comment.

An Oberlin student-athlete in another sport saw it and complained to the school's athletic director. At first, Russell received just an oral reprimand, but after members of her team confronted the athletic director and other administrators, Russell was accused of encouraging them to do so and received a written warning that she must "change her behavior."[121]

Russell told the media that the case was not about her, but instead a national issue affecting women. "I know there are many more who support me that are afraid to lose their jobs," she said. "They don't want to speak up because of the wrath that will come, and right now especially men aren't speaking up because they will get hammered."[122]

The media relations office at Oberlin declined to comment to the media about the controversy but issued a statement saying that the school "cautions all faculty and staff to be mindful when using social media."[123]

In 2023, Northwestern University was in the news following a scandal involving hazing among athletes in its football and baseball programs, a problem that caused the football coach to be fired and the baseball coach to be reprimanded. Although unrelated to free speech, the hazing story led to problems for Derrick Gragg, the school's athletic director, whose 2015 book was discovered as part of media coverage of the issue. Gragg, who was the athletic director at the University of Tulsa at the time of publication, described women in music videos as "booty-shaking sex kittens and materialistic gold-diggers."[124]

Gragg, who was hired at Northwestern in 2021, was criticized for what women's advocacy groups called "insensitive and sexist comments" that reflected poorly on both Tulsa and Northwestern.[125] In media interviews, Gragg defended his comments by explaining that he was "speaking to an audience of young men who are looking for role models as they pursue their own dreams both as college athletes and in life."[126]

Gragg accused women's groups and the media of "cherry-picking" only the most controversial parts of the book in order to augment the hazing story, pointing to a later chapter in the book, titled "Remember, She is Someone's Daughter," in which he advocated that men treat women with respect, especially in cases in which "alcohol is flowing."[127] He also cited his eight-month stint at the National College Athletic Association where he served as a diversity and inclusion officer.

Biting the Hands That Feed Us

While the most outspoken university professors get in trouble for opining about national and world affairs, others save their most severe criticisms for their own institutions. In a world in which non-disparagement agreements are non-existent, faculty members—sometimes with tenure and sometimes not—use their social media platforms and other communication methods to criticize their colleagues, students, faculty members in other departments, administrators, and the institutions as a whole.

In the years following *Pickering*, a series of cases at different levels of the court system resulted in similar rulings, many of them citing *Pickering* as precedent. In 1972, for example, the Supreme Court ruled that a community college in Texas had violated the First Amendment rights of an untenured professor when it fired him for simply criticizing college policies.[128] Robert Sindermann found out that one can be fired from a primary job of teaching as a result of doing a secondary job of union leadership too well. Sindermann was a celebrated teacher who earned excellent student evaluations and was well-liked by his colleagues. But when he became president of a statewide teachers' association, the job included speaking to state legislators about ongoing issues, which generated the wrath of college officials.

After four years of butting heads with administrators, Sindermann was told his contract would not be renewed at the end of the year. He received no explanation other than a reminder that he was an at-will employee and the institution was under no obligation to renew his contract or explain the reasons for non-renewal. He took his case to court, initially losing but eventually winning on appeal to the U.S. Supreme Court.[129]

University of Chicago political science professor Daniel Drezner had a bad feeling about the content of his blog, but that didn't stop the newly hired faculty member from his weekly rants about what was happening in his field, including criticisms that identified both individuals and institutions, including his own. "Here goes nothing. I shouldn't be doing this," one entry read.[130]

Drezner's concern turned out to be clairvoyant: when he came up for tenure in 2005, he was denied. Although he was not given a specific reason—only that it had something to do with his publication record—he surmised that it was the content of his postings, not that he might have spent too much time on his blog and not enough on true scholarship.

Drezner's reputation in the field and academic background—including two master's degrees and a PhD from Stanford—resulted in multiple offers without having to actively enter the job-hunting universe. He quickly landed at Tufts University, where he was given tenure at the beginning of his appointment, and where he remains today. The irony was that Tufts learned about his availability after reading about it on his blog.[131]

Even educators who are skilled at technology and go to great lengths to hide their identities online find their social media activity is not as anonymous as they might think. Megan Spohn was an instructor at DeVry University at a regional campus in Colorado and a PhD candidate at the University of Denver who had a personal blog—published under a pseudonym—on which she commented about her personal life, current affairs, and unfortunately her job. Her criticisms were aimed not at specific colleagues at DeVry, but at the quality of the students she taught and institutional policies, including those that required both instructional and non-instructional employees to take online training courses in diversity and harassment prevention. She referred to the training as "bullshit" and "useless crap" and opined that if she was going to spend so much time in front of a computer screen, the time could be better spent "watching something more useful, like porn."[132]

At the end of the fall semester in December 2005, Spohn was called into her supervisor's office and fired. Because DeVry is a private institution rather than a public one, Spohn could not claim her First Amendment rights were violated. And because she was a part-time instructor, she was not covered by the university's tenure system.[133]

Three cases illustrating the risks that faculty members take when criticizing their employers took place in 2024. One occurred at Tarleton State University in Stephenville, Texas, when Ted Roberts, an untenured senior instructor of history, did not see his contract renewed because he publicly criticized the school's parking policies. In defending their action, school officials pointed to his non-tenured status as well as the distinction between termination and non-renewal of a contract.[134]

One state to the east, a faculty member at Louisiana State University at Shreveport was terminated for "disruptive behavior" after years of publicly criticizing the school for environmental issues near campus caused by fracking and the mishandling of toxic materials. Brian Salvatore, a tenured chemistry professor, had drawn negative attention to the university. Salvatore further angered school officials by accusing the school of violating the state's public meetings laws when discussing those issues behind closed doors.[135]

That same year, an administrator at Harvard University raised free-speech concerns when he published an op-ed in the school newspaper, *The Harvard Crimson*, stating that the university had a responsibility to limit the speech rights of faculty members when their criticisms of the administrators reflected negatively on the university. Lawrence Bobo, dean of social sciences, wrote that he was concerned that faculty members' public comments might "arouse external intervention in university business."[136]

Bobo hinted that his concerns were prompted by the public positions taken by faculty members on the ongoing conflict between Israel and Hamas, which drew criticism from the board of overseers, public officials, and donors.[137]

Thrown Under the Bus

One of the most bizarre cases of professional educators fighting the free-speech fight began in the fall of 2016 when Kristie Torbick, a high school guidance counselor in New Hampshire, entered into a sexual relationship with a fourteen-year-old male student that lasted only a few weeks but devastated both families. As tragic as the criminal case was, it was not that unusual. By comparison, it was no different from other cases tried every day in courtrooms across the country. But when three Plymouth State University professors—two who knew her as a student and one serving as an expert witness—got involved in the case, they saw their careers threatened.

Full-time Professor Gary Goodnough and adjunct Michael Fischler had written letters of support, not making excuses for Torbick but rather describing for the court the former student they knew. PSU adjunct Nancy Strapko, also a mental-health therapist treating sex offenders, had treated Torbick and written a letter to her attorney providing an update on her treatment. When all three documents became public, the professors were subjected to negative media coverage as well as online threats and harassment. Decades of legal precedents established that their participation in the legal procedures was protected by the First Amendment and New Hampshire law, but that didn't stop politicians and newspaper editorial pages from accusing them of "protecting a predator" and Internet bloggers and trolls from adding their own vitriol. At PSU, a student group consisting largely of sexual assault survivors immediately formed on Facebook, demanding that Strapko, Goodnough, and Fischler be fired.[138]

The university bowed to the media coverage and public pressure, declining to renew Strapko's adjunct contract and telling Goodnough and Fischler they would be required to complete a Title IX "refresher course" before being allowed to teach again.

Some observers believed the timing of the story (2016–19) was not a coincidence, as the framing of the story against several ongoing news stories became part of the media coverage. Those stories included the sexual assault cases against actor/comedian Bill Cosby and Olympic gymnastics physician Larry Nassar and allegations against Supreme Court nominee Brett Kavanaugh. Another factor was the emerging #MeToo movement that began with accusations of sexual misconduct in Hollywood but soon spread to the larger society.[139]

"To say these individuals were thrown under the bus is an understatement," commented Zach Greenberg, program director for the Foundation for Individual Rights in Education. "It is a shame they had to 'lawyer up' in order to protect their rights."[140]

Goodnough, a full-time tenured professor, agreed to take the refresher course in order to put the controversy behind him. Fischler, who had recently transitioned from full-time to part-time and was no longer protected by tenure, refused. The university administration not only declined to renew his contract but also removed his name from the school's counseling center, which he founded in 1975.

Meanwhile, both the American Civil Liberties Union (ACLU) and the Foundation for Individual Rights in Education (FIRE) came to the professors' defense. In a statement posted on the ACLU-New Hampshire website, Executive Director Devon Chaffee claimed that protecting the welfare of children and protecting the free-speech rights of adults could be done simultaneously. "The ACLU-NH denounces sexual assault of any kind," Chaffee wrote. "Such actions against a minor are particularly egregious. The public is not served, however, by silencing the free speech of citizens speaking in their private capacity. As a society, we can and must support victims of sexual assault and steadfastly uphold the rights of citizens to participate in the criminal justice process."[141]

Strapko and Fischler sued the university and reached out-of-court settlements. The Strapko case was settled for $350,000. Fischler asked for no monetary damages but instead had his teaching credentials renewed and his name re-attached to the counseling center. The university announced the settlement with a rambling, 700-word statement praising his contributions to the institution, but it stopped short of the public apology that Fischler wanted.[142]

Goodnough, meanwhile, took a less confrontational approach. He knew that writing the letter did not constitute a violation of Title IX and saw the training requirement as largely symbolic. In addition, he was a full professor returning from a sabbatical and was looking forward to getting back in the classroom and teaching. "While there was some temptation to fight it, I decided that my overarching objective was to move past the event and get back into my career," he said. "As I said to many people at the time, this was not a fight that I was willing to give up my career for."[143]

Controversy at the University of Florida, and This Time It's Not About Football

As part of its campaign to scrutinize the role of Florida's State University System in public policy, the state legislature passed new laws in 2020 and 2021 regarding the activities of faculty members outside of the classroom. Among those rules were new conflict-of-interest standards that required faculty members to obtain permission from their university's administration before speaking out on controversial issues, whether related to their teaching and research areas or not, and especially if their positions were inconsistent with those of the state legislature.[144]

Faculty members at the University of Florida were the first to run afoul of the new rules. When Oliver Grundmann, a professor of medicinal chemistry, was asked to sign a letter to the Drug Enforcement Administration about the value of kratom, a chemical derived from a tropical plant and sold as an over-the-counter pain reliever, he faced more scrutiny from the administration than expected. He was given approval to sign the document but was later told he should have emphasized in his letter that his opinions—which dealt with both the benefits and risks of kratom without supporting one side or the other—were his and did not reflect the official position of the university.[145]

Grundmann got off easy considering what happened to five professors representing two other UF departments a few weeks later. When three political science professors were called to testify in a court case that challenged Florida's new voting laws, they were told they could not do so because their positions were inconsistent with the interests of the legislature. The conflict kicked off a months-long discussion of censorship and academic freedom that was covered by the national media and professional publications such as *The Chronicle of Higher Education*.

At the same time, a case receiving less publicity involved two pediatrics professors in the university's medical school who were told they could not serve as expert witnesses in cases involving the state's mask mandates in public schools because their views contradicted the position of the legislature and Florida Governor Ron DeSantis. One of the professors was publicly chastised by the legislature after saying in a media interview that sending a child to school without a mask was equivalent to putting them in a "toxic swamp of Covid."[146]

Eventually, the five professors were allowed to move forward with their participation in the court cases after they agreed to travel on their own time and at their own expense, not use any university resources in preparing their testimony, and clarify their testimony was based on their personal and professional opinion and did not represent the official position of the University of Florida.[147]

That decision wasn't enough to stem the criticism of the university, which came not only from the national media and legal experts, but also from several former UF presidents. As a result, President Kent Fuchs, who had already announced he would retire the following year, appointed a task force to develop new policies to deal with similar conflicts in the future.

Meanwhile, the three political science professors had filed suit in federal district court, claiming their First Amendment rights had been violated. The court agreed, prompting the university to appeal the ruling.[148] As of early 2024, the case is still pending.

Controversy at the University of Mississippi, and This Time It's Not About the Confederate Flag

During an eighteen-month stretch in 2021–2, two southern educators found themselves on the wrong side of university administrators over their anti-police and anti-prison stances, which were tangentially related to the deaths of Black citizens at the hands of white police officers and the ensuing public discourse over police reform.

Garrett Ferber, an untenured associate professor of history at the University of Mississippi, had long been a critic of the school's administration—in the classroom, in media interviews, and on social media—even though administrators denied having any objection to his progressive views on policing and prison reform. Tension between him and the university heated up when the school rejected his research agenda, including an application for an external grant, because, as Ferber claimed, it did not want to upset its mostly conservative donor base. He even tried to make a connection between the university's position and its nickname, Ole Miss, which has been criticized in some circles as having racist origins. "It's not some mythic politics vs. history binary, but that this antiracist program threatens racist donor money," Felber told *Inside Higher Education*. "And racism is the brand. It's in the name."[149]

While on research leave at Harvard University, his department chair, Noelle Wilson, wanted to have periodic discussions with him regarding what he was doing and when he would be returning to Ole Miss. Wilson wanted the conversations to be conducted on Zoom, but Felber, who already had a tense relationship with Wilson, insisted they be done by electronic mail so he could have a written record. That lack of communication was the only reason given for the non-renewal by the university, which otherwise would not comment because it was considered a personal matter and issue of ongoing litigation. Provost Noel Wilkin did, however, tell the American Historical Association that the decision was prompted when the chair "lost confidence in an untenured faculty member who would not act in good faith and be responsive to her repeated efforts to help him succeed."[150]

Rather than continuing to stay at the university, Ferber moved on to a position at Yale University, after which his lawyers negotiated an undisclosed financial settlement with Ole Miss.[151]

The following year, the dean of the Graduate School of Social Work at the University of Houston was demoted to a regular faculty position after calling for the abolition of all prisons and law enforcement agencies following the national controversy over the George Floyd murder and other police-related tragedies. Expressing his views in campus forums and in a book available at the university bookstore, Alan J. Dettlaff faced little criticism for his ideas because they were seen as largely hypothetical. But when he made the same comments in media interviews and on social media, the reaction was much different, even though he was unable to prove a connection between his views and his demotion.[152]

Even university presidents are not immune from criticism for their public comments. A 2022 article in *The Chronicle of Higher Education* pointed to the "chilling effect" that results in university presidents being afraid of speaking out on controversial issues for fear of offending students, faculty, politicians, or most importantly, big-money donors. The article was based on a survey of more than 150 college presidents who were offered confidentiality, even though a few agreed to speak on the record.

Among them was Richard L. Dunsworth, president of the University of the Ozarks in Clarksville, Arkansas. Dunsworth recalled his own experience after announcing on social media the university's new diversity effort, which came a few days after the January 2017 inauguration of President Trump and was viewed as a response to his rhetoric. Even though he denied there was a connection, Dunsworth said he received strongly worded emails and phone calls from donors that he described as "evenly split." In one category were those highly supportive; in the other category were those who implied that the university's efforts to make students from diverse backgrounds feel welcome were perceived as political and even anti-American.[153]

"The political landscape has changed, things are more didactic and divisive, so I'm less likely to take a position on a topic that doesn't have a direct bearing on the institution," Dunsworth said.[154]

Added Ora Pescovitz, president of Oakland University in Michigan, "It's a scary time to be a president. All of us are facing declining enrollment. Any attack makes life unpleasant and uncomfortable and that makes it challenging to speak your mind."[155]

The survey asked presidents to identify the most dangerous topics for them to speak about, and many listed Covid-19 policies, affirmative action and campus diversity, gender and sexual identity, racial justice, and gun rights (especially in the wake of campus shootings elsewhere).

Chronicle editors said the survey was prompted by a decade-long trend of Republican governors "meddling" in university governance and state lawmakers taking a more adversarial stance toward higher education. That issue ramped up once Trump took office, as the new president pushed measures that restricted international student enrollment and called for universities to stop silencing conservative voices on campus.

Dunsworth said that instead of worrying about what politicians think, he felt it was more important to be accountable to those paying tuition. "What I say as a university president matters to my students, and I can't shy away from espousing the values of the institution even though they may cause some controversy."[156]

The Larry Summers case (mentioned in the Introduction) is illustrative of the peril in which university presidents find themselves when speaking out on controversial public issues. Whether their institutions are public or private makes little difference, as in both situations presidents get in trouble for a variety of reasons. Prior to 2023, the most common issues causing problems for university presidents included defending their faculty members' research agendas against public criticism and defending their university's position on issues related to diversity, equity, and inclusion. In 2023, however, those issues were displaced by two items from the news: President Joe Biden's proposal to forgive federal student loans and the emergence of hate speech on college campuses related to the political tensions in the Middle East. The latter issue caused the presidents of Harvard University and the University of Pennsylvania to resign after their testimony to Congress resulted in criticism from lawmakers and the general public.[157]

Even before those presidents appeared before Congress, other university leaders—not having the protection of tenure and not confident enough to walk the political tightropes—found the best way to deal with public issues was to remain silent.[158]

Greg Lukianoff, president of the Foundation for Individual Rights and Expression, added in a *USA Today* interview, "I wouldn't exactly envy university presidents in the current environment. We are likely to see an uptick in cancel culture coming from the right."[159]

And Then This Happened

In late 2023, the idea of an "outspoken university leader" took on a new meaning when the chancellor at the University of Wisconsin at La Crosse was fired after the school's board of regents discovered that he and his wife had appeared in online pornography. Joseph Gow and his wife admitted that they had posted their homemade sex videos using pseudonyms for years, but had recently decided to do so using their own names. Board President Karen Walsh said Gow's revelation "showed a reckless disregard" for his role as a leader in the state university system. In his defense, Gow told the media that the creation of books and videos exploring consensual adult sexuality fell within his rights to free speech under the First Amendment. "There's nothing said about the University of Wisconsin (on the videos)," he told reporters for the *Milwaukee Journal*

Sentinel.[160] Protected by tenure in his role as a professor of communication but not as chancellor, Gow returned to his teaching role in early 2024 while still appealing his dismissal.[161]

Notes

1 "Free Speech or Harassment? Controversial Professor Tests the Limits," *NBC News*, November 30, 2016.
2 "Enough Is Enough: Calls for Mike Adams' Dismissal Grow Louder," *Encore*, June 16, 2020.
3 Greg Lukianoff, *Unlearning Liberty: Campus Censorship and the End of American Debate* (New York: Encounter Books, 2014), pp. 208–9.
4 Mike Adams, *Welcome to the Ivory Tower of Babel* (Augusta, GA: Harbor House, 2004).
5 Mike Adams, *Feminists Say the Darndest Things: A Politically Incorrect Professor Confronts "Womyn" on Campus* (New York: Sentinel Publishing, 2007).
6 Lukianoff, *Unlearning Liberty*, pp. 208–9.
7 Kate Murphy, "UNCW to Pay $500,000 to Controversial Professor in Deal Over Early Retirement," *Raleigh News & Observer*, July 23, 2020.
8 Mike Adams, *Letters to a Young Progressive: How to Avoid Wasting Your Life Protesting Things You Don't Understand* (Washington, DC: Regnery, 2013).
9 Scott Jaschik, "University Pays to Get Rid of Professor," *Inside Higher Education*, July 6, 2020.
10 Jose V. Sartarelli, "Message from Chancellor Sartarelli," July 2, 2020.
11 Murphy, "UNCW to Pay $500,000 to Controversial Professor in Deal Over Early Retirement."
12 Alan Charles Kors and Harvey A. Silverglate, *The Shadow University: The Betrayal of Liberty on America's Campuses* (New York: HarperCollins, 1998), pp. 53–7.
13 Susan Jacoby, *The Age of American Unreason* (New York: Pantheon Books, 2008), pp. 232–4.
14 Ellen Schrecker, "Academic Freedom and the Cold War," *The Antioch Review* 38, no. 3 (Summer 1980): pp. 312–27.
15 Erwin Chemerinsky and Howard Gillman, *Free Speech on Campus* (New Haven, CT: Yale University Press, 2017), pp. 61–3.
16 *Keyishian v. Board of Regents*, 385 U.S. 589 (1967). See also: Chemerinsky and Gillman, *Free Speech on Campus*, pp. 80–1. See also: Bruce Barry, *Speechless: The Erosion of Free Expression in the American Workplace* (San Francisco: Berrett-

Koehler Publishers, 2007), p. 68. Keith Fink, *Free Speech in the Workplace* (San Diego: Cognella Press, 2013), pp. 247–71.

17 Matt Krupnick, "Tenure Limits Drive Away Professors," *USA Today*, January 9, 2024, p. 1-A.

18 Ibid.

19 Ibid.

20 Paul Horowitz, *First Amendment Institutions* (Cambridge, MA: Harvard University Press, 2013), p. 107.

21 Jonathan Zimmerman, *Campus Politics: What Everyone Needs to Know* (New York: Oxford University Press, 2016), p. 58.

22 Keith E. Whittington, *Speak Freely: Why Universities Must Defend Free Speech* (Princeton, NJ: Princeton University Press, 2018), p. 26. See also: Krupnick, "Tenure Limits Drive Away Professors."

23 Krupnick, "Tenure Limits Drive Away Professors."

24 Whittington, *Speak Freely*, p. 141.

25 Ibid.

26 Ibid., p. 145.

27 William A. Kaplin and Barbara A. Lee, *The Law of Higher Education* (San Francisco: John Wiley & Sons, 2007), p. 120.

28 Ross K. Baker, "If Academic Tenure Is in Trouble at Colleges, So Is Academic Freedom," *Pensacola News Journal,* October 25, 2021, p. 8-B.

29 "The First Amendment and Free Speech on Campus," National Association of College and University Attorneys Webinar, June 3, 2004.

30 Kirsten Powers, *The Silencing: How the Left Is Killing Free Speech* (Washington, DC: Regnery Publishing, 2015), p. 19.

31 Eric Kelderman, "The Silent Treatment: Why College Presidents Find It Hard to Speak Up," *The Chronicle of Higher Education,* August 5, 2022, pp. 11–16.

32 *Wieman v. Updegraff*, 344 U.S. 183 (1952).

33 *Keyishian v. Board of Regents*, 233 F. Supp. 752 (1965).

34 Ibid.

35 Ibid.

36 *Adler v. Board of Education of the City of New York*, 342 U.S. 485 (1952).

37 New York Education Law No. 3021.

38 Zach D'Amico, "Former State Rep. Rick Saccone Resigns From SVC After Capitol Involvement," *The Latrobe Bulletin*, January 8, 2021.

39 Ibid.

40 Peter F. Lake, "How to Shield Faculty Members from Outside Attacks," *The Chronicle of Higher Education,* July 7, 2022, pp. 42–3.

41 Ibid.

42 Robert M. O'Neil, *Free Speech in the College Community* (Bloomington, IN: Indiana University Press, 1997), pp. 27–43.
43 William A. Wines and Terence J. Lau, "Can You Hear Me Now? Corporate Censorship and Its Troubling Implications for the First Amendment," *DePaul Law Review* 55, no. 1 (Fall 2005): pp. 119–67.
44 Christopher Finan, *From the Palmer Raids to the Patriot Act: A History of the Right for Free Speech in America* (Boston: Beacon Press, 2007), p. 271. See also: David Glenn, "The War on Campus," *The Nation*, December 3, 2001.
45 Glenn, "The War on Campus."
46 Finan, *From the Palmer Raids to the Patriot Act*, p. 271. See also: Glenn, "The War on Campus."
47 Stanley Fish, "Conspiracy Theories 101," *The New York Times*, July 23, 2006.
48 Ibid.
49 Dan Berrett, "ESU Professor Suspended for Comments Made on Facebook Page," *The Pocono Record*, February 26, 2010.
50 Ibid.
51 Lori Andrews, *I Know Who You Are and I Saw What You Did: Social Networks and the Death of Privacy* (New York: Free Press, 2011), pp. 76–7. See also: Berrett, "ESU Professor Suspended for Comments Made on Facebook Page."
52 *McAdams v. Marquette University*, 383 Wisc. 2d 358, 914 N.W. 2d 708 (2018).
53 Ibid.
54 Whittington, *Speak Freely*, p. 158.
55 *McAdams v. Marquette University.*
56 Ibid.
57 Ibid.
58 Robert Mackey, "Professor's Angry Tweets on Gaza Cost Him a Job," *The New York Times*, September 12, 2014.
59 Ibid.
60 Ibid.
61 Zimmerman, *Campus Politics*, pp. 57–8.
62 Perry Chiaramonte, "Florida Professor Who Denied Sandy Hook Shooting Now Claims Boston Bombings a Drill," *Fox News.com*, April 24, 2013.
63 Ibid.
64 Ibid.
65 Zeeshan Aleem, "Why Carnegie Mellon's Condemnation of Professor's Viral Tweet Is Troubling," *MSNBC.com*, September 10, 2022.
66 Ibid.
67 Ibid.
68 Ibid.

69 Ibid.
70 Snejana Farberov, "Professor Who Wished Queen 'Excruciating Death' Explains Defiant Stance on Podcast," *New York Post*, September 15, 2022.
71 A. J. McDougall, "LSU Prof Resigns After Politician He's Shared Years-Long Beef With Is Elected Gov," *The Daily Beast*, October 17, 2023.
72 Ibid.
73 Ibid.
74 Ibid.
75 Ibid. See also: Megan Zahneis, "A New Republican Governor Is In, and This Professor Is Out," *The Chronicle of Higher Education*, October 17, 2023.
76 Julia Glum, "Who Is Kenneth Storey? Professor Fired After Tweeting That Hurricane Harvey Was Karma for Texas Republicans," *Newsweek*, August 29, 2017.
77 Ibid.
78 Colleen Flaherty, "Twitter, Faculty Hangman," *Inside Higher Education*, April 12, 2017.
79 Ibid..
80 Scott Jaschik, "Twitter Blowback: Lost Jobs and Lost Money," *Inside Higher Education*, August 1, 2017.
81 Ibid.
82 Ibid.
83 Ibid.
84 Philip Roth, *The Human Stain* (New York: Random House, 2000).
85 O'Neil, *Free Speech in the College Community*, pp. 27–33.
86 Ibid.
87 Laura Krantz, "Controversy Trails New Professor to BU," *The Boston Globe*, June 27, 2015.
88 Ibid.
89 Conor Friedersdorf, "The New Intolerance of Student Activism," *The Atlantic*, November 9, 2015. See also: Rahel Gebreyes, "Yale Student Explains Why Students Were Offended by Halloween Costumes Email," *The Huffington Post*, November 12, 2015.
90 Friedersdorf, "The New Intolerance of Student Activism."
91 Ibid..
92 Ibid. See also: Gebreyes, "Yale Student Explains Why Students Were Offended by Halloween Costumes Email."
93 Suzanne Nossel, *Dare to Speak: Defending Free Speech for All* (New York: Dey Street Publishing, 2020), p. 35.
94 Robert P. George, "Free Speech Prevails at Princeton," *First Things*, July 28, 2020.

95 Ibid.

96 Ibid.

97 David French, "The Problem with Amy Wax's Immigration Argument," *National Review*, July 22, 2019.

98 Amy Wax and Larry Alexander, "Paying the Price for Breakdown of the Country's Bourgeois Culture," *The Philadelphia Inquirer,* August 9, 2017.

99 "Not All Cultures Are Created Equal, Says Penn Law Professor in Op-Ed," *The Daily Pennsylvanian,* August 10, 2017.

100 Aiden Pink, "Is This Penn Law Professor a Truth-Teller or a Bigot?" *The Forward,* March 31, 2018.

101 Ibid.

102 Jessica Schladebeck, "Penn Law Professor Loses Teaching Duties for Saying Black Students 'Rarely' Earn Top Marks," *New York Daily News*, March 15, 2018.

103 Michael Levinson, "Georgetown Law Fires Professor for 'Abhorrent' Remarks About Black Students," *The New York Times*, March 11, 2021.

104 Ibid.

105 Ibid.

106 Tom Bartlett, "I Didn't Want to Be Canceled," *The Chronicle of Higher Education,* June 11, 2022, p. 6.

107 Ibid.

108 Ibid.

109 Laura Kipnis, "My Title IX Inquisition," *The Chronicle of Higher Education,* May 29, 2015. See also: Ellis Cose, *The Short Life and Curious Death of Free Speech in America* (New York: Amistad Publishing, 2020), pp. 144–5.

110 Kipnis, "My Title IX Inquisition."

111 Ibid.

112 Ibid.

113 Cose, *The Short Life and Curious Death of Free Speech in America*, pp. 144–5.

114 Kipnis, "My Title IX Inquisition."

115 Rachel Cooke, "Sexual Paranoia on Campus, and the Professor at the Eye of the Storm," *The Guardian*, April 2, 2017.

116 Addie Slanger and Andy Tallman, "Computer Science Prof Resigns Amid Blog Controversy," *The Montana Kaimin*, October 22, 2021. See also: Muri Assuncao, "Montana Professor Resigns Amid Investigation into Alleged 'Homophobic and Misogynistic' Views," *New York Daily News,* October 23, 2021.

117 Ibid.

118 Ibid.

119 Jack Stripling, "This Professor Officiated at a Gay Wedding. Then He Lost His Job," *The Chronicle of Higher Education,* April 27, 2022.

120 Ibid.

121 Ingrid Jacques, "Coach Feels 'Burned' for Speaking Out," *USA Today*, August 30, 2023, p. 7-A.

122 Ibid.

123 Ibid.

124 Josh Peter, "NU AD's 2015 Book Remarks Surface," *USA Today*, June 27, 2023, p. 1-C.

125 Ibid.

126 Ibid.

127 Ibid.

128 *Perry v. Sindermann*, 408 U.S. 593 (1972).

129 *Perry v. Sindermann*. See also: Barry, *Speechless*, pp. 72–3.

130 Robert Boynton, "Attack of the Career-Killing Blogs," *Slate*, November 16, 2005.

131 Ibid.

132 Barry, *Speechless*, pp. 166–7.

133 Ibid.

134 Nell Gluckman, "A Tarleton State University Instructor Complained About Parking Fees. He Said It Cost Him His Job," *The Chronicle of Higher Education,* June 25, 2024.

135 Ryan Quinn, "LSU Fires Tenured Shreveport Professor, Environmental Advocate," *Inside Higher Education*, June 27, 2024.

136 Jeffrey Flier, "An Attack on Free Speech at Harvard," *The Atlantic,* June 21, 2024.

137 Ibid.

138 Randy Bobbitt, *The View From Under the Bus: A Case Study in Media Influence, Public Opinion, and Moral Outrage* (Pensacola, FL: Windchase Bay Publishing, 2020), p. 64.

139 Ibid., p. 6.

140 Ibid., p. 56.

141 Ibid., p. 42.

142 Ibid., pp. 65–6.

143 Ibid., p. 52.

144 Emma Pitt and Jack Stripling, "Inside the Academic-Freedom Crisis at Florida's Flagship," *The Chronicle of Higher Education,* September 30, 2022, pp. 11–19.

145 Ibid.

146 Ibid.

147 Ibid.

148 Ibid.

149 Colleen Flaherty, "Ole Miss Settles with Professor," *Inside Higher Education*, July 29, 2021. See also: Megan Zahneis, "Scholar Claims He Was Fired for Speaking Out Settles with U. of Mississippi," *The Chronicle of Higher Education*, July 29, 2021.

150 Ibid.
151 Ibid.
152 Ibid.
153 Kelderman, "The Silent Treatment."
154 Ibid.
155 Ibid.
156 Ibid.
157 Ibid.
158 Ibid.
159 Alla Wong, "University Presidents Are Feeling the Chilling Effect," *USA Today*, January 5, 2024, p. 3-A.
160 Kelly Meyerhofer and Rory Linnane, "Chancellor Fired for Appearing in Porn Videos," *Milwaukee Journal Sentinel*, December 29, 2023.
161 Ibid.

9

Free Speech in Sports

Fan Engagement versus Team Reputation and Locker Room Harmony

Golden Boy

Early in his career with the Cincinnati Bengals, quarterback Joe Burrow ignored the risks of speaking out on public policy matters, taking on issues such as gun violence, abortion, and food insecurity. Burrow grew up in Ohio but says he got his passion for social causes from his father, who grew up in Mississippi in the 1960s and saw the effects of poverty and racism close-up. The younger Burrow first became known for his views when he accepted the Heisman Trophy for his play at Louisiana State University in 2019, where fans nicknamed him the "Golden Boy."[1]

"Coming from southeast Ohio, it's a very impoverished area and the poverty rate is almost two times the national average," he told the audience at the Heisman presentation. "There's so many people there that don't have a lot, and I'm up here for all those kids that go home to not a lot of food on the table, hungry after school."[2] In the first month after the speech, donations to the Athens County Food Pantry, which was not mentioned in the speech but was on Burrow's social media pages, totaled more than $65,000.[3]

After he moved on to the Bengals, Burrow continued his advocacy for school food programs and then got the support of his teammates and some of his fans when he spoke about gun violence after the May 2022 murder of nineteen students and two teachers at an elementary school in Uvalde, Texas. "You've got to make it harder to get those crazy guns that everyone's using," Burrow told the Cincinnati media, referring to the assault rifles like the ones used at Uvalde. "I don't think you should be able to walk in there and buy one. You got to be able to go through a rigorous process to buy something like that."[4]

Burrow was supported not only by his teammates but Bengal players from the past. "I was very impressed with his courage in going into subject matter that could put him at odds with certain conservative fans," said Reggie Williams, who played for the team in the 1980s.[5] He received similar support from teammates and fans when he spoke out in favor of abortion rights after the U.S. Supreme Court overturned *Roe v. Wade* and gave states the right to pass anti-abortion legislation.

The support was far from unanimous, however. Chris Dorr, executive director of Ohio Gun Owners, said that Burrow should "focus on trying to get the Bengals their first Super Bowl ring rather than trying to become the orator for the liberal left."[6] Kevin Martin, owner of a gun club in Athens, Ohio, said he was a Burrow fan but added, "he represents the great state of Ohio, but he should learn more about firearms."[7]

Abortion opponents were a bit kinder. "He's a young guy. We've got to give him a chance to learn," said Laura Strietmann, executive director of the Greater Cincinnati Right to Life. "You don't teach anybody or bring them along to your side by bashing them."[8]

Recurring Themes

At least to this point in his career, Joe Burrow's experience in speaking out on social issues has produced only a modicum of controversy, as illustrated by the fan comments described above. His ability to have opinions without drawing negative attention to himself or his team may be due in part to his ability to balance his dual roles of athlete and spokesperson and not allow his advocacy to overshadow his on-field accomplishments.

Professional sports leagues and the individuals who own the teams have long struggled with the issue of free speech of athletes. On the one hand, the leagues and owners like to see players conduct media interviews and engage with fans on social media—all in an effort to market the teams and sell tickets and merchandise. But when those same athletes use their platforms to get involved in social causes, the attitudes of team owners are mixed.

One factor that makes cases involving professional athletes, coaches, and team owners different from the examples in previous chapters is the source of the punishment. Instead of coming from courts of law, the consequences more often come from fans and the media. In addition to the court of public opinion, professional athletes are sometimes sanctioned by their teams or leagues, with the discipline coming in the form of fines or suspensions.

There is a noticeable dichotomy in how much transparency is involved in the discipline system. In team sports, players are disciplined in the form of fines and suspensions from games—sometimes administered by team management and sometimes by a league, with the nature of fines and suspensions released by the teams' or leagues' media relations offices. In the matter of suspensions, it would be difficult not to do so, as there would be no other explanation for why an athlete is not in the lineup.

In individual sports such as golf and tennis, governing bodies such as the United States Tennis Association, Association of Tennis Professionals, PGA Tour, and LPGA Tour do not announce the length of suspensions nor the amount of the fines. Golf journalists say that the lack of information about player fines is due to a "Soviet-style veil of secrecy" over the process of fines and suspensions—regardless of the type or severity of the offense—in order to "better uphold the image of tour players as perfect gentlemen."[9] Journalists reporting on player transgressions instead use the euphemism that an athlete found himself "lighter in the wallet."

When it comes to team owners and offensive speech, their punishment comes in the form of occasional condemnation by fellow owners or league commissioners and negative public opinion, but any noticeable loss of ticket sales or team revenue is usually short-term. In rare cases, owners are forced to sell their franchises, but that is usually related more to conduct than speech, as in the cases of Donald Sterling of the Los Angeles Clippers and Daniel Snyder of the Washington Commanders.

Much like they are in other work environments, free-speech controversies in the world of professional sports fall into three categories: those that are work-related, those related to social issues outside of the work environment, and those involving personal expression. In the case of professional athletes, work-related complaints are not about working schedules but instead team ownership, venues, or pay (not their own salaries, but rather the disparity between men's and women's compensation in the same sport). Non-work-related social issues include racial justice and sex and sexuality (including LGBTQ rights), and other matters related to national and world politics. While athletes are taking on those issues, coaches have generated news in recent years by speaking out against gun violence.

Factors involved in free speech for athletes include:

1. *Fan engagement*. Owners like to see their athletes conducting non-controversial media interviews and engaging with fans on social media, knowing that such interaction leads to greater sales of tickets and merchandise.
2. *Attracting and retaining talent*. Much like any business, teams with owners who recognize the importance of players speaking out on social issues are rewarded with a locker-room culture that helps retain players while attracting top free agents for whom free speech is a major consideration. When players draw attention to their teams by speaking out on public issues, owners may be reluctant to reprimand them, partly in deference to the principle of free speech and partly because punishing a player would simply draw more attention to the issue.

There are two factors working against free speech in sports:

1. *Maintaining team reputation*. Organizations such as the National Football League, Major League Baseball, and the National Basketball Association claim to uphold the principles of "fair play and sportsmanship" when they fine or reprimand players for public comments about their teammates, coaches, team or league officials, or opposing players and coaches.

   One example happened in 1986 when Tampa Bay Buccaneers coach Leeman Bennett cut three starting players—tight end Jimmie Giles, wide receiver Kevin House, and running back Ron Springs—in mid-season. While their on-field performance was part of the problem, a bigger issue for Bucs' management was the locker room disruption caused by the players repeatedly bashing their teammates and the coaching staff in (pre-social media) newspaper and television interviews.

   "These players weren't going to be with us when we get to the Super Bowl anyway," Bennett told the media. "But we can't get to the Super Bowl with these guys running their mouths."[10] Even though some of the players' comments may have been defamatory, the team chose not to pursue litigation, instead using the cuts to send a message to the team. Owner Hugh Culverhouse supported the move, telling the media, "We can't get to where we want to be with guys talking out of school . . . I still want to get to the Super Bowl before I cross the creek."[11]

   Today, when players use media interviews or social media platforms to comment on social issues such as race relations or police conduct, the owners might worry about offending ticketholders or sponsors or otherwise attracting negative attention to the team. While unable to (or at least reluctant to) discipline players for speaking out, they might privately ask players to "tone it down."

2. *Demographic factors in team ownership*. While the teams' fan bases are diverse, the demographics of the owners are not: in most professional leagues, the owners are largely older, white, male, and politically conservative. In some cases, that allows owners to exercise a "good to be king" approach to limiting the speech rights of players. Explaining the tendency of NFL owners to do so, one prominent sportswriter commented that "rich men do exactly as they please, and NFL owners are always very rich men."[12]

Work-Related Issues: How the Sausage Is Made

On and off the tennis court, Chris Evert and Billie Jean King were classic rivals, dominating women's tennis in the late 1960s and early 1970s. Although they competed for tournament titles and sponsorship and endorsement dollars, they were united in demanding that female players earn prize money equal to that of men competing at the same events. For years, tournament organizers claimed the money gap was based on the differences in attendance and television ratings. By the mid-1970s, those claims were refuted, and under the threat of boycotts, tournament sponsors increased the women's purses to match that of the men's. Much of the credit, sports journalists say, goes to Evert and King for their willingness to speak out on that issue.

In 2019, the fight for equal pay for women athletes reached the world of soccer. In previous years, female soccer players representing the United States in international competitions such as the World Cup earned about twenty-five cents for every dollar earned by their male counterparts, even though the women had more success on the field—winning the World Cup four times in the previous decade—and generating larger television ratings.[13] Among the most outspoken athletes was Megan Rapinoe, who told the international media that she and her teammates would "refuse to accept anything other than what we felt like we deserved."[14] In 2023, the organizers of the World Cup met the women's demands, and the organizers of other international competitions promised to do the same.[15]

In women's golf, the issue was seldom about money but rather the quality of the golf courses hosting tournaments. When sports marketing executive Carolyn Bivens became the commissioner of the LPGA in 2005, players embraced her as the first woman to hold that post. But they were unhappy with the overall state of the organization, and they said so in media interviews. While the men's tour was playing on world-famous courses in glamorous locations in Florida and California, the women complained their events were relegated to "mediocre courses" in "backwater towns."[16] While no specific courses or cities were mentioned, golf journalists covering the tour at the time speculated they were referring to poorly conditioned courses in the Southeast. Bivens said she was upset by the comments and frustrated that they were made anonymously. While she had no power to limit the players' free-speech rights, those complaints tainted her four-year tenure as the tour's leader.[17]

For long-time golf journalists and fans, the unhappiness among LPGA players over the quality of their courses was reminiscent of comments made by a male golfer nearly fifty years earlier. During the 1970 U.S. Open Golf Championship in Chaska, Minnesota, competitor Dave Hill was displeased with the layout of the course and told the media that the owners "ruined a good cow pasture" when they built it (along with other disparaging remarks).[18] Even though the course was located in a rural and agricultural area, officials of the PGA Tour, who technically were not in charge of the event but were responsible for the behavior of its members, didn't care for the "cow pasture" remark and fined Hill $150. Hill responded with humor, telling reporters he would write out a check for $300 because he planned to criticize the course again the next day.[19]

In the five decades that followed the Hill matter, male golfers seldom made news for criticizing courses, sponsors, and other management issues. That was partly due to the improved quality of courses and increases in prize money. When players did make such comments, they were quickly admonished by tour executives or more experienced players, who deemed such comments were out-of-bounds.

That scenario changed in 2020, when players began complaining about rules that they believed limited their playing opportunities. For decades, the PGA Tour had policies that required players to participate in a minimum number of domestic tournaments per season and required them to obtain "releases" when they wanted to play in overseas events that conflicted with those on American soil. The purpose behind the rules, Tour officials said, was to allow Tour executives to promise sponsors that the biggest names would be at their events. Those rules didn't sit well with the players, who said so in media interviews and on their social media platforms. In addition, players complained that the Tour was generating ever-increasing revenue for media and publicity rights without sharing it with the players. While Tour officials were not pleased with the criticism, they made no attempt to fine or suspend players.

That unhappiness laid the groundwork for the emergence of LIV Golf, an international tour that would be funded by Saudi Arabia's Public Investment Fund and promised the best players from around the world more prize money and fewer rules. To run the operation, the Saudis hired former player Greg Norman, an outspoken Australian with his own history of butting heads with the PGA Tour. The two organizations engaged in a two-year battle that played out on social media, traditional media, and in courtrooms. The legal position of American golfers—including some of the biggest names—was that the PGA Tour had become a monopoly and was violating the spirit, if not the letter, of American anti-competitive laws.[20]

Phil Mickelson was one of the leading American golfers leaving the PGA Tour to participate in LIV Golf. During his transition, he was one of the most outspoken players who supported the new venture while bashing the American tour on his way out the door. Mickelson was suspended by the PGA Tour, not only for his own defection but for allegedly recruiting other big-name players to join him, including Dustin Johnson and Bryson DeChambeau.[21]

Those disciplinary measures started months-long Twitter feuds between him and the PGA Tour management, and between him and golf journalist Alan Shipnuck, author of a 2022 biography of Mickelson[22] and a 2023 book chronicling the PGA Tour-LIV saga.[23] Mickelson claimed he was misquoted in both books and pointed out other cases in which he confirmed the accuracy of the quotes but claimed his comments were off-the-record.[24]

When it became apparent the PGA Tour could not win the battle, the two tours began to discuss a possible merger in the summer of 2023. As part of the tentative merger agreement, the Saudi side suggested a disparagement clause that would prevent players from criticizing the new organization either in either media interviews or on their social media platforms (the PGA Tour has loosely enforced rules prohibiting players from criticizing host venues, sponsors, or other players, but seldom objects to players criticizing the organization itself). When players and sports journalists questioned whether such a rule would be or could be enforced, a PGA Tour spokesperson simply answered that "the players' free-speech rights would be respected."[25] The proposed rule caught the eye of the U.S. Senate, with one member calling for the PGA Tour to lose its tax-exempt status, partly due to free-speech concerns.[26] As of the fall of 2024, the fate of the proposed merger, along with the disparagement clause, was still undecided.

One of the ironies of the conflict between the PGA Tour and the rival tour seeking to take away its star players is that a similar scenario unfolded sixty years earlier when there was only one organization involved in professional golf: the Professional Golfers Association. From its founding in 1929 until 1963, the PGA fulfilled its original purpose of training and serving golf instructors, but it also operated tournaments. In 1963, tournament players began grumbling to each other and the media that the organization had become too complex and needed to split into separate enterprises, which it did—the PGA of America, which would serve instructors and the clubs that employ them, and the PGA Tour, which would operate tournaments. That scenario was repeated a decade later when the players, led by superstars Arnold Palmer and Jack Nicklaus, complained that it was now the PGA Tour that was trying to do too much, having grown into a cumbersome organization that was selling merchandise, designing and operating courses, and entering into other business enterprises unrelated to its primary purpose of running tournaments. The difference between the 1963 and 1973 situations was that the former was done in public; the latter in private. When Norman and the LIV organizers charted their strategy in 2021, they did so in public.[27]

Social Issues: Racial Justice

The phenomena of athletes protesting for social and racial justice did not begin with professional athletes but amateurs not previously known for public protests. In the 1968 Summer Olympics in Mexico City, one of the most anticipated events was the men's 200-meter sprint, where Americans were heavily favored. Two Americans—Tommie Smith and John Carlos—finished first and third, respectively. For Smith, the victory was the culmination of an outstanding career, which saw him set twelve world records—all while a full-time student at San Jose State University.

What made the event historic was not their medal-earning performances, but what happened when they took the podium. While the U.S. National Anthem played, Smith and Carlos faced the American flag and raised clenched fists, making what was perceived as the "Black Power" salute. In addition, Smith and Carlos removed their shoes and took the medal stand wearing black socks to represent Black poverty in the United States. The silver medalist, Australian runner Peter Norman, did not make the salute but wore an internationally recognized human rights emblem on his jacket, as did Smith and Carlos.[28]

Coming just six months after the assassination of Dr. Martin Luther King Jr. and shortly after a summer of racial violence in major American cities, the gestures of Smith and Carlos generated widespread condemnation in the United States, including vitriol in the media and in election-year political discourse. In his biography, published nearly thirty years later, Smith claimed the gesture was not "Black Power" but rather a recognition of the Olympic Project for Human Rights, an idea that started with a group of athletes talking about boycotting the 1968 Olympics but deciding instead to use their platform to speak out against discrimination and oppression around the world.[29] The animosity toward Smith spread to his coach and even the president of SJSU, who both reported getting hate mail after the incident. In addition, numerous SJSU alumni stopped donating to the university, and California Governor Ronald Reagan and the Republican-led state legislature threatened to withhold funding from the school.[30]

One year earlier, football great Jim Brown of the Cleveland Browns had convened a meeting with civil rights leader Carl Stokes and a dozen prominent Black athletes of the day, including boxer Muhammad Ali and basketball players Bill Russell and Kareem Abdul-Jabbar. The purpose of the meeting—called the Cleveland Summit—was to discuss the future of the civil rights movement and what role athletes could play using their public platforms.[31]

Despite the energy emerging from the meeting, the issue of racial justice was seldom discussed in sports circles for the next five decades, but it resurfaced in 2014. Following a series of tragedies in which unarmed Black men were killed by police—many of them at traffic stops—athletes in several sports began speaking out. The phenomenon started during the National Football League season when the St. Louis Rams entered their stadium for home games with their hands in the air, a gesture parroting the "hands up, don't shoot" chant heard during protests about police misconduct. Shortly before the season started, an unarmed Black man had been shot and killed by police in nearby Ferguson, Missouri. The team's gesture drew support from civil rights advocates and most of its fans, but condemnation from police unions.

At the beginning of the 2016 National Football League season, San Francisco 49ers quarterback Colin Kaepernick refused to stand during the pre-game performance of the national anthem. At first, he merely sat on the bench while his teammates stood, but once asked about it by sportswriters, he began kneeling in a way that was much more visible. By the end of that season, a handful of teammates and players on other teams also knelt. Players claimed their protests were aimed at drawing attention to the treatment of Black motorists by white police officers, and they were not intentionally disrespecting the flag.

At the beginning of the 2017 season, hundreds of players across the league began kneeling as well, as did athletes in other sports. As a result of the trend, then president Donald Trump commented that team owners needed to "get that SOB off the field right now. He's fired!" The last part of that comment was based on the catchphrase that Trump used on his reality television programs, *The Apprentice* and *Celebrity Apprentice.*[32] In 2017, Trump tweeted about the issue fourteen times in a day, referring specifically to Kaepernick and basketball player Steph Curry for "disrespecting our Great American Flag."[33]

As Trump continued to exacerbate the controversy, many players responded by locking their arms with each other, their coaches, and team owners.[34]

Trump and other critics of the NFL cited a 12 percent decline in television ratings for the first half of the 2016 season as evidence that the influence of the league was waning, but owners and league executives blamed the decline on Americans being distracted by the presidential election campaign. Some observers were skeptical of that defense, but the owners and executives were vindicated when ratings for the last half of November and all of December rebounded and were down only 8 percent compared to the same weeks in 2015. Throughout the playoffs and the Super Bowl (January and early February 2018), ratings had fully recovered.[35]

With some athletes, free speech comes not in the form of what they say, but what they don't say. In 2014, members of the Los Angeles Clippers protested racist comments by team owner Donald Sterling by wearing their T-shirts inside out to obscure the team's logos during warmups.[36] Six years later, players for the Atlanta Dream of the Women's National Basketball Association took the T-shirt protest idea a step further. Part owner Kelly Loeffler, also a U.S. senator representing Georgia, was an outspoken critic of Black Lives Matter in media interviews and on the Senate floor. When she ran for reelection that fall, her players protested by wearing T-shirts promoting the candidacy of her opponent, a Georgia pastor named Ralph Warnock, who won the race.[37]

One of the most celebrated American athletes of all time resisted the public pressure to get involved in social issues, fearful of how his participation might affect his "brand."[38]

At the height of his career in the late 1980s, Michael Jordan was one of the most recognized and marketable athletes in the world, and by his own choice, perhaps the least controversial. Jordan was already seen in television commercials for his own line of athletic clothing and shoes as well as companies such as Hanes, Coca-Cola, Wheaties, Gatorade, and McDonald's. But when he declined to endorse Charlotte Mayor Harvey Gantt when he was in a tight race for the U.S. Senate seat against Republican incumbent Jesse Helms, a known segregationist, his fans and national media were puzzled. Asked to explain his reluctance to speak out on the Gantt-Helms race or other political or social issues, Jordan quipped, "Republicans buy shoes, too."[39]

One of those disappointed fans was future president Barack Obama, who remembered Jordan's comments thirty years later. Interviewed for *The Last Dance*, ESPN's 2020 documentary series about Jordan's life and career, Obama recalled, "that for somebody who was at that time preparing for a career in civil rights law and knowing what Jesse Helms stood for, I would've wanted to see Michael push harder on that," Obama said. "On the other hand, he was still trying to figure out, 'How am I managing this image that has been created around me, and how do I live up to it?'"[40]

Elsewhere in the documentary, Jordan tried to distance himself from the comments, claiming they were taken out of context. However, he also drew a contrast between himself and another athlete from another sport who was equally famous.

"I do commend (boxer) Muhammad Ali for standing up for what he believed in," Jordan said. "But I never thought of myself as an activist. I thought of myself as a basketball player. I wasn't a politician when I was playing my sport. I was focused on my craft. Was that selfish? Probably. But that was my energy. That's where my energy was."[41]

Three decades later, two other National Basketball Association players made different choices, although they came from different ends of the political spectrum. Jonathan Isaac, an ordained minister and four-year starter for the

Orlando Magic, proudly spoke about his Christian conservative views against the backdrop of the NBA players kneeling during the national anthem and wearing Black Lives Matter clothing during pre-game warmups during the 2020–21 season. Isaac was one of the few players who refused to kneel during the anthem. "I do believe that black lives matter," Isaac said during a post-game press conference. "A lot went into my decision, and part of it is, I thought that kneeling or wearing the Black Lives Matter t-shirt doesn't go hand-in-hand with supporting black lives."[42]

On social media, Isaac added that he believed the answer to racial conflict is not in symbolic behavior such as kneeling or wearing shirts, but rather through applying biblical principles. He said he knew there would be consequences for his comments, and while fan reaction was evenly divided between the supportive and the critical, much of it was subdued. NBA officials had no reaction, and the Magic front office said only that it "supports their players' right to speak out, or to not speak out."[43]

For much of that season and part of the next, Isaac was sidelined with multiple injuries but was still sought out for comment on racial issues as the national media covered events such as the murder of George Floyd by a police officer in Minneapolis. In addition to media interviews, he also appeared on conservative television networks, spoke at religious and political conferences, and authored a book titled *Why I Stand*.[44]

In 2021, Isaac launched his own clothing line called Unitus, which is targeted at young conservative buyers who do not want to purchase clothing manufactured and sold by companies that publicly supported Black Lives Matter. "I believe that values matter, and in today's day when we do give our money to companies that don't support our values we're cosigning their message," he said in media interviews. "So what I wanted to do was give Americans—freedom-loving, faith-loving Americans—the option to buy with their values."[45]

Elsewhere in Florida, another NBA player took a more confrontational approach. Forward Udonis Haslem of the Miami Heat said he and his teammates were often criticized by opposing fans on road trips because of the controversial positions on racial and LGBTQ issues taken by the Florida Legislature and Governor Ron DeSantis.

"I ask people out there to stop Florida-shaming us," Haslem said as his team prepared for Game 2 of the NBA Finals against the Denver Nuggets in Colorado. "Everybody ain't down with what's going on in Florida. People think that because you live in Florida, you're down with that shit. We're not. I'm not happy about it."[46] Much like Isaac, Haslem saw the reaction to his comments mixed but subtle. He heard little from the fans and got only a modicum of support from his teammates, team officials, and the media that cover the team.

Athletes taking public stands on social issues have even reached the previously non-controversial sport of professional golf in 2021. After Georgia enacted restrictions on voting rights the previous year, fan-favorites Phil Mickelson and Rory McIlroy used their pre-tournament press conferences at the Georgia-based Masters Tournament to criticize the new laws.[47]

Ironically, one golfer not injecting himself into the discussion of voting rights—or any other issue involving race—is the most successful Black golfer in the history of the game. Tiger Woods was not at the 2021 Masters due to an injury, but long before that event, he took the Michael Jordan approach ("Republicans buy shoes too") and didn't use his platform to address social issues, even when baited by the media or others. When he first became a global celebrity in the mid-1990s, he was annoyed by repeated questions about his political views and voting choices. The fact that he was usually the only Black golfer participating in a tournament and the only one being asked questions about politics and race was not a coincidence, he noted.[48]

Woods's preference for avoiding speaking out on racial topics dates back to his first major tournament win at the 1997 Masters. The following week he declined an invitation to appear with President Bill Clinton at a ceremony marking the fiftieth anniversary of Jackie Robinson's first appearance in a Major League Baseball game. Tired of the comparison of his success to that of Robinson, who broke MLB's color barrier in 1947, Woods said through his agent that his decision was based partly on the desire for "down time" after his victory and partly on the timing, questioning why "if it was so important, why didn't he ask before?"[49]

Social Issues: Sex and Sexuality

One of the most successful female athletes in the United States has also been one of the most politically outspoken. Megan Rapinoe, an openly gay soccer star and leader of the United States Women's National Team who calls herself a "walking protest," was already an advocate for LGBTQ rights and a critic of proposed laws regarding gay marriage and pay inequities for women in professional sports.

She became more controversial during the 2016 season when she knelt during the national anthem at one home game in sympathy with San Francisco 49ers quarterback Colin Kaepernick.

"Being a gay American, I know what it means to look at the flag and not have it protect all of your liberties," Rapinoe told reporters after the game. "It's important to have white people stand in support of people of color on this."[50]

When her National Women's Soccer League team, the Seattle Reign, played a road game against the Washington Spirit, that team circumvented her protest by playing the anthem before the players took the field. A statement issued by the Spirit claimed that it chose "to not subject our fans and friends to the disrespect we feel such an act would represent . . . To willingly allow anyone to hijack this tradition that means so much to millions of Americans and so many of our own fans for any cause would effectively be just as disrespectful as doing it ourselves."[51] Rapinoe criticized the move in her post-game media comments, citing the upcoming anniversary of the September 11, 2001, terrorist attacks. "It was incredibly distasteful, four days before (the anniversary of) one of the worst tragedies in our country, to say I tried to hijack this event," she said.[52]

Three years later, she drew the wrath of President Trump when she and her teammates declined an invitation to visit the White House after the United States Women's National Team won the World Cup in 2019. At the time, Rapinoe told CNN, "Maybe America is great for a few people right now, but it's not great for enough Americans in this world," a reference to Trump's Make America Great Again (MAGA) slogan. She added that the Trump administration "doesn't fight for the same things we fight for" and that she and her teammates "would not go to the fucking White House."[53]

Rapinoe eventually went to the White House, but did so without her teammates when President Joe Biden presented her with the Presidential Medal of Freedom in 2022. Biden praised Rapinoe not only for her athletic accomplishments but also for her role in securing equal pay for the U.S. women's soccer team and her advocacy for LGBTQ rights.[54]

Trump might have had the last word in the dustup in 2023 when he used his own social media platform to claim that the American team's unexpected loss in that year's World Cup tournament was because of Rapinoe's political views and the team's "wokeness."[55]

When the 2022 Men's World Cup Soccer Tournament was held in Qatar, a Muslim country where homosexuality is illegal, European teams were forbidden by FIFA, their home league, to wear rainbow armbands bearing the "One Love" logo or any other accessories that might offend the host country. Officials threatened to issue yellow cards to any players who flouted the rules. It wasn't noticed until after one game that the German team wore shoes with smaller versions of the rainbow logo and placed their hands over their mouths when posing for a post-game photograph.

The following year, the women's tournament was held in Australia and New Zealand, where no government taboos were in place. Players were not only allowed to wear armbands or other accessories related to social issues but were encouraged to do so. Players chose from eight options, including those advocating for LGBTQ rights as well as issues such as gender equality, world hunger, education, or domestic violence.[56]

The organizers of the World Cup were not the only sports organization dealing with athletes' support of social causes. In 2022, the Federation Internationale de l'Automobile, the governing body for Formula 1 racing in Europe, began prohibiting drivers from displaying advocacy of or opposition to social issues on their helmets or clothing. The move was prompted by the case of Lewis Hamilton, a British driver who wore a T-shirt reading "Arrest the Cops Who Killed Breonna Taylor" to draw attention to the killing of a Black woman by police officers in Louisville, Kentucky.[57] Other drivers had been criticized for wearing clothing or helmet decals related to global climate change or LGBTQ rights.[58]

During the 2020 presidential campaign, forty-one-year-old Scott Piercy, winner of four professional golf tournaments during his twelve-year career, shared a homophobic meme aimed at openly gay candidate Pete Buttigieg. Piercy already had a reputation as a social media loose cannon, reposting nonsensical news stories that were easily discredited as conspiracy theories about political events and the Covid-19 pandemic, but those were those seldom generated any controversy.

The Buttigieg meme was the final straw for three of his sponsors—those that provided him with financial backing as well as his golf clubs, shoes, and clothing—and they terminated their contracts immediately. The deals were estimated to be worth $2 million. The Scandinavian fashion brand J. Lindeberg was the only one of his former sponsors to comment publicly on the matter, issuing a statement that Piercy's comments "were unacceptable and far from our views and beliefs. As a company, we want to make sure our customers, employees, and other ambassadors know we support all communities and have no room for hate or discrimination in our company."[59]

Piercy showed up at the following week's tournament with a new golf bag and clothing bearing no sponsor logos and issued what journalists called a "hasty non-apology."[60] He told reporters that "whenever I post, my intent is NEVER to offend . . . I want to apologize if any of my recent story posts have been offensive. I will do better!"[61]

As mentioned in the Preface, this book does not deal with cases of comments that are "blurted out" or made during moments of duress—especially when they involve athletes—as those are examples of immaturity rather than malice. Instead, it deals with thoughts that are premeditated. That's exactly the distinction made by Eamon Lynch, an openly gay golf journalist, when he commented on the difference between the Piercy case and that of Justin Thomas, which happened ten months later. The twenty-seven-year-old rising star was playing in the season-opening tournament in Hawaii when he missed a short putt and blurted out "faggot" loud enough to be picked up on nearby microphones.[62]

Thomas lost only one of his sponsors as a result, but it was a big one: Ralph Lauren, maker of the popular brand of Polo golf clothing. Eamon was one of many journalists willing to excuse the slip, commenting that "there's an enormous difference between angrily muttering a disgusting comment to oneself and taking the time to post a loathsome image on social media that targets an openly gay individual. Piercy got what he deserved. Thomas does not warrant the same."[63] Lynch and other journalists also pointed out the hypocrisy of Ralph Lauren dropping Thomas as an example of "maintaining its image" while simultaneously having a reputation for allegedly using "sweatshop" labor.[64]

Both Piercy and Thomas were fined undisclosed amounts for their conduct, but per PGA Tour policy, the amounts of those fines were not disclosed.

Piercy was not the only athlete ending up in hot water over LGBTQ issues. In May 2023, Toronto Blue Jays pitcher Anthony Bass apologized for posting videos on social media in which he endorsed anti-gay campaigns that advocated boycotts against Target and Bud Light for their advocacy of LGBTQ issues. One of those videos called on Christians to stop patronizing those companies.[65]

"Here's the reason biblically why I believe Christians have got to be boycotting Target, Bud Light, and any other corporation that's pushing the things they're pushing," Bass said on the video. "This is evil, this is demonic, we won't stand for it, we're not going to go to the stores anymore and we're not going to give you our money."[66]

The twelve-year veteran apologized through the media, telling reporters who cover the team that he had removed the offensive video and

> recognized that post was hurtful to the Pride community, which includes friends of mine and close family members, and I am truly sorry for that. I just spoke with my teammates and apologized to them, and as of right now, am using the Blue Jays' resources to better educate myself to make better decisions moving forward. The ballpark is for everybody. We include all fans at the ballpark and want to include everybody.[67]

The Blue Jays's front office later issued a statement explaining that "individual player sentiments are not representative of the club's beliefs."[68] Bass's apology wasn't enough for the fans, and he was cut from the team two weeks later. General Manager Ross Atkins told the media the move was necessary because "the pitcher's stance had become a distraction in the clubhouse."[69]

Social Issues: World Politics

In 2023, a year after Russia invaded Ukraine, numerous athletes from both countries competed in the All-England Lawn Tennis Championships, better known in the sports world as "Wimbledon." Anticipating that at some point it was likely that players from those countries would face each other, Ukrainian players said that win or lose, they would not be shaking hands with their Russian opponents after their matches. They asked tournament organizers to explain their decision to the crowd so they would not be accused of being bad sports, but officials declined. Earlier in the year, a Ukrainian player refused to shake hands with her Russian opponent, drawing boos from the crowd.[70]

Athletes and Coaches Say the Darndest Things

Phil Mickelson's conflicts with the PGA Tour and Shipnuck were not Mickelson's first brush with free speech and the consequences of impromptu comments picked up by the press. While still an amateur playing in an international competition in Ireland in 1991, Mickelson hit an errant drive into the gallery. In a post-round interview, he told local reporters that he was happy no one was injured, "even though the Irish women are not that attractive." That quote ended up on the front page of newspapers all across Ireland, and media portrayals of Mickelson as "an arrogant American athlete" continued even after he left the country.[71]

In 2000, Atlanta Braves relief pitcher John Rocker was fined $20,000 and suspended for three months for racial and ethnic comments that Commissioner Bud Selig said "offended practically every element in society."[72] Rocker later apologized for his comments and saw his fine reduced to $500 and suspension cut to two weeks but was required to undergo "sensitivity training."[73] Three years later, New York Yankees pitcher David Wells was fined $100,000 by his team for comments in his autobiography in which he criticized his teammates, as well as team administrators and coaches, and claimed he pitched one 1998 game while "half drunk."[74]

Carolina Panthers offensive lineman Michael Oher lost his last chance at NFL success in 2016 with a careless Instagram post. Oher, whose life story became the basis for the controversial 2009 film *The Blind Side*, had won a Super Bowl as a member of the Baltimore Ravens and then spent a year with the Tennessee Titans. After moving to the Panthers in 2015, he spent much of that season out with a series of concussions. His post showed a lineup of ten medicine bottles over the caption, "All for the brain smh (shaking my head)."[75] After public criticism, he deleted the post, but the Panthers soon deleted him from the roster, and he never played again.[76]

Early in the 2023 NFL season, San Francisco tight end George Kittle was fined $13,659 for displaying a T-shirt that read "F Dallas" underneath his jersey during his team's win over the Cowboys in a nationally televised prime-time game. The shirt was thought to be the same as one sold on the Internet and around San Francisco the week prior to the game, but instead of reading "Fuck Dallas," Kittle covered the last three letters of the first word with white tape. League officials say that wasn't enough to prevent the fine, however. Before the penalty was imposed but knowing it was likely, Kittle was asked by a reporter if it was worth it. "One hundred percent," he said. "I'd do it again."[77]

Later that fall, Kansas City Chiefs tight end Travis Kelce began a romance with pop singer Taylor Swift. That led to gentle teasing by other players and fans commenting on social media, and Kelce took it all with good humor. But then New York Jets quarterback Aaron Rodgers took a more serious swipe at Kelce, ridiculing him and his mother for appearing in a television commercial for Pfizer in which they promoted the importance of both the Covid-19 and influenza vaccines. Rodgers later challenged Kelce to a televised debate over Covid-19 vaccination policies.

Rodgers, who two seasons earlier had publicly questioned the efficacy of the Covid vaccines while flouting the league's mandatory vaccination policy, called Kelce "Mr. Pfizer" in his appearance on The Pat McAfee Show on ESPN, and then repeated his criticisms on social media.[78] The previous year, while still playing for the Green Bay Packers, Rodgers used his own social media platforms to accuse the pharmaceutical industry of spreading "Covid panic" and called Dr. Anthony Fauci, who headed up the federal government's response to the pandemic, a "pharmacrat."[79] As with most mini-controversies fueled by social media, the battle lines were predictable: other Covid-19 skeptics supporting Rodgers, and public health experts backing Kelce for his support of science. The issue also drew the attention of sports journalists, many of them already knocking Rodgers for allowing his social media antics to overshadow his on-field accomplishments.

"Every Tuesday, Aaron Rodgers emerges from his rathole to say something really, really stupid about vaccines," wrote Gregg Doyel in a 2023 column in *USA Today*, referring to Rodgers's weekly appearances on McAfee's show. "And because we live in this cult of fame, liking and believing and even electing people only because they're rich or famous, people believe Rodgers. So he's out there every Tuesday, saying something that makes us less safe."[80]

Added Mike Freeman, another *USA Today* columnist: "I still don't think Rodgers understands the power he yields. There are people who look at Rodgers and believe he knows more than the people who dedicate their lives to studying vaccines and infectious diseases. Rodgers appears smart on these topics and speaks with authority on them. It's ignorant authority, but it's authority."[81]

Shortly after the Rodgers-Kelce dustup, the quarterback renewed his feud with television comedian Jimmy Kimmel, who had ridiculed him on his nightly talk show over the Covid issue as well as the quarterback's appetite for conspiracy theories. The day before a New York court was scheduled to release documents related to the criminal case against convicted sex trafficker Jeffrey Epstein, Rodgers used his allotted time on McAfee's show to suggest that Kimmel's name might emerge as a participant in Epstein's sex parties. For years, Kimmel had ignored online vitriol and death threats that resulted from his nightly jokes about Donald Trump, but he took this issue more seriously. Through media interviews, Kimmel told Rodgers that his comments were "full-blown nonsense from a soft-brained wacko" and that his "reckless words put my family in danger . . . keep it up and we will debate the facts further in court."[82]

After that response from Kimmel, McAfee apologized to him on-air, and ESPN apologized privately. When given the chance to apologize on McAfee's show, Rodgers declined, saying instead that his comments were "taken out of context" and he never said that Kimmel's name appeared in the Epstein documents, only that Kimmel should be "nervous about the documents being released." He added that the criticism he has received is an attempt to "cancel" him because he was "stating the truth" about Covid-19 and other issues.[83]

As of March 2024, nothing further has been said about the issue, and some legal observers speculated that because the two employers involved—ESPN for McAfee and ABC for Kimmel—are both owned by Disney, executives with the parent company may have stepped in to stop the debate.[84]

Saying strange and attention-getting things is not limited to athletes; often coaches venture into dangerous territory while trying to motivate their players. In 2020, Pat Chambers resigned at Penn State after telling a Black player that he wanted to "loosen the noose that's around his neck."[85] During the 2020–1 season, Creighton coach Greg McDermott was suspended for one game after telling his team after a loss to "stay on the plantation" as a way to remind them to stick together.[86]

When Mark Adams was hired as head basketball coach at Texas Tech University in 2021, there were high hopes among the team's fans and boosters that he was the right choice to turn around the struggling program. Within two seasons, Adams found himself suspended and then forced to resign. The problems began when Adams referenced Bible verses in pre-game and post-game talks, including those in which he analogized players following the instructions of coaches to "slaves serving their masters."[87]

Late in the 2023 NFL season, Buffalo Bills Coach Sean McDermott found himself in trouble for comments he made behind closed doors four years earlier. When the Bills were in the 2019 summer training camp in preparation for their third season under McDermott, the coach wanted to motivate the team to improve in the areas of communication and teamwork. He chose a poor analogy. According to multiple players who were in the meeting room that day—some still with the team and some who had moved on—McDermott cited the terrorist attacks of September 11, 2001, as an example of people who came together to achieve a common goal through effective teamwork and communication. "What tactics do you think they (the terrorists) used to come together?" McDermott admitted to asking the players, along with, "What do you think their biggest obstacle was?"[88]

The story was first published on a sports website called Go Long but was quickly picked up by the national media, prompting McDermott to apologize to fans through the media. "My intent in the meeting that day was to discuss the importance of communication and being on the same page as a team," McDermott said. "I regret mentioning 9/11 in my message that day and immediately apologized to the team that day."[89]

While commentators in the national media called his December 7 "non-apology apology" insufficient, fans commenting on the team's website said it was time to move on from the mini-controversy, and a spokesperson for the team said it was unlikely McDermott would be disciplined by the team or the league.[90]

Ownership Issues

Team owners are often chastised for their public comments on controversial issues, and while they are often criticized by their players and the media that cover the teams, league executives, and fellow owners, they rarely face long-term consequences.

One example was Marge Schott, owner of the Cincinnati Reds from 1984 to 1999. She may have been the most disliked owner in Major League Baseball: one whom few players wanted to play for, few reporters wanted to interview, and few other owners wanted to associate with. Her most famous gaffe was when she referred to one free-agent signing as her "million-dollar (N-word)."[91] In one media interview, she praised German dictator Adolf Hitler as a man "who had good ideas, but took some of them a bit too far."[92] In yet another case, Schott publicly complained when the league cancelled one game only minutes before it was scheduled to start because an umpire had collapsed and died on the field. "Can't they just bring in someone else?" she asked.[93]

Bob McNair, owner of the Houston Texans, has made similar gaffes. When the Kaepernick situation grew from one player on one team to a league-wide issue in 2017, team owners and league executives held frequent conference calls to discuss the public relations implications. Rather than following his colleagues' suggestion that the discussions be kept confidential, McNair took his frustrations to the media, complaining that the league's lack of action was like "allowing the inmates to run the prison."[94]

In a league in which 70 percent of the athletes are Black, the comments were considered inflammatory and racist. McNair later tried to walk back the comments, claiming the "inmates" in his metaphor were not the players, but league executives.[95]

Two years earlier, McNair learned that simply donating money to controversial causes can draw public attention. McNair contributed $10,000 to a campaign aimed at repealing a city ordinance that protected gays and lesbians from discrimination. When news of that became public, many of the team's liberal-leaning fans criticized the gesture, and his half-hearted effort to defend it by explaining his born-again Christian values and quoting the Bible didn't help.[96]

Another example of a team owner known for "speaking first and thinking later" is Jim Irsay, owner of the Indianapolis Colts. Nine years after his well-publicized arrest for allegedly driving drunk, Irsay claimed he was singled out because he was a "rich, white millionaire."[97]

ESPN reporter Kimberly Martin questioned the validity of that claim on the air, prompting Irsay to call Martin "mean and ugly" and a "nothingburger" in interviews with other media.[98]

For years, Washington Redskins owner Daniel Snyder was under pressure to change the name of the team, based on criticisms from Native American tribes that claimed it was derogatory. In response, Snyder went on the record and said he would never change the name, and in written versions of the statement often capitalized the word "never."[99] After several long-time sponsors threatened non-renewal of their marketing agreements with the team, and FedEx threatened to not renew a contract to have its name on the team's stadium, Snyder relented, first assigning the placeholder name "Washington Football Team" and later choosing "Commanders" as the team's permanent name. Snyder, who also said he would "never" sell the team, eventually did so under pressure from other owners and after an investigation into claims of sexual harassment at team headquarters.[100]

NBA Coaches and Gun Violence

While athletes are often criticized by fans and non-fans when they speak out on issues such as gun violence, that blowback is seldom experienced by their coaches.

In May 2022, for example, Golden State Warriors Coach Steve Kerr criticized lawmakers for their inaction following deadly mass shootings at an elementary school in Uvalde, Texas, and a grocery store in Buffalo, New York. When he met with the media prior to a playoff game against the Dallas Mavericks, Kerr passed on questions about the game and instead launched into a calm but impassioned plea for governmental action.

"We are being held hostage by fifty senators in Washington who refuse to even put it to a vote, despite what we the American people want," Kerr said. "They won't vote on it, because they want to hold on to their own power."[101] When the reporters put down their pens and their body language indicated they were more interested in the game than in a lecture on social issues, Kerr added, "Any basketball questions don't matter."[102]

Kerr accused a group of senators of defying the will of the American people by not acting on H.R. 8, the Bipartisan Background Checks Act that the House of Representatives approved the previous year.

The following year, the murder of children and teachers at a private Christian school in Nashville led to San Antonio Spurs coach Gregg Popovich stepping up to the microphone to make similar comments. Two weeks after the tragedy, as he prepared to coach his final regular-season game after twenty-seven years in coaching, Popovich bypassed questions about his retirement and singled out Republican senators Ted Cruz, Lindsey Graham, and Marsha Blackburn for their apparent inaction.[103] He called the reporters' attention to Blackburn's response to the Nashville murders in which she said, "My office is in contact with federal, state, and local officials, and we stand ready to assist."[104] "Assist in what?" Popovich said. "They're dead. What are you going to assist with? Cleaning up their brains off the wall? Wiping the blood off the schoolroom floor? What are you going to assist with?"[105]

Popovich, who said he worries about his grandchildren when dropping them off at school, already had a reputation for being outspoken about gun violence and other issues, such as race and LGBTQ rights in previous years. "I don't think about it as using the platform that I have," he said in 2017. "I'm an individual. I live in this country. I have the right to say and think what I want. It's got nothing to do with my position. If it helps somebody else think one way or the other about something, great. But the discussion has to take place."[106]

Later that year, a mass shooting that took the lives of eighteen people in Maine prompted Sacramento Kings Coach Mike Brown to follow the precedent set by Kerr and Popovich. In a post-game gathering with reporters that took place a few hours after the shooting, Brown said, "It's a sad day for our country. And until we decide to do something about it, this is going to keep happening. We don't know how to fix a problem that's right in front of us."[107]

What made the comments of Kerr, Popovich, and Brown noteworthy is that the majority of basketball fans either supported their comments on social media or remained silent. That was different from the treatment of players who spoke out on social and political issues. In 2018, when LeBron James of the Cleveland Cavaliers used media interviews and his social media platforms to criticize President Donald Trump and advocate for gun control and racial equality, fans of the team were divided in their responses on their personal Facebook pages and that of the team. Many television political commentators weren't as kind. Laura Ingraham of Fox News told her viewers that James and other athletes should concentrate on their sports and stay out of politics. "It's always unwise to seek political advice from someone who gets paid $100 million a year to bounce a ball," she said. "Keep the political comments to yourselves . . . Shut up and dribble."[108]

Notes

1 Josh Peter, "Joe Burrow Is Rarest of NFL QBs: Speaking Up Beyond the Huddle," *USA Today,* September 16, 2022, p. 1-C.
2 Ibid.
3 Ibid.
4 Ibid.
5 Ibid.
6 Ibid.
7 Ibid.
8 Ibid.
9 Alan Shipnuck, *Phil: The Rip-Roaring (and Unauthorized) Biography of Golf's Most Colorful Superstar* (New York: Avid Reader Press, 2022), p. 159.

10 Tom Zucco, "Bucs Unload Giles, House, and Springs," *St. Petersburg Times*, October 21, 1986.
11 Ibid.
12 Tom McEwen, *Press Pass: My Life in Sports* (Tampa, FL: The Tampa Tribune, 1986), p. 188.
13 "The Fight for Equal Pay," *The Week*, August 11, 2023, p. 11. See also: Issy Ronald, Antonio Jarne, and Krystina Shveda, "Female Soccer Players Earn 25 Cents to Dollar of Men at World Cup," *CNN.com*, July 20, 2023.
14 Ibid.
15 Ibid.
16 Tim Rosaforte, "New LPGA Commissioner Faces Tour's Uncertain Future and Unhappy Members," *The Palm Beach Post*, September 11, 2008.
17 Ibid.
18 Jim Achenbach, "Dave Hill Was Unrestrained," *Golfweek*, October 4, 2011.
19 Ibid.
20 Sean Zak, "LIV Golf vs. the PGA Tour," *Golf Magazine*, September-October 2022, pp. 40–7.
21 Ibid.
22 Shipnuck, *Phil*.
23 Alan Shipnuck, *LIV and Let Die: The Inside Story of the War Between the PGA Tour and LIV Golf* (New York: Avid Reader Press, 2023).
24 Ryan Glasspiegel, "Bitter Phil Mickelson-Alan Shipnuck Feud Reignites," *New York Post*, November 27, 2023. See also: Zak, "LIV Golf vs. the PGA Tour."
25 Cameron Jourdan, "Senator Introduces Bill to Strip PGA Tour's Tax-Exempt Status," *Golfweek*, July 28, 2023.
26 Ibid.
27 Zak, "LIV Golf vs. the PGA Tour." See also: Adam Schupak, *Deane Beman: Golf's Driving Force* (Orlando, FL: East Cottage Press, 2011), pp. 1–3. See also: Zak, "LIV Golf vs. the PGA Tour."
28 Tommie Smith and David Steele, *Silent Gesture: The Autobiography of Tommie Smith* (Philadelphia: Temple University Press, 2007), p. 22. See also: "Hope and Defiance: The Black Power Salute That Rocked the 1968 Olympics," *Life*, October 14, 2013.
29 Ibid.
30 Smith and Steele, *Silent Gesture*, pp. 10, 159, and 177.
31 Richard Goldstein, "Jim Brown: Football Great and Civil Rights Champion, Dies at 87," *The New York Times*, May 19, 2023.
32 Amanda Marcotte, *Troll Nation* (New York: Skyhorse Publishing, 2018), p. 23.
33 Ibid., p. 24.

34 Anthony Crupi, "Can Anything Dethrone the NFL?" *Advertising Age*, September 11, 2017, pp. 201–21. See also: Randy Bobbitt, *Exploring Communication Ethics* (New York: Taylor & Francis, 2020), pp. 19–20.

35 Ibid.

36 Nick Swartz, "Los Angeles Clippers Turn Warm-Ups Inside Out in Protest Before Game 4," *USA Today*, April 27, 2014.

37 Ben Pickman, "WNBA Players Wear 'Vote Warnock' Shirts Opposing Atlanta Dream Co-Owner," *Sports Illustrated*, August 4, 2020.

38 Sean Gregory, "Here's How Harvey Gantt Feels, 30 Years Later, About Michael Jordan Refusing to Back Him," *Time*, May 4, 2020.

39 Ibid.

40 Ibid.

41 Ibid.

42 Sam Quinn, "Magic's Jonathan Isaac Explains Why He Didn't Take Knee or Wear Black Lives Matter Shirt Friday," *CBSSports.com*, August 1, 2020. See also: Mike Cali, "Jonathan Isaac Explains Why He Stood During National Anthem," *Orlando PinstripePost.com*, July 31, 2020.

43 Ibid.

44 Jonathan Isaac, *Why I Stand* (Nashville, TN: Daily Wire Books, 2022).

45 Quinn, "Magic's Jonathan Isaac Explains Why He Didn't Take Knee or Wear Black Lives Matter Shirt Friday." See also: Cali, "Jonathan Isaac Explains Why He Stood During National Anthem."

46 Mike Freeman, "Haslem Rips DeSantis and Says What Many Think," *USA Today*, June 13, 2013, p. 2-C.

47 Christine Brennan, "Two Prominent Golfers Speak Up in Favor of Voting Rights," *USA Today*, April 7, 2022, p. 5-C.

48 "Woods Declines Clinton Invite," *United Press International Report*, April 15, 1997.

49 Ibid.

50 "Spirit Plays Anthem Before Players' Entry to Nix Megan Rapinoe 'Hijacking,'" *ESPN.com*, September 7, 2016.

51 Ibid.

52 Ibid.

53 Harmon Leon, "A Look at Megan Rapinoe and Other Athletes Who Said They Won't Go to the White House," *The Observer*, June 27, 2019.

54 Nancy Armour, "With Lots of Love and Laughter, Rapinoe Says Goodbye," *USA Today*, September 26, 2023, p. 1-C.

55 Tara Subramaniam, "Trump Blames Megan Rapinoe and Wokeness for US Women's World Cup Exit," *CNN.com*, August 8, 2023.

56 Nancy Armour, "World Cup Players Can Wear Rainbow Armband," *USA Today,* July 3, 2023, p. 4-C.

57 Chris Medland, "F1 Drivers, Teams Banned from Making Political Statements," *USA Today,* December 21, 2022, p. 4-C.

58 Ibid.

59 Graham Gremore, "Pro Golfer Scott Piercy Bleeding Sponsors After Taking Homophobic Swing at Pete Buttigieg," *Queerty,* March 6, 2020. See also: Brian C. Bell, "Homophobic Instagram Post Costs Golfer Scott Piercy Multiple Major Sponsors," *OutSports*, March 16, 2020.

60 Graham Gremore, "The Price of Hate: Pro Golfer Scott Piercy's Homophobia Cost Him $2 Million and Heavy Dose of Public Humiliation," *Queerty,* March 17, 2020.

61 Ibid.

62 "Thomas Apologizes After Using Anti-Gay Slur at Sentry," *Reuters News Report*, January 9, 2021. See also: Eamon Lynch, "Justin Thomas Learned Something This Week. Everyone Else? Not So Much," *Twitter Post*, January 17, 2021.

63 Lynch, "Justin Thomas Learned Something This Week."

64 Ibid.

65 Scooby Axson, "Jays Pitcher Apologizes for Sharing Social Video," *USA Today,* May 31, 2023, p. 3-C.

66 Ibid.

67 Ibid.

68 Anna Lazarus Caplan, "Toronto Blue Jays General Manager Explains Why Team Cut Anthony Bass Following Anti-LGBTQ Post," *People,* June 12, 2023.

69 Ibid.

70 "Wimbledon Won't be Making Announcements on Handshake Etiquette Despite Booing," *Associated Press Report*, July 10, 2023.

71 Shipnuck, *Phil*, pp. 42–3.

72 William A. Wines and Terence J. Lau, "Can You Hear Me Now? Corporate Censorship and Its Troubling Implications for the First Amendment," *DePaul Law Review* 55, no. 1 (Fall 2005): pp. 119–67.

73 Ibid.

74 Ibid.

75 Mark Leibovich, *Big Game: The NFL in Dangerous Times* (New York: Penguin Press, 2018), p. xvi.

76 Ibid.

77 Scooby Axson, "Kittle Fined for T-shirt with Taunt," *USA Today*, October 16, 2023, p. 3-C. See also: Josh Dubow, "49ers TE George Kittle Fined More Than $13,000 for Profane T-shirt About the Cowboys," *Associated Press Report*, October 14, 2023.

78 Gregg Doyel, "By Paying Rodgers, McAfee Anti-Vax Co-Hort," *USA Today*, October 25, 2013, p. 2-C.
79 Ibid.
80 Ibid.
81 Mike Freeman, "Rodgers Makes a Fool of Himself by Attacking Kelce," *USA Today*, October 11, 2023, p. 3-C.
82 Mike Freeman, "Aaron Rodgers and Grudges Go Together," *USA Today*, January 4, 2024, p. 5-C.
83 Jordan Mendoza, "Rodgers Offers No Apology, Bashes ESPN," *USA Today*, January 11, 2024, p. 4-C. See also: Mike Freeman, "Kimmel Humiliates Jets QB Rodgers in New Monologue," *USA Today*, January 10, 2024, p. 4-C.
84 Freeman, "Aaron Rodgers and Grudges Go Together."
85 Nick Selbe, "Pat Chambers Steps Down as Penn State Basketball Coach After Internal Investigation," *Sports Illustrated*, October 21, 2020.
86 Nick Selbe, "Creighton Suspends Coach Craig McDermott Over Racist Language," *Sports Illustrated*, March 9, 2021.
87 "Texas Tech Men's Basketball Coach Resigns After Making Racially Insensitive Comments," *Associated Press Report*, March 9, 2023. See also: Joseph Salvador, "Texas Tech Suspends Mark Adams for Slavery Comment," *Sports Illustrated*, March 5, 2023.
88 Joe Buscaglia and Tim Graham, "Bills' McDermott Says He Regrets 9/11 Comments Made at Team Meeting in 2019," *The Athletic*, December 7, 2023.
89 Ibid.
90 Ibid.
91 Paul Dougherty, "Marge Schott Did as She Pleased While Owning the Cincinnati Reds," *Cincinnati Enquirer*, June 30, 2022.
92 Ibid.
93 Ibid.
94 Leibovich, *Big Game*, p. 320.
95 Ibid.
96 Ibid., p. 140.
97 Nancy Armor, "Irsay's Unhinged Rant Is Wrong, Big Problem for NFL," *USA Today*, November 24, 2023, p. 6-C.
98 Ibid.
99 Guatam Mukanda, "Goodbye, Mr. Snyder," *Forbes*, August 29, 2023.
100 Ibid.
101 Bill Chappell, "NBA Coach Steve Kerr Calls Out 50 Senators on a Bipartisan Gun Background Check Law," *National Public Radio*, May 25, 2022.
102 Ibid.

103 Ayana Archie, "NBA Coach Gregg Popovich Criticizes Lawmakers Over Gun Control," *National Public Radio*, April 10, 2023.

104 Ibid.

105 Ibid.

106 Ibid.

107 Mike Freeman, "Another Tragic Mass Shooting: NBA Coach Says Enough," *USA Today*, October 30, 2023, p. 7-C.

108 Emily Sullivan, "Laura Ingraham Tells LeBron James to Shut Up and Dribble," *National Public Radio*, February 19, 2018.

Conclusion

Everything Old Is New Again

On a hot and humid evening in July 2024, former president Donald Trump had just started speaking at a campaign rally in Butler, Pennsylvania, when a gunman opened fire from a nearby rooftop. Trump suffered only superficial wounds, but the bullets killed a member of the audience and seriously injured two others. The incident was a dramatic event within an already contentious presidential campaign, but it also began an unfortunate series of events for two Trump critics who expressed disappointment that the former president survived the shooting.

Jennifer Ripper was a teacher at Semper Elementary School in Westminster, Colorado, who posted on her Facebook page that it "looks like he ALMOST got taken out."[1] When she saw another post that said, "Dammit!!! They missed!!" she responded, "My thoughts exactly."[2] Within days, Ripper's name disappeared from the school's website, but school district officials did not say whether she had been terminated. The district issued a statement saying only that "The District has social media guidance that encourages our employees to conduct themselves in a professional manner and refrain from posting inappropriate content on personal social media channels. While our employees are entitled to their own perspectives, please know that when they share those perspectives, they are not speaking on behalf of the District."[3]

On the same day that Ripper posted her comments, an aide to a Mississippi Congressman expressed similar views on her Facebook page. "I don't condone violence but please get you some shooting lessons so you don't miss next time," wrote Jacqueline Warsaw, who worked for Democratic Representative Bennie Thompson.[4] She deleted the post within an hour, but it had already come to the attention of the *Clarion Ledger*, the state's leading newspaper. Warsaw resigned, claiming that she "got overwhelmed in the moment" and her post was meant "as a joke."[5] Not happy with only Warsaw's resignation, Republican officials in Mississippi told statewide media that Thompson should also step down.[6]

Those cases are somewhat reminiscent of one from the 1980s, when a nineteen-year-old government employee in Texas heard the news about the attempted assassination of President Ronald Reagan and told her coworkers, "If they go for him again, I hope they get him."[7] Her supervisor justified her termination by telling a court it was necessary to "maintain morale, efficiency, and discipline in the workplace."[8] A circuit court of appeals reversed that decision, and the U.S. Supreme Court confirmed the reversal. Both courts determined that the employee's low position on the organizational chart meant her comment carried little weight and was related more to her disapproval of the president's policies than a direct threat to his safety[9] (this case is discussed in more detail in Chapter 6).

The Trump shooting took place just a few months before this book was completed, and even though the employee in the Reagan case was vindicated, it's too soon to know if the individuals involved in the Trump case will fare as well in the long term.

Public versus Private

One factor the above cases have in common is that all three individuals were public employees, and as explained in the Introduction, they had more legal protection for their speech than employees in the private sector. However, in cases involving real or perceived threats to the president or other public figures, even public employees, theoretically protected by the First Amendment, still face consequences.

In explaining the dichotomy between public and private workplaces—and the level of free-speech protection that they offer or do not offer—noted criminal defense attorney Alan Dershowitz explained that the First Amendment "does not protect you (as a private employee) from your boss, who in most cases can fire you for the words you choose." Expanding his observations to the world of public commentary in general, Dershowitz added that the amendment "does not protect you from the harsh judgments of others, and the repercussions that can ensue . . . you can still be sued for defamation or charged with breaking the law."[10]

Bruce Barry, professor of management at Vanderbilt University, summarizes the dichotomy rather glibly: "In the public sector, you have the right of free speech except when you don't," he wrote in his 2007 book, titled *Speechless: The*

Erosion of Free Expression in the American Workplace. "In the private sector, you don't have the right to free speech, except when you do."[11]

In a 1995 article in *Indiana Law Review*, attorney Cynthia Estlund explained the dichotomy with a nautical metaphor, writing that "the safeguards for expression in the private-sector workplace are like islands of protection in a sea of employer discretion."[12]

The Path Forward

Suggestions for improving the legal landscape often fall along three lines: what employers can do, what employees can do, and if neither of those helps, how the courts and regulatory bodies such as the National Labor Relations Board can deal with the resulting litigation.

From the employers' standpoint, some claim that in certain fields, they need more leeway in limiting speech. Hospital administrators contend they need this authority because critical comments from doctors and nurses may cause public concern over the quality of care at that hospital and might discourage individuals from seeking care. Government agencies at all levels claim they need to limit the speech of their employees because of the confidential nature of the information they work with.[13]

And as pointed out in Chapters 5 and 6, branches of the military, as well as law enforcement agencies, claim they need to limit the speech of their employees—especially their political speech—in order to maintain public trust and the appearance of political neutrality.

Barry believes the future of the issue is up in the air. "It's hard to make a prediction going forward about employer tolerance because it seems to me there are currents pushing both ways," Barry said in a 2024 interview. "There's data showing that lots of employers do scrutinize social media of prospective and current employees, but (without data) I'd surmise that they naturally have to become more tolerant of, shall we say, flamboyant speech because it's how culture has evolved. And we see more employers trying to cultivate what the ethics consultants call a 'speak up culture' where workers feel free and comfortable raising workplace issues, which necessarily forces some tolerance. But on the other hand, firms have always exacted a duty of loyalty from workers that means they don't have to tolerate venom and toxicity directed at the firm, and given an employment climate where people change jobs more than they used to, it seems like employers should be quite willing to send their critics packing. Currents are pulling both ways."[14]

The future of workplace free speech is especially tenuous when it comes to political matters. In 2019, the Society for Human Resource Management issued an advisory that said it was acceptable to have rules barring political symbols, including the flag, as long as the policy was viewpoint-neutral and non-discriminatory. "Either everyone can do it, or no one can do it" was the consensus of the SHRM official who wrote the advisory as well as attorneys writing articles on the same topic in legal newsletters.[15]

The university campus appears to be a rare example of employers maintaining a "hands-off" policy when it comes to regulating the speech of their employees. In their 2017 book, *Free Speech on Campus*, legal historians Erwin Chemerinsky and Howard Gillman stated that administrators concerned about faculty members who "push the envelope" on free-speech issues must separate the professor's two roles. They describe a "professional zone," which includes responsibility to maintain standards in teaching and research and being accountable when those roles are scrutinized by administrators or off-campus critics. They differentiated the teaching and research roles from the "free-speech zone," in which faculty members comment publicly on matters outside of their teaching areas and are afforded more latitude in rocking the campus boat.[16]

"We believe colleges and universities can almost never punish faculty members who express controversial views outside the professional, educational context, where there are no enforceable scholarly standards and no disruption of the educational context other than that certain persons can take offense," Chemerinsky and Gillman wrote. "Faculty members who make controversial or even offensive comments on their Twitter feeds, but otherwise meet professional standards as teachers and colleagues, should not fear retaliation or harmful effects because of views they express outside their official duties."[17]

For employees, helpful suggestions for avoiding conflicts over free-speech issues are not as apparent. A reviewer of the early draft of this book posed a key question: Is there anything to be learned from the hundreds of cases involved in this book, other than "employees beware?"

The first obvious suggestion, hopefully a bit more specific than "beware," is what media executive Margaret Sullivan refers to as "self-discipline." "It's so easy to get involved in the digital equivalent of road rage," Sullivan wrote in her 2022 book, *Newsroom Confidential*. "An errant tweet can wreck your career. Delete all you want, but if someone captured a screenshot, your momentary bad judgment will live forever. Despite what you may think, exactly no one is eagerly awaiting your words of wisdom on any platform."[18]

When given the opportunity to ask questions during the interview process, prospective employees should inquire about "workplace culture" in general and "free-speech rights" in particular. Employees should ask the human resources representatives if there is a specific policy regarding the use of office computers for personal communication (assuming it is done during lunch breaks or after hours) and whether such communication is monitored. An employee should also ask how the free-speech policies, if they exist, square with policies regarding discrimination and harassment (although HR representatives would never admit it, the latter policies may be invoked to squelch criticisms of the company that management doesn't like). And employees shouldn't just take the HR department's word for it; they should talk to current and former employees about it and check the company's profile on Glassdoor or other websites.

For employees who are unionized, those organizations should insist on clear policies regarding workplace expression as part of collective bargaining agreements.

What can the courts and regulatory bodies do? One suggestion is to take the same first step that courts do in other free-speech cases: apply the long-standing standard that distinguishes between speech and conduct, with the former being protected (in most cases) and the latter not protected. That category of conduct would include threats, whether real or perceived. The courts should also respect the principles of good-faith whistleblowing and differentiate between matters of public concern and personal grievances.

Another suggestion is related to judicial restraint; lower courts could follow the U.S. Supreme Court's tradition of deferring to military leaders in free-speech cases and apply that same policy to civilian cases, allowing human resources departments to intervene and decide cases to avoid costly litigation.

One suggestion unlikely to gain any traction is the idea of removing the distinction between public and private employees in terms of free-speech protection. Legal scholar Randy Kozel suggests that courts revert to the Holmesian Model—named for Supreme Court Justice Oliver Wendell Holmes and his skepticism about the distinction—which would no longer recognize separate levels of protection.

In a 2005 article in *Northwestern University Law Review*, Kozel suggested that both types of employees, as a condition of employment, forfeit their free-speech rights. Kozel defined the model as one in which

> public employers may restrict employees' speech without implicating, let alone offending, the employees' First Amendment free speech rights . . . Under the model, employees retain their free speech and free association rights, as do all citizens, but they also must accept, as a result of their employment with the government, that the exercise of these rights may cause their employers to discipline or fire them.[19]

In short, Kozel implied, public employees must decide which value is more important: the right to free speech or the right to keep their jobs.

In the conclusion to his article, Kozel wrote that a return to the Holmesian model would produce more effective government workplaces by limiting disruption while improving morale and productivity, thus saving money for the taxpayers.[20] But he also claimed that the Holmesian model actually discourages employers from limiting speech because agencies with a reputation for doing so will "find it hard to attract and retain good employees and will have to compensate them in other ways, such as providing pay premiums."[21]

The Moving Target of Social Media

"As people conduct more business and socialize online, Facebook and Twitter have become twenty-first century watercoolers, where workers flock to grouse, joke, and vent," said labor lawyer John Polson, a partner in the Irvine, California, firm of Fisher Phillips, in a 2018 interview with a human resources newsletter. "These are conversations that previously would have happened in someone's home or in a bar or on a soccer field and would have gone under the radar. But in today's hyperconnected culture, an online comment or photo can spread like wildfire from one coworker to another and then to multitudes of strangers."[22]

Samuel Greengard, author of *The Internet of Things,* believes much of future workplace free-speech policy will be influenced by the influx of young people in the workforce. "One thing to keep an eye on is how young people think and act in regard to posts on social media," Greengard said in a 2024 interview.

> It's the proverbial canary in the coal mine. For example, not long ago, tattoos were verboten in the workplace. Now they are acceptable. When things hit a

> critical mass the powers-that-be have to adapt and adjust. The law has not kept up with technology—and the problem is getting worse. Moreover, lawmakers in Congress, state houses and at a local level are mostly ill-equipped to deal with these problems.[23]

In a 2018 article in a professional newsletter, human resources professional June D. Bell wrote that employers must take a more realistic approach when dealing with younger employees. "Businesses can bar the use of social media at work, but they can't stop employees from discussing work-related issues, whether they're venting in the break room or posting on social media," she wrote. But she adds that rule applies to employees discussing workplace issues among themselves; gripes broadcast to a wider audience are still subject to punishment.[24]

Her vague reference to privacy settings on Facebook and other social media platforms serves as a reminder to all unhappy employees: privacy settings aren't perfect, so when in doubt, limit your workplace gripes to in-person conversations or private emails.[25]

Notes

1 "Colorado Teacher Faces Backlash Over Post About Donald Trump Assassination Attempt," *The Denver Gazette*, July 16, 2024.
2 Ibid.
3 Ibid.
4 Mia Jankowicz, "A Democratic Staffer Resigned After Posting 'Don't Miss Next Time' Following the Attempt on Trump's Life," *Business Insider*, July 15, 2024.
5 Ibid.
6 Ibid.
7 *Rankin v. McPherson,* 483 U.S. 378 (1987).
8 Ibid.
9 Ibid.
10 Bill Lueders, "Speech and Consequences," *The Progressive*, October/November 2022, pp. 20–1.
11 Bruce Barry, *Speechless: The Erosion of Free Expression in the American Workplace* (San Francisco: Berrett-Koehler Publishers, 2007), p. 96.
12 Cynthia Estlund, "Free Speech and Due Process in the Workplace," *Indiana Law Review* 71, no. 1 (1995): pp. 102–51.

13 Lawrence Rosenthal, "Permissible Content Discrimination Under the First Amendment: The Strange Case of the Public Employee," *Hastings Constitutional Law Quarterly* 25, no. 4 (Summer 1998): pp. 528–84.

14 Barry, interview with the author, January 3, 2024.

15 Dana Wilkie, "When Displaying the American Flag at Work Offends Some Employees," *SHRM News,* September 20, 2019.

16 Erwin Chemerinsky and Howard Gillman, *Free Speech on Campus* (New Haven, CT: Yale University Press, 2017), p. 77.

17 Ibid.

18 Margaret Sullivan, *Newsroom Confidential: Lessons (and Worries) From an Ink-Stained Life* (New York: St. Martin's Press, 2022), pp. 248–9.

19 Randy J. Kozel, "Reconceptualizing Public Employee Speech," *Northwestern University Law Review* 99, no. 3 (Spring 2005): pp. 1007–51.

20 Ibid.

21 Ibid.

22 June D. Bell, "Firing for Online Behavior," *SHRM News*, August 24, 2018.

23 Samuel Greengard, interview with the author, January 4, 2024.

24 Bell, "Firing for Online Behavior."

25 Ibid.

References

Achenbach, James. “Dave Hill Was Unrestrained.” *Golfweek*, October 4, 2011.

Achille, Roger S. “First Amendment Protects Against Viewpoint Discrimination.” *SHRM News,* October 13, 2021.

Adams, Hall, Suzanne M. Scheuing, and Stacey A. Feely. “E-Mail Monitoring in the Workplace: The Good, the Bad, and the Ugly.” *Defense Counsel Journal* 67, no. 1 (January 2000): pp. 32–46.

Adams, Mike. *Feminists Say the Darndest Things: A Politically Incorrect Professor Confronts ‘Womyn’ on Campus.* New York: Sentinel Publishing, 2007.

Adams, Mike. *Letters to a Young Progressive: How to Avoid Wasting Your Life Protesting Things You Don’t Understand.* Washington, DC: Regnery, 2013.

Adams, Mike. *Welcome to the Ivory Tower of Babel.* Augusta, GA: Harbor House, 2004.

Aleem, Zeeshan. “Why Carnegie Mellon’s Condemnation of Professor’s Viral Tweet is Troubling.” *MSNBC.com*, September 10, 2022.

American Bar Association. *Guide to Workplace Law.* New York: Random House, 1997.

Andrews, Lori. *I Know Who You Are and I Saw What You Did: Social Networks and the Death of Privacy.* New York: Free Press, 2011.

Andrias, Kate E. “A Robust Public Debate: Realizing Free Speech in Workplace Representation Elections.” *Yale Law Journal* 112 (2003): pp. 24–9.

Archie, Ayana. “Judge Dismisses an Ex-Home Depot Employee’s Case About Not Wearing BLM on Uniforms.” *National Public Radio*, June 13, 2022.

Archie, Ayana. “NBA Coach Gregg Popovich Criticizes Lawmakers Over Gun Control.” *National Public Radio*, April 10, 2023.

Archille, Roger. “First Amendment Does Not Protect Employee’s Criticism of Supervisor.” *SHRM News,* January 26, 2022.

“Arizona County Elections Leader Promoted Voter Fraud Conspiracies Resigns.” *Associated Press Report*, September 19, 2023.

“Arkansas School Board Member Officially Resigns Over Anti-Gay Post.” *CNN.com*, November 1, 2010.

Armour, Nancy. “ESPN Personality Uses Social Media Posts as Weapon.” *USA Today,* May 30, 2023, p. 8-C.

Armour, Nancy. “Irsay’s Unhinged Rant is Wrong, Big Problem for NFL.” *USA Today,* November 24, 2023, p. 6-C.

Armour, Nancy. “With Lots of Love and Laughter, Rapinoe Says Goodbye.” *USA Today,* September 26, 2023, p. 1-C.

Armour, Nancy. “World Cup Players Can Wear Rainbow Armband.” *USA Today,* July 3, 2023, p. 4-C.
Armour, Stephanie. “Warning: Your Clever Little Blog Could Get You Fired.” *USA Today,* June 14, 2005.
Assuncao, Muri. “Montana Professor Resigns Amid Investigation into Alleged ‘Homophobic and Misogynistic’ Views.” *New York Daily News,* October 23, 2021.
Auchard, Eric. “Famed Microsoft Blogger Leaves for Startup.” *Reuters News Service,* June 11, 2006.
Axson, Scooby. “Jays Pitcher Apologizes for Sharing Social Video.” *USA Today,* May 31, 2023, p. 3-C.
Axson, Scooby. “Kittle Fined for T-shirt with Taunt.” *USA Today,* October 16, 2023, p. 3-C.
Bahney, Anna. “Interns? Bloggers Need Not Apply.” *The New York Times,* May 25, 2006, p. 1-A.
Baker, Ross K. “If Academic Tenure is in Trouble at Colleges, so is Academic Freedom.” *Pensacola News Journal,* October 25, 2021, p. 8-B.
Balasubramani, Venkat. “Court Upholds Doocing for Snarky Facebook Post.” *Technology and Marketing Law Blog,* September 21, 2013.
Balasubramani, Venkat. “Demoting Police Officer for Posting Confederate Flag to Facebook Isn’t First Amendment Violation.” *Technology and Marketing Law Blog,* February 11, 2014.
Balasubramani, Venkat. “Do Employers Really Tread a Minefield by Firing Employees for Facebook Gaffes?” *Technology and Marketing Law Blog,* January 28, 2011.
Balasubramani, Venkat. “Employee Terminated for Ill-Advised Facebook Post Gets Unemployment Benefits.” *Technology and Marketing Law Blog,* January 6, 2015.
Balasubramani, Venkat. “Facebook Complaints About Boss’s ‘Creepy Hands’ Can’t Salvage Retaliation/Harassment Complaints.” *Technology and Marketing Law Blog,* December 11, 2013.
Balasubramani, Venkat. “NLRB Invalidates Employer’s Blogging Policy and Reverses Firing Based on Facebook Posts.” *Technology and Marketing Law Blog,* September 27, 2014.
Balasubramani, Venkat. “Nurse Properly Fired and Denied Unemployment Due to Facebook Rant.” *Technology and Marketing Law Blog,* January 13, 2014.
Balasubramani, Venkat. “Police Officer’s Facebook Post Criticizing Chief’s Budget Decision Justified Termination.” *Technology and Marketing Law Blog,* January 13, 2015.
Balasubramani, Venkat. “Police Officer’s Facebook Venting Isn’t Protected by the First Amendment.” *Technology and Marketing Law Blog,* October 21, 2013.
Balasubramani, Venkat. “Texas Court of Appeals Rejects Privacy Claims Based on Facebook Firing.” *Technology and Marketing Law Blog,* October 10, 2012.
Barry, Bruce. “The Cringing and the Craven: Freedom of Expression In, Around, and Beyond the Workplace.” *Business Ethics Quarterly* 17, no. 2 (2007): pp. 263–96.

Barry, Bruce. Interview with the author, January 3, 2024.

Barry, Bruce. *Speechless: The Erosion of Free Expression in the American Workplace*. San Francisco: Berrett-Koehler Publishers, 2007.

Bartlett, Tom. "I Didn't Want to Be Canceled." *The Chronicle of Higher Education,* June 11, 2022, p. 6.

Beall, Thomas R. "Morality, Duty, and Military Ethics: The Case of Lieutenant Colonel Scheller." *U.S. Naval Institute News,* December 2021.

Beaumont, Elizabeth. "Rights of Military Personnel." Free Speech Center at Middle Tennessee State University, date unknown.

Bell, Brian C. "Homophobic Instagram Post Costs Golfer Scott Piercy Multiple Major Sponsors." *Out Sports,* March 16, 2020.

Bell, June D. "Firing for Online Behavior." *SHRM News,* August 24, 2018.

Belson, Ken and Katherine Rosman. "NFL Reporter Files Racial Discrimination Claim Against League After Dismissal." *The New York Times,* September 12, 2023.

Berntsen, Gary. *Jawbreaker.* New York: Crown Publishing, 2005.

Berrett, Dan. "ESU Professor Suspended for Comments Made on Facebook Page." *The Pocono Record,* February 26, 2010.

Bishop, Ted. *Unfriended: The Power Brokers, Political Correctness, and Hypocrisy in Golf.* Stratford, CT: Classics of Golf Publishing, 2016.

Bishop, Todd. "Microsoft Fires Employee Over Weblog." *The Seattle Post-Intelligencer,* October 30, 2003.

Black, Tiffany. "How to Handle Employee Blogging." *Inc,* April 6, 2010.

Bobbitt, Randy. *Exploring Communication Ethics.* New York: Taylor & Francis, 2020.

Bobbitt, Randy. *Exploring Communication Law.* New York: Taylor & Francis, 2017.

Bobbitt, Randy. *The View From Under the Bus: A Case Study in Media Influence, Public Opinion, and Moral Outrage.* Pensacola, FL: Windchase Bay Publishing, 2020.

Boynton, Robert. "Attack of the Career-Killing Blogs." *Slate,* November 16, 2005.

Brennan, Christine. "Two Prominent Golfers Speak Up in Favor of Voting Rights." *USA Today,* April 7, 2022, p. 5-C.

Brennan, Christine. "USFS Employee Apologies for Skater Support." *USA Today,* June 29, 2023, p. 4-C.

Brown, Janelle. "Bitch, Bitch, Bitch." *Salon,* February 1, 2001.

Buscaglia, Joe and Tim Graham. "Bills' McDermott Says He Regrets 9/11 Comments Made at Team Meeting in 2019." *The Athletic,* December 7, 2023.

Cali, Mike. "Jonathan Isaac Explains Why He Stood During National Anthem." *Orlando PinstripePost.com*, July 31, 2020.

Caminiti, Susan. "Former Levi Strauss Executive Jennifer Sey on Decision to Leave Company Over Covid 'Free Speech' Controversy." *CNBC Workforce Wire*, February 17, 2022.

Carless, Will. "Extremism in Military Still Goes Unchecked." *USA Today,* July 28, 2023, p. 1-A.

Carless, Will. "Pentagon Extremism Report is Finally Out." *USA Today,* December 28, 2023, p. 2-A.

Chappell, Bill. "NBA Coach Steve Kerr Calls Out 50 Senators on a Bipartisan Gun Background Check Law." *National Public Radio*, May 25, 2022.

Chemerinsky, Erwin and Howard Gillman. *Free Speech on Campus.* New Haven, CT: Yale University Press, 2017.

Chiaramonte, Perry. "Florida Professor Who Denied Sandy Hook Shooting Now Claims Boston Bombings a Drill." *Fox News.com*, April 24, 2013.

Clay, Nolan. "Investigation Says Oklahoma Judge Checked Facebook, Texted About Prosecutor's Genitals During Murder Trial." *USA Today,* October 12, 2023.

Clayworth, Jason. "Iowa Employee Fired for 'Offensive' Facebook Posts." *Des Moines Register,* July 27, 2016.

Cohen, Henry. *Freedom of Speech and Press: Exceptions to the First Amendment.* New York: Nova Science Publishers, Inc., 2008.

Collins, Terry. "TikTok Got Me Fired: The Pitfalls of Talking Work on Social Media." *USA Today,* July 19, 2022, p. 4-B.

"Colorado Teacher Faces Backlash Over Post About Donald Trump Assassination." *The Denver Gazette,* July 16, 2024.

"Conduct Unbecoming." *Law & Order,* Season 3, Episode 17. Original air date March 10, 1993.

Conneller, Philip. "Maine Chief Gambling Regulator Suspended for Offensive Treats." *Casino.org*, May 24, 2023.

Cooke, Rachel. "Sexual Paranoia on Campus, and the Professor at the Eye of the Storm." *The Guardian,* April 2, 2017.

Cooney, Samantha. "West Virginia Official Who Called Michelle Obama an 'Ape in Heels' Loses Her Job." *Time,* December 28, 2016.

Corkery, Michael. "How a Dollar General Employee Went Viral on TikTok." *The New York Times,* April 18, 2022.

Cose, Ellis. *The Short Life and Curious Death of Free Speech in America*. New York: Amistad Publishing, 2020.

Crupi, Anthony. "Can Anything Dethrone the NFL?" *Advertising Age,* September 11, 2017, pp. 201–21.

Dalbey, Beth. "Racist Tweet About Michelle Obama Gets Mortgage Lender Fired." *The Patch,* July 28, 2016.

Dalton, Andrew. "Ill-Considered Posts Lead to Lost Jobs." *Associated Press Report*, June 7, 2020.

D'Amato, Peter. "Nonprofit Worker Provokes Fury with Cemetery Photo." *London Daily Mail,* February 22, 2015.

"Dawkins Giving ex-Eagles Worker Tickets." *ESPN.com*, April 4, 2009.

Dean, Safid, "Ryan Clark Apologizes to Tagovailoa After 'Bad Joke.'" *USA Today,* August 25, 2023, p. 2-C.

Dees, Morris and Steve Fiffer. *A Season for Justice: The Life and Times of Civil Rights Lawyer Morris Dees.* New York: Charles Scribner's Sons, 1991.

DeGeorge, Richard T. *Business Ethics.* New York: MacMillan, 1990.

Deletter, Emily. "Former Missouri Teacher Who Created OnlyFans Account Says She Has Made Nearly $1 Million." *USA Today,* November 7, 2023.

DelPo, Amy and Lisa Guerin. *Dealing with Problem Employees: How to Manage Performance and Personality Issues in the Workplace.* Berkeley, CA: NOLO Press, 2017.

Des Jardins, Joseph R. and John T. McCall. "A Defense of Employee Rights." *Journal of Business Ethics* 4, no. 5 (October 1985): pp. 367–76.

Detert, James R. and Ethan Burris. "Can Your Employees Really Speak Freely?" *Harvard Business Review,* January-February 2016, pp. 80–7.

Deto, Ryan. "Wendy Bell is Off the Pittsburgh Airwaves Again." *Pittsburgh City Paper,* May 11, 2021.

Diaz, Laura S. and Cassie Dickman. "I Was Kicked Out: Ousted California Principal Escorted Off Campus After Graduation." *USA Today,* May 29, 2021.

"Did the Internet Kill Privacy?" *CBS Sunday Morning,* February 13, 2011.

Dienes, C. Thomas. "When the First Amendment is Not Preferred: The Military and Other 'Special Contexts.'" *University of Cincinnati Law Review* 56 (1988): pp. 779–842.

Dougherty, Paul. "Marge Schott Did as She Pleased While Owning the Cincinnati Reds." *The Cincinnati Enquirer,* June 30, 2022.

Doyel, Gregg. "By Paying Rodgers, McAfee Anti-Vax Co-Hort." *USA Today,* October 25, 2013, p. 2-C.

Dubow, Josh. "49ers TE George Kittle Fined More Than $13,000 for Profane T-shirt About the Cowboys." *Associated Press Report*, October 14, 2023.

Dwyer, Jim. "The Officer Who Posted Too Much on MySpace." *The New York Times,* March 10, 2009.

Einbinder, Nicole. "Shell Workers in Pennsylvania Were Told to Either Attend Trump Event or Not Get Paid." *Business Insider,* August 17, 2019.

Emerson, Thomas I. *The System of Freedom of Expression.* New York: Random House, 1970.

"Employees Rate Their Employers, CEOs on Glassdoor." *Associated Press Report*, March 29, 2013.

"Enough is Enough: Calls for Mike Adams' Dismissal Grow Louder." *Encore,* June 16, 2020.

"ESPN's Stephen A. Smith Suggests Racism in Chip Kelly's Roster Moves." *Pro Football Talk*, March 9, 2015.

Estes, Adam Clark. "Romney Told Bosses to Tell Their Employees How to Vote." *The Atlantic,* October 17, 2012.

Estlund, Cynthia L. "Free Speech and Due Process in the Workplace." *Indiana Law Journal* 71, no. 1 (Winter 1995): pp. 101–51.

Ewing, David W. "Employee Rights: Taking the Gag Off." *Civil Liberties Review,* Fall 1974, p. 56.
Ewing, David W. *Freedom Inside the Organization: Bringing Civil Liberties to the Workplace*. New York: E.P. Dutton, 1977.
"Ex-Cochise County Official Who Claimed Election Deniers Made Work 'Toxic' Gets $130,000." *Associated Press Report*, May 31, 2023.
Fahmy, Dalia. "More Workers Getting Fired Over Social Media Rants." *ABC News*, March 2, 2010.
Farberov, Snejana. "Professor Who Wished Queen 'Excruciating Death' Explains Defiant Stance on Podcast." *New York Post,* September 15, 2022.
"Feds Cracking Down on Pornography." *Knight-Ridder Report*, April 5, 2004.
Fields, Gary. "Military Academies Focus on Loyalty to the Constitution." *Associated Press Report*, January 21, 2024.
"The Fight for Equal Pay." *The Week,* August 11, 2023, p. 11.
Finan, Christopher M. *From the Palmer Raids to the Patriot Act: A History of the Fight for Free Speech in America.* Boston: Beacon Press, 2007.
Finder, Alan. "For Some, Online Persona Undermines a Resume." *The New York Times,* June 11, 2006, p. 1-A.
Fingerhut, Hannah, Heather Hollingsworth, and Summer Ballentine. "Meteorologists Under Threat for Climate Change Coverage." *Associated Press Report*, July 8, 2023.
Fink, Keith. *Free Speech in the Workplace*. San Diego: Cognella Press, 2013.
"Fired U.S. Employee Wins Plea." *United Press International Report*, May 19, 1967.
"The First Amendment and Free Speech on Campus." *National Association of College and University Attorneys Webinar*, June 3, 2004.
Fish, Stanley. "Conspiracy Theories 101." *The New York Times,* July 23, 2006.
Fitzgerald, Ernest. *The High Priests of Waste.* New York: Norton Press, 1972.
Flaherty, Colleen. "Ole Miss Settles with Professor." *Inside Higher Education,* July 29, 2021.
Flaherty, Colleen. "Twitter, Faculty Hangman." *Inside Higher Education,* April 12, 2017.
Flier, Jeffrey. "An Attack on Free Speech at Harvard." *The Atlantic*, June 21, 2024.
Forman, Laura. "Facebook's Politics Aren't Aging Well." *The Wall Street Journal,* June 30, 2020, p. 11-B.
Fox, Adrienne. "Politics in the Office." *SHRM News,* October 1, 2008.
"Free Speech and Profanity: A Company Enforcing Civility in the Workplace Isn't Government Action." *The Wall Street Journal,* December 1, 2019, p. 14-A.
"Free Speech and Social Media Issues Affecting Military Members." *Air Force JAG Publication*, date unknown.
"Free Speech or Harassment? Controversial Professor Tests the Limits." *NBC News*, November 30, 2016.
Freeman, Mike. "Aaron Rodgers and Grudges Go Together." *USA Today,* January 4, 2024, p. 5-C.

Freeman, Mike. "Another Tragic Mass Shooting: NBA Coach Says Enough." *USA Today,* October 30, 2023, p. 7-C.
Freeman, Mike. "Haslem Rips DeSantis and Says What Many Think." *USA Today,* June 13, 2013, p. 2-C.
Freeman, Mike. "Kimmel Humiliates Jets QB Rodgers in New Monologue." *USA Today,* January 10, 2024, p. 4-C.
Freeman, Mike. "Rodgers Makes a Fool of Himself by Attacking Kelce." *USA Today,* October 11, 2023, p. 3-C.
French, David. "The Problem with Amy Wax's Immigration Argument." *National Review,* July 22, 2019.
Friedersdorf, Conor. "The New Intolerance of Student Activism." *The Atlantic,* November 9, 2015.
Frye, Lisa. "Reviewing Employee E-Mails: When You Should, When You Shouldn't." *SHRM News,* May 15, 2017.
Gardner, Steve. "Jemele Hill Reveals Why She Had an Abortion at 26." *USA Today,* June 30, 2022, p. 5-C.
Gebreyes, Rahel. "Yale Student Explains Why Students Were Offended by Halloween Costumes Email." *The Huffington Post,* November 12, 2015.
George, Robert T. "Free Speech Prevails at Princeton." *First Things*, July 28, 2020.
German, Michael. "Hidden in Plain Sight: Racism, White Supremacy, and Far-Right Militancy in Law Enforcement." Brennan Center for Justice, August 27, 2020.
Ghachem, Malick W. "A Better Way to Protect Free Speech." *The Chronicle of Higher Education,* February 3, 2023, pp. 30–1.
Glasspiegel, Ryan. "Bitter Phil Mickelson-Alan Shipnuck Feud Reignites." *New York Post*, November 27, 2023.
Glenn, David. "The War on Campus." *The Nation,* December 3, 2001.
Gluckman, Nell. "A Tarleton State University Instructor Complained About Parking Fees. He Said it Cost Him His Job." *The Chronicle of Higher Education*, June 25, 2024.
Glum, Julia. "Who is Kenneth Storey? Professor Fired After Tweeting That Hurricane Harvey was Karma for Texas Republicans." *Newsweek*, August 29, 2017.
Gohring, Nancy. "Over 50% of Companies Have Fired Workers for E-Mail, Net Abuse." *IDG News Service*, February 28, 2008.
Goldberg, Jeffrey. "James Mattis Denounces Trump, Describes Him as a Threat to Democracy." *The Atlantic,* June 3, 2020.
Goldman, Alvin L. *Labor Law and Industrial Relations in the United States of America.* Washington, DC: The Bureau of National Affairs, Inc., 1983.
Goldman, Eric. "Facebook Rant Against 'Arial' Font Helps Reverse Sex Offender Determination." *Technology and Marketing Law Blog*, November 26, 2013.
Goldman, Eric. "More Proof That Facebook Isn't the Place to Bitch About Your Job." *Technology and Marketing Law Blog*, June 21, 2014.

Goldstein, Richard. "Jim Brown: Football Great and Civil Rights Champion, Dies at 87." *The New York Times,* May 19, 2023.

Goonen, Norma R. and Rachel S. Blechman. *Higher Education Administration: A Guide to Legal, Ethical, and Practical Issues.* Westport, CT: Greenwood Press, 1999.

Gould, William B. IV. *A Primer on American Labor Law.* Cambridge, MA: MIT Press, 1986.

Gouras, Matt. "City Drops Request for Internet Passwords." *Associated Press Report,* June 19, 2009.

Graves, Patricia. "Ask an Expert: Online Behavior." *SHRM News,* May 27, 2021.

Greengard, Samuel. Interview with the author, January 4, 2024.

Greengard, Samuel. "The Virtual Pen is Not Mightier Than the Ax." *Workplace Management,* March 1, 2005, pp. 74–6.

Gregory, Charles O. and Harold A. Katz. *Labor and the Law.* New York: W.W. Norton & Company, 1979.

Gregory, Drew. "Stephen A. Smith is Never Satisfied." *GQ,* December 11, 2019.

Gregory, Sean. "Here's How Harvey Gantt Feels, 30 Years Later, About Michael Jordan Refusing to Back Him." *Time,* May 4, 2020.

Gremore, Graham. "The Price of Hate: Pro Golfer Scott Piercy's Homophobia Cost Him $2 Million and Heavy Dose of Public Humiliation." *Queerty,* March 17, 2020.

Gremore, Graham. "Pro Golfer Scott Piercy Bleeding Sponsors After Taking Homophobic Swing at Pete Buttigieg." *Queerty,* March 6, 2020.

Gross, Doug. "Facebook Speaks Out Against Employers Asking for Passwords." *CNN News,* March 23, 2012.

Guyan, Jessica. "Microaggressions Take a Major Toll." *USA Today,* October 12, 2023, p. 1-B.

Hall, Brian. "Court Upholds Jury Verdict in Pietrylo v. Hillstone Restaurant Group." *Employer Law Report,* October 19, 2009.

Hanna, Thomas M. *The Employer's Legal Advisor.* New York: American Management Association, 2007.

Hansen, Evan. "Google Blogger: I Was Fired." *New York Times,* February 11, 2005.

Harig, Bob. "Scott Piercy Loses Golf Endorsements Over Homophobic Post." *ESPN,* March 5, 2020.

Hentoff, Nat. *Free Speech for Me—But Not for Thee.* New York: HarperCollins, 1992.

Herbert, Geoff. "Texas Roadhouse Waitress Fired After Complaining About Bad Tips on Facebook." *Syracuse.com,* July 3, 2014.

Herrington, Ryan. "Not Fit For Print." *Golf World,* February 2007, p. 17.

Heussner, Ki Mae and Dalia Fahmy. "Teacher Loses Job After Commenting About Students, Parents on Facebook." *ABC News,* August 19, 2010.

Hill, Kashmir. "East Stroudsburg University Professor Reinstated After Facebook Post About Hit Man." *Forbes Online,* March 17, 2011.

Hill, Stan. "The Multilayered Minefield of Workplace E-Mail Monitoring." *Employment Relations Today* 42, no. 1 (Spring 2015): pp. 55–62.
"The Hill's Sex Diarist Reveals All." *The Washington Post,* May 24, 2004.
Hineman, Brinley. "Can Employers Police Their Worker's Personal Lives?" *USA Today,* April 16, 2021, p. 2-B.
Hineman, Brinley. "Can You Be Fired Over Your Sex Life? Dave Ramsey Thinks So." *The Nashville Tennessean,* March 28, 2021.
Holland, Kelley. "How Office Politics and Real Politics Can Mix." *The New York Times,* October 8, 2006.
Holloway, Kali. "White Nationalist Hate is Infiltrating Our Police." *The Nation,* November 15, 2022.
"Home Depot Employee Claims He Was Fired Over 'One Nation Under God' Pin." *New York Daily News,* October 28, 2009.
"Hope and Defiance: The Black Power Salute That Rocked the 1968 Olympics." *Life,* October 14, 2013.
Horowitz, Paul. *First Amendment Institutions.* Cambridge, MA: Harvard University Press, 2013.
Huber, Lindsay. "Court Requires Glassdoor to Reveal Identities of Anonymous Users." *The American Genius,* November 15, 2017.
Hudson, David L. "Federal Appeals Court Rules Against Former Police Officer Fired for Facebook Post." *First Amendment News*, December 26, 2022.
Hutchinson, Piper. "Tenure LSU Shreveport Professor Fired for 'Disruptive Behavior.'" *Louisiana Illuminator*, June 25, 2024.
"Illinois Salesman Fired for Packers Tie Gets New Job." *Rockford Register Star,* January 25, 2011.
Imwinklerled, Daniel J. and Donald N. Zillman. "An Evolution in the First Amendment: Overbreadth Analysis and Free Speech Within the Military Community." *Texas Law Review* 42 (1975): pp. 52–70.
"Indiana Teacher with 'Kill List' of Students, Staff Sentenced to 21⁄2 Years on Probation." *Associated Press Report*, August 7, 2023.
Isaac, Jonathan. *Why I Stand.* Nashville, TN: Daily Wire Books, 2022.
Ismay, John. "The Final Fight for Black Sailors Known as the 'Philadelphia 15.'" *The New York Times,* June 16, 2023.
Jacoby, Susan. *The Age of American Unreason*. New York: Pantheon Books, 2008.
Jacques, Ingrid. "Coach Feels 'Burned' for Speaking Out." *USA Today,* August 30, 2023, p. 7-A.
Jaffe, Sarah. "Labor Rising." *The Progressive,* October/November 2022, p. 26.
Jankowicz, Mia. "A Democratic Staffer Resigned After Posting 'Don't Miss Next Time' Following the Attempt on Trump's Life." *Business Insider,* July 15, 2024.
Jaschik, Scott. "Twitter Blowback: Lost Jobs and Lost Money." *Inside Higher Education,* August 1, 2017.

Jaschik, Scott. "University Pays to Get Rid of Professor." *Inside Higher Education,* July 6, 2020.

Johnson, Danielle. "Watch What You Say—Don't Violate the UCMJ." *305th Air Mobility Wing Newsletter*, May 4, 2007.

Johnson, Gene. "Doctor Loses Job After Criticizing Hospital's Virus Response." *Associated Press Report*, March 28, 2020.

Jolly, Jennifer. "Grads, Clean Up That Social Media." *USA Today,* June 6, 2022, p. 3-B.

Jones, Charisse. "Can Your Supervisor Force You to Attend Speech by Politician?" *USA Today,* August 23, 2019, p. 2-B.

Jourdan, Cameron. "Senator Introduces Bill to Strip PGA Tour's Tax-Exempt Status." *Golfweek,* July 28, 2023.

Joyce, Amy. "Free Expression Can Be Costly When Bloggers Bad-Mouth Jobs." *The Washington Post,* February 11, 2005, p. 1-A.

"Judge: Iowa Analyst Fired Over Racist Posts Must Pay Back Benefits." *Times-Republican* (Marshalltown, IA), October 21, 2016.

Kaplan, Joseph V. *Federal Employees Legal Survival Guide.* Cincinnati, OH: National Employee Rights Institute, 1999.

Kaplin, William A. and Barbara A. Lee. *The Law of Higher Education.* San Francisco: John Wiley & Sons, 2007.

Kelderman, Eric. "The Silent Treatment: Why College Presidents Find It Hard to Speak Up." *The Chronicle of Higher Education,* August 5, 2022, pp. 11–16.

Kelleher, Susan Rowan. "Southwest Apologizes for Pilot's Trumpy 'Let's Go Brandon' Sign-Off." *Forbes,* October 31, 2021.

Kersch, Ken I. "How Conduct Became Speech Became Conduct: A Political Development Case Study in Labor Law and Freedom of Speech." *Journal of Constitutional Law* 8, no. 2 (2006): pp. 1–44.

Kersey, Lori. "WV Delegate Calls for Clinton to be Executed." *Charleston Gazette-Mail,* July 16, 2016.

Kester, John G. "Soldiers Who Insult the President: An Uneasy Look at Article 88 of the Uniform Code of Military Justice." *Harvard Law Review* 81 (June 1968): pp. 1697–769.

Kipnis, Laura. "My Title IX Inquisition." *The Chronicle of Higher Education,* May 29, 2015.

Kluger, Mark F. Interview with the author, January 2, 2024.

Kohler, Jeremy and Ryan Krull. "A Detective Sabotaged His Own Cases Because He Didn't Like the Prosecutor." *ProPublica,* October 10, 2023.

Kors, Alan Charles and Harvey A. Silverglate. *The Shadow University: The Betrayal of Liberty on America's Campuses.* New York: HarperCollins, 1998.

Kozel, Randy J. "Reconceptualizing Public Employee Speech." *Northwestern University Law Review* 99, no. 3 (Spring 2005): pp. 1007–51.

Krantz, Laura. "Controversy Trails New Professor to BU." *The Boston Globe,* June 27, 2015.

Krishnamurthy, Pavin S. and Javier Perez. "Contemptuous Speech: Rethinking the Balance Between Good Order and Discipline and the Free Speech Rights of Retired Military Officers." *Harvard National Security Journal* 12 (2021): pp. 288–328.

Krouse, Sarah. "The New Ways Your Boss is Spying on You." *The Wall Street Journal,* July 20–21, 2019, p. 1-B.

Krupnick, Matt. "Tenure Limits Drive Away Professors." *USA Today,* January 9, 2024, p. 1-A.

Lagatta, Eric. "An Iowa Meteorologist's Climate Change Coverage Led to a Death Threat." *USA Today,* June 22, 2023.

Lake, Peter F. "How to Shield Faculty Members from Outside Attacks." *The Chronicle of Higher Education,* July 7, 2022, pp. 42–3.

Lau, Shari. "Shari's Solutions: Can We Prohibit Political Discussions at Work in This Heated Election Season?" *SHRM News,* June 1, 2016.

Lavietes. "Tony Dungy's anti-LGBTQ History Gets Renewed Attention After Controversial Tweet." *NBC News*, January 25, 2023.

"The Law: Dissent Through the Courts." *Time,* April 27, 1970.

"Law Professor Fired, Complained About Black Students' Grades." *USA Today,* March 13, 2021.

Leibovich, Mark. *Big Game: The NFL in Dangerous Times.* New York: Penguin Press, 2018.

Lenhart, Amanda and Susannah Fox. "Bloggers: A Portrait of the Internet's New Storytellers." *Pew Internet and American Life Project*, July 19, 2006.

Leon, Harmon. "A Look at Morgan Rapinoe and Other Athletes Who Said They Won't Go to the White House." *The Observer,* June 27, 2019.

Levinson, Michael. "Georgetown Law Fires Professor for 'Abhorrent' Remarks About Black Students." *The New York Times,* March 11, 2021.

Lewis, Helen. "The Magic Kingdom of Ron DeSantis." *The Atlantic,* May 2023, pp. 41–50.

Lichtblau, Eric. "V.A. Punished Critics on Staff, Doctors Assert." *The New York Times,* June 15, 2014.

Lippke, Richard. "Speech, Conscience, and Work." *Social Theory and Practice* 18, no. 3 (Fall 1992): pp. 237–58.

Lowry, Rich. "The Life of Brandon." *USA Today,* November 8, 2021, p. 8-C.

Lu, Adrienne. "The Apolitical University." *The Chronicle of Higher Education,* January 6, 2023, pp. 16–21.

Lueders, Bill. "Speech and Consequences." *The Progressive,* October/November 2022, pp. 20–1.

Lukianoff, Greg. *Unlearning Liberty: Campus Censorship and the End of American Debate.* New York: Encounter Books, 2014.

Luna, Itzel. "Survey: Hate, Harassment Surges." *USA Today,* June 30, 2023, p. 6-A.

Lynch, Eamon. "Justin Thomas Learned Something This Week. Every Else? Not So Much." *Twitter Post*, January 17, 2021.

Madden, Kaitlin. "12 Ways to Get Fired for Facebook." *CareerBuilder.com*, date unknown.

"Maine's Top Gambling Regulator on Paid Leave Following Tweets." *Associated Press Report*, May 23, 2023.

Malinowski, Jenna. "ESPN's McAfee Apologizes, Defends His Post." *USA Today,* August 2, 2023, p. 7-C.

Maltby, Lewis. *Can They Do That? Retaking Our Fundamental Rights in the Workplace.* New York: Penguin Group, 2009.

Mandell, Nina. "Stephen A. Smith Won't be on ESPN for a Week After Controversial Comments." *USA Today,* July 29, 2014.

Marchetti, Victor. *The CIA and the Cult of Intelligence.* New York: Alfred A. Knopf, 1974.

Marcotte, Amanda. *Troll Nation*. New York: Skyhorse Publishing, 2018.

Marcu, Jeff. "Website Exposes Your Life." *Gannett News Service Report*, July 30, 2011.

"Marine's Obama Criticism Tests Free Speech Rules." *CNN.com*, March 8, 2012.

Massey, Lewis. "Can I Get Fired Over a Tweet? What NOT to Say on Social Media." Online Newsletter of Massey, Watson & Hembree, April 13, 2016.

May, Ashley. "Woman Who Wrote Racist 'Ape' Post Defrauded FEMA." *USA Today,* February 18, 2019.

"Mayor of Coastal Oregon City Resigns Over Posts in Police Facebook Group." *Associated Press Report*, July 10, 2023.

McDougall, A.J. "LSU Prof Resigns After Politician He's Shared Years-Long Beef With is Elected Gov." *The Daily Beast,* October 17, 2023.

McElroy, Tom. "Mattis Laughs at Trump at Charity Gala." *Associated Press Report,* October 17, 2019.

McEntyre, Nicholas. "Cop Recognized as OnlyFans Model by Subscriber She Pulled Over." *New York Post,* October 5, 2023.

McEwen, Tom. *Press Pass: My Life in Sports*. Tampa, FL: The Tampa Tribune, 1986.

McGowan, Jake. "Teacher's Semi-Racy Facebook Photo Doesn't Justify Firing." *Technology and Marketing Law Blog*, February 2, 2014.

McGregor, Jenna. "Can Your Off-Hours Political Activism Get You in Trouble at Work?" *The Washington Post,* May 31, 2017.

McLaughlin, Tom. "City Social Media Policy Rejected." *Pensacola News Journal,* May 12, 2023, p. 1-A.

McLaughlin, Tom. "Santa Rosa Commissioner Rails for Democratic-less Government; His Own Party Says He Went Too Far." *Pensacola News Journal,* May 31, 2023, p. 1-A.

McRaven, William H. "Revoke My Security Clearance Too, Mr. President." *The Washington Post,* August 16, 2018.

McWhirter, Darien A. *Your Rights at Work*. New York: John Wiley & Sons, 1989.
Medland, Chris. "F1 Drivers, Teams Banned from Making Political Statements." *USA Today,* December 21, 2022, p. 4-C.
Melzer, Andrew and Whittney Barth. "Whether Employees Can Be Fired for Participating in Peaceful Protests." *University of Illinois Law Review,* Fall 2020, pp. 221–34.
Mendoza, Jordan. "Rodgers Offers No Apology, Bashes ESPN." *USA Today,* January 11, 2024, p. 4-C.
Meyerhofer, Kelly and Rory Linnane, "Chancellor Fired for Appearing in Porn Videos." *Milwaukee Journal Sentinel,* December 29, 2023.
Miller, Jim. "Tax Official's Aide Quits Over 'Hangman' Tweet on Clinton." *The Sacramento Bee,* August 4, 2016.
Milligan, Susan. "Political Debates in the Workplace: Where to Draw the Line." *SHRM News,* May 12, 2015.
"Minneapolis Police Lieutenant Disciplined Over Racist Email Promoted to Homicide Unit Leader." *Associated Press Report*, November 9, 2023.
Moore, Mark. "Woman Fired After Giving Trump's Motorcade the Finger." *New York Post,* October 6, 2017.
Moore-Carrillo, Jaime. "Guns and Gags: How the Military Can Unduly Curb the Free Speech Rights of Soldiers." *Free Speech Today,* date unknown.
"More Companies Monitor Employee E-Mail." *Associated Press Report*, March 11, 2002.
Morgan, Edmund. "The Background of the Uniform Code of Military Justice." *Vanderbilt Law Review* 6 (1953): pp. 169–85.
Muhl, Charles J. "Workplace E-Mail and Internet Use: Employees and Employers Beware." *Monthly Labor Review,* February 2003, pp. 36–45.
Mukanda, Guatam. "Goodbye, Mr. Snyder." *Forbes,* August 29, 2023.
Mulgrew, Elizabeth. "Workplace Speech Issues Beyond the Profane." *The Wall Street Journal,* December 14, 2019, p. 16-A.
Murphy, Kate. "UNCW to Pay $500,000 to Controversial Professor in Deal Over Early Retirement." *The Raleigh News & Observer,* July 23, 2020.
"Myemployersucks.com: Why You Need a Blogging Policy." *Virginia Legal News,* July 2005.
Myers, A. Howard. *Labor Law and Legislation*. Cincinnati, OH: South-Western Publishing Co., 1968.
Mystal, Elie. "Biker Who Flipped Off Trump Loses Wrongful Termination Case." *Above the Law,* July 2, 2018.
Nader, Ralph, Peter Petkas, and Kate Blackwell, *Whistle-Blowing.* New York: Bantam Books, 1972.
Needleman, Sarah E. and Katherine Bindley, "Google Reins in Politics at Work." *The Wall Street Journal,* August 24–25, 201p, p. 1-A.

Negroni, Christine. "Fired Flight Attendant Finds Blogs Can Backfire." *The Washington Post,* November 16, 2004.

Nossel, Suzanne. *Dare to Speak: Defending Free Speech for All.* New York: Dey Street Publishing, 2020.

"Not All Cultures are Created Equal, Say Penn Law Professor in Op-Ed." *The Daily Pennsylvanian,* August 10, 2017.

Nydegger, Rudy. *Clocking In: The Psychology of Work.* Santa Barbara, CA: Greenwood Publishing, 2018.

Olsen, Stefanie. "Managers Tell an Employee She Stepped Over the Line, The Latest Warning Shot for Workers Who Blog." *CNET News*, August 31, 2004.

O'Neil, Robert M. *Free Speech in the College Community*. Bloomington, IN: Indiana University Press, 1997.

Pagnattaro, Marisa Anne. "What Do You Do When You Are Not at Work? Limiting the Use of Off-Duty Conduct as the Basis for Adverse Employment Actions." *University of Pennsylvania of Labor and Employment Law* 6, no. 3 (2004): pp. 625–84.

Palermo, Angela. "Judge Orders Boise Dog Day-Care Business, Ex-Owner to Pay Workers Fired Over Covid-19." *The Idaho Statesman,* October 4, 2023.

Passavant, Paul. *No Escape: Freedom of Speech and the Paradox of Rights.* New York: New York University Press, 2002.

Patterson, Steve. "Reprimand Settles Former Duval Teacher Amy Donofrio's Fight Over Black Lives Matter Flag." *Florida Times-Union,* June 14, 2024.

Patrice, Joe. "Amy Wax Defends Herself by Admitting Most of the Allegations Against Her." *Above the Law,* April 17, 2023.

"Perspective: I Was Fired for Blogging." *CNET News.com*, December 16, 2004.

Peter, Josh. "Joe Burrow is Rarest of NFL QBs: Speaking Up Beyond the Huddle." *USA Today,* September 16, 2022, p. 1-C.

Peter, Josh. "NU AD's 2015 Book Remarks Surface." *USA Today,* June 27, 2023, p. 1-C.

Peters, Charles and Taylor Branch. *Blowing the Whistle.* Westport, CT: Praeger Publishing, 1972.

Pettit, Emma. "An Unacceptable Idea." *The Chronicle of Higher Education,* June 24, 2022, pp. 16–21.

Pettypiece, Shannon and Allan Smith, "Shell Workers Would Have Lost Pay if They Missed Trump Speech at Plant." *NBC News*, August 18. 2019.

Phelan, Jessica. "Mitt Romney Tells Employers to 'Make it Very Clear' to Employees How to Vote." *GlobalPost,* October 18, 2012.

Pickman, Ben. "WNBA Players Wear 'Vote Warnock' Shirts Opposing Atlanta Dream Co-Owner." *Sports Illustrated,* August 4, 2020.

Pink, Aiden. "Is This Penn Law Professor a Truth-Teller or a Bigot?" *The Forward,* March 31, 2018.

Pitt, Emma and Jack Stripling. "Inside the Academic-Freedom Crisis at Florida's Flagship." *The Chronicle of Higher Education,* September 30, 2022, pp. 11–19.

Powers, Kirsten. *The Silencing: How the Left is Killing Free Speech.* Washington, DC: Regnery Publishing, 2015.

Pribek, Jane. "Employer Rights When Monitor E-Mail, Internet Use." *The Daily Record* (Kansas City, MO), February 20, 2006.

Priest, Dana. "Suing Over the CIA's Red Pen; Retired Operative Says Agency Unfairly Edited His Book." *The Washington Post,* October 9, 2006, p. A-15.

Quinn, Ryan. "LSU Fires Tenured Shreveport Professor, Environmental Advocate." *Inside Higher Education,* June 27, 2024.

Quinn, Sam. "Magic's Jonathan Isaac Explains Why He Didn't Take Knee or Wear Black Lives Matter Shirt Friday." *CBSSports.com*, August 1, 2020.

Rabinowitz, Hannah. "Jessica Watkins: Oath Keepers Member and Army Veteran Sentenced to 8.5 Years in Prison for January 6." *CNN.com*, May 26, 2023.

Rampbell, Catherine. "Americans and the 'F' Bomb." *The Washington Post,* February 23, 2107.

Raza, M. Ali and A. Janell Anderson. *Labor Relations and the Law.* Upper Saddle River, NJ: Prentice-Hall, 1996.

Reddish, David. "Pro Golfer Scott Piercy Posts Homophobic Meme, Immediately Backpedals." *Queerty,* March 4, 2020.

Reid, Erin and Lakshmi Ramarajan. "Managing the High-Intensity Workplace." *Harvard Business Review,* June 2016, pp. 85–90.

Richards, David A. *Toleration and the Constitution*. New York: Oxford University Press, 1986.

Roberts, Paul. "Feds Say Fred Meyer Broke the Law by Banning BLM Buttons at Work." *The Seattle Times,* September 21, 2021.

Ronald, Issy, Antonio Jarne, and Krystina Shveda. "Female Soccer Players Earn 25 Cents to 'Dollar of Men at World Cup." *CNN.com*, July 20, 2023.

Rosaforte, Tim. "New LPGA Commissioner Faces Tour's Uncertain Future and Unhappy Members." *The Palm Beach Post,* September 11, 2008.

Rosen, Christine. "The Shaming Spiral: How Social Media Moralizes for Profit." *Commentary,* June 2015, pp. 45–8.

Rosenthal, Lawrence. "Permissible Content Discrimination Under the First Amendment: The Strange Case of the Public Employee." *Hastings Constitutional Law Quarterly* 25, no. 4 (Summer 1998): pp. 528–84.

Roth, Philip. *The Human Stain*. New York: Random House, 2000.

Salvador, Joseph. "Texas Tech Suspends Mark Adams for Slavery Comment." *Sports Illustrated,* March 5, 2023.

Sandberg, Jared. "Infamous E-Mail Writers Aren't Killing Their Careers After All." *The Wall Street Journal,* February 21, 2006, p. 1-B.

Sawyer, R. McLaran, Keith W. Prichard, and Karl D. Hostetler. *The Art and Politics of College Teaching*. New York: Peter Lang, 1998.

Shachtman, Noah. "Marines Ban Twitter, MySpace, Facebook." *Wired,* August 3, 2009.

Schad, Tom. "Sage Steele Sues ESPN Over Free Speech." *USA Today,* April 29, 2022, p. 3-C.

Schladebeck, Jessica. "Commission: Parkland Judge Should be Reprimanded for Conduct During Nikolas Cruz Trial." *New York Daily News,* June 6, 2023.

Schladebeck, Jessica. "Penn Law Professor Loses Teaching Duties for Saying Black Students 'Rarely' Earn Top Marks." *New York Daily News,* March 15, 2018.

Schleller, Stuart. *Crisis of Command: How We Lost Trust and Confidence in America's Generals and Politicians.* New York: Knox Press, 2022.

Schrecker, Ellen. "Academic Freedom and the Cold War." *The Antioch Review* 38, no. 3 (Summer 1980): pp. 312–27.

Schreiber, Noam and Brian M. Rosenthal. "Nurses and Doctors Speaking Out on Safety Now Risk Their Jobs." *The New York Times,* April 9, 2020.

Schupak, Adam. *Deane Beman: Golf's Driving Force.* Orlando, FL: East Cottage Press, 2011.

Scoble, Robert. "Correcting the Record about Microsoft." *Scobleizer*, June 10, 2006.

Seglin, Jeffrey. "You've Got Mail. You're Being Watched." *The New York Times,* July 18, 1999.

Selbe, Nick. "Creighton Suspends Coach Craig McDermott Over Racist Language." *Sports Illustrated,* March 9, 2021.

Selbe, Nick. "Pat Chambers Steps Down as Penn State Basketball Coach After Internal Investigation." *Sports Illustrated,* October 21, 2020.

Sheffield, Mark. "Fifty Years of the UCMJ." *Independent News* (Pensacola, FL), May 6, 2000.

Shepherd, Leah. "Airline Employee Wins Verdict Over Anti-Abortion Speech." *SHRM News,* August 3, 2022.

Shepherd, Leah. "How to Handle Political Speech in the Workplace." *SHRM News,* June 12, 2023.

Shepherd, Leah. "Whole Foods Ban on Black Lives Matter Logo is Lawful, NLRB Judge Rules." *SHRM News,* December 21, 2023.

Sherman, Edward. "The Military Courts and Servicemen's First Amendment Rights." *Hastings Law Journal* 22 (January 1971): pp. 325–73.

Shipler, David K. *Freedom of Speech: Mightier Than the Sword.* New York: Alfred A. Knopf, 2015.

Shipley, Reice. "College Basketball Team Hires Controversial Coach." *The Comeback .com*, July 14, 2023.

Shipnuck, Alan. *LIV and Let Die: The Inside Story of the War Between the PGA Tour and LIV Golf.* New York: Avid Reader Press, 2023.

Shipnuck, Alan. *Phil: The Rip-Roaring (and Unauthorized) Biography of Golf's Most Colorful Superstar.* New York: Avid Reader Press, 2022.

Slanger, Addie and Andy Tallman, "Computer Science Prof Resigns Amid Blog Controversy." *The Montana Kaimin,* October 22, 2021.

Smith, Allen. "Court Upholds Discipline of Workers Wearing Black Lives Matter Masks." *SHRM News,* February 9, 2021.

Smith, Mable. *The Legal, Professional, and Ethical Dimensions of Higher Education.* Philadelphia: Lippincott, Williams & Wilkins, 2005.

Smith, Robert Ellis. *Workrights.* New York: E.P. Dutton, Inc., 1983.

Smith, Tommie and David Steele. *Silent Gesture: The Autobiography of Tommie Smith.* Philadelphia: Temple University Press, 2007.

Smolla, Rodney. *Free Speech in an Open Society.* New York: Alfred A. Knopf, 1992.

Snepp, Frank. *Decent Interval.* New York: Random House, 1977.

Soley, Lawrence. *Censorship, Inc.: The Corporate Threat to Free Speech in the United States.* New York: Monthly Review Press, 2002.

Solove, Daniel J. *The Future of Reputation: Gossip, Rumor, and Privacy on the Internet.* New Haven, CT: Yale University Press, 2007.

South, Todd. "Marine Vet Tells His Side of the Story in New Book." *Marine Times,* October 31, 2022.

"Speak Out Act Targets Wall Street's Silencing of Sexual Harassment." *The Seattle Times,* November 16, 2002.

"Spirit Plays Anthem Before Players' Entry to Nix Megan Rapinoe 'Hijacking.'" *ESPN .com*, September 7, 2016.

Stempel, Jonathan. "Judge Dismisses Whole Foods Workers' Lawsuit Over 'Black Lives Matter' Masks." *Reuters News Report*, January 23, 2023.

Stone, Biz. *Who Let the Blogs Out? A Hyperconnected Peek at the World of Weblogs.* New York: St. Martin's Press, 2004.

Stripling, Jack. "This Professor Officiated at a Gay Wedding. Then He Lost His Job." *The Chronicle of Higher Education,* April 27, 2022.

Subramaniam, Tara. "Trump Blames Megan Rapinoe and Wokeness for US Women's World Cup Exit." *CNN.com*, August 8, 2023.

Sugin, Linda. "First Amendment Rights of Military Personnel: Denying Rights to Those Who Defend Them." *New York University Law Review* 62 (October 1967): pp. 855–89.

Sullivan, Emily. "Laura Ingraham Tells LeBron James to Shut Up and Dribble." *National Public Radio*, February 19, 2018.

Sullivan, Margaret. *Newsroom Confidential: Lessons (and Worries) From an Ink-Stained Life.* New York: St. Martin's Press. 2022.

Summers, Clyde W. "Employment at Will in the United States: The Divine Right of Employers." *University of Pennsylvania Journal of Business Law* 3 (2000): pp. 65–86.

Swartz, Nick. "Los Angeles Clippers Turn Warm-Ups Inside Out in Protest Before Game 4." *USA Today,* April 27, 2014.

Taylor, Johnny C. "Off-Work Politics May Hurt Your Job." *USA Today,* July 10, 2018, p. 5-B.

"Texas Tech Men's Basketball Coach Resigns After Making Racially Insensitive Comments." *Associated Press Report*, March 9, 2023.

"Thomas Apologizes After Using Anti-Gay Slur at Sentry." *Reuters News Report*, January 9, 2021.

Thornton, William. "Bessemer Amazon Union Organizer Jennifer Bates Says She Was Fired: 'I Will Not be Silenced.'" *AL.com*, June 2, 2023.

Turbeville, Ryan Wyatt. "Sergeant Fired for Criticizing Alachua County Sheriff, Lawsuit Filed." *WCJB-TV*, March 15, 2023.

Umansky, Natalie. "10 Outrageous Tweets That Got People Fired." *Oddee.com*, February 21, 2014.

"Union Labor's Profanity Protection." *Bloomberg News,* November 20, 2019.

"United Airlines Suspends Pilot Who's a W.Va. Lawmaker Over Hillary Clinton Execution Tweet." *The Columbus Dispatch,* July 19, 2016.

Unnever, James D. "Allowing Governments to Purge Free Speech is Systematic Repression." *Pensacola News Journal,* June 11, 2023, p. 6-F.

Vickers, Lucy. *Freedom of Speech and Employment*. New York: Oxford University Press, 2002.

Victor, Daniel. "Pittsburgh TV Anchor Fired After Racial Facebook Post." *The New York Times,* March 31, 2016.

Vollmer, Howard M. *Employee Rights and the Employment Relationship*. Berkeley, CA: University of California Press, 1960.

Volokh, Eugene. "Private Employees' Speech and Political Activity: Statutory Protection Against Employer Retaliation." *Texas Review of Law & Politics* 16, no. 2 (2011): pp. 296–336.

Wallace, Patricia. *The Internet in the Workplace: How New Technology is Transforming Work.* New York: Cambridge University Press, 2004.

Walsh, Kenneth T. "Military Members Hold Negative View of Obama." *U.S. News and World Report,* January 9, 2017.

Walters, Kenneth. "Your Employees' Right to Blow the Whistle." *Harvard Business Review,* July-August 1975, pp. 26–34 and 161–3.

Warren, Earl. "The Bill of Rights and the Military." *United States Air Force JAG Bulletin,* May June 1962, pp. 6–21.

Wax, Amy and Larry Alexander. "Paying the Price for Breakdown of the Country's Bourgeois Culture." *The Philadelphia Inquirer,* August 9, 2017.

Wehane, Patricia H. *Persons, Rights, and Corporations.* Englewood Cliffs, NJ: Prentice-Hall, 1985.

Weill, Kelly. *Off the Edge: Flat Earthers, Conspiracy Culture, and Why People Will Believe Anything.* Chapel Hill, NC: Algonquin Books of Chapel Hill, 2022.

Weiss, Debra Cassens. "Judge Tosses Wrongful Termination Claim by Woman Forced to Resign After Flipping Off Trump." *ABA Journal,* July 2, 2018.

Westin, Alan F. and Stephan Salisbury, eds. *Individual Rights in the Corporation*. New York: Pantheon Books, 1980.

Whittington, Keith E. *Speak Freely: Why Universities Must Protect Free Speech.* Princeton, NJ: Princeton University Press, 2018.

Wilkie, Dana. "When Displaying the American Flat at Work Offends Some Employees." *SHRM News,* September 20, 2019.

"Wimbledon Won't be Making Announcements on Handshake Etiquette Despite Booing." *Associated Press Report*, July 10, 2023.

Winer, John D. "Can My Ten-Year-Old Tweet Get Me Fired?" *Legal News,* August 29, 2018.

Wines, William A. and Terence J. Lau. "Can You Hear Me Now? Corporate Censorship and Its Troubling Implications for the First Amendment." *DePaul Law Review* 55, no. 1 (Fall 2005): pp. 119–67.

Wong, Alla. "University Presidents Are Feeling the Chilling Effect." *USA Today,* January 5, 2024, p. 3-A.

"Woods Declines Clinton Invite." *United Press International Report*, April 15, 1997.

Zahneis, Megan. "A Dean Says He Was Ousted for His Opposition to Police and Prisons." *The Chronicle of Higher Education,* December 15, 2022.

Zahneis, Megan. "A New Republican Governor Is In, and This Professor Is Out." *The Chronicle of Higher Education,* October 17, 2023.

Zahneis, Megan. "Scholar Claims He was Fired for Speaking Out Settles with U. of Mississippi." *The Chronicle of Higher Education,* July 29, 2021.

Zak, Sean. "LIV Golf vs. the PGA Tour." *Golf Magazine,* September-October 2022, pp. 40–7.

Zaveri, Mihir. "Teacher Fired Over Tweets Wins Appeal to Texas Agency." *The New York Times,* December 1, 2019, p. 23-A.

Zimmerman, Jonathan. *Campus Politics: What Everyone Needs to Know.* New York: Oxford University Press, 2016.

Zimmerman, Jonathan. *Free Speech and Why You Should Give a Damn.* Buffalo, NY: New Idea Press, 2021.

Zucco, Tom. "Bucs Unload Giles, House, and Springs." *St. Petersburg Times,* October 21, 1986.

Index

About the Author

Randy Bobbitt is a Florida-based author and researcher and a veteran of twenty-eight years of college teaching. He has taught at the University of West Florida, University of North Carolina at Wilmington, Marshall University, and the University of South Florida.

He has written twelve books on topics including public relations, journalism history, communication law, communication ethics, and the intersection of politics and popular culture. His four previous titles for Rowman and Littlefield/ Bloomsbury were *Lottery Wars: Case Studies in Bible-Belt Politics, 1986-2005; Us Against Them: The Political Culture of Talk Radio*; *Free Speech on America's K–12 and College Campuses*; and *Controversial Books in K–12 Classrooms and Libraries.* His thirteenth book, *I Don't Know What I Want, But I Know It's Not This*, will explore the challenges faced by "senior" professors in the latter stages of their careers.

Prior to college teaching, he worked professionally in both journalism and public relations. He is a past president of the West Virginia Chapter of the Public Relations Society of America and is a frequent speaker at professional and student communication conferences. He earned a master's degree in communication management from the University of South Florida and a PhD in communication law and policy from Bowling Green State University.

www.ingramcontent.com/pod-product-compliance
Ingram Content Group UK Ltd.
Pitfield, Milton Keynes, MK11 3LW, UK
UKHW020221290926
15470UKWH00001B/307

9 781666 951080